ENCOUNTERING FREUD

ENCOUNTERING FREUD

The Politics and Histories of Psychoanalysis

Paul Roazen

Transaction Publishers
New Brunswick (U.S.A.) and London (U.K.)

Copyright © 1990 by Transaction Publishers,
New Brunswick, New Jersey 08903

All rights reserved under International and Pan-American Copyright Conventions. No part of this book may be reproduced or transmitted in any
form or by any means, electronic or mechanical, including photocopy, re-
cording, or any information storage and retrieval system, without prior permission in writing from the publisher. All inquiries should be addressed to
Transaction Publishers, Rutgers—The State University, New Brunswick,
New Jersey 08903.

Library of Congress Catalog Number: 89–33634
ISBN: 0–88738–295–9
Printed in the United States of America

Library of Congress Cataloging-in-Publication Data

Roazen, Paul, 1936–
    Encountering Freud : the politics and histories of psychoanalysis
    Paul Roazen.
        p.   cm.
    Bibliography: p.
    Includes index.
    ISBN: 0–88738–295–9
    1. Psychoanalysis—History.   2. Freud, Sigmund, 1856–1939.
    I. Title.
    BF173.R549   1989
    150.19'52—dc20   89–33634
                                                              CIP

For Michael Paul Rogin

In friendship

Contents

Introduction

The essays collected in this volume reflect the range of my interests over the last two decades. To have spent, as I have now, all this time writing about the implications of the work of Freud and his followers implies a commitment on my part that obliges self-scrutiny. Many have long ago made the point that the appeal of psychoanalysis is quasi-religious; it is like most other fields that attract people by virtue of the broad range of their seductive qualities. My professional background was in political theory, a subject concerned with the critical examination of great books. Matthew Arnold's definition of culture as "the best that has been thought and said in the world"[1] is one excellent way of describing the purpose of studying social philosophy. I believe that no one else has stayed working on Freud as long with a similar interest in the history of ideas. Out of my experience I can confirm that the general public's fascination with Freud is far greater today than it was at the beginning of my career as a writer; this has to be particularly striking to me because when I started out I was often told that there was nothing new to be said about Freud. And I still get asked, more often than I like to remember, what my own degree in political science could possibly have to do with psychoanalysis.

With all the changes that have taken place throughout these years, one element in the appeal of Freud for me still remains the same: it is appallingly easy to be original on this whole subject, in striking contrast to what would be the case on almost any other topic in intellectual history. I shudder at the thought of trying to express something new about Machiavelli, Hobbes, or Rousseau, but with Freud I still feel secure. Partly this is a question of the blinders that are usually brought to anything connected with Freud. Both during his lifetime as well as after the now fifty years since his death, people have been either so repulsed by the concepts associated with his point of view as to remain ill-informed in their prejudices, or else so overwhelmed by what he had to say that they retain no critical objectivity.

Otherwise sophisticated observers are capable of being surprisingly ill-informed about Freud; at the same time there are still those devout believers who are incapable of independent thinking.

Reactions to Freud include some interesting differences in the national receptions of psychoanalysis, which I discuss at the outset of this book, since they actually had a good deal to do with my own early involvement with this subject. As a graduate student in the United States at the end of the 1950s, I found it impossible in the social sciences to ignore Freud's stature. Yet when I came to study at Oxford in 1959, I found that there was almost no familiarity with Freud's work even though it was then a prevailing conceptualization in the United States; not one copy of any of Freud existed in my college library, which I recall being pleasantly reassuring to Anna Freud when I later told her about it. She, like her father, found "resistances" to psychoanalysis a sign of both merit and martyrdom, conclusively indicative of the ultimate victory of Freud's system of ideas.

By now things have changed. English intellectuals are more conversant with Freud than would then have been the case; Americans are today relatively disenchanted with the whole Freudian point of view, at least when it comes to the clinical practice of psychoanalysis, even at the same time as an American version of Freud has become culturally pervasive; and after an extensive delay when Jean-Paul Sartre and Simone de Beauvoir were isolated within the French intelligentsia in their interest in psychoanalysis, ironically now in a period when they are relatively out of fashion in Paris the city has become the center of world concern with the topic of Freud. Today it is impossible to go into almost any good Parisian bookstore and not come upon psychoanalytic texts that are so new as to be unknown elsewhere.

The issue of different national responses to Freud does raise the question of whether each country is in fact talking about the same system of ideas. In the United States it has been the therapeutic side of Freud's message and its implications for child rearing that have always attracted the greatest interest; even in 1909, when Freud made his one visit to the New World to deliver the Clark Lectures, which are discussed in chapter 3, he already knew that it would be the practical side of his work that his audience would be most interested in hearing about. By now, however, psychoanalysis seems to most medical observers like a cure that failed, although New York City's Kremlin-like orthodox psychoanalytic society may be the exception that proves the rule. Of course expectations were, no doubt, way too high, but the therapeutic claims for analysis were hardly modest, and some disappointment was inevitable. Freud himself was not at all impressed by the American reaction to his work and awaited the outcome in England and on the Continent. That would be, he foretold, where the ultimate "struggle" over his "discoveries" would take place.[2] Yet the more philosophic side of psychoanalysis has so attracted the bulk of the attention in France, to the neglect of Freud's clinical concerns, that I wonder whether he would have been at all pleased with the direction that events have taken there. His daughter, Anna, did take part in the expulsion of Jacques Lacan from the International Psychoanalytic Association. (I write about the whole issue of heresy in psychoanalysis not only in chapter 11, but also in my treatment of the Tausk problem in chapter 6.)

The mention of the name of Anna Freud, or "Miss Freud," as she was once regularly referred to by insiders, signals one of the biggest changes to have taken place in recent years. Her death in 1982 ended an era in the history of psychoanalysis, a phase that began once Freud had become an invalid dependent on his youngest child's care. It is one of the strange twists in the history of Freud's movement that he should have come with his precious daughter to England, where her arch-rival Melanie Klein was practicing; Mrs. Klein was to found the so-called British school of analysis. Klein's was an unlikely set of theories, whose improbability combined with a messianic fervor to give them a special attraction for intellectuals. When a leading English Kleinian I was interviewing once told me about analyses that as a matter of principle were supposed to last ten years, I quietly asked what could justify such an intervention in another human life; the answer I got was the word "research," and I am afraid that pretension has permanently colored my reaction to Kleinian ideas. I turned down an invitation to write a book about her work for a popular series edited by Frank Kermode, since I felt too unsympathetic, but I reacted as negatively to his offer of a book about Otto Rank's ideas, even though I admired Rank, on the grounds that I was not sufficiently in tune with Rank's whole mode of reasoning.

Although the alleged "Americanization" of psychoanalysis, as in the contributions of Erik H. Erikson, has become highly suspect, especially on the Continent, it is not a new issue in the history of Freud's school; he was initially offended that Carl G. Jung seemed to be backsliding from psychoanalysis for opportunistic reasons while on a trip to the States. And later both Rank and Sandor Ferenczi flourished in the United States during phases when they were growing ideologically independent of Freud. It seems to me, though, that from the point of view of psychotherapeutic practice the American concern with what works on symptoms is not at all a bad sort of preoccupation. I was nonetheless dismayed by a recent uncritical American study of Nazi Germany's use of depth psychology for the purpose of adapting people to its regime; psychoanalytic psychology, when divorced from moral enlightenment, can lead to some appalling social practices, conformist if not totalitarian. Theoretical sophistication is not, unfortunately, a noteworthy North American trait. I do think that the clash in

England between Anna Freud and Melanie Klein helped ensure a vitality to British psychoanalysis; the existence of rival orthodoxies meant less chance for complacency.

Despite her own personal success in North America, Anna Freud shared her father's notorious distaste for that continent. She could be more politic about her feelings than Freud himself, as she retained the mantle of his authority within the "movement." On the basis of my brief acquaintance with Anna Freud I am not surprised that nowadays analysts speak their minds more freely when they are commenting on Freud's life. When I was lecturing on psychoanalytic biography at the Applied Section of the British Psychoanalytic Society in the spring of 1987, I found a friendly picture of her more intimidating than either the formal portrait of Ernest Jones or the angry-looking etching of her father, each of which were prominently hung on the walls of the large room in which I was speaking. (Since Sylvia Payne plays so little role in history books, perhaps only those who knew her will appreciate how reassuring I found the central presence of her likeness when I finally noticed it during the intermission.) Today even the most orthodox can publish irreverent, if often wrongheaded, comments about Freud's marriage. When I knew Anna Freud, however, she was unquestionably the anointed leader of the psychoanalytic community. My seeing her in 1965, for example, was at least as much a prerequisite for my being received by others in the analytic world as it was for the sake of anything I hoped to pick up in the course of directly interviewing her. However, I know I learned something from sitting in on clinical case conferences, at her invitation, at her Hampstead Clinic in London.

Yet when I started publishing it was obvious that she was not going to be pleased. In 1979 she alluded to me in print, in the course of her reminiscing about Ernest Jones, as "a rather malicious American author."[3] She claimed to be objecting to the fact that I had discussed how Jones wrote his authorized biography of her father knowing she had her own priorities defining what constituted discretion; I can safely leave it to future historians to examine the correspondence between Jones and James Strachey, for example, to establish whether in fact she was capable of intimidating either of them. Jones's first draft of volume 1 of his biography brought forth from her, after she read it, the love letters from Freud to his future wife, Martha; Jones, who had to rework his text, certainly knew the scale of documentation she had up her sleeve, although he may never have realized how much she retained in her cabinets at 20 Maresfield Gardens.

Oddly enough, my attitude toward Jones himself has changed more than once over the last years. When I first started out I found his books exhilarating and vastly informative, but eventually I decided that his work was so biased as to be a serious distortion. Thanks to perseverence on my part in 1965 I came upon, and went through, all his papers that once made up the Jones Archives in London; I then discovered that it was possible to see around Jones's version, and I suppose that my first writings on Freud were partly designed to counteract the picture that Jones had tried to prop up. Jones's biography was in fact a studied act of statecraft, and it has to this day by and large succeeded in putting across the outlook that Freud himself wanted to publicize. Every effort on Freud's part to stifle an official biography was supported by his conviction that he had already succeeded in getting his own version of things into print.

Once I thought I had, through my books, succeeded in getting around Jones, it became possible to feel more charitably toward his achievement. No one should underestimate how savage he was toward his rivals among Freud's pupils. But as long as everyone does not swallow him hook, line, and sinker, then it can be possible to see how his own troubled beginnings had been transmuted by him into his genuine accomplishment. At the time I began Jones was, at least among those who considered themselves Freudians, treated as gospel. Doubtless Carl G. Jung's disciples, and those who identified with the side of any of Freud's many dissenting critics, would have immediately had the necessary perspective toward Jones's account. But famous literary intellectuals, for example Lionel Trilling and Steven Marcus, not only edited Jones uncritically into a one-volume edition but continued to popularize the merits of his point of view.

I doubt that people now starting out in this field can realize what conditions once were like. Twenty years ago Jones's papers were in such a state of disorder that I found there a whole stack of original letters by Freud that had yet to be returned to his family. (They have since appeared in print.) Jones's files were for me mainly leads for interviewing those of Freud's immediate pupils who were still alive. (It seems to me extraordinary that my interviews with twenty-five of Freud's analytic patients have aroused so little interest among analysts.) Right now the Jones Archives are temporarily closed since they are being reorganized for a computerized system, but documents, for example, that I once hurriedly examined in Strachey's home in the countryside outside London will soon be available for scholarly inspection.

Freud's own papers are still largely locked up in the Library of Congress in Washington, D.C. When I first undertook my research there was little known about the special means by which the Freud archives in New York had placed special restrictions on material that it gave to the Library of Congress. In the mid-1960s donors to the Freud archives were still alive and able to show me historical evidence that was at that time inaccessible in Washington, D.C. It is noteworthy that when I came to write my biography of Helene Deutsch, she and I tried to retrieve copies of Freud's few letters to her, which she had once given to the Freud archives; although the Library of Congress was perfectly willing to let us see what we wanted, we had no luck with the Freud archives themselves, and because of the existing legal agreement between the archives and the Library of Congress our efforts were frustrated. So much has now been written about the fate of Freud's papers, and the scholarly community has been made aware enough of the unnecessary effort to maintain false idealizations of Freud, that I do not think it worthwhile to explore further the regrettable effort to use the means of selective secrecy to give us a picture of Freud less interesting than the genius he truly was.

One item serves to illustrate the problem of the general state of the literature today: the issue of Freud's having analyzed his daughter Anna. In print I mentioned this for the first time in 1969 and then discussed it at some length in 1975. Although in old Vienna she denied it to at least one analyst, or at least he told me that she had, it had become known to a small circle of Freud's intimates, and he mentioned it in at least one of his letters that have now appeared in print. (Although the recipient talked to me about Freud's letter, he asked me not to mention it. I obliged him as he wished, but when my *Brother Animal* came out he was miffed at my reticence; students of recent history seem bound to lose, heads or tails.) There has never been any discussion whatever of this matter in the professional psychoanalytic literature. Once an official biography of Anna Freud was authorized, a portion of this work was devoted to interpreting the analysis by her father, without either challenging my earlier ideas or even hinting that I had preceded the author on this subject. I would have thought that in the normal course of scholarly work whatever I once wrote would have by now, almost a generation later, led to a series of new interpretations. Silence, however, is a most potent weapon of ideological purity, and I have found out the partisanly political way that bibliographies in the professional journals get put together. In a situation like this it is hard for me occasionally not to repeat myself, since it is never self-evident that enough people have been listening.

Oddly enough, it is the most religiously committed zealots of Freud's descendants who are apt to insist on the status of psychoanalysis as a science, and I have tried to examine the philosophic nature of the discipline. I think that however personal the sources of originality in psychoanalysis, in the end Freud's teaching did have an enormous impact not just on the practice of psychotherapy, but more generally on how we think about ourselves. One does not need to refer just to spectacular instances like the legal problems associated with a would-be assassin like John W. Hinkley, Jr., or the psychological evidence presented in the "Baby M." case, or even the concept of psychological as opposed to biological parenthood. As I am a political scientist, it is not surprising that these issues come up in my section on law as well as in my discussion of ego psychology. A central attraction this field had for me at the outset was that the psychoanalytic conceptualization cut across all the social sciences, and if one is interested in a variety of fields, from history to philosophy, psychoanalysis had had something new to contribute.

My point is obviously not that what is novel is necessarily valid, but to the extent that social philosophy involves thinking about how we think, a confrontation with Freud's ideas entails a live encounter with some of the central problems of traditional political theory. Bruno Bettelheim's writing on child rearing was preceded by thinkers like Plato and Jean-Jacques Rousseau, to take only two earlier figures. Yet my turning toward Freud's work over twenty years ago was already an act of heresy within political science. Doubtless one source of the many controversies in the history of psychoanalysis was that people like myself, dissatisfied with the conventional wisdom in their own fields, were attracted by the implications of Freud's system of ideas. Yet I think that despite what it sometimes looks like, psychoanalysis has not had enough theoretical give-and-take; if more disagreements were legitimized, as is usually the case in other disciplines I am familiar with, then volcanic-like blowups would be less likely to need to take place.

Even having challenged my own profession's complacencies, I remained ill-prepared for a whole new set of taboos that one encounters in psychoanalysis. Once I had learned of Anna Freud's analysis by her father there was no way I was not somehow going to get it into print, even though at least one famous New York analyst warned me that such a revelation would be "mis-used" by others. Similarly, I set out to announce the tendentious editing of Freud's letters, a matter that until then was not publicly known. My section on Freud's letter writing can be taken as a preliminary communication on the many volumes of his correspondence yet to come, the biggest single source of knowledge about the early history of psychoanalysis that is still outstanding. Starting with the publication of the Freud-Jung letters, and after I had blown the whistle on the hanky-panky with Freud's correspondence, the Freud family dropped its policy of expurgating Freud's letters. In general I have tried to approach the history of Freud's movement with as much dispassion as possible. I think that my admiration for both Freud and his early followers shows through all the attention I gave to the struggle of their lives. I hope that chapter 10, "Brief Lives," written in response to a spate of recent biographies of early analysts, communicates some of this sympathy on my part.

Curiously it seems to some that one is downgrading the significance of the achievements of early analysts if one talks about them as personalities and historical figures instead of merely the bearers of pure dessicated theoretical doctrine. All I can say is that I think there is more than enough speculation in the psychoanalytic literature about how many angels can dance on the head of a pin. In my view the task of the scholar entails emphasizing what is otherwise apt to be left out of the books. In the case of early analysis, the lives of the people make, to my mind at any rate, fascinating models of originality and daring. I have tried to generalize some of what I learned into the methodological sections on psychoanalytic biography that can be found in chapter 9.

Freud once described himself in a famous letter to Wilhelm Fliess as not properly a man of science but a "conquistador,"[4] and this passage has been quoted and invoked so often as to become almost ritualistic in the profession. Yet the implications of Freud as a daring innovator have rarely sunk in, surely not to his successful disciples who prided themselves on their organizational loyalties. Chapter 12 treats the issue of what I have called Loyalism; Freud was fundamentally a subversive figure in Western history, even though in his day-to-day life he was very much a physician of his era and social background. He laid down a basic challenge to Western thought. Chapter 15 and the conclusion raise the theoretical import of psychoanalysis in the context of some traditional sages and the issue of the concept of normality.

Philosophers, theologians, poets, and novelists have gone about asking the question how we ought to live and the means by which the good society could be organized; Freud too had something implicitly important to say along these lines of social and political thought. I think that how people conduct their lives has at least as much to teach as what they exhort and preach; the example of Freud and his followers is a notable one in modern intellectual history. Yet it has to be more than a question of exactly what Freud wrote and said about Mussolini, for instance, or the regime Freud in his old age chose to back in Austria, just as one has to go beyond the remarks he made about the fate of French aristocrats during the Reign of Terror or the political imagery of his writings to tease out the implications of his concepts for social philosophy as a whole.

On this point Freud's successors have been far more explicit than the founder of psychoanalysis himself. For example, I regularly teach and make required reading texts by Erich Fromm, Erik H. Erikson, and Bruno Bettelheim in my courses "Psychology and Politics" and "Psychology and Contemporary Political Theory." Fromm is now out of fashion, at least in North America, and Bettelheim has been challenged in key ways even if that has not been made widely known; I have expressed in print my own criticisms of Erikson's social conservatism. Nonetheless, I not only value Erikson's work, but vividly recall how in London D. W. Winnicott once told me about his almost envious appreciation for Erikson's own books. Yet because of the special role of discipleship in this field, Erikson's lack of a following of his own has meant his relative professional eclipse by Winnicott, to such a degree that it now seems unusual to notice their similarities of approach.

Each year I assign in university classes different thinkers like Fromm, Bettelheim, and Erikson, not because I necessarily agree with the various points each of these analysts was trying to get across, but for the reason that they were all moving in the general direction of filling out some possible consequences of the psychoanalytic revolution in the history of ideas. Psychology, as Dostoevsky once said, is a knife that cuts both ways, and Freud's thought can be used for a variety of ideological purposes, from the most radical to the very conservative. Marxism is only one of the most striking streams of thought to have made use of psychoanalytic ideas.

Fromm, Bettelheim, and Erikson, each of whom, incidentally, I interviewed, had a great deal more savvy about the history of their movement than they ever decided to put into print. (My slight impression of Heinz Kohut comes from meeting him in his orthodox phase of the early 1960s, when I found him an immensely cultured and literate figure, admired by Anna Freud; it still seems to me surprising that he should have become a source both of controversy and of some kind of movement.) Since they were analysts, the people I interviewed were bound by constraints that did not pertain to myself; I was without a clinical practice to protect and had no bonds of friendship to the early "cause" that might constrict my thinking. I sometimes felt obliged, however, to guard the anonymity of my sources.

I was struck by how the conformist pressures in analysis afflicted even the more daringly free-thinking of analysts. One famous so-called heretic instructed me, in the middle of an interview, not to write something down; another eminent analyst could not understand how I was proposing to publish what he knew to be true. "Anna Freud will destroy you!" was a melodramatic version uttered by one analyst of what was in store for me. These people were interesting to me to the degree to which analysis for them all was not merely a livelihood or even a scientific career, but also a means of saving their souls, and therefore one finds all the bravery and cowardice associated with mankind's most sustained efforts at introspective self-understanding. Sectarianism, alas, does seem to accompany such spiritual commitments.

Writing about Freud and his followers can never be a matter of small potatoes, except if one turns to some articles in professional analytic journals. There are, however, promising changes in this situation, so that now a handful of independent-minded analysts are beginning to pursue what we in university life would consider genuine scholarly inquiry. Even more momentously, however, scholars of intellectual history have begun to treat early psychoanalysis as a subject of research on which there can be different points of view; at the same time, in the face of the new open-mindedness of the last twenty years, there are still efforts afoot to stage an ideological counterreformation. One wipes one's eyes in disbelief at a recent effort to diminish the significance of Freud's Jewishness. Unlike the old-fashioned psychoanalytic invocation of the charge of betrayal and heresy, university subjects welcome rival interpretations; I think that the more different theories of any set of events that exist, the more solid the field of inquiry is apt to be.

It should come as no surprise that chapters 13 and 14 deal with political psychology and psychohistory. It will be clear by now that it is inevitable that my own interests would produce methodological reflections on those key areas.

One specific issue, which has only recently attracted my interest, does obviously follow from my preceding concerns. Almost as soon as I moved to Canada in 1971, I was informed that I ought to be interested in the life of W. L. Mackenzie King, who was prime minister longer than anyone in Canadian or Commonwealth history. King not only exceeded Walpole's record as prime minister, but he was throughout his career aware of his expanding longevity; one of his private secretaries was assigned the task of keeping the press galleries informed every time King surpassed some other leader's length in office. He led his political party for almost three decades and was in official power for most of that time; he had been a student of Thorstein Veblen, wrote books of his own, and was a serious reader.

Yet in his private life as a lonely bachelor it would be hard to find anyone more eccentric; his incessant diary keeping, mysticism, and peculiar devotion to his mother's memory have been known for some time now, even if the psychiatric basis for his peculiarities will come to the public as news. Psychological theory does not, I think, adequately prepare us for the idea that someone as privately odd could nonetheless function politically in a supernormal manner within a democracy. It is hard not to think that King's lack of "normalcy," which was so extreme as to lead some clinicians today to think in terms of a so-called latent psychosis or even schizophrenia, must have lent a special edge to his political capacities. One eminent political scientist has written about how paranoia could be functional for Josef Stalin. It is not possible to sustain the early hope of someone like Harold Lasswell that democratic character could be identified with psychological health or even Wilhelm Reich's conviction about the parallel between so-called genitality and normality, not to mention the suggestion once forwarded by Ernest Jones that cabinet ministers, like foreign secretaries, ought to submit themselves to psychoanalytic inspection before being appointed to their posts.

As a political theorist I remain fascinated by the problem of Mackenzie King; I do not pretend to have solved the enigmatic place of his eccentricies in his success. Early psychoanalysis focused on failure rather than adaptation, but in King's case historians are hard-pressed to find any instances of his ever politically fouling up. How does an example like that of King teach us about our conception of normality? It remains an open question what a fully developed human being might be like. I suspect that the psychoanalytic influence has too often been in the direction of encouraging an unduly conformist image of human nature.

I come back at the end to how I started out: I have spent over twenty years writing in this area, and there seems no early end in sight; I ought to mention that it is now much harder for me to reread Freud than it once was, since I find so much going on in each of his sentences. I regret, however, that in publishing about the history of psychoanalysis it is still possible to say almost anything with little fear of contradiction. The absence of normal scholarly standards and an international community securely able to signal the difference between good and bad work means that a vacuum exists where scholars in other fields can count on a shared sense of fellowship. The peculiarities of this subject were brought home to me by the instantaneous recognition of my little work on Mackenzie King; once I had come up with some genuine psychiatric evidence, Canadian historians recognized right away that I was on to something worth paying attention to, and I was immediately asked to review a relevant book for the *Canadian Historical Review*.

Although the lack of professional reinforcement necessarily has to be a source of unending frustration, it at the same time is also a continuing explanation of this subject's attraction for me, for there is almost no competition in the search for impartial truth. Whatever my inevitable mistakes in gathering interviewing material, written records have their own ways of being misleading; historians only rarely forget that words are always in need of being interpreted. A serious worker can still make an unusually valuable contribution; one gets back from the study of Freud what one puts into it, for the broader the cultural range brought to this subject the more significant the results are likely to be. As long as one can temperamentally stand not having to do as one is told, it is easy to be original in this area I have chosen. I started out in an academic environment, which taught me something about the role of discipleship and the consequences of dependencies on mentors; that organizations reward compliance seems to me regrettable. It is essential to be able to function as an outsider, since pious devotees have nothing to lose by attacking people who are not members of the trade union; if patriotism is the last recourse of the scoundrel, the terms *parlor psychoanalysis* and *gossip* can function as cruel shibboleths, taking the emotional place of nationalism's way of excluding foreigners. To the extent that an opportunity exists for genuine work being an expression of my whole self, which is relatively unusual in academic life, I think that my having found this subject matter represents a piece of unusually good luck.

As I reflect back over the literature of the last twenty years, I do sometimes wonder whether people respond as powerfully to books as my own ideology has led me to believe. It is, after all, historically essentially a liberal value that says that people do and should listen to what each other has to say. But experience teaches us that toleration arises at least as often from emotional exhaustion as from a positive conviction about the benefits of rival thoughts.

Lord Keynes once stated the liberal faith in the power of ideas in as extreme a way as possible:

> . . . the ideas of economists and political philosophers, both when they are right and when they are wrong, are more powerful than is commonly understood. Indeed the world is ruled by little else. Practical men, who believe themselves to be quite exempt from any intellectual influences, are usually the slaves of some defunct economist. Madmen in authority, who hear voices in the air, are distilling their frenzy from some academic scribbler of a few years back. I am sure that the power of vested interests is vastly exaggerated compared with the gradual encroachment of ideas. Not indeed, immediately, but after a certain interval; for in the field of economic and political philosophy there are not many who are influenced by new theories after they are twenty-five or thirty years of age, so that the ideas which civil servants and politicians and even agitators apply to current events are not likely to be the newest. But, soon or late, it is ideas, not vested interests, which are dangerous for good or evil.[5]

Keynes may have, I think, overestimated the significance of intellectual history, and yet it is in his general spirit that I have tried to work. (I should admit that twenty years ago I was just over thirty.) My allegiance to Keynes's outlook persists even though it has sometimes meant running head-on into the full force of the sectarianism bred by cultism. Freud was himself, however much he criticized some past liberal beliefs, also a historic figure in the best tradition of humane liberalism, which adds to why studying him as one of the West's great writers has continued to hold my interest.

Notes

1. Matthew Arnold, *Culture and Anarchy,* ed. J. Dover Wilson (Cambridge: Cambridge University Press, 1960), p. 6.
2. Sigmund Freud, "On the History of the Psychoanalytic Movement," *The Standard Edition of the Complete Psychological Works of Sigmund Freud,* ed. James Strachey, vol. 14 (London: Hogarth Press, 1953–74), p. 32. Hereafter this edition of Freud's works will be referred to as *Standard Edition.*
3. Anna Freud, "Personal Memories of Ernest Jones," *International Journal of Psychoanalysis,* 60, no. 3 (1979), p. 287.
4. *The Complete Letters of Sigmund Freud to Wilhelm Fliess 1887–1904,* trans. and ed. Jeffrey M. Masson (Cambridge, Mass.: Harvard University Press, 1985), p. 398.
5. John Maynard Keynes, *The General Theory of Employment, Interest and Money* (London: Macmillan & Co., 1957), pp. 383–84.

1

The Beginnings of Psychoanalysis

Freud studies have entered a new phase. At least from the perspective of one who has been following the subject for the last twenty-five years, the current scholarly output on the founder of psychoanalysis has several distinctive features. Formerly, books on Freud tended to be written by self-directed individuals driven by a passionate if sometimes idiosyncratic interest in the material. Of course there has been a steady stream of ortho-dox psychoanalytic embellishments to the portrait of Freud that Ernest Jones tried to establish. But in addition to such relatively unadventurous and professionally self-serving research, there has been a long line of inde-pendent efforts to document and appraise Freud's life.

William McGrath's *Freud's Discovery of Psychoanalysis: The Politics of Hysteria* (1986) is a sign that professional historians have entered the field in strength and with a determination to link Freud's work to its social and cultural surroundings. Professor McGrath is especially interested in the pe-riod of the 1890s, but explores whatever evidence is available about the intellectual origins of Freud's ideas.

In general, McGrath is following the inspiration of the eminent historian Carl Schorske. McGrath argues: "Freud, the most political of adolescents, turned in the wake of his political disillusionment to the philosophical, sci-entific realm to express his radical impulses."[1] Schorske had been the first professional historian to emphasize Freud's political frustrations being transformed into psychoanalytic insights. It is welcome that the study of the early Freud should now be in the hands of responsible academic scholar-ship; as long as research on Freud is distinct from the sectarian partisanship associated with the ideological wars that have marked the history of psy-choanalysis, we can be most grateful.

Yet McGrath's book, sound as far as it goes, has drawbacks that deserve pointing out. It is curious that he ignores, both in his bibliography and in his text, so many of his predecessors. I do not understand how he cannot mention, for instance, books such as David Bakan's *Sigmund Freud and the Jewish Mystical Tradition (1958)*, Martin Freud's *Glory Reflected (1957)*, Erich Fromm's *Sigmund Freud's Mission (1959)*, Helen Puner's *Freud (1947)*, Hanns Sachs' *Freud (1945)*, and Fritz Wittels' *Freud (1924)*. (None of my own books gets cited either.) Of course the Freud industry is immense, and no writer can credit everyone. But in McGrath's case, it is not just those sources that he neglects to mention that is troubling; equally striking is the excessive attention he pays to authorities who are highly suspect. There is every reason to believe, for example, that Max Schur's book on Freud was filled with partisanship both in terms of what Schur wrote as well as in what he chose to leave out, yet McGrath does not seem to be on his toes here or regarding other orthodox psychoanalytic books and articles on Freud.

McGrath's book is fine for what it does. But the problem is that he approaches his subject with too narrow a frame of reference. Like others before him, he has been unduly taken in by Freud's own point of view. For example, he devotes altogether too much attention to Freud's relationship to his father, while excluding any attention at all to Freud's conflicted ties to his mother. Even when it comes to Freud's father, McGrath is too credulous in accepting Freud's version of the impact on his life of the death of Jakob Freud. Otto Rank long ago suggested that Freud's account of his father's death was mixed up with, if not a defense against, Freud's feelings about the loss of his friendship with his mentor, Josef Breuer. In any event, McGrath not only fails to explore Freud's relationship with Breuer, but also does not go into any discussion of Freud's marriage to his wife Martha. McGrath's bare mention of Freud's sister-in-law Minna will not do, because Freud is reliably said to have declared that she was as much a support to him in the 1890s as his now famous intimate friend Wilhelm Fliess.

As Carl G. Jung pointed out long ago, childhood memories can be reconstructed for purposes of serving adult conflicts; therefore, Freud's accounts of his earliest years need to be approached with the skepticism bred by psychoanalytic teachings. It is surprising that McGrath takes so seriously Freud's idea about the significance of the death of his one-year-younger brother Julius in infancy. Although other writers have recently blown Freud's interest in cocaine out of proportion, McGrath scarcely mentions it here.

He does devote many pages to ingenious interpretations of Freud's account of his dreams. Yet such exercises have a scholastic air, not just due to Freud's being capable of disguising his dream material, but because, after all, we lack the dreamer's genuine free associations, which Freud considered essential to dream interpretations. Moreover, given the restricted range of McGrath's outlook, it hardly seems that this minute attention to details succeeds in focusing on the forest rather than the individual trees.

Strangely enough, McGrath does not seem to appreciate adequately the uniqueness of Freud's genius. It reads flatfootedly to be told that Freud's "disillusionment was deeply significant and constituted a substantial barrier to the normal process of maturation. Having lost faith in the example of manhood presented by his father, Freud had no adequate model to follow and had difficulty completing the process of growing up."[2] Such psychologizing smacks of the historical sin of presentism, looking at the past through the spectacles of the most pedestrian of contemporary outlooks; it should instead be the job of the historian to put us into a world wholly unlike our own rather than to view Freud as a garden-variety 1980s' neurotic.

In general, McGrath would have done well to keep in mind Freud's later career as well; in that way he could not possibly have written that "there is no reason to believe" that Freud in the 1890s was "then a more active or talkative analyst than later."[3] On the contrary, all the evidence indicates that after Freud contracted cancer in 1923 he did indeed change his practices as an analyst.

It is a welcome relief that McGrath's book indicates that the study of Freud is now an accepted part of the academic historical profession. I hope, in light of what I have already written here, that it does not sound patronizing if I say now that McGrath's book is wholly serious and lacking in partisanship. The limitations of his work only serve to remind us how little we still know about Freud's early struggles and the history of psychoanalysis's beginnings despite all the available literature.

Marianne Krüll's *Freud and His Father* (1986) first appeared in German in 1979 and influenced McGrath's *Freud's Discovery of Psychoanalysis;* both books consequently share some of the same problems. *Freud and His Father* was, however, written by a sociologist inspired by a clinical concern with family therapy and focuses on the problem of Freud's theory of seduction; its appearance in an English translation had to be delayed temporarily due to the sensationalism associated with Jeffrey M. Masson's *The Assault on Truth: Freud's Suppression of the Seduction Theory* (1984). The New York publisher of *Freud and His Father* reasonably feared that any apparent similarity between Krüll's thesis and that of Masson would damage *Freud and His Father,* yet in contrast to Masson's baffling success in seducing the interest of the media, little attention has been paid to Krüll's book.

Krüll, like Masson, is fascinated by the Freud of the 1890s and she too regrets Freud's abandonment of the seduction theory, but her reasons are entirely different and lead in another theoretical direction. Her objection to Freud's concept of the Oedipus complex sounds similar to Masson's, since it is couched in terms of a preference for the earlier seduction hypothesis. But for Masson childhood sexual abuse is the be-all and end-all of existence; he literally defines reality by that perversion. In contrast, Krüll regrets that Freud failed to rid the seduction theory of an unnecessary fixation on sexuality.

Krüll's central idea is that Freud's self-analysis was blunted by feelings of guilt associated with the 1896 death of his father; according to Krüll Freud yielded to a taboo not to delve into Jakob's conflicts and therefore Freud "never reached his own real childhood experiences."[4] She regards it as a guilt-laden mistake for Freud to have extended his early emphasis on instinct; he had originally proposed that sexual frustration lay behind the so-called actual (current) neuroses, and after 1896 he went on to argue that sexuality, in the form of fantasy, encompassed all the psychological suffering of the psychoneuroses (hysteria and obsessionality). In Krüll's view a true psychoanalytic theory would not have seen neurosis as caused by forbidden desires. Freud's elaboration of his theory of libido and his concern with phylogenetic inheritance meant that he did not have to look "to the experiential context for the explanation of human behavior."[5]

Although Krüll does not mention Alfred Adler in any way as a precursor in this connection, she has in mind that Freud should have "expanded his seduction theory into a 'misguidance' theory: the child is misguided by his or her parents or primary caretakers and hence develops neurotic aberrations."[6] Such an approach could "at one and the same time . . . have been a theory of 'guidance' toward socially acceptable behavior."[7] The preface to *Freud and His Father* by Helm Stierlin hails "the new paradigm of family therapy,"[8] and Krüll's book constitutes a biographical explanation of the reasons Freud missed out on insights that seem important to therapists today.

Krüll's book is full of hard work, but I cannot agree with her general thesis, which suffers from the historiographic mistake of thinking that what we now hold to be true must have somehow been missed by Freud. Nobody but God can know everything. The study of the history of ideas ought to expand the limits of our toleration and show us how different writers in past eras tried to come to terms with enduring human dilemmas. I find the notion of progress in intellectual history mistaken and repellent; I do not believe, for example, that Freud knew more than Jean-Jacques Rousseau or even that the most brilliant of contemporary family therapists, like Helm Stierlin, could be somehow superior to Freud. Certainly many others long before now have objected, both as feminists as well as humanists, to the patriarchalism of Oedipal thinking.

Concentrating more narrowly on Krüll's argument: I think she is absolutely right in thinking that Freud's theory of the "actual" neurosis was based on Freud's own sexual difficulties. In the early 1890s Freud gave an account of both neurasthenia and anxiety neurosis that demonstrably sounds

like a self-confession. Freud left us so much evidence in the way of correspondence, and it has been possible to reconstruct enough about his sexuality that his public denunciation of masturbation, as well as his cardiac
neurosis, can each be readily linked to his unsatisfactory sexual practices.
Freud accepted his situation of the 1890s, bowed to his fate, and lived with
his neurosis. Long ago Wilhelm Reich criticized both Freud and his followers for not being as emancipated in life as their theories might have justified. One of Freud's former patients from the 1930s that I interviewed in
the mid-1960s stressed Freud's continued belief in the toxic effects of ''abnormal'' sexual practices, whatever the alterations in some of Freud's other
theoretical views.

Krüll does convincingly establish that Freud dropped the whole subject
of the actual neurosis because he ''believed he had solved it once and for
all.''[9] His theory did, as she says, help Freud ''explain his own neurotic
symptoms, albeit not holding out the promise of a cure.''[10] Krüll however,
then proposes that it was the death of Freud's father in 1896 that propelled
him to think that the Oedipus theory, with its emphasis on the role of fantasy, could account for psychoneuroses. Freud thought that these neuroses
of defense, in contrast to actual neuroses, were to be accounted for by *past*
sexual experiences. Krüll proposes that when Freud talked about the patho-
genicity of the sexual strivings of children, rather than the seduction by
adults, he went wrong; she knows of course most historians take the view
that instead of it being an error to have replaced the seduction theory with
the Oedipus complex, that is when psychoanalysis proper began.

But it seems to me that, like McGrath, Krüll is naively wrongheaded in
believing that Jakob Freud's death was in any way as momentous to Freud
as he himself claimed. Freud often chose to escape from the threatening
present into the safety of the distant past. Krüll does write, in connection
with Freud's conflict with Carl G. Jung, that Freud ''once again invented a
theory that shifted the cause of his anxiety back into a legendary past.''[11] It
would have been helpful to highlight that Jung was the first to emphasize
that it is a neurotic characteristic to use the past defensively.

One would have thought that scholarly thinking meant not taking Freud
at his every word. It is all very well and good, and no doubt clinically
sound, to highlight the significance of family dynamics and the limitations
of mechanistic instinctualist reasoning. But why on earth insist that Freud
must be like us? It is too rationalistic to propose that if we see something as
important that Freud did not, then he must have been hiding from it, and
that an adequate explanation can be found in any solitary trauma such as
that associated with the death of his father.

Freud did indeed give up the notion that his own father was perverted, a
sexual seducer of at least some of his children. But if Freud abandoned his

no doubt nutty idea, it may have been this bizarre reproach of Jakob, not to mention the errors Freud imposed on patients by alleging that they too had been sexually abused in childhood, that helped Freud to some self-analysis in the 1890s. Krüll, however, thinks that Jakob's death put an end to Freud's efforts at self-understanding.

Approximately half of *Freud and His Father* consists of fascinating material that Krüll has assembled, partly on the basis of fieldwork of her own, about Freud's childhood and youth. She has tracked down details of Freud's early beginnings, both the people and the social circumstances, that constitute a real addition to the previous literature. (I am puzzled by her completely ignoring what I was told by Edward Bernays about the financial reasons for the Freud family move from Freiberg to Vienna: Jakob's good-natured bailing out of Freud's older half-brothers. It strikes me as without sufficient evidence, if not wild, for Krüll to postulate an affair between one of Jakob's sons and Freud's mother.)

It has to be mistaken of Krüll to title the chapter on Freud's early years "The Trauma."[12] Surely we have got away from the crude thinking that a genius can be reduced to any infantile emotional conflict. Krüll sometimes does understand that since most of the data we have come from the dreams and associations that Freud reported, much that gets written must remain speculative. While once it was taboo among analysts to dare to interpret a dream of Freud's, now the wheel has turned in completely the opposite direction. It should not take any special training to see sexual significance in Freud's famous dream about closing of eyes, but such a point is not part of Krüll's argument or the conventional literature either. On the whole, though, I am in favor of a moratorium in publications about Freud's dreams until people start remembering Freud's own warnings about trying to understand a dream without a dreamer's associations. Like McGrath, Krüll does not keep clearly enough in mind that anything Freud told us in print does not add up to real free associations. Anyway, if Krüll and others are capable of being so skeptical about psychoanalytic theory as a whole as to regret Freud's conviction about the significance of Oedipal fantasies, ought they not at least wonder whether there might not be a few things wrong with Freud's theory of dreaming?

I find the whole concern with the distant past as a valid explanation of Freud's thought an unsatisfactory way of proceeding. In a disturbing way I fear that Krüll's kind of approach, which starts out with the aim of encouraging an interest in real-life family dynamics, may end up reinforcing some of the most orthodox Freudian concentration on the traumas of early life. If, for example, it is agreed that Freud's account of the actual neuroses was autobiographical, did not Freud's wife take some part in his sexual life? Martha Freud plays altogether too little a role in Krüll's account of things, as for that matter does Freud's mother. Krüll may be right that our knowledge about Freud's mother's later life—she died in 1930—remains "very sparse indeed,"[13] but it is vast compared to the almost nothing that we know for sure about Freud's father.

Krüll has chosen to concentrate on "Freud's crisis of 1896–97,"[14] and proceeds to trace it back not just to his childhood, but to his conflicted feelings about his father and then of Jakob's about his own father. Supposedly Freud's research was "cut short by his father's death, which must have rekindled the repressed childhood fear that forbidden investigations invite terrible punishment."[15] Freud, according to this account, could assimilate his repressed childhood experience only by "fantasy—that of the universal Oedipus conflict, according to which the child's own sexual desires are responsible for his guilt so that the parents can be exonerated."[16] Krüll's argument that Freud's conflict with Jakob was a repetition of Jakob's struggle with his own father is at odds with Krüll's claim to have succeeded in getting away from Freud's emphasis on heredity.

Krüll thinks that it is "very sobering that Freud should have invented psychoanalysis because his father most probably had problems with his own sexuality and fought with his own father about matters of religion. . . ."[17] I do not think it is at all helpful to think that any one-track explanation for Freud's creation of psychoanalysis emancipates us from the notorious excesses of psychoanalytic traditionalism. It does not seem to me that we have moved away from the worst in Freud by using his life history to argue, as Krüll does, that "in our deepest feelings we have all remained the little children we once were."[18] That sort of reasoning might have been radical in Freud but now will strike most as boring.

Those who are already sophisticated about Freud and the beginnings of psychoanalysis will find many rewarding insights in *Freud and His Father*. But others will conclude that its search for early childhood secrets, and its general theme of how human beings keep repeating primitive patterns, do not sound like recent thinking yet have absorbed many of the soundest of the earliest critiques of psychoanalysis. Freud may often have been mistaken, and sometimes outrageously so, but intellectual historians can agree that despite the necessary existence of predecessors, his career was thoroughly original.

In the whole series of now famous controversies that marked Freud's career, the issue of cocaine and its uses was the first of the public quarrels. *Cocaine Papers,* edited by Robert Byck (1975), brings together the primary historical documents about Freud's involvement with cocaine, and the editor has also tried to place the drug's properties within modern psychopharmacology.

The problem of Freud's early recommendation of cocaine and his own personal use of it is of more genuine significance and perplexity than once might have been thought. He was highly intolerant of alcohol, which helped bring about at least one of his fainting spells, and fiercely resentful of any of his dependencies, yet of course he did smoke all those cigars: twenty a day. It is still surprising that in 1884 he began experimenting—on himself, his future wife, and his sisters, as well as others—with the way cocaine could relieve anxiety and depression. He even prescribed cocaine to counteract the morphine addiction of a friend.

One can fairly ask how cocaine affected Freud's dream life, accounts of which are in his *Interpretation of Dreams,* and wonder whether his proselytizing in behalf of the drug had a parallel later in his forwarding of psychoanalysis. The unexpurgated Freud/Fliess letters now demonstrate that Freud did use cocaine far longer than anyone, including even the editor of *Cocaine Papers,* had realized.

The editor has contributed a fine introduction, which points out the influence on Freud of medical reports about cocaine in American journals. One cannot help wondering if Freud's later prejudices against the United States were not partly due to the help from that continent in his early mistake about that drug. It is worth remembering that Coca-Cola contained cocaine until 1903.

At the risk of raising what may seem a side point, I think it is worth pointing out as an aspect of American intellectual history that the cover of *Cocaine Papers* proclaims "Notes" by Anna Freud; the title page is more accurate in announcing, with her name in large letters, that the notes on the Freud papers are by Anna Freud. In reality her editing amounts to an inconsequential contribution to this book, and to our understanding of the relevant texts. But it is a sign of the enormous standing she achieved in the United States, despite her own sharp reservations about that country, which she shared with her father, that her notes should characteristically be so blown out of proportion.

Although Anna Freud's work has long been viewed with appropriate skepticism in Great Britain, on the other side of the Atlantic she almost never has been criticized; such religiosity in psychoanalysis is always a mistake. Exaggerated views of her stature amount to an invitation to subsequent debunking. A rereading of her *The Ego and the Mechanisms of Defense* would easily demonstrate the theoretical untenability of her position; it is tellingly phony that the supposedly revised edition of this book in her *Collected Papers* appears textually unchanged. Her finest writing, in my opinion, came with her World War II descriptions of the emotional lives of small children at her nursery. But once it becomes possible to put in perspective the veneration of her as the symbol of her father's genius and his cause, we will be better able to counteract the baleful impact of her collaboration in injecting questionable middle-class biases into legal doctrines affecting the welfare of children. The influence she had in her lifetime on studies of Freud is another story altogether, but it is worth noting, in connection with *Cocaine Papers,* that at the time of the first preparation of Siegfried Bernfeld's now famous paper on Freud and cocaine, which is included here, she took a dim view of it; although she found its factual side interesting, she wrote Ernest Jones that she considered its interpretations loose, in error, and sometimes ludicrous.

Cocaine Papers is an authorative collection, and I was able to find only two howlers. The proposition that "Ernest Jones was Freud's personally selected biographer"[19] is of course untrue. Freud wanted no biography, and it was his daughter Anna who, long after her father's death, authorized Jones and gave him the primary source material that he used. The other striking mistake in this book comes in the partial description of Julius Wagner-Jauregg as "a professor of Freud's in Vienna;"[20] in fact, Freud and Wagner-Jauregg had been contemporaries at school and shared a complicated rivalry between them. It is true, as this book does indicate, that Wagner was a psychiatrist who won the Nobel Prize, but the crux of the problem between him and Freud was that they were colleagues who went in different directions and achieved contrasting kinds of success.

Cocaine Papers is thorough on the details of what happened in the 1880s, although it underestimates Freud's continued personal involvement in the use of cocaine throughout the 1890s. Cocaine presumably bears on the interest in the nose that Freud shared with Wilhelm Fliess. The editor also misses some documentary evidence connected with Freud's obsessive-sounding concern with Karl Koller's earning world fame for the discovery of cocaine as a local anesthetic in eye surgery. Hanns Sachs, among others, remembered a discussion by Freud of the cocaine incident, in which Freud attributed to Koller a method of working that sounds like Freud's own single-minded style of discovery; Sachs put this account into his well-known little book on Freud, which the editor might well have included here or at least called attention to.

In reading once again Freud's commentary from his autobiography, the relevant fragment of which is contained in this book, on how he had missed out on Koller's breakthrough, I wondered for the first time whether when Freud blamed his fiancée for losing out on Koller's discovery, because of a trip Freud made to see her in Germany, he was not engaging in one of his subtle jokes. In any event Freud, who at the time thought that Koller had only exploited one of the possible beneficial uses of the drug, later laid claim to an analytic patient for the credit of Koller's achievement. In pursuing the issue of assertions to scientific priority in Freud's career, which becomes a repetitious theme in many of the controversies associated with his name, the cocaine episode represents an important chapter.

The whole matter of cocaine was damaging to Freud in Vienna because he had irresponsibly foreseen none of the dangers connected with the drug. He had earned public denunciation for his recklessness. Freud recommended in a medical publication the use of cocaine in promoting withdrawal from morphine addiction, on the basis of Freud's experience with only one such case. (The patient soon afterward developed a toxic psychosis.) We still need to know more about the effects of cocaine, sexually as well as otherwise, in order to evaluate properly its full role in Freud's life and in the history of psychoanalysis.

Cocaine Papers now stands, over a decade after its first appearance, as an indispensable source book in connection with the important subject it documents. The stature of the issue of cocaine is not, I think, undermined by a recent polemical attempt, which I will now discuss, to discredit Freud's psychoanalytic theories by tracing their origin to cocaine intoxication.

It is true that sectarian feelings have led to hero worshiping, which has made it hard to advance the cause of impartial inquiry into the history of psychoanalysis. On the other hand, E. M. Thornton's *The Freudian Fallacy* (1983) (published in England under the title *Freud and Cocaine*) is testimony to the undisciplined prejudices that still exist about Freud. He is even today capable of arousing the most intense feelings.

The brief foreword, by the late Raymond Greene, a Harley Street endocrinologist, will be enough to make most people toss *The Freudian Fallacy* aside. The book, Dr. Greene tells us, "might well be called 'The Demolition of Sigmund Freud.' It is difficult to understand the strength of his influence over modern medicine, for his teaching lacks any scientific support." The quality of Freud's hypotheses is alleged to be illustrated by "his ridiculous theory of infantile sexuality." And the explanation of how Freud went wrong can supposedly be found in his "addiction to cocaine," an answer that, according to Dr. Greene, "has much to recommend it."[21]

It is a pity that Thornton's research should be introduced by so partisan an endorsement. She herself, however, can be self-indulgently extremist. She believes that " 'the unconscious mind' . . . does not exist, that his [Freud's] theories were baseless and aberrational, and, greatest impiety of all, that Freud himself, when he formulated them, was under the influence of a toxic drug with specific effects on the brain."[22] She singles out for attention "the paranoid delusions of persecution peculiar to the later stages of cocaine addiction. . . . "[23]

Freud never argued, despite what Ms. Thornton says, in favor of "the overriding supremacy of sexuality over all other facets of civilized existence and the urgent necessity that it should suffer no restraint or impediment if mankind were not to fall victim to mental illness of the gravest kind."[24] Such a theory would be preposterous if not pathological; Freud was in reality writing on the premise that people were capable of an inordinate degree of sexual self-restraint.

Thornton's attempt to explore the physical side of the complaints of Freud's early patients is ruined by the polemical tone that especially pervades her early and last pages. For example, she tells us that "with the shrewd calculation often displayed by the psychotic, Freud selected as disciples writers and other leaders of lay opinion."[25] Freud had his failings, but Thornton states without qualification that "psychoanalysis has no curative value"[26] and that Freud's theories are both "invalid and aberrational."[27] She also alleges that hypnotism can cause epilepsy.

The Freudian Fallacy has insights that merit attention. Yet Thornton cannot even fathom the source of Freud's interest in Sophocles' *Oedipus Rex* without dragging in cocaine intoxication here, too. It is too bad that so much work had to be ruined by the partisanship of this unfortunate book.

In reflecting on the origins of Freud's work many have found it appropriate that a Jew founded psychoanalysis. Members of an oppressed group are well placed for appreciating what outsiders like neurotics are up against. The marginal social position of Jews helped them to take the risks involved in becoming members of the new profession of analysis. Jews have always made up an unusually large share of the psychoanalytic movement and have had a special affinity for Freud's psychology. It would appear to be impossible to overemphasize Freud's Jewishness; I think there is no more important part of his background. In *From Oedipus to Moses: Freud's Jewish Identity* (1976) Marthe Robert quotes an eloquent letter of Franz Kafka's to illuminate our understanding of Freud's position as a Jew; after reading a book by the Viennese Karl Kraus, Kafka wrote:

What appeals to me more than psychoanalysis [in this book] is the observation that the father complex from which more than one Jew draws his spiritual nourishment relates not to the innocent father but to the father's Judaism. What most of those who began to write in German wanted was to break with Judaism, generally with the vague approval of their fathers (this vagueness is the revolting part of it). That is what they wanted, but their hind legs were bogged down in their fathers' Judaism, and their front legs could find no new ground. The resulting despair was their inspiration.[28]

Marthe Robert addresses herself to a central feature in understanding psychoanalysis. She discerns in Freud a characteristically Jewish spirit of revolt and a notably Jewish passion for ideas. Her approach is the more noteworthy in that orthodox psychoanalysts have downplayed Freud's Jewish identity. Ernest Jones was a rationalistic Gentile who sought to make psychoanalysis appear as a universally valid contribution to science. Freud's doctrines, therefore, were treated by Jones as beyond cultural influences, as well as immune to distortion by personal conflicts in Freud himself. According to traditional psychoanalytic ways of thinking, any discussion of Freud's Jewishness entails the anti-Semitism that Freud accused Carl G. Jung of sharing.

One source of Robert's relative lack of success in her valid project is a curious biographical principle: "We shall do well to concentrate on what he himself, in his voluminous correspondence and in the directly autobiographical part of his work, said on the subject. . . . "[29] Freud's own view of his Jewishness and his conscious attitude toward Christianity are obviously important. But it is necessary to go beyond what Freud himself wrote, to weigh more critically the implications of his conscious thoughts, to assess the contradictions and tensions in his ideas, not to mention taking into consideration what others, even while Freud was still alive, had to say on the same subject.

Robert labors under the identical kind of unconscious restrictions from which too many other writers on Freud have suffered. It is true that she tries to unravel the text of Freud's *Moses and Monotheism,* but she isolates the subjective distortions in this book from Freud's studies of Leonardo and Dostoevsky. If Freud wrote mainly about his conflicted feelings for his father and very little about his mother, Robert accepts Freud's view of things; we are offered the remarkable proposition, also endorsed by McGrath and Krüll, that Freud's father was "the main and perhaps the only source of his psychic difficulties. . . . "[30] Robert bases her own approach on Freud's "express opinions," in contrast to those who have looked for unconscious motives on the assumption that Freud was "lacking in self knowledge."[31] Yet Freud taught that everyone suffers from self-deception, and it can be no tribute to his system of ideas to exclude the creator of psychoanalysis from the scrutiny of his own conceptualization. In fact, psychoanalysis turns out to be a highly autobiographical creative form.

Robert's book is marred by distressing historical mistakes, all of which seem to stem from her credulous acceptance of partisan accounts of the beginnings of psychoanalysis. She renews the claim, initially started by Freud and repeated by Jones, that there was a friendship between Edoardo Weiss and Mussolini that was responsible for protecting the Italian Psychoanalytic Society. In reality, the only relationship between Weiss and Mussolini was a distant one: Weiss treated the daughter of one of Mussolini's cabinet ministers. When Robert tells us that Freud's 1928 letter to Morselli shows that Freud "was by no means the uncompromising doctrinaire that some people choose to see in him,"[32] she is evidently unaware that Freud simultaneously wrote others letters that damned Morselli with invective worthy of Freud at his most embattled. To take just one more glaring error: "Far from being wealthy at the time when he emigrated he was unable to pay the ransom demanded by the Nazis (the money was raised by Princess Marie Bonaparte)."[33] The truth of the matter is that Freud wisely had not kept money in Vienna but had had it deposited abroad, so he temporarily allowed Princess Marie to help him out; when he died a year later in London, he left an estate of sixteen thousand English pounds, making him by 1939 standards a "wealthy" man.

Despite a certain amount of such misinformation and some lack of interpretive skill, Robert's *From Oedipus to Moses* is a pleasant series of well-written essays. She is aware of the tendentious editing of Freud's letters; such censorship is bound in the end to be counterproductive, for that which Freud's children have seen fit to omit from publication will in the end get heightened attention, far more so than if Freud had been permitted to appear without such cuts. Nonetheless, although Robert's book is an advance beyond what was written about Freud thirty years ago, it is still woefully inadequate to state: "Freud never attacked the Jews as such and was never irritated by them or ashamed of them; he always felt a kind of attraction or sympathy for them."[34] On such a critical subject as Freud's Jewishness we must be more sensitive to the ambivalences that Freud taught us must accompany all deep emotional attachments.

Peter Gay's *A Godless Jew: Freud, Atheism and the Making of Psychoanalysis* (1987) is a short but peculiar book, all the more odd since the author is a professional historian. It grew out of three lectures he gave at Hebrew Union College in Cincinnati, in which he tells us he "had a single argument to make."[35] In fleshing out the lectures for publication Gay retained his singleness of purpose, despite the fact that at its best history communicates multiplicity and diversity: he wanted to reflect "on Freud's atheism and on its meaning for his creation, psychoanalysis."[36]

Gay has undergone formal psychoanalytic training in New Haven and is now an honorary member of the American Psychoanalytic Association. But instead of his dual set of training experiences having led him to a genuinely broad effort at encouraging interdisciplinary cooperation, Gay sees himself as trying to lead the loyalist cause within the history of psychoanalysis. If others within the last generation, ever since the publication of Jones's biography of Freud, have sought to show signs of the master that the more politic of the Freudians tried to disguise, Gay appears to be an apologist putting what he conceives as the best face on everything connected to Freud. In the past other famous intellectuals besides Gay himself, such as Stanley Edgar Hyman, were eager to accomplish the same objective, but it is remarkable that Gay is undertaking his task now, after so much of the revisionary (or "post-Freudian") water has already gone under the dam.

As with others who define themselves as defenders of Freud, what Gay is up to is not only unnecessary but fundamentally wrongheaded. Gay insists on the positive significance of Freud's atheism; if psychoanalysis arose precisely because of its lack of contamination by religious thinking and Freud's Jewish background, then the implication seems to be that the standing of psychoanalysis as a neutral science has been enhanced. Such would appear to be the propagandistic upshot of the "single argument" Gay has chosen to advance.

Freud was, however, far more open-minded than a rationalist like Gay can appreciate. As a historian, Gay should have remembered how Freud could, late at night at a coffeehouse and in the presence of a horrified skeptic like Jones, speculate about the existence of God. The fact that Freud was able to take so seriously the possibilities of the reality of telepathy and occultism meant that he possessed the temperament that made him able in the first place to come up with the daring set of ideas that we now know as psychoanalysis.

Freud did write his *Future of an Illusion* in 1927, when he was dying of cancer, but Gay cannot see that the essay reflects only one shallow side of Freud's understanding of human emotions. As a therapist Freud could be intolerant, certainly by today's standards; he expected people to be able to change, overcoming themselves. But Freud's most radical expectations about patients could blind him to necessary elements of humaneness. He could be so impatient of the infantile and the regressive as to fail to understand their functions. Elsewhere in Freud's work, especially when he was younger, he would not have been so superficial as to say of religion, as he did in *Future of an Illusion,* that "ignorance is ignorance,"[37] as if superstition could possibly be all there was to it.

Gay has earlier published on the Enlightenment, and he is correct as an intellectual historian to place Freud within the legacy of eighteenth-century rationalism. I found every one of Gay's references to eighteenth-century thinking fascinating, although I do believe there was much more to Freud than can be reduced to that solitary rationalist strain of thought. But it is weird in *A Godless Jew* how Gay moves, almost in the same breath, from examining some of the greatest thinkers in Western thought to considering banal writers like Joshua Loth Liebman. Surely there is a difference between the highest intellectual history and the study of such low-level texts.

Furthermore, Gay's scholarship on Freud is strikingly faulty. Gay quotes as the epigraph to his book a well-worn passage from a letter of Freud's to Oskar Pfister, but Gay ignores the full scale of Pfister's response to Freud. *A Godless Jew* contains a twenty-page bibliography, yet both it and Gay's text omit Pfister's 1928 "The Illusion of the Future," which was written as a direct answer to Freud's *Future of an Illusion*. If Gay does not even report the ever-loyal Pfister's rebuttal of Freud's position, that tells something about how narrow a range of ideological scope Gay is willing to place Freud's argument within.

Gay has done a good deal of archival work, as part of his research for a biography of Freud. Gay has examined some newly available letters of Freud's that can be found, for example, at the Freud Museum in London as well as at the Library of Congress in Washington, D.C. Gay has also obtained the permission of the Freud Copyrights to quote from hitherto unpublished material. But it looks to me as if Gay's partisanship does not allow him to make full use of what he has seen.

Freud advertised his religious unbelief, and he also paraded his lack of responsiveness to music, but just as there is far more to be said about Freud's relationship to music there has, I think, to be more than just an atheist in Freud. It is peculiar of Gay, when he cites Freud's admittedly "religious metaphors," to try to argue that they "were only metaphors,"[38] as if a great writer's language was somehow not to be taken seriously. Gay gives a sympathetic account of William James's attitude toward the rivalry between science and religion, and then Gay tells us that Freud would have regarded James's position as "sheer blasphemy."[39] Are we to take Gay's metaphor seriously, or is this just the loosest of talk? In any event, I believe that Gay is wrong and that Freud himself was more philosophically sophisticated than Gay wants to allow. As Freud used to quote Hamlet, "there are more things in heaven and earth, Horatio, than are dreamt of in your philosophy."

Gay persists in talking about Freud's "discoveries." I now think that it would be better if we abandoned that particular metaphor. Freud put forward a conception of the unconscious, he had an idea about a theory of infantile sexuality, he invented a new treatment setting, and he created a powerful movement of thought that attracted articulate disciples. If we abandon the imagery of "discovery" it might be easier to tolerate more give-and-take about the drawbacks as well as the merits to Freud's particular world view. Gay rightly tells us that "the researcher holds literally nothing sacrosanct,"[40] and I believe that that principle should be applied to all Freud's own work.

Details in Gay's book are as questionable as his general outlook. For example, he acknowledges that in practice, for example with the "Wolf-Man," Freud took a position at variance with the thesis of *Future of an Illusion*, but Gay cannot acknowledge the full gulf between Freud's speculations as a theorist and his conduct as a clinician. All Gay tells us is that "it is interesting to see Freud's scientific, wholly 'disenchanted' view of religion at work in his case histories.''[41] That is no kind of way to alert a reader to the news that Freud viewed religion's effects on the young Wolf-Man in wholly positive terms.

Gay advances Freud's eldest child Martin's version that Christmas was a special festival in Freud's household, yet I happen to have interviewed an old non-Jewish neighbor in the Berggasse, who told me that Freud children used to come by to see the Christmas decorations, which they did not have at home. Gay is so determined to work from the premise of psychoanalysis being a universal body of truths that he cannot accept Freud's Jewishness, even though it patently pervaded every aspect of Freud's life and work.

Gay promotes many of the old myths that Freud first put into the history books: that Josef Breuer in his treatment of Anna O. ''shied away from the sexual roots of her spectacular hysteria'' and that the ''provocations'' for the break with Alfred Adler and Carl Jung ''did not principally come from Freud.''[42] It is also strange for Gay to quote an anecdote of Sir Isaiah Berlin's, about an exchange between Freud and his wife on the issue of lighting candles on Friday evening, without identifying Berlin as the source and instead citing an anonymous ''private communication.''[43] Berlin long ago told me the story, exactly as Gay reports it here, and I used it in my *Freud and His Followers*. (Jones had exaggerated and distorted the whole business for the sake of constructing a polemical straw man.) On the basis of Berlin's contact with Freud, Berlin did not, however, consider Freud a great man, a judgment Berlin repeated to a distressed Kurt Eissler during the course of an interview to be locked away in the Freud archives.

In my opinion it is possible to appreciate Freud's genius without minimizing in any way the momentous role of Jewishness to his creativity. Despite the many advances in recent scholarship, the history of early psychoanalysis, even when written by professionals, is still likely to be influenced by ideological considerations. Freud was great enough to withstand our most unblinkered scrutiny, and it should also be possible to explore the variety of national responses to his work without detracting from the unity of structure that he came up with in his system of ideas.

Notes

1. William J. McGrath, *Freud's Discovery of Psychoanalysis: The Politics of Hysteria* (Ithaca: Cornell University Press, 1986), p. 109.
2. Ibid., p. 207.
3. Ibid., p. 225.
4. Marianne Krüll, *Freud and His Father*, trans. Arnold J. Pomerans (New York: Norton, 1986), p. 69.
5. Ibid.
6. Ibid., p. 70.

7. Ibid.
8. Ibid., p. xiii.
9. Ibid., p. 20.
10. Ibid.
11. Ibid., p. 193.
12. Ibid., p. 103.
13. Ibid., p. 71.
14. Ibid., p. 177.
15. Ibid.
16. Ibid., p. 178.
17. Ibid., p. 180.
18. Ibid.
19. Robert Byck, ed., *Cocaine Papers: Sigmund Freud* (New York: New American Library, 1975), p. 5.
20. Ibid., p. 402.
21. E. M. Thornton, *The Freudian Fallacy: An Alternative View of Freudian Theory* (New York: Dial Press, 1984), p. vii.
22. Ibid., p. 15.
23. Ibid., p. xi.
24. Ibid., p. xii.
25. Ibid., p. xiv.
26. Ibid., p. xv.
27. Ibid., p. xvi.
28. Marthe Robert, *From Oedipus to Moses: Freud's Jewish Identity* (New York: Anchor Books, 1976), p. 9.
29. Ibid., p. 27.
30. Ibid., p. 122.
31. Ibid., pp. 171–72.
32. Ibid., p. 183.
33. Ibid., p. 185.
34. Ibid., p. 35.
35. Peter Gay, *A Godless Jew: Freud, Atheism, and the Making of Psychoanalysis* (New Haven: Yale University Press, 1987), p. xi.
36. Ibid.
37. Sigmund Freud, "Future of An Illusion," *Standard Edition*, vol. 21, p. 32.
38. Gay, *A Godless Jew*, p. 18.
39. Ibid., p. 26.
40. Ibid., p. 46.
41. Ibid., p. 40.
42. Ibid., p. 139, p. 143.
43. Ibid., p. 153.

2

The Old World

Initially Freud's loyal disciples, in all countries, saw their task as that of rounding off what he had introduced in only a fragmentary way. Any successful movement, however, has a way of absorbing into itself some of the best ideas of the opposition, and by now there has been so much silent incorporation within psychoanalysis of ideas unknowingly taken over from Adler, Jung, and Rank that it is all too easy to read back into past "orthodox" doctrine what is accepted only today. It can be hard for even the best of contemporary analysts to find out much about their own history, for the training they undergo is highly selective in what it covers. An unspoken degree of conformism, as in most professions, melds together some of the most cohesive of the existing group ties. Freud's own power lay in his capacities as a writer, clinician, and pioneering leader; only in America has psychoanalysis rested on an institutional base intimately bound up with the official psychiatry Freud scorned.

In Great Britain, however, twentieth-century psychiatry has developed along a very different course from that which it has followed in the States. While Freudian concepts have long pervaded American culture, more old-fashioned attitudes have prevailed in England. Today Freud is still looked upon with a higher degree of suspicion in Britain, and medicine as a whole is accorded nowhere near as high a status as in the United States. Famous British analysts have tended not even to be English; Jones was Welsh, Edward Glover a Scot, and Melanie Klein and Anna Freud both emigrated from the Continent. As happened in the early days of Central European psychoanalysis, the lack of popular acclaim has meant that in England psychotherapy as a career attracted highly talented practitioners, able to resist pressures to conform. A few of the British analysts who write are, I think, far ahead of any American rivals in clarity and scope.

Although Jones led a tiny band of analysts in London before the outbreak of World War I, the important history of British psychoanalysis does not start until the early 1920s. The analytic group was then not yet intellectually sure of itself but had already attracted some remarkable figures to its ranks. Once Melanie Klein moved from Berlin to London in 1926, British analysis began to acquire its distinctive ideological character. Klein's version of child analysis was not merely a challenge to Anna Freud's practices, for Klein increasingly began to offer a full-scale variation on the Freudian outlook. Things in Britain were developing so at odds with the Freudians on the Continent that some suggested that the British Psychoanalytic Society was becoming schismatic.

The 1938 arrival in London of Freud and the Viennese analysts marked the end to the relative freethinking that had prevailed beforehand. During World War II the so-called Controversial Discussions took place within the British Society. Although it was numerically much smaller than its American counterpart, the group was wracked by a quarrel over whether Melanie Klein's ideas were "deviationist."

The level of controversy in psychoanalytic circles is normally quite low. In the light of all the attention given to the splits in the history of psychoanalysis this claim may seem surprising, but having discouraged controversy and promoted conformity to the group's will (if not Freud's own), psychoanalysis has benefited less than might be expected by the ventilation of differences of opinion. When the occasional blowup has occurred, it has generally been disproportionately violent. Admittedly, as Freud himself once pointed out, the nature of the evidence in psychoanalysis is such that one cannot hope for the same degree of certainty as in other disciplines that aspire to scientific status. Observers do not share the same evidence—and excommunication becomes more likely as a method of settling a dispute. But while in retrospect the wrangling over Melanie Klein may look like too much washing of dirty linen in public, the continuing presence of rival systems of thought in Britain has stimulated the growth of new ideas. In contrast, the broad American endorsement of Freudianism has led to a less lively atmosphere.

The issues in Britain during World War II were power and the training of candidates, since Klein's approach was being accused of constituting a new heresy. The groups around Anna Freud and Melanie Klein presented their sides of the case. Jones's autocracy was in abeyance, since he had semiretired to the country, but he was known to be sympathetic to Klein. In the end the controversy petered out, with Anna Freud's group being allowed to have their own separate training facilities within the British Society. A devoted band of committed Kleinians continued their own work, and the largest group of analysts, called the Middle Group or the Independents, who wanted to be free from either of the two rival doctrines, sought to evolve a separate path of their own.

*   *   *

The British School of Psychoanalysis: The Independent Tradition, edited
by Gregorio Kohon (1986), is an attempt to present the mature ideas coming from the Middle Group of analysts. The book contains a lengthy introductory note about the history of the psychoanalytic movement in Britain,
which provides an overview of the distinctly British contributions, and then
the rest consists of relatively recent professional papers, almost all of which
first appeared either in the *International Journal of Psychoanalysis* or its
sister, the *International Review of Psychoanalysis.*

The fierceness of the quarrels between Melanie Klein's party and that of
Anna Freud meant that British analysts have had to come to term with two
quite different ways of thinking. Both these highly sectarian groups had
more money and power than the numerically larger Independents. While in
the United States a monolithic Freudian view held sway at the most fashionable centers of training, at least until the recent advent of so-called plu-
ralism, in Britain there was a chance for more distance from received
wisdom. But British analysts have never earned the professional status or
charged fees as high as across the Atlantic.

Kohon tries his best to keep his narrative impersonal. He does not highlight any of the human tensions between the leaders in British analysis. If
Jones, for example, backed the cause of "lay" (nonmedical) analysis despite personal misgivings, it was in part because medically untrained therapists would pose less threat to his control of the British Society. Kohon's
account of the Controversial Discussions avoids such distasteful stuff as one
of Melanie Klein's chief accusers being her own daughter, Melitta Schmide-
berg.

Kohon does successfully highlight how the Independents made a special
contribution to elucidating the role of countertransference in treatment. Analysts have unconscious reactions of their own, especially to the patients'
obscure feelings that stem from their distant childhood past. Countertransference can be a useful therapeutic tool as well as an interference, but the
concept highlights that what happens in treatment is an encounter, a relationship between two people. Kohon hopes that British thinking has escaped the "sterility"[1] that he acknowledges too often marks the
productions of psychoanalytic writers. A little less historical piety on Kohon's part—he alleges, for instance, that "it was from his patients that
Freud learned psychoanalysis"[2]—would doubtless have succeeded in emancipating him even more.

The worst papers appear in the first section of the book, which focuses
on early childhood. All the writers have the worthy aim of concentrating on
what Freud excluded—the relation of mother and child. But the papers are
dull because they are too abstract, really theological, since they discuss

early infancy as if its psychology has been established neutrally. It is disturbing that some of these writers not only do not treat children but seem never to have had any children of their own.

All the papers in this volume share a genial kind of harmony. But one of the problems in the history of psychoanalysis is that there has been an inadequate number of reasonable disagreements. No one throughout this book challenges the merits of regressions, although it is true that Michael Balint draws a distinction between benign and malignant regression. More fundamentally, the concept of the legitimacy of therapeutic dependency has promoted much more extended analyses than Freud originally envisaged. Writers here talk about the first, second, and third years of analysis without any apology; nobody questions what the disadvantages of long-term treatment might be. At least until someone starts asking about the infantile gratifications for analyst as well as patient in such long-term treatments it is hard not to think that a large subject is being ignored needlessly.

Furthermore, why is no one worrying about the extent to which the analytic situation contributes to clinical phenomena? Some years ago Erik H. Erikson suggested that the classical psychoanalytic setup resembled a sensory deprivation experiment and that much so-called transference material was in fact a response not to the patient's own problems but to the difficulties in coping with the peculiar circumstances of psychoanalytic treatment. It should not be heresy to entertain such ideas, which serve as a check on the unverifiable speculation that goes on in the British Society about the nature of infancy.

The clinical illustrations in the book are always engrossing. This is partly because these analysts have been so bold as to treat psychotic patients; here one worries when the therapists are untrained medically and there is no sign of biochemical knowledge. All the lives and problems of these patients are unusual enough to command our attention. But the reactions of the analysts can be just as bizarre, as they struggle over a conflict between what they have been taught as the technical rules of their training and what they feel to be the demands of their common humanity.

For me the best section of the book was one on "The Psychoanalytic Encounter: Transference and Counter-Transference" where one gets live reports of the treatment itself. One analyst even bravely conceded having bawled out a patient and admitted that hardly any analyst talks about laughter in a clinical session. If analysts did not feel so prim, they would write much more about how second analyses differ from first analyses; they would explore the rigidities in technique that lead to therapeutic failures; they might discuss the processes of referral by which a patient gets sent to one analyst rather than another, and they would acknowledge how psychoanalytic training can interfere with the creativity of candidates. How do patients in psychotherapy compare with those in psychoanalysis, and what are the grounds for one type of treatment as opposed to the other? It would be good to know how countertransference feelings differ toward patients in different forms of therapy. Although one writer here does acknowledge "the state of *malaise* existing in the relationship between our theory and our clinical work,"[3] this book will do little to ameliorate that problem.

The final unit in this volume has as its topic female sexuality, but there is little that is genuinely innovative or even broadly based on the available literature. It is too late in the day for ritualistic utterances like "as we all know, Freud was a true scientist. . . . " or such in-group fears as the "danger of going the way of Jung."[4]

This book reminds us of the extraordinary personal dedication within the Freudian tradition. Perhaps there can never be a final reassurance that psychoanalysis has succeeded in avoiding becoming the illness for which it purports to be a cure. But the Middle Group of British analysts could go a lot further in an independent direction and still lay claim to its ties to the Freudian heritage.

The widespread influence of Freud's work has meant that the literature on psychoanalysis continues to multiply into an avalanche. The extensiveness of the available knowledge only underlines how embarrassing certain books can be in their conception.

Freud and the Humanities, edited by Peregrine Horden (1985), consists of a series of seven Chichele Lectures given at All Souls College at Oxford during 1984. The individual contributors were supposed to trace Freud's impact on aspects of the arts and the humanities. In the course of this meritorious project each of the lecturers makes a number of worthwhile observations. Freud had thought that the real test of his work would come at the ancient centers of culture, and therefore the existence of this lecture series is a sign that Freud has at least temporarily succeeded in coming into his own at Oxford. Although a sister-in-law of Virginia Woolf taught psychoanalytic concepts at Cambridge as early as the 1920s, on the whole Oxford has successfully resisted the invasion of ideas associated with Freud's system of thought.

The editor's introduction is, however, an amateurish piece of work. When he maintains that "the seven essays collected here form part of a far larger enterprise that, despite the volume of commentary psychoanalysis has engendered, is only now beginning in scholarly and critical earnest,"[5] he would seem not to know that the literature about Freud has been accumulating for almost one hundred years. Can it seriously be suggested that in this past century writers have not known something of what they were talking about? The lectures themselves are far too slight to bear out the purpose the editor claims for them. Serious yet respectful criticisms of Freud and his ideas have been available for generations, and one would have thought that any historian of ideas would be aware of the prior literature on the subject.

It is simply not accurate to state, as the editor does in his introduction, that the "neo-Freudians" took "their cue from the schismatic Alfred Adler."[6] It is true that there are analogies in the ideas of Freudian revisionists to the "heresies" of both Jung and Adler, but that does not prove any historical influences were necessarily at work.

Despite the naive conceptual underpinning offered to *Freud and the Humanities*, some of the lectures, particularly those by Charles Rycroft, Anthony Storr, and Richard Ellmann, make sophisticated reading. But if All Souls College wanted to correct an imbalance at Oxford in the appreciation of the importance of Freud for the arts and the humanities, more attention should have been paid to how to make a coherent whole out of seven such disparate contributions.

Books about figures from the Bloomsbury group in London have continued to multiply. At the same time studies of the international early followers of Freud have also grown to comprise a separate scholarly industry. Such circles of creative people that inspire and support each other are historically not that common; therefore, *Bloomsbury/Freud: The Letters of James and Alix Strachey, 1924–25*, edited by Perry Meisel and Walter Kendrick (1985), a collection of letters between James Strachey and his wife Alix, both of whom were members of the Bloomsbury set as well as disciples of Freud, arouses great interest.

James Strachey, literary biographer Lytton Strachey's younger brother, authorized Michael Holroyd to write Lytton's own biography, and until now James has probably best been known for the crusty letters he wrote protesting a draft of Holroyd's book; Holroyd was shrewd enough to print portions of James's letters as entertaining footnotes to his excellent text.

Both James and Alix were, like the rest of Bloomsbury, educated at Cambridge and were friendly with such people as John Maynard Keynes and Virginia Woolf. But the accomplishment for which the Stracheys will best be remembered was their success in carrying out Freud's mandate to translate him from German into English. Freud first appointed them to this task in 1920, when they were in psychoanalytic treatment with him in Vienna; it was unusual for Freud to treat a married couple simultaneously, and if one of them had to miss an analytic hour the other would see Freud for two sessions a day. Freud's command of English was excellent, and he spotted the Stracheys as reliable interpreters; they consulted him as they worked on their translations. James also found Freud a publisher, Leonard

Woolf at the Hogarth Press. After Freud's death, James took charge of translating into English the Standard Edition of Freud's works, which ran to twenty-four volumes.

Bruno Bettelheim recently has challenged some of the Stracheys' translations, as he has tried to blame their use of words for the course psychoanalysis has taken in the English-speaking world. In particular, Bettelheim thinks that the Stracheys' personal animosity toward religious terms and their commitment to psychoanalysis as a scientific discipline meant that the humanistic and spiritual side of Freud's thought has been underestimated and the practice of psychoanalysis unnecessarily confined to physicians. Both James and Alix themselves were, however, nonmedical practitioners of analysis, and the scrupulously fine editing of this new collection of letters is able to speak out in defense of how they proceeded as translators. Freud was not only immensely pleased with their work on his texts, but he even used some of the terms they coined (such as *cathexis*[7]) in his own manuscripts. The editorial apparatus of Strachey's Standard Edition is so impressive that the latest comprehensive edition of Freud's works in German has translated the Strachey notes.

The Stracheys were separated during 1924 to 1925, while Alix pursued her second analysis with Karl Abraham in Berlin. Like others, Alix considered Freud deficient as a therapist. While Alix was in treatment with Abraham, James had returned to London, where he started analyzing patients himself. The letters in *Bloomsbury/Freud* remind me of my own first impression of the Stracheys, when I interviewed them on Freud and the history of psychoanalysis in 1965. It seemed to me then, and even more so now, that it was altogether unlikely that either could ever have gone on to be psychoanalysts. They regarded an effort to ameliorate the suffering of patients as a "therapeutic stunt."[8] According to a reliable story in London psychoanalytic circles, James once had a patient in analysis whose free associations in treatment seemed incomprehensible. At that time there was a technical rule of thumb that when an analyst did not understand what was going on with a patient, the analyst should say nothing, and supposedly for one year Strachey remained silent. The patient, incidentally, remained in treatment with Strachey for years and went on later to become a famous psychoanalyst himself.

Both James and Alix Strachey were attractive as eccentrics; they were remarkably bookish and could survive because of their secure private incomes. But these letters demonstrate how misanthropic they could be. They were snobbishly upper-class (they referred to "filthy lower-class figures"[9]), anti-Semitic, and they distrusted things American.

The Stracheys did not care for children either, which makes their support for Melanie Klein's program of child analysis all the more interesting.

Klein was, like Alix, a patient of Abraham; at one point Alix calls Klein's mind "an awful mess."[10]

Melanie Klein's rather weird ideas about the mental life of children fascinated Alix, and it was Alix who wrote James in London about Klein, and James in turn who contacted Jones in Klein's behalf. Klein's proposal that all children ought to be analyzed fitted Alix's view of what the "turd-manipulating"[11] "little brats"[12] deserved. Klein's work also fed the animosity the Stracheys felt toward parents.

The letters document the official and uncharitable party line about Otto Rank's supposed "defection" from Freud. Although the Stracheys knew little of what was really going on between Freud and Rank, they were harsh about Rank's side of things. Carl G. Jung also gets insultingly dismissed.

Bloomsbury/Freud is not momentous in its contribution to the history of psychoanalysis, but it is a lively read. Both James and Alix knew how to write in an engaging manner. Only a small portion of their letters bear on their calling as translators. As long as one discounts their characteristic exaggerations and biases, they become indispensable witnesses to a past era.

Since they both had enjoyed homosexual affairs, it may be a little surprising to read how devotedly in love with each other they were. (It was not without reason that D. H. Lawrence detested all of Bloomsbury.) When James first met Alix, he wrote his brother Lytton how delighted he was with her as "an absolute boy."[13] Like their psychoanalytic colleagues and Bloomsbury friends, the Stracheys ignored everything that had been thought about conventional definitions of femininity and masculinity. They both cherished their solitude, and yet each made up the world for the other. They were childless, and after James died in 1967 Alix had a breakdown.

The editors have written a first-rate introduction and epilogue to this correspondence, and their footnoting is a worthy tribute to the example James Strachey himself had set in his memorable edition of Freud's works.

Charles Rycroft, who like the Stracheys also went to Cambridge, is one of the few illustrious intellectuals in British psychoanalysis. His 1978 departure from the London Psychoanalytic Society came long after he had first been bored by the papers of his colleagues. Before becoming an analyst in 1947, he failed to appreciate the significance of sectarianism to the psychoanalytic movement. By the mid-1960s he was a notably sophisticated commentator and reviewer on psychoanalysis. He was so outspoken that, although it is curiously not mentioned in the fascinating autobiographical pieces contained in *Psychoanalysis and Beyond,* edited by Peter Fuller (1985), Anna Freud once used her influence with David Astor to try to prevent Rycroft from writing reviews for the *Observer.*

Psychoanalysis and Beyond, in which Rycroft is at his best, consists of a series of lovely essays, covering a wide range of topics, written over a period of many years. There is a fine chapter about the analysis of a paranoid personality, an excellent piece on the psychology of orgasm, and an exceptional essay called "On Continuity." The most notable chapter, which had been circulated only privately before, is titled "On the Ablation of Parental Images, or the Illusion of Having Created Oneself." Here Rycroft is trying to understand some of the psychopathological reasons that may lead people to become psychoanalysts and how psychoanalysis itself can perpetuate a unique kind of human dilemma. The patients Rycroft has in mind seek ideal ancestors to take the place of the real ones they have dismissed; they appear to lack the usual internalization of their parents; they are incapable of feeling grief and construct a myth about themselves, after having disowned their parents. Persons of such a kind, Rycroft proposes, are drawn to the psychoanalytic movement, but in a way that may be harmful to the integrity of the discipline.

Rycroft connects the denial of indebtedness to the origins and nature of creativity, and uses Jean-Paul Sartre to illustrate self-idealization. Psychoanalysis appeals to "ablators" because it enhances the illusion of self-creation; it strengthens their defensive system. Analysts who choose their own analysts subsequently become proponents of their analyst's theories in large part out of personal vanity, thereby reversing the biological humiliation of not being able to pick one's own parents. In Rycroft's own interesting essay "On Autobiography," however, he implies that the autobiographical enterprise leads to an inevitable use of privacy to understand theorizing, and in this context one wonders why Rycroft has decided so to downplay his professional indebtedness to one of his own analysts, Sylvia Payne.

These essays, which a useful bibliography shows to be only a portion of Rycroft's output, are uniformly levelheaded, down-to-earth, and at the same time broadly cultured. Yet Rycroft can be curiously narrow. For example, he writes about Freud: "One wishes Freud could have reported forgetting the name of a tree or cooking utensil or losing a shopping list."[14] Whatever Freud's relationship to trees might have been, in that era few middle-class gentlemen knew in which direction within the house the kitchen was located. In a dreadful self-confession Rycroft writes: "Hegel and Nietzsche are not in my bones."[15] A psychoanalyst can do fine without Hegel, or at least Freud did, but Nietzsche, the man Freud once said knew more about himself than anyone who ever lived, is another matter.

Rycroft shares a few crudities about Freud. The idea that the aim of all activity is to decrease tension may be questionable, and Rycroft does challenge it, but it is improper to reduce Freud's concept to the "tendency"[16] he had to fainting attacks. Rycroft, like many others, questions the rationalistic premises behind Freud's therapeutic approach. But Rycroft suffers from a kind of ahistoricism. Just as a few isolated instances of Freud's fainting do not, I think, constitute a tendency, so Freud's actual practices as a clinician were more variegated than Rycroft supposes. It should be said that although Rycroft has succeeded in going beyond Freud, he is writing in Freud's own best spirit; for instance, Rycroft believes that "it is the capacity to love which makes us feel good."[17]

Peter Fuller, who tells us he was a patient of Rycroft's, has admirably edited the book into a readable whole, but wrote an introduction that is on a distinctly lower level than Rycroft's own work. Although Rycroft is always interesting, I would expect him to be embarrassed by Fuller's claim that these essays constitute "a major, innovative contribution to our understanding of ourselves and our species."[18] Rycroft has sought to combat such idealization of therapists. Fuller, like Rycroft, is not sufficiently broad to appreciate when an insight has been anticipated by Jung.

Rycroft is a descendant of the Middle Group of British analysts, and it is in keeping with Rycroft's own continuity with his ancestry that one of this book's best essays consists of a memorable tribute to D. W. Winnicott, a man whom, in Winnicott's lifetime, Rycroft viewed as the genius of British psychoanalysis.

Ernest Gellner's *The Psychoanalytic Movement: Or the Coming of Unreason* (1985) is a brilliantly written book, every page sparkling with intelligence, style, and substance. The author's name first came to public attention in 1959 with his daring dissection of the dominant school of late 1950s British philosophy. Although Gellner indicates here his appreciation of the reasons why denouncers thought his *Words and Things* an atrociously bad book, its publication was a memorable event in intellectual history.

Gellner, who now holds a chair at Cambridge, has written a book that, although a generation from now he might repudiate it, is a marvel of civilized intelligence. He has attempted to explain the bases for the success of psychoanalysis. He is correct in thinking that an astonishing revolution in our ideas has come about. Freud's system of thought, with all its flaws, has so fundamentally altered how we think about human behavior as to become "the dominant idiom for the discussion of the human personality and of human relations."[19]

In this book Gellner tries to show the ways in which cultural patterns account for the success of the psychoanalytic belief system. In an intellectually deterministic way, he interprets the flourishing of psychoanalysis as part of a backlash against a sickly and complacent vision of humankind.

Bloodless and unrealistic accounts of motivation inspire dubious counter-theories. Gellner treats psychoanalysis respectfully; at the same time he understands the defects in the logic of some psychoanalytic propositions and, in an original and lively way, points out the reasons why such beliefs should have gained wide currency.

Provincialism is hard to escape, however. David Hume, and the whole British philosophical tradition for that matter, may be sacred, but they do not exhaust the ambitious problem Gellner has set out for himself. If one wants to understand why Freud triumphed, then some comparative cultural perspective is necessary. Why did books simultaneously published in English do so much better in the United States than England? The uneven rate of Freud's influence in France has not yet been accounted for, and the current obsession with psychoanalysis in Paris is astonishing. The Dutch responded to Freud as quickly (before World War I) and as permanently as the Americans, while the Israelis have never paid much attention to psychoanalysis. How Stalin closed down depth psychology in the Soviet Union in the late 1920s is another chapter. Gellner makes a flip comment about the Japanese and psychoanalysis, yet a history exists of what happened to Freud's concepts there. Both India and Latin America have their own tales. John Stuart Mill thought that comparative culture was the equivalent in social science of experimentation in the natural sciences, and Gellner might have followed through this insight of a heroic forefather in social thought.

Gellner understands the logic of psychoanalysis as a guild, though the title of his book is misleading about the core of his discussion. He is interested in the problem of the power relation of analysand and analyst but does not pursue the history of the relationship of psychoanalysts and their pupils.

This book will enlighten all who yearn for the latest and most sophisticated answer to Adolf Grünbaum's critique of psychoanalysis. Karl Popper succeeded in permanently raising the issue of the testability (i.e., falsifiability) of psychoanalytic thinking. Gellner provides a welcome and literate overview of the latest philosophic controversy about the logical status of psychoanalytic propositions.

If Gellner has sought to make the "central aim" of his book that of specifying how "the intricate and elegant structure of that system fitted in with the distinctive social and intellectual condition of mankind in our age,"[20] he has failed. But just as no real encounter, with a person or an idea, should be assessed a mistake, this book is—whatever its inadequacies—still a marvel. Its every page instructs and enlivens and represents a tribute to humane intelligence.

Gellner is particularly strong on analogies between religious convictions and psychoanalytic ideologies. But the breadth of his knowledge does not excuse a few howlers. Freud was not a psychiatrist, and Jones's biography of Freud ought to be cited in its full three-volume edition. Janet Malcolm is an incompetent source about Karl Menninger's analyst's analyst, as on most psychoanalytic issues, and it is a pity that some of Gellner's citations to local pundits are insular, although it is a universal fate to be bounded by one's own cultural horizons.

Psychoanalysis in France has had a fascinating history, one that highlights that which has been exceptional in the British reaction to Freud. Although the founder of psychoanalysis studied in Paris and idolized Jean-Martin Charcot, the early history of psychoanalysis has to be understood in the context of developments within French medicine. France was one of the slowest countries to respond to the significance of Freud's teachings. For some time Jean-Paul Sartre and Simone de Beauvoir, notably in her great novel *The Mandarins,* seemed to stand alone among the French in their sophistication about things psychoanalytic. Right now, though, it is as if Freud has, for the time being, so succeeded in France that every major philosophical or social issue has to be cast within psychoanalytic categories for the subject to be legitimized for intellectual discourse.

While years earlier others (such as Alfred Adler, Wilhelm Reich, Erich Fromm, and Herbert Marcuse) tried to reconcile Marx and Freud, the French have now come to this issue in their own manner. The psychoanalyst Jacques Lacan's difficult thought has been the main focus for the controversies that have surrounded French thinking in this area of social philosophy.

Sherry Turkle's *Psychoanalytic Politics: Freud's French Revolution* (1981) is the best single introduction to this complicated school of thought. Lacan, along with his opponents as well as those he has influenced, wrote in a deliberately obscure style; he believed he had to destroy ordinary language in order to communicate what he had to say. Turkle takes nothing for granted except the need for clarity. She undertook field research in France, interviewing as many people as she could who have participated in France's psychoanalytic culture.

In contrast to the fate of Freud's work in North America, where it became part of the medical establishment and therefore to some extent an instrument of social control, in France the critique of psychiatry has become allied with psychoanalysis. Radical antipsychiatric thought has also been highly politicized. Lacan tried to return to the so-called true Freud, a visionary subversive of contemporary culture. After being expelled from the International Psychoanalytic Association in the early 1950s, Lacan then led several schisms within French training institutes. Turkle admirably describes how he fought against the normalizing and professionalizing of psychoanalysis.

One of the sources of Lacan's appeal has been the specifically anti-American cast to his thought, for he was the resolute enemy of the ego psychologies that have flourished on the North American continent. In contrast to someone like Erik H. Erikson, Lacan did not think that the ego exists as a coherent entity; he conceived of it instead as a distorted reflection of processes of mirroring and believed the self gets built up on the basis of misrepresentation. The ego becomes the carrier of neurosis.

Lacan was not interested in therapeutic "cure," nor in allowing social problems to be masked as psychiatric ones. From his perspective, psychoanalysis's radical possibilities have been undermined by the successful integration of Freud's ideas into the North American establishment. To Lacan, widespread conformist implications of psychiatric practices have been allowed to go unchecked.

Various neo-Freudians long ago challenged the biologistic bias in Freud's thinking; such critics sought to emphasize the role that culture plays in defining human feelings. Lacan too wants to get at the symbolic, rather than the anatomical, side of human psychology, and so while Freud has been taking a beating lately from North American feminists, in France Lacan's brand of psychoanalysis has been in the vanguard of the movement for female emancipation.

Lacan tried to show how society succeeds in invading the individual; the unconscious gets influenced by the social situation through the use of language. He has not only had an enormous impact on practitioners and the general public, but has persuaded French Marxists that Freud complements a positivistic side to socialism. Without trying to romanticize mental illness, it can teach something unique about the nature of human freedom.

Even aside from French culture's notorious inaccessibility to outside influences, psychoanalysis in France got off to a slow start. French medicine regarded Freud in particular as a German thinker whose contributions had been anticipated by earlier French writers. A French psychoanalytic institute did get started in the 1920s, but it remained relatively unfashionable; now not only is Freud at the center of French intellectual life, but French analysis had become one of the leading sources of stimulating thinking in the West.

From a pedestrian, English-speaking point of view this turn of events has been a mixed blessing. Lacan himself was deliberately hard to follow and notoriously controversial; his books cannot be read line by line, the way most others can. Even commentaries about Lacan's ideas are hard to follow. Yet in François Roustang's *Dire Mastery: Discipleship from Freud to Lacan* (1982), inspired by Lacan's influence, we find fragments of challenging ideas that are jarringly bold and original.

Dire Mastery, which first appeared in France in 1976, grew out of the French analytic milieu; it is a surprisingly enjoyable book to read. Passages in it will come as a shock to many conventional North American students of analysis. Roustang, for example, is outspoken about why all psychoanalytic societies have to be inadequate for the life of the mind. (Lacan broke apart numerous organizations that he had founded.) Roustang may seem insulting about the conformism of Anna Freud's work. She was, among other things, a prim schoolteacher, and her pedantic approach has been vastly overrated on the North American continent.

The main body of the book is directed at reconsidering Freud's relationship with a few of his disciples. The popular success of D. M. Thomas's *The White Hotel* in part reflects how widely known among contemporaries is the story of early analysis. Roustang's book is unusual in looking at the controversies from the side of followers struggling to fill themselves out; he has not just taken Freud's view of things and treated it as accurate history. The main evidence from which Roustang works is published correspondences, even though he knows that most of what has appeared has been tendentiously edited from a standpoint partisan to Freud.

Karl Abraham is the first disciple to get discussed in this account of the construction of a new church. Roustang believes that every psychoanalytic society reproduces the church or the army. He uses each of his historical chapters to say something interesting about current analysis. He examines, for example, the relation between faith and transference: "One has to believe in it for it to work, for the discovery to occur, but once it works, one no longer needs to believe."[21] Roustang's book is sequential enough that the paradoxes are genuinely challenging: "Neurosis is always an inability to speak, to fantasize, to desire on one's own, but it is also a longing, the deep-rooted longing to be an echo or a mirror of what others say or think."[22] Roustang contends that analytic groups inevitably maintain, in order to transmit their teachings, the transferences that analysis aims to dissolve.

The section on the Freud-Jung letters is particularly outspoken, especially given the virtual ban on Jung's writings among the French brought about by his collaboration with the Nazis. All the participants in the early history of analysis must be understood in terms of their personalities in order to make sense of their theories. Roustang believes that in this field above all the argument from authority can have no place. The psychoanalyst is, according to him, "a solitary who cannot lean on anyone," "an auditor of the inaudible, the one who takes a chance with language even in the analysand's unspoken speech."[23] Roustang is able to be independent of orthodoxy in assessing Victor Tausk's tragic struggle with Freud, as well as in describing Georg Groddeck's effort to be both liberated and a Freudian.

If analysis is essentially a structure of discovery, then its theories should continue to call into question all beliefs. Roustang admires what he calls clear-sightedness, "the ability to express opinions that leave people flabbergasted and to ask questions to which no answer can be found. . . . "[24] In behalf of this kind of insight *Dire Mastery*, an unusually interesting book, closes with a chapter titled "Toward a Theory of Psychosis."

Roustang seems to me outstanding to the extent that other French psychoanalysts do not communicate in lean, spare prose. While so many good writers in the English-speaking world strive for a plain style, French thinkers are apt to be opaque, confusing, and yet sometimes dazzling. Just because some of the most original analytic thinking is now going on in Paris, it behooves us to try to make sense of what is being proposed.

Roustang's *Psychoanalysis Never Lets Go* (1983) is rather more difficult than his *Dire Mastery*, if only because the broad familiarity with the story of the history of Freud's school provided a background to Roustang's own interpretations. In *Psychoanalysis Never Lets Go*, where he concentrates on therapeutic method, Roustang constructed a special framework for the text through a preface for the English-language edition. (The book was first published in 1980.) He worries that treatment often ends in a form of alienation either on the patient's part or the analyst's, since neither side questions enough the dogmas that can become central to their existence. Roustang wants to ask the most subversive questions of analysis. A key thesis is that the irrational feelings Freud set out therapeutically to call forth, the transference, is close to hypnosis and old-fashioned suggestion; the blindness that results accounts for the title of Roustang's book. He thinks that such binds are an exaggerated form of what happens in every serious human relationship. He wants to touch on the seduction necessary to love and the underlying human quest for imitation.

At the outset of the book Roustang dissects Freud's own stylistic techniques of persuading readers. Some of Freud's hypotheses can sound like certainties because his system was built to hang together so well. Roustang then goes on to demonstrate what he considers the true nature of an analyst's interpretations: unverifiable constructions that nonetheless have a therapeutic impact. But the analyst should not partake of the illusion that he can bring forth the "whole truth,"[25] lest he impose closure on the patient's discourse. Patients otherwise can be forced to break away from treatment, to protect themselves from being psychologically annihilated in the analyst's preconceptions.

An important chapter deals with the proximity between transference and telepathy. The interest Freud took in occultism has never been more adequately accounted for. Roustang insists on the legitimacy of the connection between the analyst and the medium; thought transference is "the very heart of analytic experience."[26] The analyst's task is to sustain with equanimity the emotional deformations imposed upon him by the patient's inner requirements.

An analyst's silence is no solution, since it is "a language the patient learns quickly."[27] Roustang speak of biases that are only hinted at in the professional literature: "anyone who has been to several different analysts knows very well that the past he discovers with each is different. . . . "[28] He warns against the "grotesque power,"[29] beyond the time of an analysis, the treatment situation allows analysts to wield. The essence of the suggestion that concerns him lies not so much in what the analyst says but in the readiness of the patient's suggestibility. Archaic emotions, like the desire for fusion, can be mobilized in therapy, and everyone who participates should recognize the fascination of symbiosis. The analyst, along with patients, has unconscious reactions that ought not to be mystified.

Roustang is aware that some of what he is advocating is not entirely novel; he even mentions the name of Jung, who has remained a taboo figure among French intellectuals. There are so many challenging ideas in this difficult book that it is bootless to pick a fight with any of its particular points. *Psychoanalysis Never Lets Go* makes for demanding reading, since it is not what we are used to hearing about. One of the most rewarding chapters is the final one, where he argues that patients are like writers, creating a narrative account of their lives. This inspired capacity to be inventive is, he holds, essential to the curative impact of treatment.

Although analysts like Rycroft in London and Roustang in Paris have emerged out of different contexts, their work is reassuring about the enduring strength of the tradition of thought initiated by Freud and currently being reinvigorated in both Great Britain as well as France.

The story of psychoanalysis in Germany is inevitably in the shadow of the rise to power of the Nazis, the single most important political event, I think, in twentieth-century history. But despite the importance of its subject, Geoffery Cocks' *Psychotherapy in the Third Reich: The Göring Institute* (1985) is the worst book I have read in ages; its central conceptual flaw can be detected in the title. Cocks believes that psychotherapy existed in Hitler's Germany. Just as students of jurisprudence have persuasively argued against the misuse of the word *law* in connection with the Third Reich, since everything "legal" was arbitrary and contrary to natural justice, so the term *psychotherapy* is misleading to those who want to understand what happened under Hitler.

The author lacks any real understanding of the ethical dimensions to what he purports to be writing about. He is fascinated by the degree of alleged professional institutionalization that so-called psychotherapists achieved under Hitler. Only when describing the link between the Göring Institute, headed by a cousin of Hermann Göring, and the SS does Cocks comment: "To the extent that this history should include a degree of moral judgment, it must be said that these activities involved a higher degree of culpability in their contributions to Nazi projects."[30] If indeed the author is correct in claiming that what he calls psychotherapy flourished under Hitler and had its roots in pre-Nazi Germany and its continuity in the post–World War II Germanys, then Germany as a country and culture stands indicted anew. What we have then is no success story but the tale of a collapse of Western civilization.

The kindest way of treating passages in the book is to declare that their author is morally out to lunch. He is centrally concerned with the affairs of the Göring Institute, led by Dr. Matthias Göring, pretty much to the exclusion of old-line psychiatrists. A few choice quotations about Matthias Göring are in order. We are told that "it is difficult to gauge the degree of anti-Semitism in Göring," but that "his words and actions between 1933 and 1945 leave no doubt over his condemnatory public stance then toward Jewish influence in his profession."[31] The author writes that Göring "did not join the Nazi party in order to exercise his anti-Semitism; he joined as part of a process of professional necessity and national-cultural loyalty."[32] In 1933 and 1934 Göring made *Mein Kampf* required reading for all "psychotherapists." His relationship with his own deputy, Schultz, deteriorated "to the point of rupture early in 1945 with Göring's insistence that they, as those in charge of a psychotherapeutic institute, serve as psychological advisers to the last German units defending Berlin against the Russian invaders. When Schultz refused and pointed to the futility of such an action, Göring branded him a defeatist and continued to badger him about it."[33] The author thinks that Göring's party membership "carried a certain degree of sincerity and conviction."[34] The complex of motives in Göring's reviewing of Nazi books and articles was, we are informed, "typically human."[35]

For reasons that are chilling in terms of the history of Western culture, earlier philosophical ideas, and in particular a Romantic tradition in German psychology, could be made use of by the Nazi regime. As one reflects on World War II and the fate of Western culture, it seems to me mistaken to assert the alleged "benefit to patients as well as to the evolving profession itself."[36] I refuse to agree that "the composite of these beliefs, actions, inactions, choices, compromises, opportunisms, improprieties, and outrages presents a peculiarly human picture, devoid of either heroes or true villains."[37] There were, in my opinion, no "major strides"[38] in any features of this story.

One would be inclined to say something positive about the notes in the back of the book, which do show that the author has read with zeal selected primary sources. But he maintains in an early citation that "as the history of the Göring Institute once again makes plain, Nazi Germany was not a perfect totalitarian order. . . . "[39] The concept of totalitarianism may no longer have the respectability that it had in the late 1950s, but I cannot imagine anybody in the field ever having tried to prove "perfection" in how Hitler's Germany illustrated the type of system called *totalitarianism*. One holds one's head in despair at the malignant irony of the Nazi conviction that "mental disorder within the master race could not be genetic or essentially organic"[40] and that therefore applied depth psychology had a special role to play in the Third Reich.

Only a small portion of this sorry tale has hitherto been widely known. Jung's collaborative activities, although early on condemned by a Swiss colleague as well as by Wilhelm Reich, have been weighed and assessed. The way Jung's ideas could be used to suit Nazi purposes is unfortunately only part of a much wider picture. It is not as broadly understood how Jones also was able to work successfully with Matthias Göring. Nor are most people aware of Freud's authoritarian leanings in the last decade of his life. Freud's attitude toward Austrian politics in the 1930s was heartbreaking to his politically idealistic followers.

One bit of light emerges from the text to reassure us that there was a solitary sanity of resistance to Hitler's tyranny. A member of the Göring Institute, John Rittmeister, was arrested by the Gestapo (in late 1942) and accused of being part of an espionage plot that fed information to the Russians. Rittmeister had compromised the "integrity" of the Göring Institute and aroused "the patriotic wrath of the institute's director."[41] On the charge of high treason Rittmeister was executed in 1943.

The author does not seem to recognize that the success of the Göring Institute and its part in helping the Luftwaffe and in promoting the war effort itself besmirch the whole tradition of German so-called psychotherapy. All of us should be wary of the implications of any system of ideas that aims to "harmonize" the individual and the social order, a point made in a different context by the French analysts influenced by Lacan. I think that any book that argues that psychoanalysis was "preserved through the departure of Jewish analysts and by the cover of the Göring name"[42] has to be fatally flawed. To the extent that German culture once represented some of the best in the Western tradition, the account this book gives is more ethically worrisome to me than the horror stories about the abuse of psychiatry under the Soviet regime.

Almost at the outset of the book the author informs us that "psychotherapists at the Göring Institute, of course, were not permitted to treat Jews. . . . "[43] After he has made some formal bows in the obligatory direction of morality, the author states: "To treat Jews or to protest the Nazi dictum was to risk not only personal destruction but also destruction of the profession and practice of psychotherapy itself. And then what of the patients who needed treatment?"[44]

The author does not understand that the Nazi regime destroyed psychotherapy as it should be known and that the German practitioners of their craft owed an obligation to their patients, to humanity at large, and to the patients in countries that the Nazis assaulted. One suspects that only in a success-oriented culture like the United States (William James stigmatized that "bitch-Goddess success") could an academic study of such a situation thrive into publication without encountering the most savage criticism reviewers could marshal. The notion of a "German psychotherapy" is, I think, on all fours with the concept of an "Aryan" physics.

Notes

1. Gregorio Kohon, *The British School of Psychoanalysis: The Independent Tradition* (London: Free Association Books, 1986), p. 65.
2. Ibid., p. 74.
3. Ibid., p. 215.
4. Ibid., p. 344, p. 360.
5. Peregrine Horden, ed., *Freud and the Humanities* (London: Duckworth, 1985), p. 22.
6. Ibid., p. 5.
7. "Psychoanalysis," *Standard Edition*, Vol. 20, p. 26.
8. *Bloomsbury/Freud: The Letters of James and Alix Strachey 1924–25*, ed. Perry Meisel and Walter Kendrick (New York: Basic Books, 1985), p. 210.
9. Ibid., p. 231.
10. Ibid., p. 195.
11. Ibid., p. 82.
12. Ibid., p. 180.
13. Ibid., p. 23.
14. Charles Rycroft, *Psychoanalysis and Beyond*, ed. Peter Fuller (London: Chatto and Windus, 1985), p. 84.
15. Ibid., p. 90.
16. Ibid., p. 32.
17. Ibid., p. 263.
18. Ibid., p. 2.
19. Ernest Gellner, *The Psychoanalytic Movement: Or the Coming of Unreason* (London, Granada, 1985), p. 5.
20. Ibid., p. 11.
21. François Roustang, *Dire Mastery: Discipleship from Freud to Lacan*, trans. Ned Lukacher (Baltimore: Johns Hopkins University Press, 1982), p. 62.
22. Ibid., p. 19.
23. Ibid., p. 72.
24. Ibid., p. 138.
25. François Roustang, *Psychoanalysis Never Lets Go*, trans. Ned Lukacher (Baltimore: Johns Hopkins University Press, 1983), p. 35.

26. Ibid., p. 55.
27. Ibid., p. 59.
28. Ibid., p. 61.
29. Ibid., p. 63.
30. Geoffrey Cocks, *Psychotherapy in the Third Reich: The Göring Institute* (New York: Oxford University Press, 1985), p. 202.
31. Ibid., p. 114.
32. Ibid.
33. Ibid., pp. 115–16.
34. Ibid., p. 118.
35. Ibid.
36. Ibid., p. 248.
37. Ibid., pp. 248–49.
38. Ibid., p. 249.
39. Ibid., p. 252.
40. Ibid., p. 12.
41. Ibid., p. 167.
42. Ibid., p. 9.
43. Ibid., p. 21.
44. Ibid.

3

America

It is by now well established that the special interaction of Freud and the United States is a notable feature of our century's cultural history. Although one might think that psychoanalysis led to a greater degree of toleration of nonconformity, Freud's ideas could be used for intolerant social purposes. For example, the United States of the 1880s might have been able to absorb a higher degree of deviant behavior than would be the case today; the pre-Freudian era was sometimes more tolerant of a greater diversity of personality types than our own time. It is of course impossible experimentally to test what the United States would have been like without the influence of psychoanalysis. But a comparative national approach can serve as a laboratory in social science, and the contrast between Britain and the United States, for example, can highlight certain key issues.

I am reminded of a contemporary American psychoanalyst who was working on a biography of T. E. Lawrence and traveled about interviewing those people who remembered Lawrence; the analyst chanced upon the English soldier whom Lawrence paid to administer an annual beating to him and eagerly awaited the possibilities of accumulating psychodynamic data. The soldier, however, was perplexed by the analyst's whole approach, since to this old-fashioned Englishman there seemed nothing especially bizarre or pathological about Lawrence's behavior. He was simply "a bloke who liked to get beaten," a view that may make us realize the way in which Freudian ideas can have a constricting and puritanical impact on our image of man.

The contrast with Great Britain highlights the fact that the reception of psychoanalysis in the United States is in part a problem in comparative history. Very early in volume 1 of *Freud and the Americans* (1971) author Nathan G. Hale asks the questions: "Why did America welcome psychoanalysis more warmly than any other country? What was there in the nature of psychoanalysis and what in American conditions that created this affinity?''[1] From the period before World War I on, Freud (to his consternation) found a far more responsive audience in the States than anywhere else; in his last years the wealthiest patients who came to him for treatment were Americans, and Freud's dependency on them for his livelihood only added to his resentment. Unfortunately, we know relatively little about the history of modern psychotherapy and even less within a comparative cultural framework.

Hale's book is an extremely patiently documented account of psychoanalysis in the United States up until 1917; the next volume may tell the tale down to our own time. Although at the outset of his study Hale raises the question of a comparative historical approach to the problem of Freud's success in the United States, he apparently has little interest in pursuing the subject, even vis-à-vis one other country, say England. English neurology was (and still is) among the best in the world, and doubtless this inhibited the rise of a powerful psychotherapeutic movement capable of exerting as much influence as Freud had in the States. In addition, England possessed an ancient culture, with a long-standing appreciation of its past, whereas only at the end of the last century were Americans forced to realize that with the closing of the frontier and the end of free lands their future was acutely constrained by the limitations of history.

Hale's strength lies in his devotion to the documentary evidence, rather than in any broad-gauged interpretative analysis, and given the woefully limited character of prior work in this field perhaps his approach was all to the good. Even in comparison to Freud's own prudish attitude toward sex, the turn-of-the-century Americans seem to have been puritanical. According to Hale, the sweeping scope of Freud's theories gave the Americans a sense of unity (and security) in their approach to problems of mental health, yet characteristically the Americans ignored the intellectual interconnections that gave Freud's system coherence, and as Hale puts it, "they muted sexuality and aggression, making both more amiable. They emphasized social conformity. They were more didactic, moralistic, and popular than Freud."[2] Despite the highly individualistic character of Freud's own practice as a therapist and the liberationist aims he upheld at his best, Hale is right in emphasizing that "much psychotherapy was oriented toward binding up the wounds of those who failed or assuring the ambitious of new personal powers."[3] To the extent that "neuroses prevented the successful fulfillment of a social role," that "kind of failure psychoanalysis could cure." And so "medical psychology always . . . operated to reinforce social norms."[4]

Hale is also accurate in disposing of the myth Freud's "followers furthered of a pre-psychoanalytic period of therapeutic impotence and despair."[5] In fact, the Americans before Freud were developing a school of mental healers, at least some of whom had adopted the Frenchman Pierre Janet's "clinical conception that subconscious, dissociated memories were a major cause of nervous symptoms."[6] Before Freud, however, gross insanity was largely traced to brain lesions or inherited predispositions, and interpreting neuroses thus, Hale points out, "as entirely somatic" had the advantage for the patients of freeing them of "the stigma of breaking the [Victorian] norm of control over the emotions."[7] Hale's thesis is that "psychoanalysis became important in America during the crystallization of crises in two subtly interconnected fields—the social realm of sexual morals and the professional realm of the treatment of nervous and mental disorder."[8]

Freud did suggest that heredity was an overestimated factor, and the Americans were quick to put the blame (much more so than Freud) on parents and the environment. Freud had argued that both insanity and neurosis were degrees of exaggeration of the normal, and following this line of reasoning "physicians not only could feel a closer rapport with their patients but they could also interpret these illnesses in terms of their own feelings and experences."[9] Freud assumed that patients could be trusted to work out their own individual solutions to inner conflicts, and if he stressed the demonic forces that underlay symptomatology, he also took for granted the intensely moral nature of those patients who found themselves at odds with their instinctual life.

It is hard to overestimate how far we have come from the American conception of sexual morality at the beginning of the twentieth century. Hale persuasively argues, for example, that "the physician's stereotype of woman became progressively 'purer' from the 1870's to about 1912,"[10] which suggests that women and other social groups were being newly stigmatized at the same time Jim Crow legislation was being enacted against Negroes. Perversions were to be condemned as unhealthy, and both excessive masturbation and undue amounts of intercourse were deemed dangerous; if Freud himself wondered whether masturbation could lead to a loss of virility he was only a man of his time. To argue, as he did, that masturbation was a symptom and not a vice was, after all, only to transmute the undesirable from a purely moralistic to a seemingly scientific level.

In contrast to the partisanship that mars many studies of the early days in psychoanalysis, Hale is fair and evenhanded. For example, he notes that Freud's opponents used the theme of sexuality to discredit psychoanalysis, but Hale is aware that "the psychoanalysts themselves also used the issue to make their opponents seem hide-bound, obscene and squeamish."[11] Whereas Jones's account of an attack on Freud made it seem "unprovoked," Hale's research reveals that a follower of Freud's had indeed "provoked"[12] the denunciation. While some authors write as if Freud were alone in his special approach, Hale understands the work of Freud's predecessors such as Havelock Ellis and Pierre Janet, who, while relatively forgotten figures today, were responsible for writings that made the public more receptive to Freud's brand of psychotherapy.

Psychoanalysis before World War I was rather different from what it later came to be. For instance, catharsis, the expression of suppressed conflicts, was the central therapeutic goal. Freud's curative aims were originally far bolder than they were to become in his more resigned, postcancerous phase from 1923 on. (It was this later, dying Freud who trained most of the therapists who carried his technique back to the States; they were identifying, however, with a man taking leave of his human contacts, whom it pained to talk, and who was less and less interested in therapeutic success.) Psychoanalysis' early adherents were passionately committed to "the cause":[13] the initial campaign for Freudian approaches was manned by practitioners unlike today's. While better educated than the traditional hospital psychiatrists, Freud's early followers were less well trained and from humbler social beginnings than the eminent neurologists of their day.

William James's own work on the irrational not only preceded Freud's, but he also initially welcomed Freud's contributions. Yet James had his legitimate doubts about the early analysts and Freud personally, having met him in 1909 for the Clark Lectures: " . . . they can't fail to throw light on human nature, but I confess that he made on me personally the impression of a man obssessed with fixed ideas."[14]

Morton Prince, Hale points out, "initiated the enduring American interest in hypnotism and the subconscious,"[15] and yet Jones treated him as a most dangerous enemy. Prince in turn resented Jones's attempts to discredit his work and viewed Jones as a fanatic in behalf of psychoanalysis. Prince had "insisted that the neuroses were perversions of normal memory processes and that buried memories were best reached by hypnosis,"[16] but his view of the unconscious was decidedly not that of Freud: "I conceive of the unconscious not as a wild, unbridled subconscious mind, as do some Freudians, ready to take advantage of an unguarded moment to strike down, to drown, to kill, after the manner of an evil genie, but as a great mental mechanism which takes part in an orderly, logical way in all the processes of daily life, but which under certain conditions involving particularly the emotion-instincts becomes disordered or perverted."[17] As psychoanalysis began to take hold in the United States, and it did so medically before popularly, the argument pro and con grew more belligerent. Prince thought the analysts were becoming more of a "cult" than a scientific group and argued that "Freudian literature was sprinkled with such expressions as 'proved,' 'established,' 'well known,' 'accepted.' Such expressions take the place of 'theory,' 'possibility,' 'probability,' to which we are accustomed in progressive science. . . . "[18]

Freud's therapeutic approach, although more hopeful in its pre–World War I form than in later years, still seemed too austere to many Americans. For example, Freud had thought that it was the analyst's job not to provide guidance, not to inject his own values, but to take away hindrances, to get rid of obstacles, on the assumption that the patient knew best how to order his own life. While the analysis of dreams, the technique of free association, and the revival of old memories appealed to the American desire to overcome excessive reticence, the Americans were reluctant to think that analysis was automatically synthesis. They were inclined to believe, along the lines that Jung suggested in his 1912 lectures at Fordham University, that not only was the unconscious more beneficent than Freud thought, but the analyst should not restrict his activities so narrowly as Freud proposed. Jung is, in my opinion, an unduly underestimated figure in current intellectual life, in the United States as in France; this neglect is partly due to his having made his appeal more on the artistic than a scientific level, but also of course to his collaboration with the Nazis. Those who are apt to admire recent so-called advances in psychoanalytic thinking would do well to find out how extensively Jung anticipates much of what seems most admirable in today's fashionable writers.

In contrast to Jung's approach, Freud and a long line of his disciples, especially in the United States, sought to present psychoanalysis as neutral and "value-free." My own guess is that a discussion of the relationship between moral values and Freud's work would have made the founder of psychoanalysis extremely uneasy and discontented. Freud never doubted that his ideas were revolutionary and therefore bound to have effects far beyond the understanding and treatment of the neuroses. At times Freud could even thunder like a modern prophet, challenging the values and practices of Western Christendom.

Yet Freud always feared that his empirical insights might get swallowed up in mankind's search for ethical direction. As he aged, his devotion to science grew increasingly pronounced, and as his illness restricted his activities, he drew back somewhat from therapy. After contracting cancer in 1923, Freud never again wrote a case history. The writings of his last sixteen years, as he gradually withdrew from the world, contain some of the most sustained abstract restatements of his findings that can be found anywhere in his work.

But even as Freud kept insisting more and more on the status of psychoanalysis as a science, he found himself giving freer reign to his own speculative impulses. In his later years he wrote about the roots of religion, the future of civilization, and pondered other age-old quandries. His hope was that some of his students would perceive the moral implications of psychoanalytic principles, and that workers in other fields would be able to revolutionize their disciplines as he had altered the shape of modern psychology. In the United States, however, the clinical side of psychoanalysis was kept insulated from the more theoretically abstract of Freud's endeavors.

When it comes to the issue of what Freud's own practices as a clinician were like, it is almost as if some of his American followers preferred to keep this matter in the dark. It is hard not to suspect that how unorthodox Freud could be was inconsistent with a myth about his supposed detachment that suited the story which his American disciples chose to propagate. Far too little is known about what Freud did in the conduct of his analyses, although more was preserved in the oral tradition among analysts than ever succeeded in making its way into print.

For all his genius, Freud was not exempt from many of the social prejudices of his day. By our current standards Freud the therapist was decidedly moralistic. "Be better next time!" was the way one of Freud's patients once summarized to me Freud's own approach. Addicts, psychotics, delinquents, and male perverts—precisely those cases for whom the scope of psychoanalysis has been expanded since Freud's death, especially in the United States—would have seemed more or less repugnant to him. Though he wanted to understand as much of human behavior as possible, he could not help being a man of his time. Unless one can acknowledge how different Freud was from what would be acceptable in a therapist today, it is impossible to see just how great were the forces of social prejudice, both in the world at large and in his own soul, with which he had to contend.

Seeing Freud in proper historical perspective can also illuminate some characteristic clinical shortcomings of our own day, for if Freud was more intolerant as a therapist than would now be considered usual, he was also much more boldly individualistic than many of the followers who pay him homage. The Central Europe of his time was far more cosmopolitan and less narrowly bourgeois than, for example, some contemporary New World practitioners of Freud's art. Standards of belief and value were more multiple and less uniform than a modern mass society like the United States tends to produce.

In one case a middle-aged woman came to Freud because of her guilt over homosexual urges. Freud recommended her to a Viennese pupil for an analysis; as a result of a year of treatment the patient was free of her guilt feelings but actively homosexual. With some anxiety the analyst reported to Freud the outcome of the analysis. But Freud surprised his disciple by concluding that it was an appropriate point at which to terminate the analysis. The patient's children had grown up, her sexual affair was discreet, and her husband was now interested in her mainly for social purposes. One can be pretty sure that most North American candidates in training today would not get off so easily were this the upshot of a supervised analysis.

Freud could be remarkably emancipated from some middle-class values. In another case he actively intervened in behalf of a specific marriage choice, one that today might seem bizarre. This patient had had a long-standing sexual relationship with his brother's wife. As a result of an analysis with Freud, the man was freed from his incestuous bond, only to fall in love with his niece, the daughter of his former mistress. Freud considered that this new relationship represented a solid step forward for his patient. The girl, however, was recalcitrant and resisted the advances of her uncle. Freud thereupon recommended that she undergo an analysis. The girl's analyst was told by Freud that there was a secret in the case and that when the analyst discovered it she should report it to Freud. Within a week or so the analyst returned with the news that not only was the secret uncovered, but there was a secret to the case that Freud himself did not know.

This case fits the archetype of the legendary Viennese love tangle. The young girl did indeed know about the long-standing liaison between her suitor and her mother, as Freud had wanted to find out, but he did not know that the girl had the fantasy that she herself was the child of the illicit union between her uncle and her mother, which fully explained her hesitancy to get involved with him sexually. Once Freud was made aware of the girl's inner world, he dropped the idea of the match. The fact that Freud would countenance, even try to promote, such a match should demonstrate what a world away from today's middle-class values was his own private therapeutic practice.

Freud's distance from the values of conventional society played a role in his individualistic conception of treatment. The analyst was not supposed to burden a patient with extraneous problems, either analyst's or society's. Ideally, the aim of an analysis was to help the patient, enriched from his inner resources, to become his own best self. Freud hoped and expected that in each patient the analyst could find an ally, the struggling self that had been weighted down by mistakes in upbringing and misconception of goals.

Freud took for granted what nowadays, at least in the United States, seems so rare in patients, a self that knows what it wants. The patients Freud worked best with were those with already well-constituted egos. As Freud remarked to a patient at the end of a three-months' analysis in 1908: "What I liked best about working with you was that as soon as I gave you something you were able to make use of it.'' Freud took for granted, at least in the early period of his practice, a well-functioning personality capable of integrating the insights he could offer.

Bold as he was as a practicing clinician, Freud remained shy about discussing the aims of analytic therapy. In his earlier years he had been far more outgoing and interventionist than later on, especially after he had his cancer; in those last years of his life he was more disillusioned about the prospects of therapeutic success and more preoccupied with the future of his findings as a scientific body. Yet almost nowhere did Freud seek to define the concept of psychic health. It was characteristic of him to relegate the problem of freedom, for example, to a mere footnote.

The healthy was not just the same as the worthy—on that point Freud was insistent. One might be healthy and still good-for-nothing; it was also possible to be quite sick and yet, in Freud's mind, valuable as a human being. He did not want to have to give advice or preach to patients, for that would be to duplicate the techniques of hypnotic treatment and suggestion, as well as some of the mistaken tasks of traditional religion. Freud assumed in his patients the role of a well-integrated, even if overly severe, superego, which may in part explain his relative lateness in coming to discuss this concept. Even though people of fancy and imagination could hold a special place in his heart, Freud steadfastly admired the conscientious and the upright.

Freud could scarcely have foreseen the uses his concepts would be put to since his death. As much as he had not wanted psychoanalysis to become a mere "handmaid," as he liked to put it, to psychiatry, in the United States at any rate it would be hard to overestimate the impact of his ideas on psychiatric theory and practice. Dr. Spock's child-rearing manuals would be inconceivable without the backdrop of Freud's work.

Psychoanalysis has had its successes, and analysts in the United States are now hardly in the position of being an underpaid revolutionary band at odds with conventional wisdom. Analysts have direct as well as indirect influence not only on psychiatric departments, but on schools, law courts, universities, professional training centers, business corporations, and so on. As long as Freud and his followers were themselves on the outside they could scarcely be accused of advocating conformism. They could even afford to evade certain issues, thanks to the social position in which they found themselves. To the degree that today's analysts have become members of the establishment, however, Freud's ideas need to be clarified lest they be pressed willy-nilly into service in behalf of the status quo. Problems such as that of moral values need especially to be reexamined in the very different historical conditions under which we now live.

For some time now psychoanalytic theory has been separated by a rather wide gulf from psychoanalytic practice. For those of a bookish cast of mind it is disquieting that theoretical understanding is of so little help in orienting oneself in psychoanalysis. On theoretical grounds one may find little cause for worry that psychoanalytic ideas will be used to promote conformism or mere adjustment, but the widespread influence of psychoanalysis today, as well as the background and training of those who now become therapists, can lead to legitimate concern over the role certain types of values have come to play in clinical practice.

It is simply not possible to exclude from psychoanalytic thought the problem of moral values. To attempt to do so is only to encourage the uncritical acceptance of the prevailing standards of morality. No one, of course, can choose goals for other people; the task of good theory should be merely to make it as hard as possible for psychoanalysis to be used unthinkingly for a given political or social end.

Let me cite a few examples from my own limited experience in the mid-1960s. I remember seeing the case of a young Jewish girl presented at a fine psychiatric hospital in Boston, Massachusetts. She came from the proverbial good middle-class family, but had run away, across the country, for the sake of adventure and "sleeping around." Her parents had finally retrieved her and put her in the hospital. She seemed to me a not especially intelligent young lady, and her rather standard manner of complying with the way young people dressed then did not make her look any more interesting.

To the clean-cut, hardworking resident who was treating her, however, she was schizophrenic, and with psychoanalytic theory in hand everyone in the room tried to examine the roots of her troubles. About two-thirds through the discussion the senior psychiatrist, an analyst, reacted with fury; he demanded to know what was the evidence for schizophrenia in the girl. Groping for justification, the resident finally had to admit that he did not like the way the girl dressed and wore her hair. By the end of the meeting the "diagnosis" of a hippie—or, more troubling for the girl's prospects, a diagnosis of a pseudo-hippie—had been agreed upon.

From my participation in case conferences at that time two other illustrations of the role moral values can play in clinical practice come to mind. A depressed black man was having an affair with a white woman. As the psychiatrist explained his handling of the case, "I didn't exactly criticize the affair, but I tried to make him see that a white woman who has an affair with a black man must have a devaluated sense of herself." Perhaps this was so, and possibly the hippie was also schizophrenic, but such pat ways of dismissing behavior that deviates from middle-class norms does seem humanly offensive and scientifically questionable.

At another meeting a Peace Corps psychiatrist described his work as largely focused on preventing young men from "going native" and marrying young girls in the field. He regarded it as axiomatic that college-educated white Americans who wanted to marry "barefoot girls with only a third-grade education" must be suffering from mental disturbance. In one case, the psychiatrist said that a young man in love had "shaky ego boundaries," which justified psychiatric intervention—as if any impending marriage were not an appropriate time for such an upheaval.

From many such instances one acquires the feeling that almost any prejudice can be defended by means of modern psychology. Since psychoanalytic concepts aim at being scientific, they should be capable of being used for very different political and social purposes, from the most conservative to the most radical. What is impermissible, however, is for someone to assume his values and beliefs in such a way that rather striking moral positions are taken via clinical categories without an awareness that the same categories might justify very different moral alternatives.

In one area of contemporary psychology the role of values has crept in rather notably, although surreptitiously, and that is in developmental models of personality growth. To what extent are these conceptions descriptions of how things do happen, and to what degree are they accounts of what we would like and approve? Have we, in fact, examined anything like all the possible human potentialities that it might be logical to try to foster? These are questions that on formal grounds alone psychoanalysis must try to answer. After all, to say that an act is immature or neurotic is to imply a standard of maturity or health. Yet how little attention is paid to what we could possibly mean by normality.

At his best Freud stood for the ideal of autonomy. It is a commonplace by now that the psychoanalytic revolution has contributed to the liberalizing trends in our time. It can never be enough, though, to call upon a heritage that values individual freedom of choice and labors against deceit and coercion. Hypocrisy arises precisely when, under the guise of glittering ideals, objectionable conformist practices are permitted to flourish. The more psychoanalytic theory pays attention to problems of ethics and values, the harder it is going to be to make moral choices in undercover ways. Suggestion is still very much an element in treatment, even in the hands of well-trained psychoanalysts, and hidden ethical advice is all the more likely in those who think of themselves as morally aloof and neutral. New threats to human freedom are always arising, and psychoanalysis has to adapt to these if it is not to become one more component in the social hierarchy at odds with the growth of humane individualism.

When Freud paid his memorable trip to the United States in 1909, he spent a few days in New York City before going to Clark University to receive an honorary degree. A. A. Brill, then Freud's leading disciple in the United States, was living on Central Park West; Freud expressed his approval of the spot and strongly encouraged Brill to remain there, and from that beginning arose one of the main geographic clusters of the New York analytic community. Even in those pre–World War I days, psychoanalysis was attracting the interest of Greenwich Village intellectuals; Walter Lippmann, for example, brought Brill for an evening to one of Mabel Dodge Luhan's salons to explain the import of these new ideas. However welcome Freud's system might have been in the United States, he himself remained resolutely convinced that his work was in danger of being corrupted. Freud was not content that psychoanalysis become a mere medical specialty; since he sought a triumph in the life of the mind, the North American continent was to him not cultured enough to be as worthy a battlefield as the Old World.

Janet Malcolm's *Psychoanalysis: The Impossible Profession* (1981) is a slightly expanded version of articles that originally came out in the *New Yorker*. It is odd how different one's reaction can be to pieces that seem to be journalistic, as opposed to the consideration due a book later nominated for a national award in nonfiction. At the time these articles first appeared, I read them dutifully, wondering whether the author's purposes were clear to herself, for she began one of her pieces with such a banal quotation ("If two people are repeatedly alone together, some sort of emotional bond will develop between them"), reiterated here, that I questioned whether she did not harbor some unconscious savage intent.

The idea of interviewing in depth one anonymous psychoanalyst, whom she called "Aaron Green," was an imaginative one. It sometimes appears as if she has adopted the device of creating a fictionalized alter ego to represent the thinking of a contemporary New York Freudian purist. To the extent that there are so many of America's analysts now in New York and more analysts in the United States than in any country in the world, it was daring to try to enter the inner sanctum of the establishment of Freud's heirs. Yet the *New Yorker* articles made hard reading, as one had to slog through some elementary expositions of analytic concepts to glean bits and pieces of inside dope.

As a book it is possible to assess the author's work in a different light. On the second time around it makes a lively, quick read. Yet carefully considering the import of her approach, one can only conclude that she has succeeded in constructing a myopic view of the current state of psychoanalysis. Her narrow focus stems from her having accepted a series of questionable premises: that the New York Psychoanalytic Society and its doings are of weighty import; that other training centers in New York, not to mention elsewhere on the continent, are beneath consideration; and that American psychoanalysis is "a great cut above psychoanalysis elsewhere in the world. . . . "[19] Lillian Ross's own *New Yorker* pieces some years back on New York's analysts, collected in her *Horizontal and Vertical*, were implicitly far more sophisticated.

The result of Janet Malcolm's efforts becomes a species of propaganda in behalf of a therapeutic approach that by now is justifiably widely suspect. One would like to believe that analysts like Aaron Green, since they still seem to exist, are not doing too much harm. He thinks of himself as a surgeon, impersonally working in a laboratory; after fifteen years of analysis himself, he does not consider it out of the ordinary to see patients five times a week on a couch for eight or ten years. The existence of such a fossil is a tribute to the persistence of human credulity, the fears of human contact that link both therapists and patients, and the quest for solutions to human dilemmas in the realm of secular religions.

We are given a narration about the creation of a "transference neurosis," how a patient's emotional life can come to revolve around the person of the analyst, without any questioning of the advisability of mobilizing such human feelings. Abundant evidence exists to lead to doubts about the traditional analyst's capacity to meet the kind of regression evoked by the only apparently neutral setting of the analytic situation. Yet Janet Malcolm steadfastly presents things from Aaron Green's point of view, simplistically tracing any alternative therapeutic procedures back to Sandor Ferenczi, Freud's talented Hungarian follower.

The truth of the matter is that few of the early analysts, including Freud himself, would have behaved with such literal-minded coldness toward neurotic suffering. Freud, at his best, treated every patient as an exception, and the therapeutic rules or recommendations he laid down for others were intended as provisional guidelines, places where a beginner might go wrong. The author, however, treats Aaron Green's musings on the magic of so-called scientific technique as the reasoning of some kind of soul expert. She quotes the head of the New York Psychoanalytic Society's Treatment Center as saying of his cases, "There are no surprises, we haven't had a surprise since 1974."[20] Anybody with horse sense should scoff at the mumbo jumbo underlying such pretentious arrogance. Even worse than the assumption that the likes of Aaron Green are privy to secrets of the human psyche unknown to other practitioners, she treats him as a kind of modern grand inquisitor, sorrowfully bearing the hardship of the burdens that others are too weak to undertake.

Psychoanalysis: The Impossible Profession fits into a line of apologetics for fundamentalist psychoanalysis that too many intellectuals have unashamedly undertaken. Well-meaning people easily might be misled by this book. If Aaron Green had an "unsmiling face"[21] for Janet Malcolm, what are the clinical implications of humorlessness (or smugness)? Jokes are not just defensive maneuvers, as Green seems to think; Freud's own analyses were rarely the "ordeal"[22] that Green proposes his patients undergo. Although the creator of psychoanalysis had a more tolerant outlook on human diversity than some of his loyalist epigones, he might be amused by this fully analyzed analyst's admission of his desire to be a beautiful woman.

What is really askew about this book is the misjudgments about the relative standing of the writers she has undertaken to talk about. It is as if she believes that the leaders of the New York Psychoanalytic Society are some sort of giants. Does she not learn anything from Aaron Green's admission that his classes during his training were disappointments? At least some courses in old Vienna or Berlin were spectacles of intellectuality. Being infantilized toward a genius like Freud is different from being childish in a contemporary parochial bureaucracy. (In discussing Victor Rosen's fall from grace with the powers-that-be in New York, for some reason she does not mention his name nor his subsequent suicide.) She cites some of the most creative figures in recent psychoanalysis, such as D. W. Winnicott in England, as if they were just the equal of some local New York logic chopper. Heinz Kohut of Chicago does get a good deal of attention, altogether too much in terms of the history of the development of technical innovations, but then he is treated as a sinner against the alleged primacy of the Oedipus complex. Nowhere does she critically examine what there could be about unswervingly "classical" Freudianism that might have struck so many as appallingly destructive, if not sadistic.

It has long been established that to sell books in the United States one need only successfully appeal to the New York City market. It is unfortunately true that elsewhere in North America decent bookstores scarcely exist. New York's cultural life is a high attainment, and if Janet Malcolm had given any account of the bases of the psychoanalytic schisms or revisionism over the years, she would at least have served the history of ideas. As it is, this apparent exposé may help reinforce authoritarianism and cultism in conservative training centers. The book reflects too much a mood of cultural self-congratulation characteristic, alas, of "God's own country." Given the objective problems of contemporary analysis, it would be a mistake to accept this version of orthodoxy as any less dubious than many of the other existing approaches for people in trouble.

Books are my business, as a reader, writer, and teacher, and therefore I have long been distressed with the instruction offered North American candidates in analytic training and our students of psychiatry at medical school. To the extent that training facilities are designed for psychologists, social workers, and social scientists as well, I think my basic disquiet is reinforced. In contrast to the complacency implicit in Janet Malcolm's account, I do think we have grounds for alarm, which at least in part confirm the criticisms of American psychoanalysis that are heard today on the continent.

For instance, the practice of assigning sequences of Freud's papers without any critical secondary literature has become conventionally acceptable. Yet the real excitement to Freud's thinking can get lost if the significance of the dates in Freud's life is not kept in mind. It is impossible to understand what was going on in any of Freud's work apart from the larger context in which he was thinking. If lay analysis were ever to be widely accepted in the United States, that would immensely help the problem I am addressing. Right now, however, I believe there should be an effort, both by reading assignments as well as from lecturers, to provide a framework, ethical as well as social, in which Freud was writing. It should be accepted that analytic training groups have knowledgeable outsiders to help candidates make sense of early psychoanalysis. So often Freud was apt to be combatting another writer, sometimes even a former disciple, and yet the fascination with the isolated logic of his ideas can easily take over the center of our training attention.

I am proposing that we study Freud as all good historians proceed, in order to be clear how different his world was from our own. Once one can understand what he had to fight against, then his genuine achievement becomes clear. Yet I am making a point that I think is at odds with how much contemporary analytic literature proceeds. We need to know how our work links up with Freud's or how his ideas can fulfill our own needs only in order to establish the continuity of the psychoanalytic tradition. But there should be an end to papers that purport to extend knowledge by means of beginning (or ending) with pious quotations from Freud. Being a writing analyst should not be identified with textual exegesis. Of course we need to know what Freud thought, but his ideas cannot be successfully understood as artifacts, nor can his mind necessarily satisfy what we need to think now.

It is immensely difficult to become well educated in the history of psychoanalysis, and this is in large part because of all the sectarianism that has blinded people over the years. But even while Freud was still alive there were respectful criticisms of his work being advanced, most of which have been forgotten today—or sometimes reinvented by thinkers unaware of their predecessors. Not many candidates in training, or even medical students, ever get anything to read by Carl G. Jung, for example, even though Jung was not only an excellent critic of Freud's but wrote some pioneering papers in the 1920s on short-term psychotherapy; some of his ideas about dreaming, character, and the legitimacy of symptoms were way ahead of their time. Realistically there is no pope able to excommunicate anyone for now having a good word to say about some of the people whom Freud himself saw as heretics.

At the same time it has never been clear to me how some writers succeed in getting put on the reading lists of our hospitals and institutes. I suspect that provincial or national prejudices play a larger role than they might. Psychoanalytic literature has been accumulating for almost a century now, and there ought to be more of a consensus on which papers and books are classics. One does not have to be a Sullivanian to acknowledge how he pioneered in the treatment of psychosis or to be a Kleinian to assign, for instance, her work on depression. One should not have to travel to London to discover that Donald W. Winnicott was probably the most original thinker in the history of the British Society, nor should one have to accept any of Jacques Lacan's technical recommendations to appreciate his criticisms of North American analysis. Erich Fromm's early papers on the liberal ethics implicit in Freud ought surely to be widely read, and still other recent influential figures, such as Bruno Bettelheim and Erik H. Erikson, also deserve a hearing.

Part of the problem is that each of these different conceptualizations has had such a variety of terminology attached to them that it is not easy to make one's way in the world of these writers. Teachers have the job, however, of helping students cope with alien concepts. I am not, of course, implying that only those people about whom there was in the past a brouhaha need to be read; it has been possible to be original in analysis without inventing new terms for everything. But too often analysis, for all its ritualistic citation of dates connected with the earlier literature, lacks genuine historical consciousness. When recent literature is being assigned and acknowledged landmarks get ignored, one suspects that our educational system is faulty.

I do think there has not been enough willingness to disagree without threatening someone else's reason for being; the level of everyday conformity, which I think can be detected in today's psychoanalysis, gets communicated willy-nilly in the training of future practitioners. It is the lack of enough critical thinking and the absence of rival thoughts that is a breeding ground for the tumultuous conflicts that have marked the history of analysis.

Those of us who consider ourselves liberals in analysis, open to new ideas and interpretations, face an uphill struggle against the entrenched power of orthodoxy. The influence of the establishment in any field rests partly on unthinking agreement and the fear of outsiders as well as on the privileges of trade unionism.

Unfortunately, psychoanalytic liberals have an uncertain heritage to rely on. One thinks of too many instances of intolerance: Jung criticizing Alfred

Adler as well as Freud; Sandor Rado, in an orthodox phase, siding against Klein; Franz Alexander reviewing Karen Horney negatively; and Fromm seeing Otto Rank in terms of the rise of fascism. The power of Freud's work comes from his genius as a writer, but the difficulty in going beyond him stems partly from the failure of toleration among those who have tried to come up with alternatives.

At the same time we should be aware of how fashions change among analysts, as they do in every field. Twenty years ago Heinz Hartmann's ego psychology was, at least in most journals in the United States, cited as avidly as theorists of narcissism are now being quoted. But one wonders whether in another generation it will be any clearer why, for example, Kohut's self psychology was important than it is now why Hartmann once seemed central. It is impossible to assign everything in the course of training, but I doubt that we have come anywhere near the outer limits of what might be possible in the direction of catholicity.

As long as I am making a plea in behalf of historical generosity, I should add that it even behooves us to be clear what psychotherapeutic thinking was like before Freud. The case histories of the old-fashioned psychiatrists are still noteworthy; the attention to detail of the pre-Freudian thinkers was remarkable. It is easy to overlook the achievement of classical psychiatry in encouraging case histories that are ample enough to allow for later self-correction. By now the pendulum has swing so far that throughout the literature individual patients tend to get lost in abstract speculations.

At his best Freud emphasized how little we know. He was sounding that note not just by means of his concept of the unconscious, but even after he had constructed psychoanalysis as a system he was capable of caution and reserve. He had invented this field out of his own autobiographical understanding, yet created a discipline enough beyond himself to qualify as a science; others after him have been able to use his work for the sake of coming to conclusions that he might well have wanted to repudiate. It would be, therefore, in Freud's best spirit to communicate to students the variety of the field, as well as the uncertainties, which would show why the excitement of discovery will, we hope, always be associated with the study of psychoanalysis.

The five lectures Freud delivered at Clark University in September 1909 are justifiably famous; a critical examination of his text is an appropriate way to conclude our discussion of the relationship between Freud and the United States. The 1909 occasion was a memorable one; Clark University in Worcester, Massachusetts, under the leadership of G. Stanley Hall, was to be the only institution ever to award Freud an honorary degree. For Freud the trip to North America, which included some steps across the border into Canada at Niagara Falls, represented a taste of dearly sought academic recognition. If Freud retained a lasting disdain for most things American, some of the people he met at Clark, such as William James, were to be among the exceptions that for Freud always proved his rules. Many readers have been first introduced to psychoanalysis by the clear exposition of his ideas that Freud worked out for his American audience.

Freud began his first lecture with a bow to Josef Breuer. In giving his account of the history of the psychoanalytic "method of examination and treatment,"[23] Freud generously claimed that it was Breuer who merited the credit for having created psychoanalysis. Within five years, however, after the splits with Adler and Jung, Freud corrected his remarks in connection with Breuer, assuming (as he put it in a footnote added in 1923 to his Clark Lectures) "the entire responsibility for psychoanalysis."[24]

Freud began his discussion at Clark by moving immediately to Breuer's famous case of "Anna O." Over half of Freud's first lecture was taken up with some of the details of Anna O.'s afflictions and the course of Breuer's cathartic treatment of her in 1880–82. She suffered from florid symptomatology that ought not, Freud contended, be mistakenly attributed to physical aetiology. Anna O. had a paralysis and loss of sensation at the extremities of one side of her body—and suffered from the same problem sometimes on her other side. Her sight was restricted and her eye movements peculiar. She coughed nervously and had a problem with the way she held her head. She ate with extreme difficulty and was unable to drink for some weeks in spite of being intensely thirsty. At several points she was unable to speak or understand German, her language, while communicating instead in English. She could also be subject to what the French called "absences," or confusional states. She had, in the terminology of the nineteenth century, taken to her bed.

Freud expressed satisfaction that the majority of his audience was a nonmedical one, since according to his experience conventional medical wisdom of that time was too apt to be therapeutically pessimistic. The Freud of the pre–World War I era was unlike the aloof victim of cancer of his old age; in 1909 he was centrally concerned with symptoms and the alleviation of mental suffering. In an interview he gave then he declared, "As you ask me about my own method of psychotherapy I must first mention that there are of course many sorts and ways of psychotherapy. All are good if they accomplish their objective, that is effect a cure."[25]

Anna O.'s kind of "hysteria" deserved, Freud held, the sympathy and understanding of the therapist. Paradoxically, a favorable prognosis for the patient's recovery too often deprived the physician of the caring attitude he would have for sufferers of organic disease. Novel theories were needed to undermine a simplistic moral injunction for the patient to pull herself together. Furthermore, the hysteric's symptomatology violated commonsense assumptions about the mind and the body. Freud thought the ailments of Breuer's patient could be explained satisfactorily by Breuer's technique of going back to their earliest appearance. Through what Anna O. called the "talking cure" or "chimney sweeping," it proved "possible to bring about the disappearance of the painful symptoms of her illness, if she could be brought to remember under hypnosis, with an accompanying expression of affect, on what occasion and in what connection the symptom had first appeared."[26] Freud was convinced that Anna O.'s symptoms proved to be the outcome of unresolved emotional experiences.

Oddly enough, Freud had picked a patient who had not in fact been successfully treated by psychotherapy. It is true that in later life she became a famous German social worker; the government of West Germany honored her after World War II by printing a postage stamp with her picture. Perhaps her successful career helps explain why Jones revealed the patient's name, "much to the family's displeasure."[27] But Prof. Henri Ellenberger has convincingly unearthed material that fully supports a contention of Jung's that Freud had told him about Anna O. as a therapeutic failure. In addition to her other problems, after Breuer's cathartic treatment Anna O. was addicted to morphine. Full recovery took place only later, but the recuperative process remains shrouded in mystery.

It is hard not to question why Freud chose to repeat Breuer's reluctant use of this particular case history. Early on Freud felt the need to surround his own beginnings with a historical context, and evidently by 1909 he still wanted to establish a heritage behind his own characteristic therapeutic approach, a continuity with forerunners. Freud complained afterward that Breuer had failed to include his own countertransference feelings toward his attractive and highly intelligent young patient. (It has not been possible to document the stories Freud told people like Jones and James Strachey about Breuer's reactions to Anna O.'s transferences.) In 1914 Freud wrote: "It will be remembered that Breuer said of his famous first patient that the element of sexuality was astonishingly undeveloped in her and had contributed nothing to the very rich clinical material of the case."[28] Breuer's report, however, does not conform to Freud's description, for while Breuer pointed out Anna O.'s lack of sexual development, he had not gone on to deny any role erotic feelings might have played in her disturbances.

Enough time has passed so that we have a clearer picture of how much both Breuer and Freud left out. Despite Freud's interest in Anna O.'s particular symptoms, he tells us nothing about her religious background. (Her family was an Orthodox Jewish one.) Although one might infer material about her social class, Freud isolates individual symptoms from their human context. For example, Anna O. had a lady companion she evidently did not care for, yet at Clark Freud focused on a symptom like "disgust" at her lady companion's dog, and how this influenced her own problems, without drawing attention to the larger social dilemma Anna O. found herself in. It is not just that Freud, as well as Breuer, overlooked the cultural situation of talented young women of that era. But even in describing the effects on Anna O. of the death of her father, Freud reports no curiosity about what the father might have been like, nor the quality of his relationship to his daughter. It therefore becomes impossible to accept Freud's confident prediction of exactly what kind of additional symptoms she might have developed without the benefit of Breuer's treatment.

Symptoms must be evaluated in the context of interpersonal, social, and somatic data. Jones characterized Anna O. as having developed "a museum of symptoms."[29] His metaphor is suggestive: if patients no longer fall ill that way, what can account for it? Sex and biology are not the same thing; even if Anna O. were sexually disabled, it does not follow that it was improper for some people to remain, as did Anna O., childless and unmarried. Any concept of symptomatology has to include, in addition to physical components, moral as well as social elements. Symptoms can be a warning signal, a challenge to beware of self-betrayal. From the point of view of a therapist, helping people has to be understood in terms of the preexistence of certain social norms. Implicitly Freud may have been aware of some of these problems, for although he had started out as a clinical worker, by the end of his life he preferred to take his stand as a pure scientist.

Essentially, in 1909 Freud was using Anna O.'s case history for the sake of illustrating the psychological principles he had evolved by then; detours, which might seem warranted today, would have contradicted his purposes and distracted his audience. Every neurotic, Freud held, clings emotionally to the past. Emotions consist in "displaceable magnitudes."[30] If affects were "strangulated," they had to find an "abnormal"[31] outlet. Here Freud was bent on summarizing the now-famous concept of conversion. Symptoms arise from inappropriate discharge. Through correcting gaps in memory the therapist can hope to remove the conditions from which symptomatology originally arose.

Freud found historical consciousness a useful means of introducing novices to his psychology, and so he began his second lecture by recounting his experiences as a student of Charcot's in Paris. Freud and Breuer had started out by equating psychological traumas with the effects of somatic ones, although as Freud pointed out, it had not been Charcot, for all his interest in demonstrating hysterical paralyses, but his student Pierre Janet who followed up on the psychological train of thought.

Freud then introduced a concept distinctive to his own way of thinking: resistance. Neurotics suffer from forgotten memories, but lost recollections survive unconsciously. Although that which is defended against seeks release, inner obstacles interfere with forbidden gratifications. According to Freud, those blocks in turn resist the therapist's efforts to revive past memories. Freud's concept of resistance, however, has proved a controversial one, since it opens the way to the patient's healthy ego feeling the analyst must always possess superior knowledge. Yet in terms of his own era Freud was attempting to be less authoritarian than others in approaching "nervous" difficulties.

From our own standpoint Freud seems excessively confident about his ability to attain therapeutic success. He based his theory of the necessity of removing resistances on supposed processes of recovery. "Starting out from the mechanism of cure, it now becomes possible to construct quite definite ideas of the origin of the illness."[32] Patients, Freud argued, suffer from inner conflicts; rather than face the pain of acknowledging wishes at odds with ethical and aesthetic standards, repression comes into play. A conflict between opposing mental forces characterizes psychological problems. Freud thought that the technique of free associations, rather than hypnosis, is valuable precisely because it enables the therapist to observe resistances and repressions. Symptoms are a sign of unsuccessful handling of wishes that are intolerable. Ailments are substitutes for repressed ideas.

Freud had believed that his American hosts were a practically oriented people, and only in his third lecture did he try to outline the broader implications of his theories. Jokes were illustrations from normal life of the operation of distorted substitutes for underlying complexes. Slips and above all dreams were other everyday avenues to knowledge of the repressed unconscious. Since Freud's death there has been so much attention given to ego psychology that it is worth pointing out how restricted a view of the ego he had as of 1909; when Freud spoke about "the ego's forces of defence" he specified that he had in mind "resistances."[33] The distortions behind symptoms help to explain the disguises that take place in dreaming. Freud proposed that we only fulfill repressed wishes by means of a variety of unconscious subterfuges.

Although by now we take the principle almost for granted, Freud's 1909 pronouncement about the momentous significance of childhood experiences was by no means a commonplace. In dreams he thought "the child that is in man pursues its existence. . . . "[34] In the face of the human capacity to transfer past problems onto the present, Freud's aim was that of enlightenment. He was fully confident of the ability of his techniques "to bring the pathogenic psychical material into consciousness and so to get rid of the ailments that have been brought about by the formation of substitutive symptoms."[35]

But as we look back at Freud in 1909 it is hard to believe that he was justified in advocating his techniques as if they could be learnt in anything like the manner of the methods of histology or surgery. Instead of living up to the ideal of self-knowledge, Freud had succeeded in deceiving himself about the objectivity of his conclusions. From today's perspective it is clear, as it was to many of Freud's contemporaries, that what he had to offer were best described as hypotheses rather than as "findings." In science hypotheses are valuable to the extent that they are capable of being fruitful of further developments, including alteration and correction; as a scientist, therefore, Freud should have been more cautious.

Only in his fourth lecture did Freud pinpoint the role in his system of erotic factors. He assigned "predominant significance" to "erotic disturbances" in mental life.[36] Freud was, like every other figure in intellectual history, a man of his times, and whatever the ultimate significance of his ideas, he had to share many preconceptions of his society. In reaction against conventional Central European wisdom Freud took what now seems an arbitrary approach to symptoms; he saw them as psychogenic in character, not social or somatic, whereas we now believe that all factors can play their part.

If Freud was boldly original in his willingness to treat symptoms as psychologically meaningful, he was also sticking out his neck in condemning prevailing sexual morality. He objected to the lack of candor about sex, as people veiled their feelings in lies, prudery, and prurience; although he did not say so publicly, Freud thought Americans were particularly guilty on this score. Freud attributed neurotic symptoms not just to the persistence of childhood impressions, but in particular to the survival of powerful erotic experiences. Infantile sexuality was for Freud the root of later troubles, for under stress adults regress back to earlier, "not completely conquered"[37] complexes.

Freud was concerned with both the mental as well as the physical side of sexual life. Oedipal conflicts were for him the essence of neurosis—"the *nuclear complex* of every neurosis"[38]—which he thought explained the significance of barriers against incest. The moral Freud drew from the Oedipus complex reflects the liberal ideological framework from which he worked. It is, Freud held, inevitable and "perfectly normal"[39] for a child to be erotically attached to its parents. But later the oedipal constellation must be defused. Each individual should take parents as models and transfer libidinal involvement to new, nonfamiliar "objects." The child must gradually detach himself from his parents, which Freud considered "a task that cannot be evaded if the young individual's social fitness is not to be endangered."[40] Education has its role to play in helping the individual to emancipate himself from his family, and Freud recommended psychoanalysis as a kind of after-education "for the purpose of overcoming the residues of childhood."[41]

At the outset of his fifth and final lecture Freud brought his system together. The frustration of erotic needs lies behind neurotic illness, and he saw this frustration as stemming from outside impediments as well as from internal inflexibilities. Yet frustration cannot be logically defined apart from a given social and moral context, for what is considered illegitimate in one class or era will be deemed satisfying elsewhere. For all his philosophical skepticism, Freud proceeded as if absolute norms could be universally agreed upon. This issue is a key one, since he treated illness as a surrogate satisfaction. According to Freud, "pathological symptoms constitute a portion of the subject's sexual life or even the whole of his sexual life. . . ."[42] Freud's theory of resistances supported his contention that a patient, despite an effort to overcome difficulties, will unconsciously oppose recovery. To Freud the flight from reality was one way of defining neurotic illness. But psychological problems had to involve "biological damage"[43] for Freud; neurotics are infantile, regressed, unable to get beyond their childhood beginnings.

Neurotics are not alone in being wish-fulfilling creatures. Freud believed that everyone resorts to fantasy to make up for unsatisfying realities. It is typical of him to have viewed fantasy in a negative light. Failure leads to withdrawal into fantasy, and in the event of "illness" substitute satisfactions explain symptomatology. For Freud reality appears hard and unappeasable. One way of satisfying the inexorable demands of life is through artistic creation instead of symptoms. But "persistent rebellion against the real world," in the absence of adequate artistic creativity, leads to the isolation of neurosis. Freud took a critical view of religion but at the same time saw neurosis on the increase, due to the decline of religious faith. Perhaps his fundamental antagonism to Catholicism can be seen in his choice of a specific analogy: "Today neurosis takes the place of the monasteries which used to be the refuge of all whom life had disappointed or who felt too weak to face it."[44]

Despite his eagerness to leave his audience with a comprehensive view of psychoanalytic psychology, most of Freud's last lecture was devoted to advocating the significance of his chosen method of treatment. He introduced it by elucidating the concept of transference, which Freud modestly called "the most important of the observations which confirm our hypothesis of the sexual instinctual forces operating in neuroses." The patient's irrational feelings, directed in the course of treatment toward the analyst, indicated to Freud the existence of unconscious wishful fantasies. He repudiated the notion that transferences might be "*created* by psychoanalytic influence"; it arises "spontaneously in all human relationships just as it does between the patient and the physician."[45] But one can question whether Freud had chosen the proper alternative. Transference does not have to be "created" by the psychoanalytic situation in order for it to be influenced by it, and the question of its spontaneous arousal "in all human relationships" is superlatively a matter of degree.

Freud proposed that transference was to be psychoanalysis's means of therapeutic influence. He was confident that after the patient was shown in therapy the existence of irrationally infantile feelings it would be possible to gain mastery over neurotic processes. But as we shall see, Freud's ideal of rationalism misled him. It is noteworthy from our own perspective that as clear as Freud attempted to be and as consistent as he tried to make his system, he does not state what limits on transference reactions should be therapeutically set. Nor is he explicit how, besides the use of rational explanations, the therapist ought to meet transference complexes once they appear in a treatment setting. If it is agreed that the analytic situation can itself mobilize transferences, Freud missed how his techniques generally influence the material they uncover.

Freud was aware of one so-called resistance to psychoanalysis—"people are afraid of doing harm. . . . " Since Freud set out to stir up repressed sexual instincts, he conceded the legitimacy of the question of whether the patient's higher self would be in danger of being overwhelmed. Freud's answer, though, was firm. A surgeon does not fear the consequences of taking measures to cure a disease. All operations temporarily increase pain for the sake of the ultimate recovery. Most of us have witnessed the catastrophe of severe mental collapse, and the disease model is hard to get out of one's mind. But is neurosis an "illness" like a physical disorder? It is in any event highly doubtful that in the sphere of the psyche there can be any such thing as what Freud confidently had in mind, "a permanent cure." It is questionable how many today could go along with Freud in thinking that psychoanalysis "can make the same claims as surgery. . . . " Freud thought that the mental suffering of analysis was much less than the pain of surgery and "quite negligible in proportion to the severity of the underlying ailment."[46]

Freud was uncompromising in rejecting even the possibility of negative therapeutic results: "the final outcome that is so much dreaded—the destruction of the patient's cultural character by the instincts which have been set free from repression—is totally impossible." Once again Freud's drastic alternative, "the destruction" of the patient's higher capacities, can be rejected. Freud gave the narrow logic for his self-assurance: "our" experiences as analysts "have taught us with certainty" that the lifting of repressions can "only" be to weaken the power of unconscious drives.[47]

Freud believed that the patient's critical judgment is more reliable than continued self-deception, and he thought that sexual drives are especially capable of being sublimated into more "socially valuable"[48] directions.

But without more explicit attention to moral values it is impossible to be sure of the merits of any therapeutic results. Freud did not generally advocate sweeping problems under rugs, but he tried to evade the philosophical implications of his clinical practices. On one social point alone Freud was clear, and it was on this note that he concluded his Clark Lectures: society has been unduly sexually restrictive, and social patterns have thereby had neurotic consequences.

Freud had begun his first lecture by offering the case of Anna O. as an illustration of his principles. If confronted with the actual clinical history that we now know, he might rationalize the therapeutic failure in her case on the grounds that analysis, instead of catharsis, had not been carried out. Even so it is bound to seem utopian, misleading to therapists as well as patients, to hold out the hope of "complete success" in any kind of psychotherapy. Freud was in reality at his best as a therapist when he maintained a sense of the limits of what can ever be therapeutically accomplished. Yet the ideal he promulgated at Clark, the creation of a neutral technique capable of transforming human nature, helps explain one source of Freud's appeal to his New World audience.

It would be erroneous to conclude that criticism of any parts of Freud's writings implies a lack of appreciation for his stature in the history of ideas. If Freud was wrong on a point, it is in his own best scientific spirit to try to point it out. The passage of eight decades since Freud delivered his lectures at Clark has given historical distance to what he was then proposing. Too much of what Freud inaugurated has been credulously accepted by the public. His capacities as a stylist have not been equaled by anyone in the history of psychoanalysis. George Bernard Shaw once relevantly wrote: "He who has something to assert will go as far in power of style as its momentousness and his conviction will carry him. Disprove his assertion after it is made, yet his style remains. Darwin no more destroyed the style of Job or Handel than Martin Luther destroyed the style of Giotto. All the assertions get disproved sooner or later; and so we find the world full of a magnificent debris of artistic fossils, with the matter-of-fact credibility gone clean out of them, but the form still splendid."[49]

Freud's writings are historical documents, not sacred texts. One problem is that no one since his death has been able to come up with a synthesis that matches the systematic power of his own mind. A lot of post-Freudian work has been like the adding of epicycles to the Ptolemaic conception rather than looking toward an entirely new view. But there is no agreed-upon alternative yet to psychology as Freud left it.

It is at least clear that Freud's exposition of psychoanalysis was designed to convince; readers have not often enough seen how he could stack the deck in favor of persuading others to his own point of view. If Anna O. was at best a therapeutic standoff, then Freud should not have begun with her case at Clark and then ended his lectures on a note of therapeutic optimism. Perhaps she would not now be seen as neurotic. By the end of his life Freud was a good deal less sure of himself diagnostically as well as therapeutically. But he continued to deceive himself about the scientific status of what he had come up with earlier.

Historical conscientiousness requires that we acknowledge how bold Freud was in an area still so uncertain today. On some points, like the significance of childhood, we are too apt to take for granted insights based on one of Freud's central contentions. Yet another of his key points, the sexual origins of neurotic symptomatology, sounds obviously wrong, a product of Freud's own culture and probably his personality as well. In a fundamental way, however, Freud was challenging traditional conceptions of the mind and the body. Symptoms can have a meaning, even if not the ones Freud emphasized, and psychotherapeutic interventions, even if Freud's particular recommended techniques are not adopted, can affect bodily processes. In a sense it was his idealism that led him to hope that through changes in sexual practices one could directly influence suffering in the mental sphere. Freud was a prophet in addition to being a scientist, a seer as well as a psychologist. His artistic capacities ensured his triumph in intellectual history, and no doubt artistry played a role in his therapeutic practice as well. Yet to the degree that later workers have been able to pursue his leads and even come to different conclusions, Freud deserves his ranking place in the history of modern science. For all the callowness Freud saw in his audience at Clark, it symbolized how American culture as a whole was the first to assess accurately Freud's standing in the history of ideas.

Notes

1. Nathan G. Hale, Jr., *Freud and the Americans: The Beginnings of Psychoanalysis in the United States, 1876–1917* (New York: Oxford University Press, 1971), p. 4.
2. Ibid., p. 332.
3. Ibid., p. 248.
4. Ibid.
5. Ibid., p. 47.
6. Ibid., p. 168.
7. Ibid., p. 57.
8. Ibid., p. 434.

9. Ibid., p. 220.
10. Ibid., p. 39.
11. Ibid., p. 300.
12. Ibid., p. 301.
13. Ibid., p. 177.
14. Ibid., p. 19.
15. Ibid., p. 67.
16. Ibid., p. 305.
17. Ibid., p. 307.
18. Ibid., p. 285, p. 283.
19. Janet Malcolm, *Psychoanalysis: The Impossible Profession* (New York: Knopf, 1981), p. 51.
20. Ibid., p. 68.
21. Ibid., p. 3.
22. Ibid., p. 126.
23. Sigmund Freud, "Five Lectures on Psychoanalysis," *Standard Edition*, vol. 11, p. 9.
24. Ibid., p. 9.
25. Quoted in Adelbert Albrecht, "Professor Sigmund Freud," in *Freud As We Knew Him*, ed. Hendrik M. Ruitenbeek (Detroit: Wayne State University Press, 1973), pp. 23–24.
26. Freud, "Five Lectures on Psychoanalysis," p. 14.
27. Henri F. Ellenberger, "The Story of Anna O: A Critical Review with New Data," *Journal of the History of the Behavioral Sciences*, 8, no. 3 (1972), p. 270.
28. Sigmund Freud, "On the History of the Psychoanalytic Movement," *Standard Edition*, vol. 14, p. 11.
29. Ernest Jones, *Sigmund Freud: Life and Work*, vol. 1 (London: Hogarth Press, 1954), p. 247.
30. Freud, "Five Lectures on Psychoanalysis," p. 18.
31. Ibid.
32. Ibid., p. 23.
33. Ibid., p. 35.
34. Ibid., p. 36.
35. Ibid., p. 38.
36. Ibid., p. 40.
37. Ibid., p. 45.
38. Ibid., p. 47.
39. Ibid., p. 48.
40. Ibid.
41. Ibid.
42. Ibid., p. 49.
43. Ibid.
44. Ibid., p. 50.
45. Ibid., p. 51.
46. Ibid., pp. 52–53.
47. Ibid., p. 53.
48. Ibid., p. 54.
49. C. Wright Mills, "Introduction," in Thorstein Veblen, *The Theory of the Leisure Class* (New York: New American Library, 1953), p. vi.

4

Letter Writing

Freud was one of the world's great letter writers; his capacities as an artist can be highlighted as one follows how he could perform off the top of his head. He regularly set aside time for correspondence and usually answered every bit of his mail almost immediately after receiving it. Almost all his letters were in his own handwriting, for only late in his life did he dictate anything; a few letters were taken down by his favorite Otto Rank, and still later Anna Freud performed some secretarial chores. By means of his correspondence Freud kept in touch with his followers all over the world, clarifying his psychoanalytic theory and giving tips for handling difficult patients. The pleasure he took in composing letters was clearly that of a born writer.

The Letters of Sigmund Freud and Arnold Zweig, edited by Ernst L. Freud and translated by Prof. and Mrs. W. D. Robson-Scott, was in 1970 only the sixth volume of Freud's letters to appear. Zweig was already established as a leading German literary figure before 1927, when he first got in touch with Freud by mail; Zweig had long since made a mark with his novel *Claudia* and was just completing a new piece of fiction, *The Case of Sergeant Grischa.* From the outset Freud and Zweig exchanged letters as two dignitaries, and throughout the twelve years in which they wrote to each other they remained on relatively formal terms. As representatives of the best in Central European culture, they were both appalled at the rise of Nazism and both were drive to exile (Zweig to Palestine, Freud to London) by the barbarians of their era.

Zweig, who died in East Berlin in 1968, was Freud's junior by thirty-one years. He regarded himself as Freud's faithful pupil, a "foster son," and he came to address the master as "Dear Father Freud."[1] His letters convey a heartfelt adulation: "Your achievement will . . . be sufficient to guarantee the immortality of Viennese cultural life in the nineteenth and twentieth centuries."[2] As a writer himself Zweig could speak with some authority about Freud's prose: "You are *the* one living writer whose every sentence, without haste and without pause, communicates knowledge."[3] Zweig could even divine the true though unexpressed aims of Freud's singular contribution to intellectual history: " . . . analysis . . . can bring about the slow unshackling of mankind. . . . Analysis has reversed all values, it has conquered Christianity, disclosed the true Anti-Christ, and liberated the spirit of resurgent life from the ascetic ideal."[4]

Freud was a fascinating writer, and nothing from his pen has ceased to be interesting. His correspondents, however, could rarely touch his capacities, intellectual as well as stylistic, so that following Freud's letter-writing relationships often leads to losing some respect for his disciples. Karl Abraham, for example, seems rather a boring straight man in his letters to Freud, Lou Andreas-Salomé an adroit diplomatist, Wilhelm Fliess a dotty romantic, and Oskar Pfister a virtuous, though not very deep, man of God.

In this correspondence Arnold Zweig comes across as a garden-variety neurotic. In and out of analysis throughout much of his friendship with the master, Zweig, like other men of great talent, chose analysts who were scientifically undistinguished. Thus when he writes of his latest novel that "thanks to my analysis, the last sections, the last third, are really successful,"[5] he does seem a poor devil in need of some perspective on himself and the power of psychoanalysis. It is good to discover that some people fully recognized the great man's stature in his lifetime. But when Zweig writes that he will "never tire of reading you and seeing your findings confirmed" and when he describes the gift of Freud's collected papers as "the foundation stone of a library as well as of life,"[6] then for Zweig's sake one does wish he could have been less hung up on himself (which led to this slavish devotion to Freud) and more fulfilled in his art.

These letters seem, therefore, one-sided in that they are, quite properly, more taken up with Freud's life and work than with that of his younger and less distinguished partner. Yet unlike some of Freud's other correspondence, this collection of letters has little scientific value. It was as an artist that Zweig could give Freud great pleasure; the one time Zweig wrote an essay on psychoanalysis Freud sent back a short, petulant note picking Zweig up on a few trifling inaccuracies. "I am always very touchy about little things,"[7] Freud immediately apologized. Freud was capable of being interested in everything, but when it came to his own discoveries he could be hard and possessive.

The Freud we see in these letters is not primarily the revolutionary in psychology or even the leader of a large and growing movement, but a formidable old man measuring death stalking him. Less and less open to new influences, Freud spent his seventies and early eighties suffering terribly from cancer of the jaw. But he rarely gave himself up to anything approaching self-pity. He seems dispassionate in referring to "weeks of pain,"[8] being "old, feeble, and tired,"[9] his "increasing feeling of helplessness,"[10] his painful disillusionment with people, and his conviction that he had less and less left to publish.

Yet despite a harrowing illness Freud retained his vitality and energy almost to the very end of his days. At the age of seventy-nine he writes: "I still have so much capacity for enjoyment that I am dissatisfied with the resignation that is forced upon me. . . . I also find it hard to adapt myself to the role of the hero suffering for mankind, which you kindly assign me. My mood is bad, little pleases me, my self-criticism has grown much more acute."[11]

When the fire was up in Freud he could be a great hater, bitter and vindictive. There is little mention of his erring pupils in these letters (save for calling his ex-pupil Rank a "mountebank").[12] But Freud gave full vent to his unremitting sense of being badly treated by the world at large, despite the honors that he received. When Freud was awarded the Goethe Prize for literature from the city of Frankfurt in 1930, Zweig commented that "your deep pessimism about the future of analysis is not quite justified after all."[13] Freud wrote back that he could not deny being very pleased at the honor. "The thought of a closer connection with Goethe is very tempting, and the prize itself is more an act of deference to the person than an appraisal of his achievement. . . . For a reconciliation with my contemporaries it comes pretty late and I have never doubted that long after my day analysis will finally win through."[14]

In response to the many birthday greetings when he reached eighty, Freud wrote: " . . . what nonsense to try to make up for all the ill-use of a lifetime by celebrating such a questionable date! No, let us rather remain enemies."[15] Freud acknowledged having "all kinds of uncharitable prejudices with regard to humanity."[16] He maintained his "wholly non-scientific belief that mankind on the average and taken by and large are a wretched lot."[17] It was one of the great man's contradictions that such convictions did not interfere with his capacity to be a cultivated charmer.

Although these letters sound very much like the Freud of old age we have already come to know (and it should be remembered that almost no one who wrote about Freud knew him before he was quite old), they give us almost no direct insight into his private life. But they do bear the unmistakable stamp of Freud's character. When Zweig said he was toying "constantly with the idea of writing your biography—if you would permit me,"[18] Freud wrote back:

> . . . alarmed by the threat that you want to become my biographer—you, who have so much better and more important things to do, you who can establish

monarchs and who can survey the brutal folly of mankind from a lofty vantage point; no, I am far too fond of you to permit such a thing. Anyone who writes a biography is committed to lies, concealments, hypocrisy, flattery and even to hiding his own lack of understanding, for biographical truth does not exist, and if it did we could not use it. Truth is unobtainable, mankind does not deserve it, and in any case is not our Prince Hamlet right when he asks who would escape whipping were he used after his desert?[19]

It is unlikely that publishers will give up encouraging the Freud family to bring out more books of such letters. Freud sent, for example, approximately two thousand letters to Sandor Ferenczi in Budapest, almost none of which have ever appeared in print and which are now all being edited in Paris. There are also several hundred letters between Freud and Jones, but Freud often wrote Jones in English, and since Freud's written English was not very elegant or even wholly grammatical, this particular set of letters has been slow in being published. There is a legal rule that divides the right to sell a letter from the right to publish it, so while the recipients (and their heirs) of Freud's letters may get what money they can through sales or tax-deductible gifts, Freud's estate retains the right to publish his letters until fifty years after his death. Since Freud died in 1939, it has taken some time before his letters started appearing in unexpurgated form. (In the past the Freud Copyrights has demanded payment for the publication of any photographs in which Freud might have appeared, even group ones; he himself sometimes gave away, unasked, portrait shots of himself.)

Unfortunately there has been a good deal of hanky-panky, well beyond the realm of medical discretion, in the editing of Freud's letters. While it is impossible as yet to check the Freud-Zweig correspondence against the uncensored originals, enough is known about the fate of Freud's other letters to make one appropriately wary.

The editing of this correspondence is not entirely successful in its footnoting. At one point Zweig mentions having heard from a close pupil of Freud's about the existence of a biography of the master by Isidor Sadger; a footnote[20] attempts to "explain" that this is evidently a mistake for a well-known book by Fritz Wittels. Unknown to the editor (Freud's longest surviving son), Sadger did in fact write a biography of Freud, and this was probably the very book Arnold Zweig had heard about. But Sadger's account was deemed either so irreverent or malicious that a few of Freud's disciples succeeded in suppressing its publication. The history of psychoanalysis is no better, alas, or more open than the history of other major intellectual movements.

Nathan G. Hale, Jr., chose to help resurrect an American figure from the early days of psychoanalysis, James Jackson Putnam. In *James*

Jackson Putnam and Psychoanalysis (1971), translations by Judith Bernays Heller, Hale edited the correspondence between Putnam and William James, Freud, Jones, Sandor Ferenczi, and Morton Prince. Putnam was a founder of the American Neurological Association and a distinguished professor at Harvard Medical School who had been experimenting with hypnosis and psychotherapy since the 1890s. Like Prince, Putnam was disenchanted with heredity as an etiological factor, and like Jung, his method of treatment was partly inspirational. As an Emersonian, Putnam was avowedly optimistic and environmentalist, and as a New Englander with a social conscience he felt (like Adler) that the "social instincts" in neurotics had to be cultivated. For Putnam, Freud's psychoanalysis meant a new burst of hope.

As Freud wrote, Putnam represented "altogether a wonderful acquisition"[21] to the psychoanalytic movement, and the master was willing to overlook many differences between his views and those of Putnam for the sake of the latter's sterling character, as well as in behalf of psychoanalysis in the United States. Putnam was not only well connected socially but also a Gentile, a representative of the "English race"[22] Freud admired. The founder of psychoanalysis would have been foolish not to cultivate this elderly gentleman. Janet had earlier dedicated his 1906 Harvard Lectures to Putnam.

Like others who came under Freud's influence, Putnam felt that Freud's visit to the States in 1909 had "helped to change radically the whole course of my life and thought,"[23] and this was true even though Putnam was sixty-three years old when he became an advocate of the cause of psychoanalysis. Essentially, Putnam's psychoanalytic essays were propaganda in behalf of Freud's ideas. Putnam once referred to a patient of his as "a thorough convert"[24] to psychoanalysis. Freud knew Putnam's worth; as he wrote Putnam at the end of 1910: "I do not want to let this eventful and troublesome year close before having thanked you for many things; for your valuable articles, for the inestimable aid which you have lent our cause, for allowing your name to be used in America as a protection against the possible misunderstandings and abuses to which I otherwise would have been subjected. From the bottom of my egotistical heart I wish you untroubled health and energy."[25] Freud was writing tongue-in-cheek with that reference to his own egocentricity, since Putnam's New England altruism made Freud rather uncomfortable. But it was typical of Freud's intransigent spirit also to mention in the same letter that "our cause is doing very well here; the opposition is at its height."[26]

During his trip to the United States in 1909 Freud paid a visit to a camp in the Adirondacks owned by Putnam and some of his old friends. Freud arrived at the camp with Jung and Ferenczi, only to find that in honor of the visitors—an Austrian, a Swiss, and a Hungarian—the buildings had been decked out with the emblems of Imperial Germany. The intended honor must only have reminded them of the sorry state of American understanding of European realities. Partially in reciprocation of Freud's visit, Putnam went to Weimar for the 1911 International Congress of Psychoanalysis. During his trip he spent six hours in analysis with Freud in Zurich, which should give some idea how rough-and-ready by today's standards was the practice of early psychoanalytic technique.

As a therapist Putnam seemed to Freud a bit on the "ambitious" side, too eager to find means of helping and curing. When the controversies arose within the psychoanalytic movement over the personalities and ideas of Adler and Jung, Putnam remained wholly loyal to Freud while hoping that some compromise arrangement with the "dissidents" could be worked out. Putnam had long been interested in treating relatively more serious cases than those to which Freud preferred to confine his technique. Putnam's catholicity comes through in his defense of Morton Prince in writing to Jones: "I think it would be utterly unfortunate if those of us who really care about psychopathology in the larger sense should drift apart, no matter what the provocation."[27] As late as the fall of 1912 Putnam cannot quite see what all the fuss about Jung was: "I cannot think that any serious breach would be occasioned by this present movement on his part."[28] A former patient of Putnam's had introduced him to American Hegelianism and this convinced him of the need patients have for ideals to encourage their sublimations. Putnam sympathized with Jung's insistence that the analyst help the patient with his present-day problems. In describing Putnam's differences with Freud, Hale is right in saying that Putnam "anticipated many of the questions later pursued by psychoanalytic ego psychologists as well as by psychotherapists outside the movement."[29]

James Jackson Putnam and Psychoanalysis, since it covers the years of the great pre-World War I public battles in psychoanalysis, contains some of Freud's most polemical letters. For example, the break between Freud and Wilhelm Stekel gets referred to as "treason"[30] on Stekel's part. Freud characterized Jung by his "lies, brutality and anti-semitic condescension toward me."*[31] As for Adler, after his "defection" Freud referred to him as "a gifted thinker but a malicious paranoiac."[32] While later on Freud described the "loneliness"[33] that surrounded him, he does not seem to have fully acknowledged how he had himself brought that state to pass. He only knew that he had to protect himself "against people who have called them-

---

*These comments about Jung are omitted from the version of Freud's letter to Putnam that appears in *Letters of Sigmund Freud,* ed. Ernst L. Freud, trans. Tania and James Stern (London: Hogarth Press, 1961), p. 314.

selves my pupils for many years and who owe everything to my stimulus. Now I must accuse them and reject them. . . . I am not in favor of sloppy compromises, nor would I sacrifice anything for the sake of an unproductive reconciliation.''[34]

Yet Freud tolerated considerable differences between his own position and that of Putnam. To the old New Englander Freud's conception of the unconscious was ''too *negative* to be fully satisfactory.''[35] Putnam was a decent man who, though he appreciated the novelty of Freud's approach, drew back at all its consequences. ''I cannot convince myself that life, with all that makes it admirable, is to be explained purely and simply through the study of conflicts . . . we have to reckon all the time with *positive,* rather than *negative,* factors in the world.''[36] In anticipation of later analysts' interest in problems of the superego, well ahead of his time Putnam expressed his ''longing to get all that metaphysics has to offer,''[37] and this was to get away from Freud's reductionism or from what Erik Erikson was later to call the excessive ''originology'' of early psychoanalysis. Putnam hoped and believed that Freud's ''terribly searching psycho-genetic explanations correspond only to one pole of human life, and that there is another pole in which he takes no interest.''[38]

Putnam could not accept Freud's view that religion was an outgrowth of infantile helplessness and the need for an all-powerful father. Putnam objected, as did Jung, that the real '' 'unconscious' contained not only the 'shady' side of human nature, but an implicit recognition of the good.''[39] Therefore Putnam held that ''no patient is really cured unless he becomes better and broader morally, and, conversely, I believe that a moral regeneration helps towards a removal of the symptoms.''[40] Putnam saw his patients in terms of their position in society and wrote Freud that ''the individual is not to be thought of as existing alone, but should be considered as an integral part of the community in which he lives. . . . ''[41]

Freud replied by evading the substance of Putnam's argument and simply stated: ''I do not share your great respect for Adler's theories.''[42] Putnam then sent an abject reply in which he promised to take ''to heart''[43] Freud's reference to the danger of Adlerian heresy. Unlike Putnam, Freud was determined to keep psychoanalysis clear of philosophy, in order to establish his new field on independent grounds. Freud never held that analysts had to be perfectionists, either about themselves or their patients, and therefore he could write to Putnam: ''I feel no need for a higher moral synthesis in the same way that I have no ear for music.''[44] (Music is known to have irritated Freud.) Freud elaborated his position in his correspondence with Putnam: ''If we are not satisfied with saying, 'Be moral and philosophical,' it is because that is too cheap and has been said too often without being of any help. Whoever is capable of sublimation will turn to it inevitably as soon as he is free of his neurosis. Those who are not capable of this at least will become more natural and more honest."[45]

Whatever the differences between Putnam and Freud, the American was steadfast in his defense of psychoanalysis. The early analysts, including Freud, shared a literalistic fear of seducing their children, and Putnam's daughter Molly said he was afraid of holding his daughters on his lap; he even fixed the seat on Molly's bicycle lest she be unduly stimulated. Apparently Putnam's work in behalf of Freud hurt the American's medical practice, and it certainly offended his wife. She regarded him as gullible and too easily taken in, and Molly (later a psychoanalyst herself) reported her reacting with "tragic bitterness, feeling that he had been mistakenly lured into a false path which would ruin his professional standing."[46] Putnam's death at the end of World War I was a keen disappointment to Freud, since the American future of psychoanalysis would now be left to less certain hands.

Any reader should be warned, however, that Putnam's letter writing is fairly boring, and it is to Freud's credit that, although usually he responded immediately to his mail, he is often uncharacteristically slow in replying to Putnam's most windy missives. For the sake of his cause, however, Freud could be patient in putting up with Hegelian metaphysics. But it does not make the reading any easier for the editorial apparatus of *James Jackson Putnam and Psychoanalysis* to be so pedantic. The book is marred by superfluous footnotes, such as "See preceding letter,"[47] as if the reader cannot be trusted to remember what he can safely be assumed to have just finished reading. The typesetting of the book is strange, and one suspects that without such large empty spaces around less than earth-shaking letters the price of the book could have been kept down. But maybe American scholarship on a figure like Putnam is bound to have a self-inflated quality to it—which might have reassured Freud in some of his prejudices.

From Freud's point of view, Carl Gustav Jung led the most painful of the "secessions" from psychoanalysis, for of all the pupils in Freud's life, Jung played the most substantial intellectual role. Jung was declared a "heretic" by Freud some time after his troubles with Adler and Stekel, yet the three pre-World War I controversies were historically interrelated. These men established the revolutionary tradition within psychoanalysis. All later analysts would be both tempted and frightened by the prospect of open rebellion; by the 1920s it would even be possible, as in the case of Rank, for leading pupils to help push another into being a "deviant." Nevertheless, a wide range of evasive strategies existed, enabling an analyst to be his own person and yet a Freudian as well.

Of all possible accusations, "Jungian" is still probably the most devastating among Freud's spiritual descendants. Every subculture has its villains, and to them Jung seems a particularly odious figure, partly because Freud had placed such high hopes on him. His later contact with the Nazis only put the final seal of disapproval on a man Freud's pupils had learned to detest. Jung is still often dismissed today, following Freud's lead, as a "mystic," supposedly as unscientific as the socialist Adler.

The extent of the Freudian bitterness over Jung can be inferred from the difficulties the Jung archives encountered in gaining access to Jung's part of his correspondence with Freud. When, long after Freud's death but while Jung was still alive, the Jung archives offered to exchange with the Freud archives its half of the many letters between the two men, Anna Freud was unable to find Jung's letters to her father. The Jung archives then sent copies of Freud's letters, but without reciprocation. As soon as Jones needed Jung's letters for his biography of Freud, however, they somehow turned up, and even to the Freud archives it seemed awkward timing.

The Freud/Jung Letters, edited by William McGuire and translated by Ralph Manheim and R. F. C. Hull (1974), is, however, the product of full cooperation between the children of Freud and Jung. Unlike the previously published editions of Freud's letters that have come out with his family's approval, all of which were bowdlerized save for those to Putnam, this volume of Freud's correspondence has been presented intact. A few cuts have been introduced, but only in Jung's side of the letters. Until now Jung scholarship has been appallingly slack compared to the care with which Freud's writings have been edited. Evidently the Jung family has not yet faced the inevitable loss of privacy that will be involved in establishing Jung as a historical figure, and therefore Toni Wolff is described in a footnote as merely "Jung's close friend and collaborator for more than forty years,"[48] instead of as a former patient of Jung's and his lover for many years.

Jung first wrote to Freud in 1906, and although Jung was less dedicated to the art of letter writing than Freud, their correspondence remained intense until the falling out in 1913. It was typical of Freud not to strike up intimate friendships readily, yet when he did allow himself to grow dependent on someone, the intimacy was often sustained by letter writing. Whereas to Jung the correspondence between himself and Freud was not so crucial, to Freud it meant that as long as letters went back and forth the relationship was under his control as a writer.

For some years before their famous split Jung labored to forward psychoanalysis. At that time Freud's ideas had not yet won psychiatric recognition. Nevertheless, it was a sign of the low esteem in which psychiatry was then held that when Jung decided to specialize in it, well-meaning friends were afraid he was jeopardizing his career. As a leader of the Burghölzli, a famous Swiss psychiatric facility, Jung represented to the neurologist Freud a new realm in which he might hope to extend the influence of his ideas;

future analysts such as Jones, Ferenczi, Karl Abraham, and Abraham Brill spent research time at the Burghölzli.

Freud was encouraging and supportive of his new Swiss student, and even though in later years Jung might sometimes prefer to trace his indebtedness to Eugen Bleuler, the Swiss expert on schizophrenia, there can be little doubt of Jung's extended discipleship to Freud. For a time Jung even wanted to exclude from attendance at a Swiss psychoanalytic society those who were inadequately stalwart in support of Freud's cause. Jung had as a youth been sexually assaulted by a man he had worshiped, and Freud had to point out to Jung that his kind of religious reverence for the founder of psychoanalysis could end only in apostasy.

There were, however, long-standing sources of difference between Freud and Jung, which eventually culminated in their separation. Jung had hesitated to extend the concept of sexuality as broadly as Freud wished, and Jung came to interpret much so-called infantile clinical phenomena as of secondary rather than primary causal importance; current difficulties, he held, could reactivate past conflicts. Although half a century later many therapists were inclined to agree with Jung that the past can be used defensively to evade the present, at the time Freud saw Jung as merely retreating from the boldness of psychoanalysis's so-called findings. In later years, when Freud and his followers castigated Jung's "cowardice" in the face of the "facts" of infantile sexuality, it may have seemed ironic to Jung that in reality he had lived a far less sexually frustrated life than Freud evidently had. Jung may have rejected Freud's concepts of sexuality, but then he had less personal need to make sex seem so all-important.

For Freud the period from 1906 to 1909 constituted a break with his past, as he emerged from the narrow sphere of Vienna onto European psychiatry as a whole. Freud named Jung his heir in psychoanalysis, his "crown prince,"[49] and offended many of his leading Viennese followers (like Adler and Stekel) for the sake of making Jung president of the International Psychoanalytic Association. Freud was convinced that history was on his side, and for the sake of his cause any sacrifice seemed appropriate. Most of the early analysts were Jews, and Freud sought to broaden his movement's support by going beyond the confines of his own background; as a Gentile, Jung was a valuable ally in Freud's attempt to save psychoanalysis from being dismissed as a psychology suitable only for Jewry. Although in 1914 Freud in print accused Jung of anti-Semitism, no hint of such prejudice appears in any part of their correspondence.

Perhaps the most striking new information these letters supply bears on the final break in their relationship. Jung had urged that all future analysts be analyzed, a suggestion for which Freud was grateful and one that has for many years now been standard practice. But it seems that Jung's proposal arose from his perception of some of the human failings of Freud, who had himself never been analyzed. Freud had, however, confided in Jung's wife about the gradual termination of sex in his own marriage.

As Jung had grown in stature he felt Freud's organizational demands to be increasingly onerous. Freud had to chide him about not taking his functions as a leader seriously enough, and Jung ultimately came to the conclusion that his own work had to take precedence over his labors for the International Psychoanalytic Association. Less rationalistic and suspicious of the unconscious than Freud, Jung began to formulate his own views on the important compensatory functions of symptoms; he also suggested that one can interpret characters in dreams as standing for aspects of the dreamer's own ego. Freud began to suspect that Jung's innovations (he later pioneered the practice of short-term psychotherapy) meant that he harbored death wishes toward Freud.

Freud's inner conflicts led him to faint twice in Jung's presence, and although Jung forebore to interpret these incidents in letters to Freud, the issue of Freud's neurosis could not readily be evaded. Freud then picked up a slip of Jung's pen in order to substantiate his suspicion of Jung's heresy. Jung replied with an insolent letter, admitting his own ambivalence but pointing out Freud's need to use symptomatic interpretations for the sake of maintaining his own power and enabling him to remain blind to his own weak spots. Freud never forgave Jung for this letter, although it took over a year for Freud to excommunicate Jung from psychoanalysis. Freud composed *Totem and Taboo* as part of an effort to drive a public wedge between himself and Jung. Despite the surprisingly personal nature of their falling out, the stature of Freud and Jung means that no one interested in the history of our century can afford to miss their correspondence collected in this book.

Skeptics have often pointed out that Freud was obsessed with fixed ideas; he was, in fact, a plunger and a reductionist, as his critics have often charged. It is harder to appreciate how Freud's intolerance of distraction, his insistence on letting his mind follow its own course, was part and parcel of that drive so essential to his creativity.

Freud's friendship with the Berlin physician Wilhelm Fliess has long been established as a key to the origins of psychoanalysis. But Freud, who destroyed Fliess's part of their correspondence, had not wanted his intimate letters to Fliess to become public. Anna Freud decided to cooperate in publishing Freud's letters to Fliess, but the 1950 edition was sliced and cut in an almost incomprehensible manner. Throughout Freud's published letters, deletions, without marks of omission, have been introduced; no consistent principle, such as medical discretion, has been followed. Until *The Com-*

plete Letters of Sigmund Freud to Wilhelm Fliess, 1887–1904, translated and edited by Jeffrey Moussaieff Masson (1985), only in the one volume of Freud's letters to Jung had Freud's correspondence been presented intact.

This new 1985 edition of Freud's letters to Fliess is complete; it is bound to be read alongside the censored version of the same correspondence. Unfortunately, no editorial marks indicate which passages constitute restorations of earlier cuts. It requires an effort not to leap on the newly revealed passages, and there will be a natural tendency to overemphasize their importance. But it should not be too hard to maintain a balanced perspective, since what once was expunged was censored on capricious grounds of family propriety.

If one asks what this book tells us that we did not know before, it must be admitted that the earlier picture of Freud remains essentially the same. Throughout his life he was avid in his letter writing, and the complete text shows him at the height of his literary powers. He and Fliess jointly entertained a variety of dotty ideas, ranging from the hypothesis of a male sexual periodic cycle to the alleged significance of the nose in neurotic disorders. In connection with Freud's speculative follies it is worth keeping in mind an aphorism of a German philosopher, Theodor Adorno: in psychoanalysis only the exaggerations are true.

Reading these letters does lead one to rethink the nature of Freud's position in intellectual history. From today's perspective, Freud sounds curiously behavioristic in writing about sex. Throughout his life he treated sexual energy as a fixed quantity, capable of being directed into either neurosis or creativity. He often refers here, for instance, to the physical consequences of the abuse of masturbation. Yet in private he could verbally joke that the problem with masturbating is knowing how to do it well.

In the 1890s Freud was struggling with his own intolerance of available contraceptive methods. In letters to Fliess he wrote about both his abstinence and impotency with his wife, Martha. But nothing in these letters supports the proposition that Freud became sexually involved with his sister-in-law Minna. Of course, written evidence has its own way of being misleading; despite these hundreds of letters to Fliess, and the relative absence of those to Minna, Freud's comments in old age indicate that she played as critical a role in overcoming Freud's self-doubts as did Fliess. If there is an overwhelming impression that comes through from this correspondence with Fliess, it is of Freud as an exceptionally devoted family man.

The intimacy between Freud and Fliess—although ultimately it soured over personal issues as well as questions of scientific priority—shows how warm and outgoing Freud could be. The friendship is also part of the story of the publication of Freud's greatest book, *The Interpretation of Dreams.*

Freud was making a contribution to autobiography as well as to the world of science; Fliess was not only a key figure in many of Freud's dreams, but Freud sent him galleys of the manuscript for correction and revision. It turns out that throughout the 1890s Freud resorted to the use of cocaine more often than anyone realized, and it doubtless had effects on his dream life.

In the end, however, it is Freud, not Fliess, who really matters, although Freud took from Fliess concepts such as latency, erotogenic zones, and bisexuality. Freud's misjudgment of Fliess as "the Kepler of biology"[50] is bound to leave a reader shaking his or her head in disbelief. Freud had plenty of curious quirks of belief. And he obviously misled many of his patients with his own personal hobbyhorses. Since, as Freud himself believed, self-analysis is impossible, the creator of psychoanalysis turned out to be the only analyst incapable of ever being analyzed.

The editorial apparatus of this book is appalling. Jeffrey M. Masson either reviles or ignores established work in the field. He silently relies on the editor of the first edition of these letters when it suits him and criticizes him when it does not.

Unlike Masson's edition, however, the previous editing was done with a thorough knowledge of all Freud's writings, and serious workers will have to use the notes attached to the earlier, truncated version of these complete letters. Masson's editorship of this book was part of the divorce settlement between himself and the Freud archives; after Masson was fired from the archives the publication of these letters was included along with the money in the separation agreement.

On the lecture circuit Masson has relied on his involvement with this edition of these letters as support for the scholarly credentials behind his own obsession about the sexual seduction of children. Yet his brief introduction is sanitized of the thesis contained in his sensationalist book *The Assault on Truth: Freud's Suppression of the Seduction Theory.*

Masson's editorial job on Freud's letters to Fliess fails to place the correspondence within the history of ideas. On completing the reading of this book, one's mind inevitably turns to the need for yet another edition of these same letters.

Notes

1. *The Letters of Sigmund Freud and Arnold Zweig,* ed. Ernst L. Freud, trans. Professor and Mrs. W. D. Robson-Scott (London: Hogarth Press, 1970), p. 47, p. 45.
2. Ibid., p. 155.
3. Ibid., p. 113.

4. Ibid., p. 51, p. 23.
5. Ibid., p. 99.
6. Ibid., p. 67, p. 72.
7. Ibid., p. 71.
8. Ibid., p. 143.
9. Ibid., p. 6.
10. Ibid., p. 60.
11. Ibid., p. 101.
12. Ibid., p. 107.
13. Ibid., p. 8.
14. Ibid., p. 9.
15. Ibid., pp. 122–23.
16. Ibid., p. 2.
17. Ibid., p. 3.
18. Ibid., p. 126.
19. Ibid., p. 127.
20. Ibid., p. 179.
21. *James Jackson Putnam and Psychoanalysis: Letters Between Putnam and Sigmund Freud, Ernest Jones, William James, Sandor Ferenczi, and Morton Prince, 1877–1917*, ed. Nathan G. Hale, Jr., trans. Judith Bernays Heller (Cambridge: Harvard University Press, 1971), p. 43.
22. Ibid., p. 133.
23. Ibid., p. 147.
24. Ibid., p. 140.
25. Ibid., p. 110.
26. Ibid., p. 110.
27. Ibid., p. 259.
28. Ibid., p. 277.
29. Ibid., p. 2.
30. Ibid., p. 150.
31. Ibid., p. 189.
32. Ibid., p. 146.
33. Ibid., p. 200.
34. Ibid., p. 176.
35. Ibid., p. 94.
36. Ibid., pp. 185–86.
37. Ibid., p. 79.
38. Ibid., pp. 78–80.
39. Ibid., p. 54.
40. Ibid., p. 118.
41. Ibid., p. 172.
42. Ibid., p. 173.
43. Ibid., p. 174.
44. Ibid., p. 105.
45. Ibid., pp. 121–22.
46. Ibid., pp. xii–xiii.
47. Ibid., p. 109, p. 112.
48. *The Freud/Jung Letters: The Correspondence Between Sigmund Freud and C. G. Jung*, ed. William McGuire, trans. Ralph Manheim and R. F. C. Hull (Princeton: Princeton University Press, 1974), p. 440.

49. Ibid., p. 218.

50. *The Complete Letters of Sigmund Freud to Wilhelm Fliess, 1887–1904,* trans. and ed. Jeffrey M. Masson (Cambridge: Harvard University Press, 1985), p. 320.

5

Insanity and the Law

Even though the problem of the legal disposition of assassins rather suddenly once again became a grim reality to American society in the 1960s, assassination is in fact an ancient part of political life. What is new, however, is that the legal argument over the assassin is now apt to be couched in psychodynamic categories, leaving the legal profession as well as the public often bewildered about what to do with this sort of psychological evidence. Law has always been, along with history, one of the closest professional allies that political scientists can count on, yet both lawyers and historians have been rather more receptive to the implications of psychology for their own fields than is usually the case within political science.

Unlike the pattern in most other countries, American assassinations (at the presidential level) have tended to be the product of more or less disturbed individuals rather than the work of political groups. Charles Rosenberg's *The Trial of the Assassin Guiteau: Psychiatry and Law in the Gilded Age* (1968), a book begun before the wave of assassinations that included John F. Kennedy, Martin Luther King, Jr., and Robert Kennedy, is an engrossing narrative of the death of President Garfield and the trial of Charles J. Guiteau; at the same time it is a fascinating exposition of the relation between psychiatry and law in the pre-Freudian era. As a man, Guiteau sounds to modern ears very much like a classic paranoid schizophrenic. The creator of a complicated delusional system, Guiteau traveled from city to city, moved from project to project, descending "from charlatanry to petty fraud."[1] He grew more and more detached from other people; without a family and apparently never having had any friends, Guiteau could eventually no longer keep a job or prevent his personal appearance from deteriorating. Just then, apparently at the end of his rope, he conceived the mission of "removing"[2] President Garfield.

Like other assassins, Guiteau quite consciously enjoyed all the publicity associated with being a figure of national importance. He was convinced of having a special tie to the Almighty; the assassination was God's deed and not his own. Although it may seem bizarre, Guiteau believed he had executed God's command, and he remained proud of having been chosen as the Lord's instrument in such a grandiose matter. (A religious delusion in the twentieth century may have a much more pathological inner meaning than in previous centuries; at any rate, such a religious delusion would probably go far nowadays in getting one off the legal hook.)

Guiteau's trial informs us how a dispute over diminished responsibility could be argued in pre-Freudian terms. A little less than a hundred years ago insanity was commonly viewed not only as a mysterious and uncanny illness, but sometimes as the result of a form of satanic possession. True insanity, it was widely held, must always be accompanied by physical disease and ill health. In Guiteau's case the prosecution successfully appealed to the principle that a man's character had to be ultimately his own responsibility. The notion that insanity might exist throughout life was, by and large, rejected in late-nineteenth-century America as a logical impossibility. Insanity was thought to be a disease that could not be hereditary. Since Guiteau's life pattern showed no gross discontinuities, his crime was consistent with his other acts and hence the "result of evil impulse, not mental illness."[3] Guiteau was to be treated, then, as an example of depravity and vice.

The prosecution relied for its expert psychiatric testimony on the intellectually conservative authority of asylum superintendants, who were mainly (until the Freudian revolution) bureaucrats with little scientific training. The defense relied for its witnessness, in behalf of an insanity plea, on a new group of neurologists. Dr. Edward Spitzka in particular, a young foreign-trained physician, argued in support of the thesis that Guiteau's morbid mental processes had indeed existed since his birth. Guiteau's crime, as well as his pathetic life, were the outcome of his mental disease. Curiously enough, the defense psychiatric position also made use of the significance of head shape in the diagnosis of mental illness.

Throughout the trial Guiteau interrupted the proceedings with strange and irrelevant comments. Americans of 1881, however, according to Professor Rosenberg, "especially those living in rural areas, seemed able to tolerate a far greater degree of deviant behavior than is ordinarily the case today"[4] and so paradoxically that age's human tolerance for the full diversity of personality types led to a result that may seem antihumanitarian to some today.

For the whole issue of insanity and criminal responsibility had little effect on Guiteau's fate. He had murdered an American president, and there was never much doubt as to the outcome of the court's decision. How an offender like Guiteau gets treated does seem to depend on the importance of the slain man to society, and perhaps there are sound pragmatic reasons why this should be so. Professor Rosenberg's book does show, however, the hollowness of the history books' treatment of Guiteau as a "disappointed office-seeker," motivated by "a thwarted desire for office."[5] This book also shows how greatly American attitudes toward crime, heredity, and insanity have shifted in the last century.

Nevertheless the whole issue of insanity and diminished responsibility is as vexing now as then, although the problem in any particular case would today be debated in a very different intellectual context. Unfortunately, the training of psychiatrists, lawyers, and political scientists—and perhaps, even more important, their daily experiences—are so different that little agreed-upon wisdom exists among them. A psychiatrist in a courtroom is in an alien world, and he is apt to see the contestants in the legal process as engaged in a sadistic battle. Even aside from the issue of getting the better psychiatrists to participate in courtroom work, it is likely that precisely those therapists who are best at dealing with extremely disturbed patients are apt to have the greatest difficulties in coping with a lawyer's kind of verbal demands.

No person, whether "healthy" or "sick," can be safely or fully described by any known set of labels. (One of the merits of Professor Rosenberg's book is that it does not embark on such a sterile course.) Even the greatest lunatic, at some level and in some areas of his functioning, will sometimes be quite sane. Schizophrenics accordingly should be looked upon as people with schizophrenic problems, not as creatures who can be clearly demarcated from other human beings. As Professor Rosenberg describes the defense attorney's reasoning, "it was not complete irrationality that ordinarily marked insanity, but rather a failure of reason and proportion, an acceptance of false premises and an inaccurate view of practical matters."[6] It is still so today that "true madness might coexist with acute intelligence."[7]

The Trial of the Assassin Guiteau is the work of a historical craftsman, whose aim is to use as many perspectives as possible to shed light on an incident in an era long past. The book gives historical distance to the problem of assassination in the United States and illuminates a most vexing area of law and political science. In the end it may turn out that the medical standards of sanity must be at cross-purposes with legal notions of responsibility, and the best of modern psychodynamic theory may have limited uses for law and the rest of social science. But the impact of the Freudian revolution will be with us for some time to come, and the issue really is not whether such psychological concepts will in fact be used, but whether they will be employed with intelligence and sophistication.

A historically minded study of a nineteenth-century assassin and how concepts of mental illness were once used in the United States can help to introduce the issue of how one evaluates today the enduring riddle of insanity. Freud, although not a psychiatrist himself, by his own writings and those of his followers managed to have a major impact on all our modern thinking.

For some people insanity has long been fashionable. It is not solely a heritage of the Romantic era to see a madman as a spiritual hero, and madness and genius do seem curiously interconnected. R. D. Laing, who was trained as a psychoanalyst, is only the most notable recent exponent of the view that sees in mental illness a legitimate challenge to the social status quo. Otto Friedrich's *Going Crazy: An Inquiry into Madness in Our Times* (1976), however, is a grim but wholly touching reminder of the terrible suffering involved in psychotic breakdowns. To "go crazy" may seem an unscientific expression, but Friedrich applied it mainly to those who have had to enter mental hospitals.

In sheer quantitative terms the extent and cost of insanity need underlining. In 1973, for example, 444,777 Americans were admitted to 337 state and county medical institutions; approximately another 100,000 patients entered America's 156 private hospital facilities. (Such hospitalization then cost as much as $165 a day.) About 1.7 million people are currently in American mental institutions, and even the best facilities are filled with sadness and fear.

Friedrich discusses other instances of mental disturbance as well, such as alcoholism, crime, and self-destructive behavior in general, and he reports that suicide has become, after accidents, the second highest cause of death among college-age people.

In contrast to so many authors of contemporary clinical literature, Friedrich avoids abstraction and self-satisfaction. It might seem that his book is theoretically unsophisticated. But by relying on examples from literature, music, politics, and art, Friedrich has put together a moving series of stories of human failure and tragedy. He tells us that he had "dug only a shallow trench in this mountain of misery,"[8] but in the end he succeeds in giving a disturbingly accurate account of what happens when someone has a nervous breakdown. Convinced that most of us can share the experience of going crazy, if only through the analogous upheaval involved in falling in love, Friedrich uses plain English to communicate his painful tale.

All too often there is a gulf between practitioners devoted to insight psychotherapy and those committed to physical means of treatment. If one has ever witnessed the catastrophe of serious mental collapse, it is hard to scoff at the prospect of symptomatic recovery. Nor—if one has seen how frequently suicidal patients can change their minds, often after it is medically too late—can one entertain lightly the right to kill oneself.

No intelligent therapists can be entirely happy with existing clinical results. The literature is hardly littered with examples of effective therapeutic approaches, and treatment failures are almost never written about. Even if it could be proven that the real sources of a patient's trouble are not in his or her past experiences but in large-scale social factors, pragmatic success in helping the victims of the world as we know it would be no minor matter.

Friedrich tells us early of the increasing skepticism about the whole field of psychiatry—largely due, he thinks, to the success of modern drugs. He feels that psychiatrists too often have little understanding of what they are doing. Only at the end does he admit to a "bias"[9] against psychiatry; his preconceptions were reinforced, he says, by two years of research on this book. He does not know what causes or cures insanity—still an unsolved mystery—and he insists that nobody else knows either. He believes, however, that madness is a part of each of us, completely human even if inexplicable.

Oddly enough, he exempts Freud from criticism. Friedrich does argue that psychoanalysis is apt to fail with those who have already gone mad, he does criticize many of the rituals of psychoanalytic interviewing, and he believes that Freud's colleagues were often unbalanced people in search of their own salvation. Yet it would be more consistent for Friedrich to admit Freud's own lack of interest in therapeutic success, especially with the most seriously disturbed cases.

Friedrich might well have questioned some of the scientific claims of psychoanalysis. Not only do the personality and training of an analyst have a suggestive impact on treatment, but also the apparently neutral psychoanalytic situation has its own biases as it creates experimental stress. He does remind us of the Hippocratic principle that the physician's main job is to help nature perform its own processes of self-cure, and he repeats the warning: "If you can do no good, at least do no harm."

Friedrich is right in questioning the legitimacy of much psychiatric vocabulary, and his book is convincing precisely because of his belief that "those who have actually gone crazy seem . . . to have a more earthy and concrete understanding of insanity than do the psychiatrists who pose as experts."[10] He is correct in thinking that many psychiatrists are too complacent about their traditional activities, and he is open to discussion of how dietary deficiencies may underlie craziness. Nevertheless, he proposes that there is usually a link between the form of a breakdown and the sufferer's sense of identity and therefore psychology can be a means of bridging the gulf between those who have and those who have not "lost" their minds.

Friedrich's study constitutes an impersonal narrative; he skillfully interweaves vignettes from his own experience and that of friends, but tells us that he has never consulted psychiatrists or taken their drugs. Nonetheless, his version of madness in our times is thoroughly absorbing and plausible.

One only worries that his unremittingly somber account may succeed in being such a collection of pathological cases as to encourage the illusory feeling in the reader that such problems belong to others, not ourselves.

Psychiatry is, I think, a more than usually conformist profession. The lines of orthodoxy do shift periodically; however, at any one time it is possible to find devout defenders of received wisdom scattered in most major metropolitan areas. A successful church breeds heresy, and Thomas Szasz, a trained analyst as well as a psychiatrist, has been a troublemaker unlike anybody else in the modern history of the field, and his special area of interest has been in the law. *Schizophrenia: The Sacred Symbol of Psychiatry* (1976) was his thirteenth book to have appeared within twenty years, and cites the forthcoming publication of two more books.

Szasz has asked some key and embarrassing questions: what sort of expert is a psychiatrist, and as whose agent, the individual's or society's, does he serve? During the use of psychiatric testimony in the 1975 trial of Patty Hearst, Szasz performed a useful function in calling a spade a spade; he pointedly insisted in print on the influence of the Hearst power and money in engaging professional psychiatric evidence at odds with moral and political common sense. He has also helped publicize the psychiatric collaboration in the Central Intelligence Agency's experimental administration of drugs like LSD. Psychiatry has had an especially broad impact in the United States, which helps account for Szasz's polemical tone.

Szasz has been challenging the power of psychiatric authority and, in particular, the practices that take place within large institutions. The founding fathers of modern psychiatry, Emil Kraepelin and Eugen Bleuler, seem to Szasz mere clinicians rather than medical investigators. Kraepelin and Bleuler, along with psychoanalysis's Freud, aimed to extend the bounds of medicine over morals and law, and to Szasz that means they were religious and political conquerors, not scientific leaders.

Schizophrenia, as the leading paradigm of psychiatry, is for Szasz "the greatest scientific scandal of our scientific age."[11] Szasz holds that so-called schizophrenics merely speak in metaphors unacceptable to their audience. The use of the concept of schizophrenia as a "diagnosis" really points, Szasz argues, to "a religious symbol rather than to a medical disease."[12] Too often psychiatrists label problems as diseases without the existence of physical lesions, and then treat patients as if they had no ethical rights. Szasz thinks that these practices support his contention that psychiatry controls not diseases but deviants. Instead of restricting themselves to illness and treatment, psychiatrists have engaged in ethical and political decision making. Wherever psychiatry has become popularly successful it has impinged on "the domains of ethics and politics, rhetoric and law, aggression and defense, violence and war."[13]

It is a well-known principle that most patients wind up in mental hospitals because their families can no longer put up with them. Szasz believes that psychiatric thought has not done enough to encourage the toleration of eccentricity and the acceptance of the inevitability of suffering. Szasz may be right in thinking that under the banner of progress psychiatry has been an agent of social control, segregating certain disturbing persons and making scapegoats of deviants. Compulsory psychiatric interventions ought always, Szasz says, to be suspect. The Soviets have for a long time been using treatment as a form of torture for dissidents, but it is not only there that one finds "the unjust and unjustifiable incarceration of innocent persons in insane asylums."[14]

Szasz seeks to demythologize psychiatry. As he broadly concedes about schizophrenia, "we know neither what it is nor what causes it."[15] Our ignorance leads us often to apply the term to almost any kind of behavior of which we disapprove. Szasz holds that it is not just modern psychology, but social science in general, which is in part fake or pseudo-religious. As Szasz puts the matter in its extreme: "Modern writers are given to rediscovering that 'alienists' are usually alienated from themselves and their society, and that if their clients suffer from anomie, they usually make them more, rather than less, anomic."[16] Many people have discerned similarities between Szasz's critique of psychiatry and that of R. D. Laing. But Szasz makes no bones about his distaste for Laing's idealization of insanity, as well as Laing's reliance on public funds for collectivist purposes. For Szasz it is no more proper to construe anomie as authenticity than it is to demean whole groups or societies as insane. Szasz in the end upholds a stoic view: life is necessarily an arduous struggle, compassion can be won through confronting conflict, and patience and modesty go with being able to endure life with decency and humility.

Szasz maintains that he is not against "voluntary psychiatry, or psychiatric relations between consenting adults."[17] He has a sense of humor. One wonders, though, whether Szasz is not excessively rationalistic. Can psychotherapy truly be conceived as a contract with clearly defined rules of the game? To what extent do inevitable human dependencies undermine even the most clearly defined programs of treatment? For purposes of his argument in *Schizophrenia* Szasz makes only one single reference to the problem of manic-depressive insanity, and yet he persists in using *schizophrenia* and *madness* as interchangeable terms. One doubts that Szasz believes there are no circumstances whatever under which people are entitled to be protected against themselves. But Szasz's tenacious social purpose is above all worthy of praise. He is right that consent should justify psychiatric treatment and that the aim of "cure" ought to be personal autonomy and self-control. Amidst the clashes between the variety of psychiatric schools that our century has witnessed it can be too easy to forget that a patient, whatever the fashionable label, should always be treated as a person.

Part of Szasz's notoriety comes from his being an enormously intelligent person writing in a field whose practitioners rarely read books. He has already managed to make a notable contribution to contemporary psychiatric thinking. But he arouses controversy because he challenges the self-satisfaction of those who are successful in worldly terms as so-called experts of the mind. In the United States particularly the public excessively defers to psychiatrists out of the naive faith that they are adequately trained to be exceptionally knowledgeable about people. For those in psychological trouble it is hard to know what to recommend. Too often there are varied psychiatric schools of thought that each ignore the other's achievements. Szasz is right in advising that people should never stop thinking for themselves.

Over the years Szasz has had his impact, most strikingly in the United States Supreme Court's decision requiring that hospitals either treat or release harmless patients who have been involuntarily committed. Szasz's politics can be characterized as laissez-faire liberal. He did support Richard Nixon in 1972, but he does not deny it, just honestly groans over the mistake. Since Szasz and Herbert Marcuse could enjoy each other's company, it would seem that the life of the mind can still transcend the most obvious ideological differences.

In *Karl Kraus and the Soul-Doctors* (1976) Szasz assembled dazzling satire by one of the greatest figures from old Vienna. Kraus (1874–1936) was born in Bohemia, then a part of the Austro-Hungarian Empire, and brought to Vienna at the age of three. In 1899 Kraus founded a new periodical—*Die Fackel* (*The Torch*)—that became a famous Viennese institution and his life's work. As a poet and polemicist, above all a master of the German language and its Viennese dialect, Kraus coined superb aphorisms. Through his artistry and command of words he became a leading social critic in Vienna. The German edition of his works comes to fourteen volumes, and the complete edition of his magazine runs to thirty-seven volumes. In addition Kraus was an actor-lecturer. Szasz suggests that Kraus is relatively little known today because he went against the grain of so many trends that have dominated much of twentieth-century thought.

Szasz has put together here the crux of Kraus's critique of Freud and modern psychiatry. Szasz has seen so many devout followers of Freud that Szasz forgets that the creator of psychoanalysis had a considerable sense of humor. Freudian analysts who attempt to analyze without jokes are imposters. If Kraus and Freud had not become opponents, Freud would have been free to love Kraus's wit. As Szasz points out, many admirers of Kraus were also adherents of Freud. Kraus and Freud shared the conviction that their world was coming to an end, and they refused to see progress in the destruction of everything they cherished. Freud was by eighteen years the older man and sought Kraus out, but Kraus rejected Freud's overtures, and Freud reacted by disparaging Kraus.

Kraus did not see the mental health movement as a liberating scientific advance. Instead he warned against it as a new threat to human dignity. Perhaps his most famous saying was: "Psychoanalysis is the disease of which it claims to be the cure."[18] Kraus also ridiculed those who thought that it was "progressive"[19] to consider anti-Semitism a disease. Kraus was a radical individualist who challenged the key social norms of his time and place. Consequently his writing still retains its subversive strength.

Like George Orwell, Kraus feared that through the debasement of language people would be undermined as spiritual beings. He fought against those who threaten to destroy our words and therefore our world, and Szasz has picked from Kraus some superb illustrations of psychiatric and psychoanalytic demagoguery. Szasz thinks that Kraus, like himself, is a "rhetorician,"[20] defined as someone who uses language to influence how others think.

For Kraus psychoanalysis became a problem because it was not real treatment although it paraded pseudo-medical jargon. Kraus discerned that behind a facade of therapeutic humanitarianism could be the destruction of personal responsibility. Freud saw too much of human action as symptomatic of psychological diseases and treated people not enough as free moral agents but instead as foolish patients. Kraus attacked forensic psychiatry in particular, and the contemporary relevance of his point of view can be seen in the widespread use of psychiatric testimony in almost every celebrated trial of our time, from Leopold and Loeb in the 1920s to the recent "Baby M." case.

Szasz does miss, in my opinion, the tragic element in Freud, the degree to which he deceived himself over what he had accomplished. But Freud has been too often invoked as a prophet rather than as a realistic model to live by. Szasz offers us selections from one of the immortals of Western history. A few paragraphs by Kraus on sex are worth the price of the whole book. As Szasz sees it, Kraus's task was to bring people to themselves. We can still laugh with him today.

E. Fuller Torrey in *The Roots of Treason: Ezra Pound and the Secret of St. Elizabeth's* (1984) tells a tale of psychiatric whitewashing that makes compelling reading. During World War II Ezra Pound, an American citizen, was paid by the Fascist government of Italy to broadcast propaganda, aimed at American troops, that supported Benito Mussolini and Adolf Hitler. Psychiatrists became involved because of Pound's stature as a poet and his use of the insanity plea.

The early chapters of the book, recounting Pound's life as a youth and his contribution to twentieth-century poetry, are relatively lifeless. The texts of Pound's poems that Torrey cites are not convincing of Pound's genius. Torrey does establish, however, the extent of Pound's influence on modern literature. Among his friends and associates were almost everyone of any literary standing in the English-speaking world. Pound edited T. S. Eliot's *The Waste Land,* helped give Ernest Hemingway his start, and published James Joyce before anyone appreciated his talent; William Butler Yeats was also indebted to Pound. Yet somehow the literary portion of the book fails to come alive, and one impatiently reads on to get to the meat of Torrey's story.

We do get a clear picture of a demonstrative, colorful, eccentric individual at odds with his conventional American background. Even at the age of sixteen Pound was a "non-conformist and social outcast raging against his fellows for mistreating him."[21] At least as self-centered as any other aspiring young poet, Pound led a tumultuous life of affairs and entanglements with other brilliant artists. He found pre–World War I America uncongenial, but Europe was more receptive to his talents.

In addition to his poetic calling Pound had, even in his early years, prophetic ambitions. His interest in monetary reform was allied with anti-Semitism and hatred of blacks. Pound also "urged discrimination against the immigrant groups that continued to flock to America's shores."[22] According to Torrey, Pound "increasingly perceived his role as a social critic and reformer rather than as a poet."[23]

After Mussolini came to power Pound made his home in Italy from 1925 on, having found a compatible political regime. But Torrey misses an important cultural point—the extent to which other Americans, even members of the Left, were attracted by Italian Fascism. Mussolini's so-called experimentalism appealed to an entire group of pragmatic liberals, including Charles Beard, Lincoln Steffens, and Herbert Croly. In contrast to these mainstream thinkers, however, Pound's commitment to Fascism stemmed from fixed ideas about landlords, bankers, and stockholders. He was obsessed with what he considered parasitic userers.

Starting in 1931 Pound dated his personal letters with the Fascist calendar, and in 1932 Pound wrote a manuscript that compared Mussolini with Thomas Jefferson. Even after Mussolini's 1935 invasion of Ethiopia, Pound remained devoted to Fascist principles. Pound also corresponded with the English Fascist Oswald Mosley, seeking to "solve" the problem of international armament manufacturers.

Pound accepted the notorious *Protocols of Zion* as authentic, although from early in this century they were known as an anti-Semitic fabrication of the czarist police. (Hitler praised the *Protocols* in *Mein Kampf.*) Pound believed the Jews not only caused wars but also corrupted sex. His politics grew more strident: Franklin D. Roosevelt was an instrument of Jewish financial interests. Old friends worried about Pound's diatribes.

Torrey's book becomes spellbinding when he gets to World War II. Beginning in 1941 Pound made radio broadcasts in Italy's behalf. (The Englishman William Joyce, later executed for treason, performed the same service for Hitler to Berlin.) Two or three times a week Pound publicly blamed the Jews for the war, and there were over three hundred of these speeches. Pound was increasingly sympathetic to Hitler's objectives, and he allowed some of his broadcasts to be replayed from Berlin. In 1943 Pound (with seven others) was indicted for treason in the District of Columbia.

Even while Pound was still broadcasting, Hemingway thought of using the insanity defense in Pound's behalf. When the war ended and Pound was brought back to the United States, his powerful friends orchestrated a psychiatric escape hatch. In a second indictment Pound was accused of nineteen acts of treason, but an insanity plea was successfully used to declare him unfit to stand trial.

Torrey is devastating toward the psychiatrists who used professional jargon in order to save Pound from standing trial. (For some reason Torrey omits to cite Thomas Szasz's interest in this case.) Torrey mixes things up by bringing in the Nuremberg and Japanese war crime trials; nor is Pound's case anything like that of the French collaborators of the Vichy regime. But Pound was certainly as sane as he had ever been, and his defenders—including the psychiatrists—consciously knew how technical terminology was being abused for partisan purposes.

Torrey documented his book with material he gained access to through the Freedom of Information Act. Torrey shows how the head of St. Elizabeth's, Dr. Winfred Overholser, Sr., an analyst and a psychiatrist, bears the chief responsibility not only for the psychiatric testimony that resulted in Pound's not standing trial, but also for how Pound was cared for at St. Elizabeth's from 1946 until his release in 1958. A host of intellectual luminaries continued to visit Pound. No psychiatric treatment of any kind was ever undertaken. Pound's Fascist beliefs persisted, and he helped promote the cause of a rabid segregationist. Pound flourished at St. Elizabeth's. For the first time in his life he was free from financial worries. He had disciples, good food, and even the privacy for sexual satisfaction.

Overholser continued legally to shield the man he later called his "guest."[24] As one German poet observed: "Pound was the first insane poet with whom I have ever had a conversation, and the only genuinely insane thing about that conversation was that Pound was not insane."[25] The reports of the attending nurses indicated a continuing absence of pathology, a judgment with which the junior psychiatrists concurred. In 1958 Pound's friends secured his release—he was said to have been insane continuously since the beginning of World War II—and he soon returned to Italy. "Standing on the ship's deck on arrival in the Naples harbor, Ezra Pound posed for reporters and gave the Fascist salute."[26]

Torrey's book adds up to a tale of an outrageous confusion of psychiatric and political categories. Yet Torrey does not seem to me unfairly biased against Pound. The last chapter of the book is the most poignant part of all. After Pound's return to Italy he grew seriously depressed and genuinely ill. Without the support of the hospital environment and his visitors, he began to realize how mistaken his politics and economics had been, and the failures in his life were highlighted for him. Pound spent his last years unable to write and regretting his life; he died in his sleep in 1972.

Pound was so constituted that the well-meaning efforts of his supporters may have compounded his problems. "Of the seven other Americans indicted with him in 1943 for broadcasting for the enemy, three had had their indictments dismissed, two had died before they could be brought to trial, and two had been convicted and sentenced to life imprisonment. . . . Even Tokyo Rose . . . had been released from prison after only seven years."[27] Pound's story reminds us that political evil and clinical insanity are wholly different concepts, and that law and psychiatry are separate disciplines whose interconnections demand the most rigorous kind of philosophic exploration.

Notes

1. Charles Rosenberg, *The Trial of the Assassin Guiteau: Psychiatry and Law in the Gilded Age* (Chicago: University of Chicago Press, 1968), p. 30.
2. Ibid., p. 39.
3. Ibid., p. 65
4. Ibid., p. 54.
5. Ibid., p. ix, p. 181.
6. Ibid., p. 124.
7. Ibid., p. 211.
8. Otto Friedrich, *Going Crazy: An Inquiry into Madness in Our Time* (New York: Simon & Schuster, 1976), p. 363.
9. Ibid., p. 355.
10. Ibid., p. 351.
11. Thomas Szasz, *Schizophrenia: The Sacred Symbol of Psychiatry* (New York: Basic Books, 1976), p. 190.
12. Ibid., p. xiv.

13. Ibid., p. 191.
14. Ibid., p. 189.
15. Ibid., p. 43.
16. Ibid., p. 165.
17. Ibid., p. 49.
18. Thomas Szasz, *Karl Kraus and the Soul Doctors: A Pioneer Critic and His Criticism of Psychiatry and Psychoanalysis* (Baton Rouge: Louisiana State University Press, 1976), p. 24.
19. Ibid., p. 11.
20. Ibid., p. xi.
21. E. Fuller Torrey, *The Roots of Treason: Ezra Pound and the Secret of St. Elizabeth's* (New York: McGraw Hill, 1984), p. 28.
22. Ibid., p. 69.
23. Ibid., p. 89.
24. Ibid., p. 245.
25. Ibid., p. 253.
26. Ibid., p. 263.
27. Ibid., p. 277.

6

The Tausk Problem

Many innovators in the history of ideas have founded organizations that, in time, have acquired an ideological life all their own. In Freud's case he himself was responsible, whatever the merits of his case, for taking part in the pre–World War I battles that led to the exclusion and withdrawal of Adler and Jung from the ranks of the psychoanalytic movement. But by the 1920s, when Freud tried to keep Rank, who was a personal favorite, from following in the rebellious footsteps of Adler and Jung, other orthodox analysts like Karl Abraham and Jones helped make any reconciliation between Freud and Rank impossible.

Since Freud's death in 1939, a small band of highly talented and influential European analysts, many of them living in New York City, have kept a zealous watch over the public image of Freud. Despite Freud's considerable and, especially in America, unquestioned stature in intellectual history, any portrayal of Freud that conflicted with this group's idealized conception of him has always been challenged by one of these analysts.

Among the well-known upholders of orthodoxy has been Kurt R. Eissler. In 1950 he published a critique of the heterodoxy of what had been one of the most lively and original centers of psychoanalytic training, the Chicago Institute of Psychoanalysis, led by Franz Alexander. When in 1956 the distinguished art historian Meyer Schapiro published an essay on Freud's study of Leonardo, Eissler answered it, five years later, with a huge book, part 1 of which is titled "Polemics."[1] Erik H. Erikson has easily done as much as any other contemporary writer to ensure the widespread acceptance of Freud's basic concepts, yet the originality of some of Erikson's ideas, which he himself has consistently traced to their Freudian bases, has led Eissler to question publicly whether Erikson ought properly be called a psychoanalyst at all. In an appendix to a book Eissler has articulated the kind of reservations his friends have had all along about Erikson's work, by pointing out that "despite the marks of its psychoanalytic origin," Erikson has "built a theoretical system which . . . deviates from accepted psychoanalytic theories," and because of this "deviation" (the long-standing designation of Freudian heresy) Erikson ought merely to be called a "psychotherapist."[2] The value of Erikson's ideas, in this view, is a secondary matter.

Eissler has written that "by the proper use of psychoanalysis"—that is, in its more "orthodox" form—"a new world, a new culture, and the means for the survival of the Occident could be built."[3] Of Freud's relationship to truth, Eissler feels "inclined to compare him . . . with Moses, who did not seek God—but God sought him, and he was strong enough to bear it."[4] At the same time, Eissler's view of the character of contemporary psychoanalysts seems strangely at odds with what Freud himself believed about the possibilities of human nature; "there is no other science," writes Eissler, "in which the reliable collection of primary data necessitates a perfectly equilibrated personality."[5] Since Eissler does not appear to find this demand in any way inconsistent with the growing number of practicing analysts, it is hard not to begin to speculate about the role of trade unionism in such self-proclaimed Freudian orthodoxy. Freud himself referred numerous patients to analysts who would count as deeply disturbed by Eissler's utopian standards.

Eissler not only tells us that "Freud presented almost the complete human cosmos scientifically," but also observes that it is "most impressive to note that, in the month Freud closed his eyes, the evening glow of Western culture took its brutal beginning."[6] As far as the "deviants" in psychoanalysis go, Eissler is unremitting: "It is in my opinion a proof of the greatness of Freud's work that it grew like a powerful trunk from which twigs branched off. I say purposely twigs and not branches."[7] Eissler tells us that although he "never met Freud, he is as much alive within me as though he were still with us. If one owes understanding, profession, and probably psychic survival indirectly to one personality, no other outcome is possible."[8]

Eissler has also been the founding secretary to the Freud archives, established, curiously enough, partially with Jungian money. He has claimed that in order to persuade Freud's former colleagues, patients, and friends to tape-record their memories and deposit them along with all the available Freud letters in the Library of Congress, he had to guarantee that the material would be sealed for fifty to a hundred years. However, in my own research on Freud and his circle I encountered many donors who not only had no idea their material was now locked away, but who positively objected to the secrecy with which Eissler was determined to protect Freud from the scrutiny of independent historians.

Eissler wrote an explicitly polemical assault on one of my books, *Brother Animal: The Story of Freud and Tausk* (1969). In his *Talent and Genius:*

The Fictitious Case of Tausk Contra Freud (1971) Eissler openly conceived of his task as that of "defending" Freud against what he interprets as the "attack" on him in *Brother Animal*. In preparing this defense, Eissler did relatively little research; he did not, for example, get in touch with the Tausk family, who had many unpublished articles and letters in their possession. On the other hand, he fished through his otherwise sealed Freud archives to find whatever he could to support his case.

Eissler's denunciation of my book has to be answered, not because he interprets the silence of previous writers in the face of his abuse as a confession of error on their part, but rather because Eissler is an established analyst who has chosen to attack not merely my interpretations and reconstructions (which in the spirit of free historical inquiry I am quite willing to see challenged) but also my accuracy and, most important, my integrity as a scholar.

In the course of writing a book on the moral and political implications of Freud's work (subsequently published as *Freud: Political and Social Thought*), I decided to try to meet and interview everyone still living who had ever known Freud. I eventually saw over seventy people who knew Freud, in addition to another forty or so who were either professionally interested in the history of psychoanalysis or who had themselves actively participated in the early psychoanalytic movement. In the end I succeeded in meeting twenty-five of Freud's analytic patients, three of his children, his surviving sister-in-law, two daughters-in-law, and some nieces and nephews as well.

Early on I was told by an elderly analyst, Helene Deutsch, "Nobody will tell you about Tausk!" Although I already owned a book with one of Tausk's technical papers in it and vaguely associated his name with that of Lou Andreas-Salomé (friend of Nietzsche, Rilke, and others), as a figure in the history of psychoanalysis he was unknown to me. Thus my curiosity was aroused, and as I conducted my interviews on Freud I always tried to ask about Victor Tausk.

Some older analysts—like Willi Hoffer in London and Otto Isakower in New York—specifically knew of a story connected with Tausk and suggested that Helene Deutsch would be the one to get it from. Another analyst, Herman Nunberg, bitterly rejected my inquiry, saying, "You are not going to get our secrets." At a later interview, however, when I then knew parts of the story that even Nunberg was unaware of, he cooperated and told me what Freud had said to him after Tausk committed suicide in 1919. (I am giving these details since Eissler has now maintained that the story of Tausk was always well known and never a secret and that "the only three surviving psychoanalysts who had known Tausk shared willingly their knowledge with the inquirer. Had Roazen met with obstacles, we may rest assured that he would have let us know about them. . . . "[9]) A Swiss analyst could tell me what Freud had said to him on Tausk, and a Chicago analyst, Edoardo Weiss, who had been a friend and classmate of Tausk's at medical school in Vienna, was to be a continuous help to me in unraveling the problem of Tausk's life and death.

From Adler's daughter I learned the whereabouts of one of Tausk's sons, and after I had gotten in touch with him he sent me a copy of his father's precious suicide note to Freud. Eissler finds reproaches against Freud where none were intended throughout my narrative; for instance, in explaining why this note was signed "Tausk" rather than "Victor," I mention that Freud and he were never on such intimate terms, which Eissler interprets as some accusation on my part. That final letter of Tausk's, written on the morning he shot himself, was to be a key document in my work. For although Helene Deutsch had already given me a great deal of her time (in the end about two hundred hours in the 1960s) discussing Tausk as well as other aspects of the history of psychoanalysis, only on the occasion of my uncovering the suicide note, of whose existence she had not known, did she tell me the "secret" that she had predicted would "go to the grave" with her.

She had readily related that Tausk had been her first analytic patient, at a time when she herself was still in analysis with Freud. According to her, Tausk—whom she, like Lou Andreas-Salomé before her, regarded as the best in the Viennese psychoanalytic circle—would not have considered asking to be analyzed by someone other than by Freud himself. Freud, however, refused him an analysis and instead sent him to Helene Deutsch, an experienced psychiatrist but a relative newcomer to analysis. This was an insult to Tausk, according to Dr. Deutsch, and the same interpretation was independently confirmed later in a letter from one of Tausk's sons, but Tausk accepted the slight and became Dr. Deutsch's patient. Here is an example of Eissler's method of argument: he blames me for not giving specific evidence on this point and so assumes the worst, mentioning "reactions in Tausk for which he [Roazen] has no proof or else he would surely have presented them. . . . The idea of 'terrible insult' and humiliation is solely the author's idea. . . . "[10]

By the winter of 1918–19, when Tausk entered analysis with Helene Deutsch, his psychoanalytic contributions were far more extensive and established than hers. He may, however, have seen in her as a woman a suitable intermediary between himself and Freud, as Lou Andreas-Salomé had been earlier, and this may have compensated for her relative inexperience in psychoanalysis. (It is from Lou's comments about Tausk, with whom she had a love affair, that the title of my book was drawn; she wrote: "From the very beginning I realized it was this very struggle in Tausk that most deeply moved me—the struggle of the human creature. Brother-animal.

You."[11] Eissler considers my title "offensively coarse, if not downright vulgar."[12])

Dr. Deutsch was an old acquaintance of Tausk's, but as his analyst she became more familiar with the long-standing tension between him and Freud. On Freud's side, he explained when he sent Tausk to her for analysis why he would not analyze Tausk himself, and it was this that she had been so very reluctant to divulge until I presented her with the suicide note: it made Freud uncomfortable to be in close proximity to Tausk, for Tausk had a penchant for filling out and publishing Freud's ideas before Freud's own thought processes had reached their conclusions. Tausk would then tend to see these ideas as his own.

On Tausk's side, as he explained to Dr. Deutsch in his analysis with her, Freud seemed to want to put his mark on the original ideas in his circle, including Tausk's own; it appeared to Tausk (as to Adler and Jung before him) that it was going to be impossible to assert himself independently as a man in Freud's circle. Tausk grieved over Freud's standoffishness toward him, as well as Freud's failure to accord him adequate recognition.

According to Dr. Deutsch, Tausk's conflict with Freud was so fascinating to her that it came to fill some of her own analytic hours with Freud. Lest her patient interfere with her own analysis, Freud brought the whole triangular relationship to an end, giving Helene Deutsch the choice between terminating her own analysis with Freud or Tausk's with her. To Helene Deutsch it was an order, and Tausk's treatment, which had lasted three months, was abruptly ended. Three months later he committed suicide, blowing out his brains; he had also tied a curtain cord around his neck, so that as he fell he was strangled.

Tausk had had more than his share of human troubles. Married at the age of twenty-one to a girl he had made pregnant, dissatisfied with his early career as a lawyer in Bosnia, in 1905 he separated from his wife and two sons and moved to Berlin as a journalist. Tausk was to have many love affairs, but in each one of them he drew back from the commitment of marriage; the dependency of a woman made him feel enslaved, and he deserted a whole series of women, who seem to have accepted the fact that his troubled soul was at fault and that his actions were not the result of willful irresponsibility. This picture of the reaction of Tausk's abandoned sweethearts, which I reconstructed from the account of people who knew some of them—e.g., Tausk's sister Nada and Dr. Deutsch—was independently confirmed after the publication of *Brother Animal* by two former lady friends of Tausk who then got in touch with me. Tausk's problem with women was the reason for his coming to Freud for treatment.

Freud had not turned against Tausk without recommending another analyst, nor had he tried to force the issue of his remaining in the psychoanalytic group by giving choices of unacceptable analysts in Vienna; Freud evidently thought that Helene Deutsch would be a good compromise. Instead, the unusual arrangement turned out badly and probably exacerbated Tausk's dilemma, for to Helene Deutsch, who had a wholly adoring attitude toward Freud, Tausk's incipient rebelliousness and criticism of her analyst had an extraordinarily prurient attraction. Embodying all her own negative impulses to Freud in the person of Tausk, she may well have made the problem between the two men worse (out of understandable vanity), as she submitted to Tausk's seductive appeal and transmitted his story in her analysis with Freud. She later thought that she might have been expressing some suppressed guilt feelings toward her patient in helping with my research on Tausk.

In all of Eissler's diatribe against my book, he has not chosen to discuss the sources of Tausk's analytic treatment going awry—a strange oversight for someone concerned with issue of psychoanalytic technique, who at the same time believes that analysts require a "perfectly equilibrated personality." He questions, on the other hand, Tausk's sincerity in wanting an analysis, as well as his "analyzability." Eissler states: "In terms of classical psychoanalysis, Tausk was incurable."[13] With the worst kind of psychological determinism, Eissler writes that Tausk "had been doomed, since childhood, to live a miserable and unfortunate life. . . . "[14] Eissler traces Tausk's suicide to the "orbit of his insight"[15] into himself having grown—in other words, Tausk was in reality such a wretch that he deserved to die—though Eissler does not credit the analysis with any share in this supposed heightened self-knowledge. Surely therapeutic failure is an important subject of scientific interest, not merely an occasion for diagnostic name-calling. Analyses are not—even short ones and even three months after termination—supposed to end so badly, and this perhaps accounts for much of Eissler's rancour.

Eissler has directed his ire not only at my *Brother Animal,* but also at every analyst he can find who in any way has written well of it. Charles Rycroft is only one of the many who came in for savage treatment, and Bruno Bettelheim, who has taken no public stand on the book but who has evidently strayed too far from orthodoxy in other respects, gets tossed in for good measure. Curiously enough, Eissler is by and large unaffected by the favorable reviews of my book written by mere psychiatrists who are not also psychoanalysts. Clearly, *Talent and Genius* is meant as a housecleaning operation. He feels no special loyalty to a dead analyst like James Strachey, an old ally, and Eissler accuses me of having deliberately sought out for quotation the few instances of Strachey's supposed imprecise translations.

In every case that Eissler mentions, Strachey's translations read much better than Eissler's own and differ not at all in meaning.

Eissler is exercised over my supposed "central thesis . . . that it was Freud who was ultimately responsible for Tausk's untimely death."[16] It is true that, in discussing the reaction of members of Freud's inner circle to Tausk's suicide, I quote a letter from Paul Federn in which he wrote: "The motivation was Freud's turning away from him . . . If Freud had shown him a human interest, not simply recognition and support, he might have continued to bear his martyr-like existence. . . . But *he* was not *kind* as little as Freud is kind, i.e. Freud possesses so much love for people that he can be kind, but in his old age he became increasingly harder. . . . That we could not keep Tausk is our shame."[17] Since Federn always remained a loyal apostle of Freud, it is no wonder that Eissler says "a particularly bitter taste was left by Paul Federn's letter, which should unquestionably have been published only after Tausk had become a historical figure and no one who knew him personally was around any longer."[18] Yet in contrast to Federn's view of Tausk's death, in *Brother Animal* I pointed out how strange it was that the participants in that tiny subculture so "readily believed that if Freud dropped a man it could lead to his self-extinction. Exclusion from the revolutionary community was an annihilation greater than any physical death."[19]

Eissler frequently accuses me of misquotations, a term he uses to mean quoting out of the context he would have wished. At no point do I feel obliged to retract a passage. It is true that since Eissler has written a book more than twice as long as mine (oddly enough, in order to prove Tausk less important—"an accident in Freud's life"),[20] he is able to deal at greater length with issues I just touch on. Eissler succeeds in going into details that I omitted in order to keep the central points salient, but he does not thereby succeed, as he assumes he must, in refuting the validity of those central points. He himself, moreover, is guilty of misquoting me, as for example when he implies that I only use the word *loans*,[21] where I have in fact also written that Freud *gave* money;[22] then he uses his misquotation to suggest that I did not adequately emphasize Freud's financial generosity, especially in behalf of psychoanalysis. Eissler is again inaccurate when he quotes me as describing Freud as a "fighting man";[23] he is apparently using as his source a passage in which I write that Freud was a "fighting innovator."[24]

Eissler considers it dreadful that I have in any way attributed to Freud the trait of vanity. Yet later Eissler describes Freud in this way: "From 1900 on . . . Freud's creativity became immune to the vicissitudes of object relations. . . . Freud felt responsible to himself alone."[25] If one begins with the premise that Freud's character was perfection itself (Eissler dismisses the very notion of Freud's having had any "worst qualities"), then anybody who tries to offer a more balanced and lifelike portrait of the great man is guilty as a "detractor." Eissler even finds it necessary to prove at considerable length that Tausk was merely talented, whereas Freud was a genius—as if that were in any way a contested point.

But the specific grounds Eissler has for distinguishing between Tausk and Freud seem to me unusual. Tausk had lived a sexually varied existence—what Eissler calls a "dissolute sexual life"[26]—in contrast to the monogamous Freud, who evidently tired of his wife relatively early. Martha Freud, according to Eissler, "provided the background that was optimal for Freud's creativity. . . . "[27] Although Eissler dodges the evidence for the falling off of Freud's sexual life in his forties, he goes on to discuss other great men of ideas who, he claims, did not especially enjoy sex. In Freud's case Eissler may be making a virtue of necessity. For example, he tells us that Freud was never "even for a moment" involved with Lou Andreas-Salomé "as a sexual being . . . and this despite the fact that he turned toward her with his whole person."[28] Who is running down whom, if this is what Eissler sees as Freud's "whole person"? Even of Freud's youth Eissler speaks with puritanical authority: "The full duration of Freud's engagement was spent in total sexual continence."[29] Is this supposed to make Freud more admirable as a person? How, in any case, can Eissler be so certain?

Although Eissler is ready to use any portion of the Freud archives for the sake of buttressing his picture of the master, he studiously ignores material that would help him make honest scholarly use of them. For example, it is highly likely—if not certain—that after Tausk killed himself Freud commented about it in letters to such analysts as Sandor Ferenczi and Karl Abraham, with whom he was in close communication at the time. Yet although I raised this question in *Brother Animal* and Eissler has used other portions of the archives in building up the argument of his book, he ignores the question of what Freud may have written to these analysts on Tausk's death.

Possible grounds for this omission are suggested by one of the startling published comments of Freud's that we already have. In a letter to Lou Andreas-Salomé announcing Tausk's suicide, Freud wrote: "I confess I do not really miss him; I had long taken him to be useless, indeed a threat to the future."[30] This was written of a man who went to medical school in order to become an analyst, spent ten years in Freud's circle, and then, having attacked official psychiatry in behalf of psychoanalysis, was rejected by Freud. Eissler explains away Freud's comment by referring to how Freud stood for the establishment of "freedom of emotion."[31] Eissler does not attempt to explain the contrast between Freud's private letter to Lou and his glowing public obituary of Tausk, which until I reprinted it in my book I had never seen cited in the literature.

Since I pointed out in *Brother Animal* that the offending sentence in Freud's letter to Lou had been censored from the published correspondence between them, Eissler did some detective work to discover the origin of the suppression. Anna Freud had, Eissler tells us, specifically requested that deletion, and he is so involved in the emotional life of the Old Guard analysts that he asks us to believe her request was motivated solely by a desire to protect Tausk's sons, rather than Freud's image. Are we to suppose that the suppression of Freud's comments to Arnold Zweig (in their volume of letters) on hearing the news from Zweig of Adler's death—with no marks of omission in the text—was also made out of consideration for Adler's children and not for Freud himself?

Freud's letters to Lou and Arnold Zweig are hardly the only instance of Freud's correspondence being doctored for the public. It is remarkable that with all the Freud family's protectiveness about his papers, I am blamed for not having overcome all possible obstacles. Through a piece of good fortune I gained access to Ernest Jones's papers, including those that went into the making of his official biography of Freud. Eissler claims that although I was able to read Anna Freud's letters to Jones, I have not had the benefit of seeing Jones's letters to her. What does he expect, since these had not yet been made available? In fact, Jones did leave in his files copies of a part of his correspondence, and so I have seen at least some of Jones's letters to Anna Freud. Eissler also cites unpublished material from the minutes of the Vienna Psychoanalytic Society, as if I were obliged to quote from it. The obligation went the other way: I had to promise the editors of these minutes not to use any of their unpublished manuscripts.

In Eissler's view I exhibit a "truly embarrassing emptiness of . . . psychological understanding."[32] To test this by comparison, let us take one hypothesis he advances regarding the chronology of events I set forth in *Brother Animal*. My book reports that shortly after the end of Tausk's analysis, he met and fell in love with a patient, Hilde Loewi. The precipitating cause of the suicide, according to his own account in his last will, was his inability (once again) to go through with a marriage. Eissler claims that Hilde had become pregnant, having been a virgin whom Tausk seduced on her first clinical visit to him. Eissler states that only after attempts to abort had failed did Tausk become engaged to her and that later, after Tausk's death, she miscarried.

Eissler cites no evidence for his assertions, nor names any informant, though it is hard to see how after so many years anyone could be compromised by being so identified. Even if we assume that Eissler is correct in his facts, this information need not contradict my acceptance of Tausk's own account of the immediate cause of his suicide, his inability to marry. The concept of a "seduction" is of course a loaded one, and Eissler's confident assertion of Hilde Loewi's prior virginity (how can he possibly be so certain?) is evidently intended to blacken Tausk. My book discusses the way in which Tausk's involvement with a patient may have been part of his rebellion against Freud; it could also have contributed to Tausk's disturbed feelings. If Hilde did become pregnant by him (possible, though not entirely consistent with what we know of Tausk's sexual experience), it is easy to see how trapped he must have felt. According to Eissler's own material, I would conclude that Tausk's promise to marry Hilde was prompted more by a sense of honor than by his real wishes. The similarity of this situation with that of Tausk's first forced marriage, which had ended so unhappily and with so much guilt, must have weighed heavily on him. That Tausk had been rejected by Freud and was, at the age of forty, faced with the prospect of starting a new career over again must have contributed to the demoralization of his last months.

Eissler seems determined to run down Tausk at every opportunity. In refutation of what Eissler calls Tausk's "need to destroy women,"[33] let me cite two letters written to me spontaneously after the publication of *Brother Animal,* both from former lady friends of Tausk's. One woman, who knew Tausk in his psychoanalytic period in Vienna, wrote:

> Now I am surrounded by the ghosts of yesteryear. After all those years, I now start understanding so much, which was not clear to me then. I understand why his nickname for me was "dear it," as compared to him I was indeed only an it, who did not know why he could be so kind and lovable, and then again aloof and a thousand miles away. I also understand why one day, out of the blue sky, he left me standing in the street (I'll never forget that place), telling me that he could not see me anymore; he was just following the directions of his tormented mind. He said, "for reasons I would not understand. . . . " I thank you for your book, though it leaves me sorry to know now that I had not been able to understand, who he was and what he was looking for.

Another woman, who had an affair with Tausk earlier during his years as a prolific journalist in Berlin (for what reason does Eissler assume that "apparently"[34] I had only discovered one of Tausk's numerous pre-Freudian articles?), was able to tell me that Tausk's stay in a sanitorium had been precipitated by a frustrated love affair, which I had not known of when I wrote *Brother Animal.* (Eissler, aware of the nonpsychiatric meaning of those institutions in Central Europe at that time, nonetheless turns it into a "hospital."[35]) But none of what I knew then, or know now, of Tausk's love life would fit Eissler's allegation of "duplicity"[36] in Tausk's moving letters to his former wife.

This woman, who also wrote to me after the appearance of my book, knew Tausk in artistic circles in Berlin and later married a painter; she found my account of him "so very true to nature, as I saw him, and the story of his stormy tragic ten years in science. . . . Tausk should not have gone into the world of science, he should have remained in the literary world, the world of poetry and art. . . . The other night Victor came to me—he looked the same as he did fifty years ago, he was unhappy, couldn't pay the rent for his room in the house I'm now living in—the dream was very real." Freud was, she thought, "not comfortable with Tausk because there he had been confronted with the mind of a poet and artist seeing far beyond . . . the dogma." Eissler himself is a very different type of analyst from the kind she assumed Tausk became; Eissler writes of the hope for the future that "man will have brought light to all the dark corners of that universe he carried within himself."[37]

Whatever the justice of this speculation by a woman who loved Tausk and did not know Freud, Tausk's unusual personality made a profound impression on many people—including Freud and Lou—who knew him. While Eissler tries to destroy Tausk's moral character, calling aspects of him "delinquent," "schizophrenic," and "sociopathic,"[38] he does not attempt to square this with Freud's own view of Tausk as "an intensely conscientious man": "All those who knew him well valued his straightforward character, his honesty towards himself and toward others and the superiority of a nature which was distinguished by a striving for nobility and perfection. . . . He is sure of an honorable memory in the history of psychoanalysis and its earliest struggles."[39] By the time Eissler has finished with him, is there—in Eissler's account—much of "an honorable memory" left for Tausk?

All the while Eissler is undermining Freud's obituary of Tausk, he is busy at the task of whitewashing Freud. Eissler cites my mention of Freud's having analyzed his daughter Anna and then refers to this as a "well-known"[40] fact. "Well-known to whom?" one may ask. Embarrassing to many, like Eissler, who have rigidly stuck to the rules of what is or is not a proper analytic technique. How is it possible for Freud to have been more unorthodox as an analyst? Since Eissler does not cite a single reference in the published literature to prove that Freud's analysis of Anna was "well-known"—and Jones's authorized biography of Freud contains not a word of this analysis—one wonders how he can expect readers to believe him here. Herself the recipient of an unusual form of therapy, Anna Freud advised Jones, on a trip to the United States in 1956 to celebrate Freud's centenary, that it might be a good occasion to give American analysts a slap on the wrists as a reminder of the distinction between psychoanalysis and psychotherapy.

A point of pure method in research betrays Eissler's kind of bias. Whenever, under Eissler's subsequent prodding, one of my informants has stuck to his story—as many evidently have—Eissler ignores or dismisses their information as already established. When, on the other hand, he and the rest of that generation of orthodox analysts have been in a position to intimidate any of the people I saw, reminding them of old loyalties (to say nothing of the future of psychoanalytic orthodoxy), then he has been able to get "clarifications," if not retractions. In particular, the Old Guard came down heavily on Dr. Deutsch for having been so impolitic as to have generously cooperated with me for the sake of the historical record. She told me all the details I gave in my book about her patient's analysis and about her own treatment by Freud.

What is striking, in the end, is how little of Dr. Deutsch's story they were able to shake. For example, she now seems to believe that Tausk was her third, not her first, analytic case; this proves to Eissler that she was not so inexperienced, "previously" having "carried through"[41] (for three months at the most) two other analyses. One of these "earlier" patients is supposed to have been a "close relative"[42] of Freud's, although my information has that person in treatment in 1921, not 1918. But even if Eissler were right, it is hard to see how such a minor point would alter my story significantly. Dr. Deutsch is no longer able to keep straight whether Freud sent Tausk to her or Tausk came of his own accord, although she never previously—even in the presence of my wife, one of Tausk's sons, and his wife—was in any such confused state as to whose suggestion brought Tausk to her for treatment. Would it really be better, from Eissler's point of view, if Freud had first tried to send Tausk to Federn or another unacceptable analyst and had then broken up Tausk's analysis with Dr. Deutsch, the one therapist—Eissler hopes—whom Tausk himself chose? Dr. Deutsch cannot now recall having said that the break between Freud and Tausk, verified by Paul Federn's letter, was at Freud's initiative; all I can say is that that is not what she told me and others when we were all together.

Just before the American publication of *Brother Animal*, the galleys had gone to the Hogarth Press in London, as the British publishers of my first book; they at first accepted *Brother Animal* but, when pushed by my New York publisher for better terms, gratefully withdrew their offer because, they wrote, of their close association with the Freud family. Nevertheless, pressure was then indirectly put on me, via Dr. Deutsch, to correct certain "mistakes" in my text, though she had been informed of nothing specific for me to rectify; rather, she suggested I publish everything about Tausk but leave out the fight with Freud.

When *Brother Animal* finally appeared in print, Dr. Deutsch seemed mainly worried lest she come off too well and Freud less so; her old friends might think she had misled me at Freud's expense. She wrote a few pages about my book, as yet unpublished, in which she said that whenever I brought her "in directly, as a kind of living witness of the past, it is always true and exact. . . . " However, she disagreed with some of my interpretations.

Eissler is obviously unhappy with Edoardo Weiss's cooperation with me, although Eissler puts it in special terms. I am reported to have "derived far more profit from . . . interviews with Weiss than" I have let "the reader know."[43] The late Dr. Weiss, aging and isolated at the Chicago Psychoanalytic Institute, was exactly one of those most subject to Eissler's kind of orthodox intimidation, and in letters to me Weiss discussed issues that he probably evaded in correspondence with Eissler.

My book discussed at some length the role of plagiarism in Freud's life—the way in which the scientific quest for truth can be accompanied by rival claims for priority. Eissler rebuts my illustrations at much greater length than I gave to the whole matter, and future historians can weigh the evidence. But it is noteworthy that Eissler mentions my illustrations as part of my supposed effort to detract from Freud's reputation, while he ignores the actual point I was driving at in listing these squabbles over priority. Since Eissler can see a discussion of the human origins of Freud's ideas only as an assault on the great man's character, his is unable to discuss in his self-proclaimed "polemic" how I try to relate the problem of plagiarism to Freud's interest in thought transference (telepathy) and his discovery of the technique of free associations. My hypothesis about the compatibility of Freud's therapeutic technique with specific parts of his personality may well be incorrect, but Eissler at no point indicates that I had any such historical purpose in mind.

My book *Brother Animal* was designed to restore to the public's attention the figure of Victor Tausk, whom I believed forgotten. I never intended to argue that trained analysts did not know about some of his work; indeed, it was my contention that Tausk's concepts of ego boundaries and identity, as well as his clinical interest in the study of psychoses, were the foundation of much later psychoanalytic thought. Freud himself and others in his circle had so little acquaintance with cases of serious mental disturbance that they considered paranoia one of the neuroses. Tausk made some lasting contributions to analytic theory and therapy, which have been incorporated in the works of such contemporary thinkers as Bettelheim and Erikson.

Now that Eissler's *Talent and Genius* is available, it can be left to the reader to decide whether or not what we now know of Tausk's career adds to our understanding of the early period of psychoanalysis and succeeds in helping to define Freud's standing in history. It is to be hoped that future historians, when they try to see Freud as a full human being instead of a god, will not be subjected to the charge of "prejudice" against him. Because Eissler in his multiple attacks makes himself Freud's hagiographer, it does not follow, as he assumes, that my book or the many others he criticizes constitute a derogation of Freud.

For the sake of future students of the history of psychoanalysis it seemed incumbent on me to reply to Eissler's polemics, and so I published my rebuttal in 1972. *Brother Animal* had been less than 50,000 words long, whereas Eissler's effort to discredit my work took up 160,000 words. Eissler then attacked my reply with an article, again at much greater length than my own efforts. Given Eissler's own lack of succinctness, it is odd for him to accuse me of squandering space. It is only because of Eissler's numerous factual errors and the quality of his allegations, as he zealously pursues his idealizations of Freud, that I feel obliged again to correct the record.

Eissler maintains that *Brother Animal* is "the most brutal attack ever directed"[44] at Freud. He then claims that I have written "that Freud was responsible for the suicide of Victor Tausk."[45] No such words were ever written by me, nor can Eissler cite a page reference. Eissler further asserts that I believe that "Freud planned and knowingly drove Tausk to his death."[46] Once again Eissler is wrong, and he offers no supporting evidence. Eissler appears to be puzzled that "most readers and many reviewers have overlooked Roazen's claim of deliberateness on Freud's part, yet there is no doubt that this is what he does claim."[47] Here Eissler offers a page reference to support his thesis; even reading that page in isolation apart from the rest of my work, I am not surprised that Eissler finds that "most" readers and "many" reviewers did not come to the misconception that he foists on me. Tausk's death was in my opinion a moving human tragedy and not the result, as Eissler falsely imputes to me, of any "preconceived malicious plan"—"Freud's plot."[48]

It is true that there were those in Freud's immediate circle in 1919 who did at least find as the main motive for Tausk's suicide Freud's rejecting behavior. Paul Federn, for example, like other disciples, imputed godlike powers of life and death to Freud. It is also the case that Edoardo Weiss, whom Eissler now calls "an eye-witness, who was excellently trained in classical and dynamic psychiatry,"[49] wrote the following words to me after I showed him my new material on Tausk: "Poor Tausk, *he sensed that Freud did not want him to continue to live* . . . Freud's personality has some dark sides." (The italics were Weiss's.) When *Brother Animal* appeared, Weiss congratulated me, saying that nobody had characterized so clearly and truly the personalities about whom I had written. Then in a book published in 1970, Weiss hypothesized of Tausk's suicide: " . . . he must have felt abandoned by persons close to him, perhaps particularly by Freud."[50]

Weiss's considered views about Tausk's death (like Federn's own immediate response) need not, of course, have been entirely correct. I had rejected Weiss's verbal exclamation, in the course of an interview, that Freud was Tausk's "murderer." The subtitle of Eissler's *Talent and Genius* had been: "The Fictitious Case of Tausk Contra Freud." Yet Eissler had in his closed archives the reminiscences of Ludwig Jekels, another early analyst; Jekels recalled: "Freud thought very highly of Tausk's analytic talents yet refused firmly to analyze him although Tausk had asked him repeatedly to do it: I, too, asked Freud to do that, but he replied: 'He is going to kill me!' "[51]

In my view, which I have expressed in print, Tausk's pathology led him to be vulnerable to Freud's rejection. Until the appearance of *Brother Animal* no published material existed describing Tausk's history of emotional difficulties, and in my book I listed a variety of alternative choices Tausk might rationally have made. That Tausk could not find any way out other than the course he took is, though, humanly understandable and an essential component of his tragedy.

Eissler seems offended that my initial response to him ignores many of his trivialities; he finds "at the centre" of my article "an analysis" of his "character."[52] Readers can judge for themselves. Eissler makes so many peculiar charges that it is bootless to try to answer each one. For example, he accused me in *Talent and Genius* of never having read Freud's *Interpretation of Dreams*. Now he thinks I do not know the correct publication date of Freud's essay on Leonardo. Eissler asserts that an early paper by Tausk on sublimation, which focused on the role of inhibitions in artistic creativity, was old hat in psychoanalysis in 1912, but Lou Andreas-Salomé recorded in her diary that part of Freud's response to Tausk's paper consisted in the statement that "we should not dare to move so boldly into new territory. . . . "[53] Eissler seems unaware that in any historical reconstruction details can be legitimately disputed and alternative interpretations proposed. The difficulty is Eissler's dogmatism and that he has assumed the role of prosecutor for orthodoxy.

In his denunciation of my work Eissler has chosen to ignore the material that Tausk's family was good enough to place at my disposal. He once again takes issue with my characterization of Freud's referral of Tausk to Helene Deutsch for treatment as an insult to Tausk. Eissler writes: " . . . a reaction such as Roazen ascribes to Tausk is so improbable that it can be refuted with certainty."[54] Eissler cannot accept the implications of Tausk's masochistic tendencies. Dr. Deutsch told me that for Tausk to be sent to her as a patient was humiliating to him; however, I did not take any one source as definitive. In my reply to Eissler I indicated that Dr. Deutsch's view of the matter had been confirmed for me by one of Tausk's sons. In another of his many erroneous assumptions, Eissler attributes this confirmation to Tausk's older son, Marius. In fact, it came from Marius's younger brother, Victor Hugo. As Marius wrote to me after a visit from Holland to his brother in Austria, to whom he communicated what I had been recently told of their father: "My brother tells me that he has known for many years that Freud assigned my father's analysis to Dr. Halla Deutsch but he can no longer identify the source of his knowledge. He also believes that this was considered by some as an insult." Marius himself had initially been skeptical of many of Dr. Deutsch's memories. Later, when my wife and I visited Victor Hugo in Austria, where we were joined by his Aunt Nada from Yugoslavia, he confirmed that his father considered the referral to Helene Deutsch an insult. He told us that what knowledge he had came from either his father's sister Jelka or Victor Hugo's own psychoanalyst, Eduard Hitschmann, a good friend of his father's. On reinterviewing Dr. Deutsch I read aloud Marius's account of his brother's recollections; she chortled over the passage about the "insult," since through the years she had gained such acknowledged standing. But she reaffirmed that in 1919 it had in fact been humiliating to Tausk.

From Eissler's accounts one might think that he has unique access to the truth. Wherever I have phrased conjectures about events so long past with historical cautiousness he takes this as a sign of evasiveness. On formal grounds alone his partisanship is evident. *American Imago* devoted its Winter 1973 issue to Tausk; although Eissler's bibliography in his next attack on me omitted it, that issue contains a paper written by Marius Tausk that objects to many of Eissler's accusations. Marius Tausk also disliked some portions of *Brother Animal*. But he, his wife, myself, and my wife were graciously entertained at Dr. Deutsch's home on July 15, 1966, an evening that was devoted to sorting out the whole of the "Tausk problem." If my detailed notes of all my interviews with Dr. Deutsch contain errors, I was never told by any participant in our meeting that the manuscript of *Brother Animal* contained the alleged mistakes that subsequently have so agitated Eissler. On the subject of bibliography, other items might interest the reader: my article, "Victor Tausk's Contribution to Psychoanalysis," which Eissler ignores but which was an introduction to three of Tausk's previously untranslated papers; Helene Deutsch's autobiography, which Eissler also evades, in which she states that Freud had "entrusted"[55] the case of Tausk to her, an issue Eissler had disputed in *Talent and Genius;* and a collection of Tausk's papers that was published as a book in France. (Subsequently they came out in Germany, Spain, and Italy.)

Eissler sticks to his earlier deterministic view of Tausk: he "was doomed to live a miserable life."[56] Under the impact of my defense of *Brother Animal*, Eissler has made one concession; he is now willing to entertain the subject of what might have gone wrong in Tausk's analysis with Dr. Deutsch. Eissler does not dispute that the abrupt termination of Tausk's treatment was at Freud's direction. Eissler misrepresents my argument, however, when he concludes that no transference was ever established between Tausk and Dr. Deutsch. In *Brother Animal* and in my reply to Eissler's attack I discussed what the special transference consisted in. My version is of course open to challenge.

The articles by Mark Kanzer, which Eissler does cite in part, are qualitatively of a different order from Eissler's derogatory approach to Tausk. Marius Tausk has objected to many of Kanzer's hypotheses. But it is possible to disagree about a common body of historical material without imputing base motives.

(It is a minor point, but Eissler has repeatedly referred to me as a "sociologist."[57] As the biographical information on all my books indicates, my professional training has been in political science; my special field is political philosophy and the history of ideas. A code word for "dissenters" in this field is *sociologist*. Other terms—such as *mystic, socialist, psychotic, malicious, pop historian,* or *tasteless*—each have had their own individual history in the story of Freud's school.)

Eissler continues to claim special knowledge about one of the precipitating factors in Tausk's suicide, his incapacity for going through with a planned marriage to Hilde Loewi. I had discussed her, as well as Tausk's general problem of maintaining constant feelings for women, in *Brother Animal*. Eissler alleges Hilde's virginity, seduction, and pregnancy. In *Talent and Genius* Eissler cited no evidence or informant for what he now claims is "the true reason"[58] for Tausk's suicide. To rely on any one "true reason" for a suicide seems a peculiarly rigid approach.

The concept of seduction is a complicated one, and one might consider it an offense to the dignity and autonomy of womankind. Tausk had many unhappy love affairs; nothing in my account of one of Tausk's former women friends (who thanked me for having written *Brother Animal*) justified Eissler's claim that Tausk's desertion of her "was so traumatic that the victim still suffers from it after decades."[59] Concerning Hilde Loewi, Eissler now says he has an informant, whose name his is not permitted to reveal, who received the information from Hilde herself. Eissler is here being naive as well as inconsistent; all he offers is hearsay. It is particularly odd for him to rely on such anonymous testimony. In *Talent and Genius* Eissler had attacked Henri Ellenberger's *The Discovery of the Unconscious;* Eissler criticized Ellenberger for reporting ''a personal remark that is unfavorable to Freud, despite the fact that the person who made it must have had some doubt, since he wished to remain anonymous . . . ''[60] That principle of Eissler's discredits Eissler's own reliance on his informant.

I do not endorse Tausk's treatment of women or any other aspect of his pathology. But if Eissler's informant's story could be confirmed, it would fit Freud's view of Tausk, which stressed the power of his sense of honor, better than Eissler's. Eissler's new suggestions do not alter my conviction that Tausk's rejection by Freud, which left Tausk at the age of forty with the prospect of starting a new career over again, must have contributed to the demoralization of his last months.

Eissler resents that *Brother Animal* did not go unnoticed when it appeared. He regrets that ''Roazen's sensational revelations caught the public imagination. . . . ''[61] He appears miffed that not as many people have noticed his book as mine. Eissler is too cautious, however, when he writes that *Brother Animal* has appeared in paperback and been translated into French and German; it has also appeared in Portuguese, Italian, Spanish, and Japanese. Success in publishing is of course no solid criterion for either merit or worthlessness.

Eissler is still exercised over my use of quotations from Freud that he would prefer not to have people remember. The issue of Freud's approach to psychosis is a large one, hardly to be settled by Eissler's technique of working over one solitary quote from Freud, inserting italics at several points and dropping them at another. Chapter 6 of *Brother Animal* contained a considered discussion of the concept of psychosis in Freud's thought, and the reader can turn there to help him or her form a judgment of the matter. Is Eissler so upset about the story of Freud and Tausk because if Tausk had been psychotic, he should have been treated differently by Dr. Deutsch and Freud; and if Tausk had been only neurotic, he should not have ended up a suicide?

As secretary of the Freud archives, Eissler still defends the widespread censorship that has taken place in the publication of Freud's correspondence. I first pointed out this doctoring in *Freud: Political and Social Thought*. Eissler says that Anna Freud is personally responsible for having excised Freud's harsh comments about Tausk in the published version of the letter informing Lou Andreas-Salomé of the suicide. (The cuts were first made in the German edition, but after the appearance of *Brother Animal* the full letter appeared in the English version.) When reminded by a letter from Marius Tausk that a Tausk family still existed, those words evidently be came more of an embarrassment. But all the deletions from Freud's published letters, often without marks of omission and so far without justification on grounds of medical propriety, are indefensible. They are an offense to impartial scholarship.

Eissler excuses Anna Freud's brother's part in the censorship on the grounds that he was "an architect by profession," therefore not "a trained and experienced editor."[62] Who is to take responsibility for the tendentious editing of Freud's other collections of letters—those to Pfister, those to Abraham, those to Fliess, those to Zweig? It is not the first time that a family naturally has tried to protect the image of its father. What is unusual in Freud's case, however, is that this unsavory practice has been exposed so soon after the publication of the volumes in question and that Eissler has defended it.

Eissler accuses me of "lacking in linguistic subtlety"[63] in alluding to comments of Freud in a letter to Zweig (misdated by Jones in his biography of Freud). Adler died suddenly died on a trip to Aberdeen in 1937, and Zweig mentioned in a letter to Freud that he was very much moved by the news. Freud replied: "I don't understand your sympathy for Adler. For a Jew boy out of a Viennese suburb a death in Aberdeen is an unheard-of career in itself and a proof of how far he had got on. The world really rewarded him richly for his service in having contradicted psychoanalysis."[64] (Eissler omits the third of Freud's sentences, although it clarified his meaning.) Jones, Anna Freud, and Eissler were so identified with Freud's side of his quarrel with Adler that evidently none of them seems to have minded these words appearing in Jones's biography. Jones struck out other passages at Anna Freud's request. After outsiders to the Old Guard orthodox analysts protested about Freud's unforgiving words, those passages were omitted from the volume of Freud's letters to Zweig. Now Eissler wants to say that Jones was mistaken in translating *Judenbub* as "Jew boy," since Eissler naturally prefers the sound of "Jewish boy." But Jones was correct and more linguistically subtle than Eissler; *Juden* is a noun, as is the word *Jew,* whereas *Jewish,* except when referring to the Yiddish language, is usually an adjective.

In *Talent and Genius* Eissler asked rhetorically: "What does it mean when Prof. Roazen's construction of a Freud-image is based on a selection of precisely those passages that were imprecisely translated? This alone seems to me to prove that he was essentially on the wrong track."[65] I replied that in every instance Eissler mentioned I could not find a meaningful difference between Eissler's tortured literal translations and Strachey's good English. Now Eissler retorts that he "never wrote or implied that he

[Roazen] deliberately selected imprecise translations," although Eissler immediately adds: "That would not have surprised me." Eissler is mistaken when he claims that I "demand that we treat" Strachey's "*Standard Edition* like the Septuagint. . . . "[66] I do prefer Strachey's translations; unfortunately, he relied almost wholly on printed German versions of Freud's works, not available manuscript sources. I hope scholars will one day benefit from inspecting the originals.

Eissler reproaches me for "unprecedented indiscretions."[67] Doubtless there is much in *Brother Animal* that he would have preferred kept secret. However, one of his earlier contentions had been that there was nothing very new in my book. But for Jones to claim that Freud rejected a candidate for analytic training on the grounds the man was too abnormal, to name the man, and for Eissler to repeat his idea while close members of the family are still living seems to me an impropriety. As a matter of fact, the daughter has ridiculed the alleged story, which Eissler likes to repeat, because the man won a Nobel Prize; it might seem that candidates accepted by Freud were thus in some way superior to Nobel Prize scientists.

A historian's responsibility is to the truth. One of Tausk's sons objected to passages in the manuscript of *Brother Animal*, but the other son was less sensitive, as was Tausk's surviving sister; I am glad to say that despite my determination to express the story as I saw best, Tausk's more critical son has helped maintain our good relationship. Unfortunately, Federn's son reacted with greater ambivalence. When *Brother Animal* first appeared, Ernst Federn sent me what he called his "forgiveness" for my failing to omit certain passages in his father's 1919 letter about Tausk's suicide; he credited me with good intentions in the aim of serving historical truth, and I considered the matter settled. Since I had made known and objected to the tendentious editing of Freud's letters, I felt I could not cooperate in similar censorship of my own writing. It is my conviction that Paul Federn's full sentiments, whatever their merits, were shared by others in Freud's inner circle, and the way in which Freud was regarded by his early followers was an essential part of the story I was telling.

After Eissler's *Talent and Genius* appeared and my reply was published, the ranks of orthodoxy tightened, and Ernst Federn underwent a change of heart, publishing a letter of protest at my having gone beyond the permission he had given me in 1969 to publish only "the major part" of his father's letter. It is typical of Eissler's bias that although the bibliography of his latest blast at me cites Ernst Federn's letter, it omits my published reply. Even now Eissler does not quote Paul Federn's letter in full; Federn evidently had more knowledge of Tausk's resentment and the extent of the break with Freud than Dr. Deutsch had during the analysis, which was terminated three months earlier.

Eissler's own kind of research is worth commenting on. In interesting tape-recorded interviews with Wilhelm Reich, which fortunately got into print, Reich alluded to "gossip" and then asked Eissler, "Shall we go into that?" Eissler replied, "I think gossip—for the historian, gossip is extremely important." Reich then asked, "Do I have to take part in that?"[68] and then proceeded to recount the material in which Eissler had indicated his interest. I think Eissler's point was partially sound, except that a good historian knows that gossip can be distorted and must make every effort to verify such information. The interviews with Reich show no effort at cross-checking on Eissler's part. He was distressed when the Reich interviews were published; he would have preferred them to have remained sealed in the Freud archives until the twenty-first century.

I do not know why the American taxpayers should support the housing of such a closed collection, and I know of an income tax deduction taken on material to the Freud archives and there may be others. In keeping with the implications of the legal decisions associated with former president Nixon's papers and tape-recordings, scholars might well mount an effort to question what the legal status of the control of the Freud archives now is.

Independent historians can hardly be pleased at Eissler's use of material from the archives that is barred to scholars at large. Nor can they be impressed by Eissler's lack of curiosity. I expressed the view that after Tausk killed himself it is highly likely that Freud commented about the suicide in letters to such analysts as Ferenczi and Abraham. Eissler's ideology leads him to object "that this question arouses a minimal interest in me. . . ."[69] since we already have in print Freud's letters on the matter to Lou Andreas-Salomé and Oskar Pfister. I would consider any additional information about Freud's thinking to be highly important. Eissler obviously fears that Freud might have written something even more startling than in the published letters we already have.*

Eissler is not quite right that I did not ask the owners of those letters for the information I wanted. Michael Balint told me he was too busy to research the matter, and although he had physical possession of the Freud-Ferenczi letters, he said I would need Anna Freud's approval before publishing anything. When I interviewed Hilde Abraham I found her too close to Anna Freud to make it likely that she would cooperate even as Balint had. (Historians should be alerted that Hilde Abraham insisted on

---

*Some years laters, in another obsessive book of Eissler's titled *Victor Tausk's Suicide* (1983), he quoted Freud's having written Ferenczi: "Tausk shot himself . . . eight days before a scheduled marriage. . . . Aetiology obscure. Probably psy[chic] impotence and last act of his infantile fight with the father ghost. Despite acknowledgement of his endowment, no adequate empathy in me."[70]

such strange translations in the volume of the Freud-Abraham letters that her co-translator refused to allow his real name to be associated with the book.)

Eissler claims that in *Brother Animal* I thank him "for the time, hospitality and cooperation with which I [Eissler] helped him in his research. . . . "[71] There is no such wording in my book, although I did thank a list of some ninety-seven people, including Eissler, for their help. I met Eissler only once; I saw more of many other informants, particularly those who had direct contact with Freud, as Eissler had not. (He is also mistaken in his assertion that I interviewed Lou Andreas-Salomé's literary executor, as the absence of his name from the list of the people I met should indicate. I did, however, engage in correspondence with him.)

Tausk was assuredly not the easiest man to get on with, and *Brother Animal* showed many of the personal difficulties of other early analysts. But Freud could be intolerant and arbitrary. A passage from a volume of the minutes of the Vienna Psychoanalytic Society, which I had not been able to cite until its publication, illustrates this point. At a meeting in 1915 Freud is reported to have commented that "Tausk, even though he is an exponent of the psychoanalytic view that we have held until now, is nevertheless fighting for a lost cause; in the realm of symbolism, a decision has long since been reached in favor of primal fantasies."[72] Notice Freud's ex cathedra tone: he uses the royal *we* referring to himself, and the "decision" he mentions stands for a change in Freud's thinking that analysts were now expected to follow.

Freud, despite inevitable human failings, was a great man and a powerful innovator in the history of ideas. Eissler's crusades against myself, as well as others, are unworthy of the memory of the founder of psychoanalysis. Eissler maintains again that *Brother Animal* contends that "Freud deliberately planned and caused Tausk's suicide. . . . "[73] I am not responsible for Eissler's incompetence as a reader. I know nothing special about Eissler's personality, although he declares that "the bulk" of my earlier rebuttal of him "is devoted to the low level of my [Eissler's] character."[74] Perhaps one can infer something about Eissler from the nature of the charges he erroneously levels at others. He now writes that "Roazen was certainly wrong when he wrote, referring to previous polemics of mine with Franz Alexander and others that 'he [Eissler] interprets the silence of previous writers in the face of his abuse as a confession of error on their part.' "[75] But in *Talent and Genius* Eissler had written of one of Freud's supposed recent detractors: "My rejoinder . . . was apparently not burdened by grave mistakes, because it was never answered. . . . "[76] Such inconsistency in Eissler's reasoning does leave one baffled.

Eissler tells us that Franz Alexander, a well-known and distinguished psychoanalyst, "never even read the article in which I was critical of the psychotherapeutic technique he recommended to psychoanalysis."[77] It would seem customary for Eissler to be certain without providing any supporting evidence. But having now replied twice to Eissler's attacks on my work, I think it would be sound policy for all future objects of Eissler's wrath to follow the example he claims Alexander set long ago.

In the spring of 1973 I received a series of letters from Eissler, some registered, in response to my rebuttal of his *Talent and Genius*. Eissler repeatedly proposed to me that the president of Harvard University be asked to set up an investigatory committee of scholars from his faculty in order to review the differences between Eissler and me on Freud and Tausk. I ignored Eissler's letters, since I regarded his request an expression of embarrassing grandiosity. I cannot imagine the president of Harvard caring less about myself or the issues Eissler chooses to cook up. I also believe, incidentally, that the last time a president of Harvard undertook such an investigation was in the Sacco-Vanzetti case, and the wisdom of his decision in that instance is still much doubted.

Notes

1. K. R. Eissler, *Leonardo da Vinci: Psychoanalytic Notes on the Enigma* (New York: International Universities Press, 1961), p. 7.
2. K. R. Eissler, *Hamlet* (New York: International Universities Press, 1971), p. 518.
3. K. R. Eissler, *Medical Orthodoxy and the Future of Psychoanalysis* (New York: International Universities Press, 1965), p. 237.
4. K. R. Eissler, *Talent and Genius: The Fictitious Case of Tausk Contra Freud* (New York: Quadrangle Books, 1971), p. 293.
5. Ibid., p. 309.
6. Ibid., p. 181, p. 232.
7. Ibid., p. 154.
8. K. R. Eissler, *Freud as an Expert Witness: The Discussion of War Neuroses Between Freud and Wagner-Jauregg*, trans. Christine Trollope (New York: International Universities Press, 1980), p. xvi.
9. Eissler, *Talent and Genius*, p. 333.
10. Ibid., p. 328, p. 330.
11. Paul Roazen, *Brother Animal: The Story of Freud and Tausk* (New York: Knopf, 1969), p. 58.
12. Eissler, *Talent and Genius*, p. 42.
13. Ibid., p. 125.
14. Ibid., p. 120.
15. Ibid., p. 123.
16. Ibid., p. 2.
17. Roazen, *Brother Animal*, p. 153.
18. Eissler, *Talent and Genius*, p. 131.
19. Roazen, *Brother Animal*, p. 156.

20. Eissler, *Talent and Genius*, p. 190.
21. Ibid., p. 9.
22. Roazen, *Brother Animal*, p. 26.
23. Eissler, *Talent and Genius*, p. 133.
24. Paul Roazen, "The Legend of Freud," *Virginia Quarterly Review* 47, no. 1 (Winter 1971), p. 45.
25. Eissler, *Talent and Genius*, p. 297.
26. Ibid., p. 245.
27. Ibid., p. 312.
28. Ibid., p. 46.
29. Ibid., p. 261.
30. Roazen, *Brother Animal*, p. 140.
31. Eissler, *Talent and Genius*, p. 300.
32. Ibid., p. 43.
33. Ibid., p. 75.
34. Ibid., p. 62.
35. Ibid., p. 258.
36. Ibid., p. 70.
37. Ibid., p. 314.
38. Ibid., p. 309, p. 70, p. 78.
39. Roazen, *Brother Animal*, p. 138.
40. Eissler, *Talent and Genius*, p. 81.
41. Ibid., p. 329.
42. Ibid., p. 108.
43. Ibid.
44. K. R. Eissler, "On Mis-Statements of Would-Be Freud Biographers with Special Reference to the Tausk Controversy," *International Review of Psychoanalysis* 1, part 4 (1974), p. 392.
45. Ibid.
46. Ibid.
47. Ibid.
48. Ibid., p. 395, p. 392.
49. Ibid., p. 407.
50. Edoardo Weiss, *Sigmund Freud as a Consultant: Recollections of a Pioneer in Psychoanalysis* (New York: Intercontinental Medical Book Corporation, 1970), p. 11.
51. I owe this reference to Peter Swales; see also Paul Roazen, *Helene Deutsch: A Psychoanalyst's Life* (New York: Anchor Press/Doubleday, 1985), p. 173.
52. Eissler, "On Mis-Statements," p. 392.
53. Roazen, *Brother Animal*, p. 51.
54. Eissler, "On Mis-Statements," p. 394.
55. Helene Deutsch, *Confrontations with Myself: An Epilogue* (New York: Norton, 1973), p. 135.
56. Eissler, "On Mis-Statements," p. 396.
57. Eissler, *Talent and Genius*, p. 60; Eissler, "On Mis-Statements," p. 396, p. 406.
58. Eissler, "On Mis-Statements," p. 397.
59. Ibid., p. 398.
60. Eissler, *Talent and Genius*, p. 378.
61. Eissler, "On Mis-Statements," p. 392.

62. Ibid., p. 401.
63. Ibid., p. 402.
64. Ernest Jones, *The Life and Work of Sigmund Freud,* vol. 3 (New York: Basic Books, 1957), p. 208.
65. Eissler, *Talent and Genius,* p. xi.
66. Eissler, "On Mis-Statements," p. 402.
67. Ibid., p. 403.
68. *Reich Speaks of Freud,* ed. Mary Higgins and Chester M. Raphael, with translations by Therese Pol (New York: Farrar, Straus & Giroux, 1967), p. 96.
69. Eissler, "On Mis-Statements," p. 404.
70. K. R. Eissler, *Victor Tausk's Suicide* (New York: International Universities Press, 1983), p. 140.
71. Eissler, "On Mis-Statements," p. 405.
72. *Minutes of the Vienna Psychoanalytic Society,* vol. 4, ed. Herman Nunberg and Ernst Federn, trans. M. Nunberg in collaboration with Harold Collins (New York: International Universities Press, 1975), p. 287.
73. Eissler, "On Mis-Statements," p. 409.
74. Ibid., p. 412.
75. Ibid.
76. Eissler, *Talent and Genius,* p. 345.
77. Eissler, "On Mis-Statements," p. 412.

7

Marxism

In 1955 Herbert Marcuse published an important critique of so-called revisionist Freudian psychology. With great polemical skill Marcuse punctured the inspirationalist pretensions of writers who had tried to update psychoanalytic thought. Marcuse had turned to a serious examination of Freud during the late thirties, when he felt forced to reformulate Marxist premises. Bourgeois society had survived economic crises, the proletariat was susceptible to Fascist appeals, and the Soviet Union, both domestically and internationally, had not fulfilled revolutionary hopes. In his *Eros and Civilization,* disclaiming an interest in the clinical side of psychoanalysis, Marcuse selectively picked those concepts from within orthodox Freudian writing that might support his purposes. Relying on what he called a "hidden trend" in psychoanalysis, Marcuse tried to demonstrate the feasibility of a nonrepressive society. He maintained that Freud was the true revolutionary and that Freud's cause had been betrayed by those who diluted his message for socially conservative purposes.

Russell Jacoby has extended Marcuse's thesis. In *Social Amnesia* (1975), a thought-provoking book, Jacoby rakes over writers from Alfred Adler to R. D. Laing who, he holds, have inadvertently lent support to the status quo by proposing idealist ethics. Like Marcuse, whose endorsement appears on the cover of this book, Jacoby believes that what is historically specific to capitalism need not be universalized as essential human nature. Freud is valuable because he exposed the hypocrisy of traditional values; he knew, according to Jacoby, the fraudulence of liberal individuality and the depth of social injustice. In contrast to what he views as Freud's approach, Jacoby considers the revisionists to have spiritualized social injustice. Their efforts to "humanize" psychoanalysis have supposedly dissolved its cutting edge. To Jacoby, the standard of "authentic" human relationships, as in Laing's existentialism, reinforces the power of social domination within the depths of the psyche. Jacoby proposes these theses and argues that because of social amnesia Freud's true message has been repressed; psychoanalysis, in the guise of reform, has been put to reactionary social purposes.

It is surprising that this is the work of a historian, as Christopher Lasch points out at the beginning of his introduction. But unfortunately, Lasch, who criticizes fellow historians for having tried to see Freud as a man of his times, forgets that that would be one way to use him as a source of our being detached toward today's society; Lasch tells us that he is tempted "to argue that historical understanding of Freud has to begin with loyalty to his basic concepts."[1] Lasch's opponents are supposedly unhistorical, writing "empirical" history. In these terms, though, Marcuse would also have to be considered unhistorical, since he sought to relativize Freud as the embodiment of one phase of capitalist development.

The central problem for practicing historians is that Jacoby makes statements like "it can hardly be maintained that the orthodox Freudians have simply been content to repeat Freud, fleeing any change as heresy—nor that Freud himself suppressed innovations."[2] But this contention has indeed been made, precisely by the neo-Freudians trying to revise psychoanalysis, and Jacoby, in attempting to refute it, does not examine the evidence and feels no need to develop an argument. (Franz Alexander—who is often considered a neo-Freudian and was favorably cited by Marcuse—is excluded from Jacoby's attack.)

In reality, however, Freud was more disturbing than those who fancy themselves hardheaded are willing to admit. At times he could explicitly identify himself with the devil. Twice he challenged the maxim "Love they neighbor as thyself" as both morally undesirable and psychologically unrealistic. Freud was trying to overturn the traditional ethics of Western Christendom. As an alternative he had in mind a new morality, not radical social change. He was horrified by Wilhelm Reich's attack on the traditional bourgeois family and by the uses of Marxism in psychoanalysis; his *Civilization and Its Discontents* was a reply to both.

Politically, Marcuse's tortuous philosophic reasoning about Freud amounts to romanticization. Jacoby contends that "Freud's subversiveness is derived from his concepts and not from his stated political opinions."[3] Jacoby ignores the evidence from so-called empirical history that could amplify this point. In his old age Freud supported a clerical and authoritarian regime in Austria that put down the socialists in a civil war. Marcuse might have been shocked to learn that Freud could not only flatter Mussolini by inscribing a copy of *Why War?* to him, but could entertain as a hope the mistaken idea that one of his own disciples had direct access to the Italian dictator.

Moderate and pro-establishment, Freud was, as Jacoby acknowledges, an old-fashioned liberal. In *The Interpretation of Dreams* Freud expressed his sympathy for the aristocratic leaders of the *ancien régime* who suffered from the French Reign of Terror. Jacoby, however, de-emphasizes Freud's right-wing tendencies and, curiously enough for a supporter of the Frankfurt school of critical sociology, ignores the latent bias of Freud's protest: "Politically I am just nothing."[4] Jacoby does quietly tell us, in contrast to the polemical tone of the rest of the book, that "evidently Freud was not arguing from a left position. . . . "[5]

Jacoby's capacities are shackled by his ideological purposes. He has chosen to attack R. D. Laing and Erich Fromm for the sake of purifying socialist radicalism. Although he lists concepts like identity and identity crisis among revisionist mistakes, he tactfully omits Erik H. Erikson's name from this book. Erikson's psychology has explicit conservative sides to it, but then Lasch's introduction praises Erikson's historical work. Jacoby does not state a principle of selection in explaining his choice of writers to criticize.

Marcuse misunderstood the power structure within psychoanalysis: the more orthodox analysts have exerted a professional weight that a "deviant" like Fromm never had. Marcuse was right in accusing his opponents of verging on social Pollyannaism. But he failed to understand the clinical grounds on which these writers had chosen to abandon traditional Freudian principles.

Jacoby's book also ignores the clinical literature. He focuses on the contrast between therapy and radical politics. But the contrast the revisionists had in mind was between decent and poor therapy, and this distinction need not entail social quietism. Jacoby writes in praise of a dialectical tension between psychoanalytic theory and therapy. This disjuncture has, however, often led to a hypocritical gap between what "orthodox" analysts profess and what they are sometimes willing to do in practice. He concedes the legitimacy of therapeutically aiding the victims of our society, as long as this does not glorify them or confuse therapy with revolutionary social change. But in attacking Laing's approach to schizophrenia Jacoby mentions no rival clinical theories. He regards Laing as too abstract in treating the family apart from society, and in this he may be right, but presumably he would find existing alternative approaches to treatment even harder to swallow. He seems to assume naively that the clinical literature is filled with effective therapies. The tolerance that he does extend to Laing, however, would also seem appropriate to earlier psychoanalytic reformers.

Despite the cosmopolitanism of the Frankfurt school, this book is curiously ethnocentric. In keeping with his tone of admiration for the underdog, Jacoby believes it is not an advantage to be a Marxist today. While this bias may be true for most North American circles, it does not extend to the whole of the contemporary world. In general, Jacoby fails to see weaknesses in the Frankfurt school. For example, he feels no obligation to discuss what human nature might be like under a social structure emancipated from capitalism.

Furthermore, since Marcuse years ago criticized Jean-Paul Sartre, that is the end of the matter for Jacoby. Yet Sartre has written with considerable savvy about the threats to autonomy in psychoanalysis, as well as its other inadequacies. Nor does Jacoby question Marcuse's version of the psychoanalytic concept of perversion or Freud's view of femininity. (According to Martin Jay's history of the Frankfurt school, not even Theodor Adorno or Max Horkheimer could share Marcuse's particular reading of Freud.)

Dogmatism mars this book. After having attacked Adler, for example, Jacoby tells us that the Adlerians may be right, "substantively, if not factually."[6] A victim of the amnesia he writes against, Jacoby proclaims toward the end of his book the conviction that "chronic disease . . . is not a biological statement about the poor, it is a social statement."[7] Adler said much the same thing over half a century ago. Prefabricated slogans, which Jacoby links to commonsense psychology, can also be a product of critical theory. He shares the cultism he bemoans as a reaction to our society.

This stimulating book is written with verve and intelligence and, unlike much socialist literature, takes the theoretical implications of depth psychology seriously. Yet it is unfortunate that a Marxist critique of middle-class psychology ultimately has to be self-satisfied.

Russell Jacoby is a thoroughly engaging writer who combines a sophisticated perspective with a lively style of presentation. Unlike so many other Marxists, Jacoby treats psychoanalytic thinking seriously and yet does so without any unnecessary jargon derived from the socialist tradition.

Earlier, in his *Social Amnesia: A Critique of Conformist Psychology from Adler to Laing*, Jacoby had trenchantly dissected some of the key flaws in post-Freudian thought. In a well-intentioned effort to correct the clinical negativism they found in classical psychoanalytic theory, many Freudian revisionists committed themselves to a kind of inspirationalism that had conformist overtones. Jacoby, however, was not sensitive in his first book to the clinical realities that might have led to philosophic convictions that he could easily puncture; instead, Jacoby amplified Marcuse's line in denouncing thinkers like Erich Fromm and Harry Stack Sullivan. At the same time Jacoby idealized Freud as a subversive and potential social radical, ignoring what Freud was like both as a thinker in the round and as a historical actor.

In *The Repression of Psychoanalysis* (1983) Jacoby is still indebted to Marcuse, who was in fact an impressive social thinker, but Jacoby is now relatively emancipated from the ideological blinders of the whole Frankfurt school of critical thought. Jacoby is more tolerant of diversity and open to theoretical alternatives. He can, for example, pierce through feminist strictures against Freud, because Jacoby knows how receptive early analysis was to its female practitioners. In *Social Amnesia* Jacoby rightly suspected that there was something admirably challenging about early analysis, and now in *The Repression of Psychoanalysis* he has sought to bring back to our attention one of the early Freudians about whom we have known too little.

Otto Fenichel's *The Psychoanalytic Theory of Neurosis* may have been cited as an authoritative textbook by orthodox analysts for over four decades, yet little has been known about how out-of-step with developments in the United States Fenichel remained from the time when he first emigrated from Europe in 1938. He lived in Los Angeles until his death in 1946.

Jacoby does not have enough material for a full-scale biography, nor is he really interested in reconstructing Fenichel's life. He does supply information about Fenichel's obsessionality, which should not surprise anyone who has looked at *The Psychoanalytic Theory of Neurosis*. Fenichel not only kept lists of every movie or concert he ever attended, but also seems to have saved note sheets about the women he slept with. One does wish that Jacoby, who must have encountered at least some of Fenichel's ex-patients, had given some inkling of what sort of clinician he was.

Jacoby's main interest is in telling the story of Fenichel's left-wing political commitments. For a time in Europe he would appear to have been a member of the Communist party, and J. Edgar Hoover's FBI kept a file on him. Fenichel was deeply concerned about the fate of psychoanalysis in the United States and wrote lengthy letters to a few colleagues in his circle of acquaintances. Because of the existence of a handful of such people in the history of analysis Jacoby feels entitled to call them "political Freudians" who have been forgotten.

In actuality, I think Jacoby is mythifying history by calling these isolated figures part of "a long and far-reaching tradition of dissenting and political Freudians."[8] Jacoby thinks that they shared the fate of being repressed along with classical analysis, while he ignores the degree to which Fenichel's clinical outlook became part of an oppressively standard orthodoxy. It is in keeping with Fenichel's penchant for isolating and compartmentalizing things that almost no trace of his social radicalism can be detected in his widely influential, though wooden, *Psychoanalytic Theory of Neurosis*. Jacoby thinks that Fenichel consciously hid his private heresy while proclaiming public orthodoxy.

The Repression of Psychoanalysis is invaluable if only because of the primary source material it has uncovered. The book is welcome because of Jacoby's criticism of the way analysis has developed in the United States. Medical practitioners will no doubt wince at Jacoby's strictures, but it is hard not to agree that being cultured, nonconformist, and intellectual meant more to the early Freudians than it does to today's practitioners of the analytic craft. I do not think that Jacoby is willing enough to face up to

Freud's own social and political conservatisms, but Jacoby is correct in detecting a general decline in the vitality of the profession. It does not require any nostalgia to agree that to be a psychoanalyst was once a calling; but too often it is now a career the advance of which is dependent on an organizational hierarchy that distrusts originality and the life of the mind.

Wilhelm Reich's books have enjoyed a continuing popularity, especially among youth. *The Mass Psychology of Fascism* first appeared in Germany in 1933; the Nazis banned it in 1935. Then in 1946 the first English-language edition appeared, and in 1970, almost forty years after its initial publication, a new English translation was made available. The publisher of the 1970 version announced that it intended to file suit against two west coast companies for circulating photocopies of the book. After all these years it is hard to imagine a surer index of Reich's success as an author than the existence of pirated editions of his works.

Reich began his career as a devoted follower of Freud. While he was not an intimate of Freud, he was certainly one of the most brilliant members of the talented circle that surrounded the aging founder of psychoanalysis. A trained psychiatrist, Reich made some significant contributions to modern psychotherapy. He was the first to insist on the need for a systematic understanding of the techniques of therapy, and he was also the earliest to focus on the therapeutic usefulness of understanding the negative feelings of patients toward their analysts. In addition, Reich broadened the scope of communication between patient and analyst, considering not only verbal but bodily expression as emotional data to be elucidated. Reich encouraged the psychoanalyst to look beyond symptomatic troubles to the character of the patient as a whole; much of what is known as modern ego psychology, with its study of defenses and resistances, was prefigured in Reich's work.

Adolescence was a phase of personality development that especially interested Reich. As a practical reformer he held that many adult problems would never have developed had not sexual expression been prematurely stifled. This liberationist side of Reich ensured his success in America. For, despite the talk about American sexual freedom, by the standards of other cultures this country remains, in my opinion, both prurient and guilt-laden.

To the orthodox psychoanalysts of the 1920s Reich was a troublemaker. Aggressive and difficult, he made orgastic potency the test of mental health. His insistence on trying to harmonize Freud's depth psychology with Marx's social and economic theory was also a source of controversy. By trying to understand human instinctual life along with social forms of domination he exposed himself to attack from both ideological flanks. To the Freudians he seemed to have betrayed the purity of their psychological mission. Reich had argued that only the dissolution of the traditional middle-class family would lead to the disappearance of the Oedipus complex (and the experience of the Israeli kibbutzim would later prove him right). Freud, however, was skeptical and wrote his *Civilization and Its Discontents* partly as an answer to Reich's position. From the point of view of the Marxists, Reich was too involved with the mere superstructure of bourgeois society. When in the late 1920s Reich went on a lecture trip to post-revolutionary Russia and claimed that unless the country also had a sexual revolution it would deteriorate into a bureaucratic state, the Soviet authorities were encouraged to suppress psychoanalysis. In the 1930s Reich succeeded in being expelled both from the International Psychoanalytic Association and communist organizations.

The Mass Psychology of Fascism was originally written at the high point of Reich's involvement with Freudian and Marxist concepts. The book is of uneven quality, starting off with some brilliant and subtle interpretations of the appeal of Fascist ideology to the mass mind, but then deteriorating, especially toward the end, into bombastic and propagandistic exhortations. Reich added to the book over the years, and the 1970 edition is deficient in not indicating when he wrote which portions. One can pretty well guess, though, that the most polemical parts were written during his final, almost messianic phase.

The central interpretative thesis of the book wears well: modern man is torn by contradictory impulses toward conservatism and revolution. He craves authority and fears freedom, but is simultaneously rebellious. The authoritarian patriarchal family, Reich held, distorted some of man's most generous and cooperative instincts. Fascism represents not so much any one political party as the organized expression of the average man's enslaved character, "the basic emotional attitude of the suppressed man of our authoritarian machine civilization. . . . "[9] Reich's main sociological point was that society is capable of transmuting man's inner nature, producing a character structure that then reproduces society in the form of ideologies. Unlike other Marxists of his time, Reich emphasized the independent role ideological systems played in social action. He went on to interpret ingeniously the mysticism of the Nazis in terms of the symbolic meaning of their doctrines. In Reich's time the distressed middle class became members of the Nazi radical right, and he chose to explain modern nationalism as an outgrowth of suppressed genital sexuality.

At his best Reich was a dissident thinker with a utopian appeal for those who reject the standards of conventional society. During the time when the war in Southeast Asia tarnished all the elites in American society, Reich's reputation as a modern prophet increased. At his worst, however, Reich was a crank; his obsession with "physical orgone energy,"[10] which he claimed to have discovered, was already intrusive enough in 1942 to mar his revised edition of *The Mass Psychology of Fascism*. His invention of orgone energy accumulators and his use of them in therapy set the U.S. Food and Drug Administration against him. If he was, as seems plausible, already mentally disturbed by the time of his trial, his sentence is an example of the cruelty of which our society is capable. His writings were destroyed by the government, while Reich himself died in a federal prison in 1957.

Near the end of his life Reich became aware that his own theory of genitality was not to be found in Freud's works. Yet Reich always remained deeply devoted to his former teacher. Unlike later followers, who weakened the radical aspects of Freud's concepts and junked the libido theory, Reich chose as his mentor the early Freud, the heretic who wrote and thought shocking things. So we find Reich, like Freud, struggling to prevent his basic contributions from being diluted. The revolutionary in Freud remained Reich's model, and perhaps this partly accounts for his having endured so long.

In the history of ideas it is customary for the reputations of thinkers to fluctuate cyclically. Among intellectuals Erich Fromm now commands little current interest. For example, when *To Have or to Be?*, his twenty-second book, appeared in 1976, although it was the selection of a major book club, it met with notable critical silence. This book was a restatement of Fromm's final theoretical position, and one might explain the absence of reviews by the familiarity of many of its themes. But the appearance in 1973 of Fromm's *The Anatomy of Human Destructiveness*, a major statement, did little to alert the intellectual community to the misunderstandings that have grown up around the contributions of this seminal thinker.

The publication of Fromm's *Escape from Freedom* (1941) was a notable event in modern intellectual history. *Man for Himself: An Inquiry into the Psychology of Ethics* (1947) also illustrated the power of his mind. Throughout the 1940s and 1950s students read and respected Fromm's publications and tried to keep up with the flow of his new books. Perhaps Fromm's fecundity helped to deter his success in high culture. But the climate of opinion has also shaped the response to Fromm's work. Socially he has been the most radical of psychoanalytic thinkers. He was concerned with the pathology of normality and considered it legitimate to speak of an "insane" society and of what happens to sane people within it. Paradoxically, Fromm's reputation went into an eclipse in North America during the turbulent 1960s, yet in the preceding (supposedly more conservative) decades he was widely acclaimed as a pundit. Just as Jung's reputation as a depth psychologist, despite his appalling political misjudgments about the Nazis, is finally on the upswing, in the long run Fromm will undoubtedly get the credit he deserves. No psychoanalyst tried more relentlessly to reconcile Freud and Marx.

Part of Fromm's problem came from his lack of association with one of the more prestigious research universities on this continent, and here he might well have felt vindicated in his belief that the more famous centers of learning propagate support for the status quo. It took courage and originality on Fromm's part to establish himself as someone to be heard without the support either of conventional academic life or the mainstream of the psychoanalytic movement. Other conformist pressures worked against him. Literary critics, if only by virtue of their command of language, exert a weight beyond their special fields, and they have on the whole sided, when they have been at all receptive to psychoanalytic thought, against the revisionist school.

Sectarianism has undercut the place Fromm deserves. It is not surprising, given the prior controversies in the history of psychoanalysis, that although a landmark in social science, *Escape from Freedom* was greeted with savage reviews by Freudians insistent on preserving the purity of their dogmas. Psychoanalysis, like other organizations, has thrived on having both heroes and villians, and it was Fromm's fate to become an object of scorn among orthodox psychoanalytic followers. He found himself dropped from the direct membership list of the International Psychoanalytic Association, and like other so-called heretics his writings have been blacklisted at most training centers. Although his books continue to be purchased widely by the public, professionally Fromm has been ignored rather than criticized responsibly. It is perhaps the inevitable fate of dissidents that they must each go their own way. Fromm once published a critique of Otto Rank and has been at times too hard on Jung. Fromm was allied with such original thinkers as Harry Stack Sullivan, Clara Thompson, and Karen Horney, and yet none of these people was able to match organizationally the ranks of "official" psychoanalysis.

While from an outsider's point of view Fromm remained an analyst loyal to the broad Freudian tradition, he also was a socialist. But even here sectarianism undermined his stature within the intellectual elite. Fromm was an early member of the Frankfurt school of critical sociology, and his bitterest critic was a former co-worker, Herbert Marcuse. In a famous exchange, originally published in *Dissent,* Fromm tried to defend himself against Marcuse's attack. Marcuse cannot be entirely blamed for the slavish way his own disciples have continued either to attack Fromm or to denigrate his contributions. But combined with the opposition of establishment psychoanalysis, the sectarianism of the Left (aided by Paul Goodman's critique of Freudian revisionism) gave Fromm little basis for potential supporters.

When Fromm was twenty-two he received his Ph.D. from the University of Heidelberg. He had written a thesis on the sociology of three Jewish sects. Subsequently he underwent psychoanalytic training and graduated from the Berlin Psychoanalytic Society in 1931. He recalled having spent about ten years as an orthodox Freudian, although he never had any personal contact with Freud himself. Fromm's first wife, Frieda Fromm-Reichmann, was also a pioneer, specializing in the development of new therapeutic techniques. In 1934 they moved to New York, and then in 1949 Fromm himself left for Mexico, where he launched a psychoanalytic institute. Like Erikson and Bettelheim, the breadth of Fromm's writings helped to fill the gap left by the fashionable narrowness of contemporary professional philosophy.

No revisionist Freudian wrote for as long as Fromm, nor has any reached a broader public, shown more independence of thought, or possessed more conceptual ability. He helped introduce important alterations in the 1930s brand of psychoanalysis. Turning away from the pessimism of Freud's instinct theory, Fromm insisted on the potential significance of changes in the social environment as a means of altering the human condition. In a field where it is still possible for writers to treat Freud's case histories as sacred texts, Fromm was bold in challenging Freud's clinical practices. Early on he recognized the social prejudices incorporated in the traditional psychoanalytic conception of women. Sociologists advise that the way to advance oneself professionally is to write for one's peers, but within psychoanalysis Fromm has had few equals, and his early associates all predeceased him. So in the end his strategy of appealing to the book-buying public may have been the only recourse open to him.

Freud was not much interested, aside from criticizing sexual mores, in the social sources of suffering and exploitation. Fromm, on the other hand, was intrigued by the way our culture fosters conformist tendencies by suppressing spontaneous feelings and thereby crippling the development of genuine individuality: "human beings are more afraid of being outcasts than even of dying."[11] Following the earliest interest in character structure shown by Jung and Wilhelm Reich, although loyally citing Freud's own limited efforts at character typology, Fromm developed his concept of "social character" to explain how societies produce and reproduce the personality types they need to perpetuate themselves. Social character gets molded by the economy, and in turn dominant character traits shape the social process. As external necessity gets internalized in the psyche, human energy is harnessed for a given economic or social system. In this way we become what we are expected to be.

Instead of seeing the unconscious as something frightening, Fromm held that truth is repressed by an unconscious that is basically socially determined. He also thought that too often we fear our superior potentialities and, in particular, the ability to develop as autonomous and free individuals. He traced destructiveness to the unlived life rather than to a mythical death instinct. If cruelty is one of the ways of making sense of life, it only illustrates Fromm's theory that character-rooted passions should be considered psychosocial phenomena.

Fromm, who died in 1980, was fundamentally a religious person in the prophetic tradition. His occasionally sanctimonious tone often obscured his critical acumen. To Freud sentimentality of any sort awakened fears of personal weakness and passivity. If Freud avoided piousness he could at times be moralistic; in books like *Future of an Illusion* and *Civilization and Its Discontents* he sought to uproot some traditional Western standards of ethics. Beneath Fromm's religious piety lay a genuinely bold spirit. Both Fromm and Freud likened themselves to great rabbis. In *To Have or to Be?* Fromm identified with Rabbi Jochanan ben Sakai, as Freud had done in his *Moses and Monotheism*. Even in his accounts of clinical work Freud gave his readers more comfort than he liked to acknowledge. It is reassuring to be led to think one is tough-minded. Freud's therapy was characteristically more supportive than his ideal of aloofness might lead one to suppose.

A certain snobbery deters some people from admiring a writer who becomes world famous. However lowbrow a popular book like Fromm's *The Art of Loving* (1957) may appear to be, he was doing something important for intelligent readers in need of spiritual guidance. For Fromm selfishness is not, as in Freud, the same as self-love. Fromm thought they were opposites and therefore the possibility of altruism as an aspect of self-expression becomes a real one. Yet there are grounds for questioning Fromm's capacity to convince. He lacked Freud's irony, the Viennese sense of play and feeling for the absurd. As a writer Freud had a superb dramatic sense, whereas Fromm's books began to weigh heavily. At times Fromm did not sound ignorant enough, as when he asserts in *To Have or to Be?* that "we know almost everything that is important to know about human behavior. . . ."[12] Freud was grandiose, but at least at times he liked to emphasize how little we can understand. The combination of certainty and skepticism in Freud helps account for his enduring popular appeal.

To Have or to Be? is not easy reading, but it does manage to present the viewpoint and challenge of "radical humanistic psychoanalysis." In keeping with his long-held view that selfishness and altruism are different character orientations, in this book Fromm presents two alternative modes of existence: the mode of having and the mode of being. A feature of what Fromm saw as the crisis of contemporary life was that society is too much centered around things than around persons. The "having" mode is represented in the alienation of consumerism; and the "having" mode's predominance is reflected, Fromm thought, in the growing use of nouns and the decreasing use of verbs in the Western world. Whereas Freud liked to debunk the legitimacy of altruism, Fromm tried to combat egocentricity. Too often we hold our ego as a possession, the basis for identity, a thing.

In addition to egotism Fromm set out here to combat greed and human passivity, bewailing the prevalence in the modern world of competition, antagonism, and fear. We are, he says, unduly bound to our own egos. Like other thinkers, he distinguished between subjectively felt needs and objectively valid ones. For Fromm the existence of a desire does not in itself constitute an ethical norm. He had in mind the aim of self-realization; for him self-affirmation was a process of exercising human reason in a productive activity. He attacked Marcuse for encouraging a hedonistic return to childhood instead of holding maturity as the ultimate goal of socialism.

Fromm believed that reason properly exercised will lead to an ethic of love. But he distinguished his own views from those of Freud. Love for Fromm was a process of self-renewing and self-increasing: " . . . selfishness and laziness are not the only propensities inherent in human beings. We human beings have an inherent and deeply rooted desire to be: to express our faculties, to be active, to be related to others, to escape the prison cell of selfishness."[13] Society has aimed not, as Freud thought, to repress sex, but to villify sex for the sake of breaking the human will. Social conformism succeeds to the extent that it breaks our independence without our even being aware of it. In searching for "guidance to a non-theistic, rational, yet religious, philosophy of life"[14] Fromm was no longer committed to a theory of progress. Like other Central European refugees, he came to hint that there has been a decline in the spirit of society at least since the thirteenth century. When he refers in *To Have or to Be?* to Jesus he does not have organized religion in mind, and he divorces Marx from what he called "the vulgar forgery presented by Soviet Communism."[15]

Fromm concluded *To Have or to Be?* by suggesting resolutions of what he saw as our central social crisis. Outside of proposing the creation of a new humanistic body of experts who were to create guidelines to be submitted to the citizenry for discussion, Fromm was left with mainly hortatory proposals to encourage social change. He was not optimistic in his utopianism, but he retained a "faith" in humanity's capacity to extricate itself from the catastrophic circumstances it has created.

Fromm's recommendations were in the end idealistic ones, and if they succeed only in making us feel better about ourselves they may serve conservative purposes. But when he declared that a new society presupposes a deep change in the human heart and that what we need is a new object of devotion to replace the present one, Fromm was convinced that drastic environmental reforms are necessary to improve human life fundamentally. His concepts were designed to construct bridges between the individual and society. Long ago he insisted on the inevitable role ethics play in psychology. To the degree to which Fromm overcame received wisdom, avoiding both pre-Freudian and current behavioristic views, the monument of his work has enriched our discourse.

By the early 1970s it was clear to many that psychoanalytic psychiatry had not been thriving lately. Rival therapeutic approaches to Freud's own recommended treatment procedure had proliferated; the alternative possibilities were so abundant as to perplex any conscientious observer. Dr. Joel Kovel, in his valuable and popular *Complete Guide to Therapy* (1976), tried to clarify a confusing situation by setting forth the advantages and drawbacks to the various clinical techniques.

An even more basic disquiet afflicts those idealistically associated with the tradition of depth psychology. It is not so much that fundamentally new challenges to Freud's structure are being offered; in retrospect, it is striking how earlier thinkers, not without respect, sensitively questioned both the subjective psychological bias in Freud's ideas and the cultural presuppositions in early psychoanalysis. Yet within the last couple of decades, certainly since the high point of Freud's influence in North America around the time of his centenary in 1956, an erosion of confidence has taken place. By now psychoanalysis can no longer claim vitality and elan. Its theory has become stagnant, unlikely to arouse the minds of daring young thinkers.

This state of affairs conflicts with the earlier history of ideas. Although it is possible to romanticize the past, Freud and his immediate followers were people of imagination and culture; they comprised a remarkable group of nonconformists committed to the life of the mind. If the story of Freud's work has been marked by acrimony, at least it was not beset by the self-satisfaction that arises from worldly success. Once psychoanalysis became part of the American psychiatric establishment, and this conquest was attained shortly after the end of World War II, intellectuality became a threat to the profession's trade unionism. In countries where psychoanalysis has had more opposition, one is more apt to encounter writers reminiscent of earlier figures in the history of depth psychology.

Kovel's *The Age of Desire: Case Histories of a Radical Psychoanalyst* (1982) confirms him as one of the few young analysts worth listening to. The subject of his 1970 *White Racism* marked him off from his contemporaries. In occasional pieces, like a critique of the conformist implications in Erik H. Erikson's ego psychology and more recently in an "anti-psychiatric" account of the American mental health industry, Kovel has distinguished himself for having a mind of his own. In an appendix to *The Age of Desire* he includes two notes: one is a criticism of the fashionable self-psychology of Heinz Kohut and another an appreciation of the controversial French analyst Jacques Lacan.

The Age of Desire proposes an ambitious task, a new attempt to bring together Marxism and Freudianism. Kovel has had his predecessors in this enterprise, notably Wilhelm Reich, Erich Fromm, and Herbert Marcuse. (Adler was the earliest analyst to be interested in socialism, but like so many other radicals attracted to supposedly hard-nosed "orthodox" psychoanalytic theory, Kovel would be unhappy with him as a precursor.) By now it is a commonplace that Freud and Marx are two of the most disturbing modern prophets, and Kovel has undertaken to construct his own synthesis of their divergent points of view. The central flaws of each body of thought, Marxism's positivism and psychoanalysis's subjectivism, seem to match up with the strengths of the other, so that it is possible to hope to understand historical reality, as well as the roots of imagination—what Kovel chooses to call "desire."

Unlike so many analysts who think in a socioeconomic vacuum, Kovel self-critically worries about his own complicity in the self-deception and fraudulence connected with the misuse of trickery, illusion, and the suggestibility of patients. And in contrast to most Marxist ideologues, confident that the historical process will render outmoded the remnants of bourgeois psychological problems, Kovel proposes to use case histories to illustrate the characteristic kinds of suffering produced in so-called late capitalism.

An early chapter recounting Kovel's attendance at a national convention wins the reader's sympathy; the self-congratulatory air is oppressively pervasive and realistic. Disputations about narcissistic impairment can be as metaphysical as any of the old discussions of libido theory. Learned theoreticians can heighten the level of obscurantism and mystification. Freud may have had emancipatory purposes, but the upshot has been academicism and pedantry. Instead of a critique of the status quo, psychiatry has often become a tool of social control. In contemplating his colleagues Kovel concludes that most of them are "out-and-out hacks," and yet he knows that "the virtues of practitioners have precious little relationship to the theory they espouse. . . ."[16]

In keeping with the Marxist emphasis on praxis, or labor, as the core unit of history, Kovel presents a few of his own case histories. These patients include a compulsively work-driven executive and a spoiled rich girl; he also movingly recounts the fate of a hospitalized lower-class psychotic. It is hard to criticize these case presentations, since so much of the literature now is aridly theoretical, yet his case histories lack an artistic quality that would successfully bring them alive. In attempting to recast the main issues of psychoanalytic psychiatry along the lines of radical social thought and trying at the same time to indicate certain possibilities open to Marxism, it was perhaps inevitable that this difficult, rewarding book would end up being demandingly obscure.

The case histories are designed to show how psychoanalysis has remained trapped in the world Freud is supposed to have sought to undermine. Neurotic self-alienation cannot be understood independently of alienation from others. Each of his cases are selected as representative not of the true possibilities of the human species, but of the social order we tend to reproduce. Splits in capitalist existence inevitably affect personal life; work becomes, instead of an expression of human capacities, the embodiment of a part of the self that is objectified into a commodity for purposes of exchange.

The kinds of self-estrangement Kovel describes have an underside that is potentially radical, for he argues that what is so often denied in people is a "transhistorical" potentiality and that "desire" can be found in those human strivings toward objects that "cannot yet be named in the languages of history."[17] A patient has a chance to reexperience alienated portions of the self, to recapture through a shared tie to an analyst possibilities that have been lost in "otherness." Hatred is, to Kovel, a particular thwarting or repudiation of desire. At the price of perpetuating alienation, "late" capitalism mobilizes consumption patterns for purposes of domination. It is no wonder, according to Kovel, that the mental health movement now plays so large a role, for capitalist society both inflates as it cripples the self, enhancing the possibilities of individuality yet creating a deadened public world, leaving it to psychologists to perpetuate the contradictions.

However hesitant one might be of Kovel's theorizing, his account of bureaucratic psychiatry is memorable. In a hospital setting puffed-up thinking must confront the realities of overcoming class boundaries between therapist and patient. The psychiatric emergency room is as inadequate as one could imagine. Drugs can substitute for care in a social setting that is fundamentally depersonalized. As discontented as one ought to be with the psychotherapeutic treatment of the most disturbed patients in a hospital, biological psychiatry has its own drawbacks, including the old illusion of precise diagnosis.

Kovel's discontent with his own profession, as a lifeless reflection of mass culture, appears thoroughgoing. His point is that the system itself promotes stupefying social practices. Not just the welfare bureaucracy becomes an instrument of oppression; psychoanalysis, although a protest against alienation, at the same time reinforces it. The training programs in particular are hotbeds of authoritarianism and cultism.

It is easy to agree with most of what Kovel has to say, except that his reasoning seems to be caught up in the strangulation to which he objects. He himself uses theory as a shield against the immediacy of reality. It is as if the Marxism he has turned to in order to escape from his dilemma is partly responsible for perpetuating it; in the book one longs for fewer abstractions and more concrete experiences of his own. He is reifying concepts when he tries to contrast the self-determination of "individuation," which is supposedly "a bit like divine grace," with liberalism's individualism, dismissed as a "degenerate ideology of bourgeois culture."[18]

If, as Kovel admits at the end, he is "not a very good Marxist,"[19] his humanism makes his approach more attractive. In an occupation so filled with technicians and public relations experts, Kovel admires the "ineffable caring quality" that is "evidently attainable within bourgeois professionalism, even if only by a minority."[20] In his struggle to develop a psychotherapy that is compatible with radical social practice, Kovel articulates the noninstrumental nature of therapeutic concern: true care takes place when people are treated as ends in themselves, not as the adjunct to some organizational purposes. *The Age of Desire* renews both psychoanalysis and socialism, in restating the Enlightenment ideals underlying those two traditions of thought.

Notes

1. Russell Jacoby, *Social Amnesia: A Critique of Conformist Psychology from Adler to Laing* (Boston: Beacon Press, 1975), p. xi.
2. Ibid., p. 11.
3. Ibid., p. 25.
4. Quoted in Paul Roazen, *Freud: Political and Social Thought* (New York: Da Capo Press, 1986), p. 243.
5. Jacoby, *Social Amnesia,* p. 83.
6. Ibid., p. 41.
7. Ibid., p. 141.
8. Russell Jacoby, *The Repression of Psychoanalysis: Otto Fenichel and the Political Freudians* (New York: Basic Books, 1983), p. x.
9. Wilhelm Reich, *The Mass Psychology of Fascism*, trans. Vincent R. Carfagno (New York: Farrar, Straus & Giroux, 1970), p. 13.
10. Ibid., p. 9.
11. Erich Fromm, *To Have or to Be?* (New York: Harper & Row, 1976), p. 105.
12. Ibid., p. 99.
13. Ibid., p. 100.
14. Ibid., p. 59.
15. Ibid., p. 16.

16. Joel Kovel, *The Age of Desire: Case Histories of a Radical Psychoanalyst* (New York, Pantheon, 1981), p. 175, p. 26.
17. Ibid., pp. 69–70.
18. Ibid., p. 155, p. 254.
19. Ibid., p. 260.
20. Ibid., p. 27.

8

Ego Psychology

From the earliest social philosophers in the classical world to the inception of political science as a profession, writers have agreed in principle on the relevance of psychological material for political understanding. The difficulties that we are still apt to encounter today, however, arise as soon as unreasonable demands are made for a once-and-for-all settlement of the methodological issues, either by those who remain skeptical of the upshot of the collaborative enterprise or by those who expect to be able wholly to transform our political thinking by means of psychology.

Conscientious people interested in psychology and politics retain a sense of hesitation about their work. Partly this cautiousness reflects the relative lack of professional legitimization for bringing together these two perspectives. But there are genuine difficulties with interdisciplinary work, and especially with these two disciplines, that have helped to hold back what might otherwise seem an almost self-evidently desirable cooperation. Both fields have had their orthodoxies, but it is partly by means of examining any other field that one is helped to overcome some of the provincialism inevitable in one's own professional training.

I have chosen the example of Erik H. Erikson in order to illustrate some of the problems, as well as the promise, inherent in interdisciplinary cooperation, without of course claiming that his sort of work can be said to embody all the possible contributions to be derived from psychology for political thought. Erikson is, however, one of the liveliest workers from within the Freudian school, and while the concepts of a very different kind of thinker like B. F. Skinner have already received extensive attention, Erikson's ideas, though widely influential within social science as a whole, have made relatively little explicit impact on contemporary political thought.

Given his background and training as a child psychoanalyst, Erikson is perhaps an improbable figure to have had any influence on political science. Precisely because his professional origins are likely to seem so alien, it pays to examine his work in the round, for without an overall understanding of Erikson's contribution to clinical psychology, any application of his concepts is likely to be sterile; nowadays to invoke, for example, an identity crisis may be no less truistic than the old (and justifiably frowned-upon) habit of searching for oedipal conflicts.

Erikson has recounted the casual way in which in 1927 he became a member of Freud's circle. While Erikson was traveling around Europe as a young artist, an old school friend asked him whether he would like to earn some money in Vienna painting the portraits of the children of Dorothy Burlingham, a wealthy American in analysis with Freud. In addition, Erikson's friend was going on summer vacation and needed a temporary replacement for himself as a tutor for children of analytic patients and for patients in child analysis with Anna Freud. At the end of the holiday Dorothy Burlingham and Anna Freud asked Erikson whether he would like to become a child analyst, a profession whose existence was previously unknown to him. The two women had noticed Erikson's natural psychological gifts. Furthermore, in a culture where men were not expected to be very good with small children—in the Central Europe of that era fathers were not seen pushing baby carriages—Erikson represented an acquisition for child analysis.

Erikson had been raised as the stepchild of a German-Jewish pediatrician, and his later attentiveness to various stages of the life cycle can be seen as beginning in the characteristic pediatric concern with childhood problems in the context of specific developmental phases. Erikson's focus on the role of the environment in personality development, even in earliest childhood, can be traced also to some of the specifics of the practice of child analysis. Since child analysts work with patients whose environment (parents and family) cannot be disregarded, child analysts have had to be more alert to issues that analysts of adults, fascinated with the intricacies of the unconscious, could more readily disregard.

Erikson maintained an ambivalent relationship to Anna Freud and her work. Analyzed by her at an exceptionally low fee, in an era when to be an analyst was to become a member of an underground revolutionary band at odds with established psychiatry, pedagogy, and social science, Erikson has feared that she never forgave him for giving up the practice for which he was trained. Psychoanalysis remains the only formal higher education Erikson ever had, which helps to account for his excessive deference to Freud. As with her father, when Anna Freud did not like certain ideas she tended to protect herself from her hostility by finding them "foreign"; she repeatedly said of Erikson's work that she had never been able to understand much of it. Nevertheless, Erikson dedicated one of his books to her.

Through his association with Anna Freud, who stood guard over her father's failing health, Erikson had contact with the founder of psychoanalysis. Intellectually, however, Erikson was of no known significance to Freud. (Erikson does play a part in Freud's biography; in 1936 he predicted that Freud would not come to America to receive an honorary degree, and therefore Harvard University did not go through with an intended offer.) Like others around Freud in his last years, Erikson partly played the role of a servant; Frank Lloyd Wright is reported to have remarked that once he had pupils he had solved his servant problem, and like other great men Freud made use of services from members of the movement he had forwarded.

The atmosphere around Freud could be constricting, especially for a man trying to stretch his creative powers. Erikson has commented upon what he found to be "a growing conservatism and especially a pervasive interdiction of certain trends of thought. This concerned primarily any idea which might be reminiscent of the deviations perpetrated by those earliest and most brilliant of Freud's co-workers. . . ."[1] In Vienna Erikson began to present his work on play constructions with children, but was told that such a technique was akin to Melanie Klein's approach. To be like Klein was, at least in the Vienna Psychoanalytic Society, as reprehensible as to resemble Jung, Adler, or Rank, and Erikson felt helpless in what seemed to him such an overprotective milieu. To be really like Freud was to be original, yet to identify with Freud as an innovator meant to risk ceasing to be a psychoanalyst. So to Erikson "the idea of moving on and working independently seemed . . . invigorating. . . ."[2]

Erikson left Vienna in 1933, shortly after graduating from the training program of the Vienna Psychoanalytic Institute. Nevertheless, he never ceased trying to maintain his good relations with orthodox psychoanalysis. His career is a good example of how, though Erikson came to share many of the ideas of the early "heretics" in psychoanalysis, the movement had grown so large and successful that no one tried officially to dissociate him from it. On his side Erikson, sometimes glorifying Freud's public image, has tried to make it seem that there was some inevitability within Freud's ideas pointing toward the course Erikson has taken.

Almost from the outset Erikson began to revise psychoanalysis in a more healthy-minded direction. In 1936 he published a review of Anna Freud's *Psychoanalysis for Teachers and Parents:* "Following the traditional route of psychoanalysis the book says much about what may limit and endanger the child's ego; it says little about the ego itself. Correspondingly psychoanalysis has so far been useful to pedagogy primarily as a basis for criticism of cultural progress and the dangers it involves for children. So far as further studies may illuminate the ego, psychoanalytic insight will be able to help education in its most specific problem: the strengthening and enriching of the ego."[3] Significant as Erikson's differences from Anna Freud may have been, he expressed his point of view loyally within Freud's terminology of the ego. The earlier "deviators" in the history of psychoanalysis also wanted to correct unnecessary negativism in psychoanalytic theory, but they did so by setting up rival conceptualizations. (It should be said that Erikson never mattered enough to Freud in his extreme old age for it to have seemed worthwhile to start an argument about his work.)

The earlier ideological contests in Freud's circle had created a tradition of rebellion in psychoanalysis, which confronted later analysts with the threat of expulsion and excommunication, as well as with the attraction of notoriety of differentiating their psychological thought from Freud's. Erich Fromm was another psychoanalyst who, from a Marxist orientation, had preceded Erikson's interest in the social context of personality development, and subsequently Fromm went far, as did Erikson, too, in drawing ethical conclusions from psychoanalytic principles.

But Erikson was uneasy at any comparison of his work with that of Fromm. The most orthodox had been contemptuous of *Escape from Freedom*, seeing it as a betrayal of the cause of the undiluted depth psychological orientation. Fromm, who himself had no personal contact with Freud, even went so far as to write a book emphasizing certain negative features in the master. Consequently Erikson is far more apt to be assigned reading at contemporary psychoanalytic institutes.

Freud remained a hero to Erikson, even a taboo subject. Admiring Freud's courage, while remaining himself a cautious leader in psychoanalytic reform, Erikson was afraid of being too outspoken. Conscious of the inadequacies of Freudian theories of femininity and motherhood and finally coming to see the analytic situation as an "exquisite [sensory] deprivation experiment,"[4] Erikson has revealed in his ambiguous prose the need not to clarify to himself how far he has drifted from classical psychoanalysis. Erikson has referred throughout his writings to Freud's own life, for example in books on Luther and Gandhi, and these two alternatives, outright revolution and passive resistance, represent the two poles of Erikson's possible relationship to Freud. In his preoccupation with the nature of greatness, Erikson has been continuing one of the central themes of Freud's last book, *Moses and Monotheism*.

Rebellion can be as much a sign of dependence as more positive ties, and Erikson has sought to work out his own independent path, while acknowledging that his concepts follow directly from their Freudian origins. His writing has earned widespread acclaim, yet it was not without its forerunners in the history of psychoanalysis. Long before Erikson, Fromm had insisted on the importance of external social reality. Jung had focused on later stages of the life cycle than the Oedipus complex and in particular on middle-age crises and the last half of life; Jung also emphasized the constructive functions of apparent regressions. Adler had seen the key role of the ego for the understanding of normal as well as pathological psychology and early on had wanted to explore the implications of aggressive drives. Finally, Rank had pointed out the neglected role of the psychology of creativity, as well as the significance of the non-Oedipal mothering functions. Erikson, however, succeeded in legitimizing many of the insights that had previously been deemed "deviant" among analysts.

Yet Erikson's contribution has also been an undeniably individual one. From the outset he tried to make his points through striking case histories and later through fuller life histories. He retained the artist in him, and a certain impressionistic character remained in his kind of writing. Although the upshot of his work has important implications for psychoanalytic theory as well as for social thought, he came to abstractions with the uneasy wonder of a self-proclaimed novice. It took a theoretically inclined friend, for instance, to point out how the outlines of Erikson's ego psychology fit into prior orthodox psychoanalytic thought.

If in Vienna Erikson felt cramped and uncomfortable, it was not easy at that time for analysts to earn a living anywhere they might choose to live. Erikson first tried to recover his Danish citizenship, but that would have taken years, and psychoanalysis had had little impact in Scandinavia. Viennese analysts had, however, long been living off the fees of American patients. Erikson first tried to come to New York City, but A. A. Brill, Freud's deputy there, was not sufficiently impressed by Erikson's credentials. The American analysts resented the way their Viennese colleagues treated recently graduated candidates as "export ware," good enough for the New World; Erikson was already being recommended abroad as qualified to train other analysts. The Boston analytic group was more receptive to Erikson's talents, and his clinical rise there was meteoric. Prof. Henry A. Murray invited him to participate in the Harvard Psychological Clinic, and under him Erikson published some of his earliest findings on children's play constructions.

Erikson also enrolled in the Harvard graduate program in psychology, only to drop out (or be flunked out). His "failure" can be seen as a tribute to his unwillingness to compromise with what may have seemed to him to be some of the unnecessary demands of academic psychology, and in later years the famous Harvard psychologist Edwin Boring was embarrassed about how Erikson had fared in his department. One can only wonder how different the situation would be today.

Erikson's fieldwork in the Pacific Northwest helped him to grow independently. Confronted with Indian cultures even more alien to him than the

America he had had to adapt to, he did not content himself with trying to "prove" the cultural universality of Freud's propositions. Instead he found, for example, that child-rearing practices in different societies fit the demands of different cultural and socioeconomic situations. Rather than view society, as had earlier psychoanalytic thinking, in negative terms—as frustrating, inhibiting, and the source of neurosis—he stressed how individual developmental needs were abetted and encouraged by particular cultural patterns.

Geza Roheim, an early analyst who was the first of Freud's followers to do anthropological fieldwork, quickly spotted Erikson's latent conservatism. Roheim strongly objected to his weakening of Freud's critical terminology: "Some anthropologists and evidently also Erikson seem to think that whatever a 'culture' demands must be 'good' and the main thing is 'cultural synthesis.' "[5] In Erikson's behalf, however, he has also seen in psychoanalysis "a tool for the detection of that aspect of the total image of man which in a given historical period is being neglected or exploited, repressed or suppressed by the prevailing technology and ideology—including hasty 'psychoanalytic' ideologies."[6]

Erikson's fieldwork experience also seems to have increased his awareness of the necessary personal involvement of any observer. Although psychoanalysis had had its place for the term *countertransference*, to account for the analyst's own emotional reactions to his patients' material, Freud had not done very much more than point out the possibility of the analyst's neurosis interfering with the progress of patients. But countertransference was often regarded merely as a possible contamination that one should be able to master and overcome, whereas the realistic involvement of the analyst in clinical material is bound to be more elusive and cannot be summarized by any neutral-sounding terminology.

Erikson's kind of public self-scrutiny is not without its own drawbacks. The history of Freud and his concepts shows how often psychological insight can serve purposes of self-deception as well as self-exploration; and Erikson's injunction that the psychologist should make use of his own personal reactions, by disciplined self-awareness, does have its limitations, for how open can the student of society be without becoming irrelevantly autobiographical?

Erikson's own interest in the use of psychology in history, the area he has called "psycho-history," had been preceded by his involvement in developing ego psychology. In the 1920s Freud had begun to shift away from psychoanalysis's id orientation, yet this came in the last years of his life, when he took a more and more abstract view of personality, as an object to be investigated rather than as a human being to be helped. While in the hands of some of Freud's followers ego psychology became an abstract metaphysics, a language from which human emotions have almost disappeared, Erikson tried to show, first with clinical examples and then with historical studies, how the psychologist must explicitly attend to the interaction of an individual's internal and external realities.

By stressing the sense of identity as an integrating agency of the mind, Erikson was trying to show how defects in a person's organizing ability can be responsible for his loss of control over impulses. Rage, for example, can result from someone's blocked sense of mastery, and malignant regression can stem from an inability to tolerate passivity and helplessness, since sometimes it feels better to be bad than weak. If aggressivity can be seen as a defense, for example against a sense of identity diffusion, that need not of course imply that identity processes are conscious; rather, ego identity for Erikson was largely an unconscious part of the mind, founded on ideal prototypes but developing also in opposition to models of evil, what Erikson termed "negative identity."

Although like others Erikson has seen the disadvantages of Freud's hydraulic metaphors, which are apt to connote an unduly mechanistic image of mental functioning, nonetheless he retained the metaphor of quantity in his designation of the concept of ego strength. Normality, according to Erikson, should be seen in positive terms, not just in the light of the absence of symptoms. Erikson proposed to look at an individual not from the point of view of how he or she is obstructed or what is denied or cut off, but rather from the perspective of how many inconsistencies the individual is capable of unifying. Liberalism in the spirit of John Stuart Mill has long sought for an elaboration of what a fully developed person would be like, and Erikson's sketch of the various stages of the life-cycle is at least one such model of man. Perhaps as a result of his origins as a child analyst, forced to see symptoms in terms of rapidly changing patterns of growth, Erikson was more likely than other analysts to confront the difficult problem of what we could mean by psychological health. Although psychoanalysis has been more cautious in this area than one might expect from a system of thought so ready to classify the deviant and abnormal, Erikson approvingly quoted one of the pithy sayings from Freud's last years: when asked what a healthy person ought to be able to do, Freud responded, "To love and to work."

Any psychological theory is perhaps bound to sound artificial and wooden when baldly stated. If one approaches Erikson's work from the point of view of the history of psychoanalytic ideas, it is easier to see what he was getting at. For example, Freud is reported to have once dismissed an American patient on the grounds that he "had no unconscious." To Freud this was a way of saying that the patient's conflicts were so submerged and out of reach as to render him uninteresting if not "worthless." Freud could accordingly take a special relish in bizarre dream material and launch into an interpretation exclaiming, "That's a real dream!" To Freud and the early analysts what was repressed and relatively inaccessible was somehow more real than what could be dismissed as merely superficial. On behalf of the patient's future development Freud sought to free him from his past, and it was part of Freud's cosmopolitanism that he held himself back from circumscribing too closely what options might be desirable for a patient's future. Unscramble the patient's conflicts, free him of fixations, and one can, Freud held, rely on each individual to find his own best way.

Often the difficulty was that Freud's demands left too heavy a weight on patients and too light a burden on analysts. Erikson emphasized the difference between the kinds of patients analysts are apt to encounter today and the early cases Freud treated. Today's patient "suffers most under the problem of what he should believe in and who he should—or indeed, might—be or become; while the patient of early psychoanalysis suffered most under inhibitions which prevented him from being what and who he thought he was." [7] The problem for the analyst, then, may be not so much freeing people from their pasts as helping them to establish some sense of continuity with their history in the first place, so as to have a secure sense of direction. The pendulum has in fact swung so far that continuity is now seen among analytic thinkers as almost an unquestioned good thing, whereas the possible desirability of discontinuity goes almost undiscussed.

It may be that we have here one of the special sources of the appeal of Erikson's work for Americans. To the extent that we are a nation of immigrants, severed from any deeply rooted past, analytic involvement in our individual histories offers a special kind of safety, as it helps to make up for the insecurities of our collective past. One of Erikson's central messages has been the usefulness of social institutions, such as religion, which an earlier generation of analysts looked upon as a neurotic crutch. Once one begins to emphasize the prime importance of the ego's integrative capacities, then a good deal of acceptance toward society becomes in order.

At times Erikson is guilty of having gone much too far in the direction of simply legitimizing the status quo. At least certain passages of *Childhood and Society* can be seen as an effort to use psychology to buttress post-World War II American ideology. Erikson interprets American family life in tune with that era's conventional piety; he sees in the American home

> an automatic prevention of autocracy and inequality. It breeds, on the whole, undogmatic people, people ready to drive a bargain and then to compromise. It makes complete irresponsibility impossible, and it makes open hate and warfare in families rare. It also makes it quite impossible for the American adolescent to become what his brothers and sisters in other large countries become so easily, uncompromising ideologists. Nobody can be sure he is right, but everybody must

compromise—for the sake of his future chance. The analogy here to the two-party system is clear. . . . [8]

One might not have thought that a man who so early in his American experience investigated the position of American Indians would be so obtuse to the possibilities for Americans of "complete irresponsibility." But perhaps political naivete and complacency are a deeply ingrained Freudian trait; when warned of the impending rise of Hitler, Freud had blandly suggested that "the nation of Goethe could never go to the bad." And when Erikson once had an encounter with Huey Newton, whose philosophy struck him as "foreign," after hours of sympathetic exchanges Erikson asked "one last question," which seems to me to undercut any understanding of the Black Panther's viewpoint: "Huey, what do you think of the two-party system?"[9]

Many have seen in Erikson's psychology the Americanization of Freud, and ego psychology has served as an avenue for smuggling into psychoanalysis a meliorism and hopefulness that would be hard to infer from Freud's texts themselves. As one reads Erikson's account of the life cycle, there is little sense of the costs of success or of the utter wastefulness of some human suffering. If Erikson has gone in a Pollyannaish direction, he has at the same time performed the service of emancipating much contemporary thinking from Freud's artificial determinism; the artist in Erikson has been less concerned with causes and effects than with patterns and configurations.

No doubt it is Erikson's emphasis on the ego's task of synthesizing inner and outer realities that has contributed to the conformist implications of his work. The concept of identity was not, however, intended to mean that our inner selves should be molded to fit some outer social roles; on the contrary, Erikson has insisted on the essence of the ego being a state of "active tension."[10] As he once put it: "There is no feeling of being alive without a sense of ego identity."[11]

An ego's sense of wholeness may, however, be artificially maintained through the projection of unconscious negative identities on to oppressed social groups, and at least some social conflicts can be understood in terms of how a group's sense of reality demands the established inferiority of others. But Erikson's insight into the way one set of people can live as psychological parasites on others reveals his awareness of the injustice of such a pattern. Whatever one may argue about the conservative implications of some of his ideas, his heroes—Luther, Gandhi, or Freud, for instance—have hardly been straightforward conformists.

Erikson's interest has been in ideological reformers, spiritual leaders, rather than in politicians of a more mundane, compromising sort. For years he ran a faculty seminar at Harvard on the life cycle, in which each participant was supposed to present a life history. In the end he felt that there had never been a successful study of a politician at one of his seminars, which should suggest the kind of material most accessible to Erikson's kind of psychology, for his concepts work best on introspective, self-scrutinizing people, who have left behind diaries, letters, and other autobiographical material. Primary data, perhaps interviews with people who knew one's historical subject, help the historian to avoid succumbing to the practice of simply applying psychological labels as an exercise in ingenuity.

The difficulty with so much of the work that has been undertaken on the psychology of political leaders is that it is often pursued for the sake of unspoken partisan purposes. Here Freud himself led the way, for his collaborative study with William C. Bullitt on Woodrow Wilson can hardly be taken as an unbiased use of psychoanalytic tools. (But recent revisionist diplomatic historians might see Freud's antipathy to Wilson as justified and objective.)

An anecdote can illustrate some of the difficulties in political psychology. In 1952, during an interview at the White House in which Truman was trying to persuade Adlai Stevenson to run for the presidency on the Democratic ticket, the then governor of Illinois protested that he was, for the time being at least, not suitable for the job, since he had recently gone through a divorce that had been traumatic for him. Truman brushed aside Stevenson's doubts about his capacities and continued to hector his chosen successor in a manner that was in itself traumatic. After Stevenson, a shaken man, had left Truman's office, the president exhibited a kind of insensitivity not uncharacteristic of broker-politicians; he is reported to have turned to an aide and asked, "What the hell's a 'trauma' anyway?"

It would be hard to overemphasize the natural gulf between the respective orientations of the political scientist, with his typical interest in power, influence, and status, and that of the depth psychologist and his humanistic concern with the inner, psychic dimension of political and social events. The therapist's preeminent concern is with failure and the unsuccessful, which is why people pay therapists in the first place, and in particular with those nonreality factors that can become interferences in people's lives.

Despite all that has been written professionally on psychology and politics, it would be easy to overestimate what has been accomplished. If psychologists are, in the view of many political scientists, notoriously unsophisticated politically, political scientists can be no less callow about human psychology. I can remember my first job interview, over twenty years ago, with the chairperson of a distinguished political science department at a major university; when I explained my interests, I got the reply: "Oh, so you are going to write a book on Hitler." Although volumes have been written stressing the "abnormal" character of Hitler's political behavior, any psychopathological approach to Hilter might be unduly reassuring. Erikson's own treatment of Hitler resists the temptation simply to discuss Hitler with diagnostic labels and instead focuses on the disquieting aspects of intelligent and purposeful manipulation in Hitler's public image.

Once I knew of the forthcoming publication of the Freud-Bullitt book on Wilson, I began in 1965 to do background research in order to catch up on the latest Wilson literature. When I consulted one distinguished historian of American diplomacy and mentioned the Freud-Bullitt study, his eyes lit up at the prospect as he reminded me of the relationship between Mrs. Peck and Wilson while he was in the White House and how it had almost become a national scandal; a Freudian interpretation of Wilson would, to this cultured historian, necessarily center on the president's adult sex life. Another scholar, then working on Wilson's early years, informed me that it would be a mistake to think that Wilson hated his father, for Wilson really loved his father—as if those two polar opposites were alternatives instead of being psychologically compatible.

Erikson's *Gandhi's Truth* was partly designed to illustrate for historians and political scientists the power and utility of ego concepts for the understanding of someone Erikson considers an essentially religious figure. Yet Erikson is capable of seeing Gandhi in strictly political terms, as when he cites Gandhi's rejecting the offer of others to join him in a strike with the unsaintly assertion: "Fasting is *my* business." [12] Working on behalf of an oppressed people, Gandhi managed to liberate a surrendered identity; by perfecting an active mode of nonviolence, Gandhi transformed a divisive and negative identity of the passive Indian into an inclusive and militant claim for unified nationhood.

Erikson's work on Gandhi obviously also had a moral purpose, and although Freud discussed the problem of freedom only in a footnote, it is in keeping with the Freudian heritage to value liberty and independence. Erikson has therefore made much of the importance of "leeway" to ego autonomy and in his Gandhi book specifically to the "leverage of truth." [13] Erikson believes that Gandhi's philosophy is as central to our time as Luther's was to the Reformation.

In the doctrine of nonviolence Gandhi proposed to bring out the best in his opposition, which was unlike the purpose of at least some American radicals in the 1960s, who designed strikes for the sake of eliciting the violence they held to be latent in modern institutions. Yet Erikson is capable of some political savvy, as when he quotes Tom Mboya as having said that Gandhi's technique would work against the British, but not in a conflict with the Belgians. Erikson himself aimed to publicize the universality of Gandhi's ethic, the way it tried to transcend all nationhoods, what Erikson calls "pseudo-species," in order to reach the most inclusive identity possible. The Christian concept of the golden rule, implied in Erikson's admiration for Gandhi, is reflected in his notion of "mutuality," which can be seen as displacing the earlier Freudian "genitality."[14]

We may well wonder whether, by indirection, Erikson did not in the end arrive at a position similar to that of Erich Fromm, for as the latter held to the so-called naturalist position in ethics, which says that what man should be can be directly inferred from what he has been or has aimed to become, so Erikson sees Gandhi's universalistic ethic as an inevitable part of the realities of modern life. It may seem odd that two writers like Erikson and Fromm should have gone as far in the direction of ethical preaching as they have, given Freud's own professed reluctance to draw moral conclusions from his psychoanalytic work. Yet despite his commitment to science, Freud, too, had his prophetic side, which can be seen in his *Future of an Illusion* and *Civilization and Its Discontents*.

It is a tribute to the scientific side of Freud that writers can emerge from his school, using some of his characteristic techniques, to arrive at conclusions different from his own. One could scarcely imagine a figure like Gandhi less congenial to the early Freudian perspective, which might well have seen him as laboring under repressions of both a sexual and aggressive sort. But if Freud's conceptualizations have led to a greater tolerance of human diversity than he might himself have countenanced, they have also led to a wider utility from the point of view of political theory, for psychology can be used for left-wing as well as for rightist political purposes. (If asked to defend the distinction between Right and Left, I would fall back on a maxim of the great political scientist Andre Siegfried: when you meet someone who claims that the old distinctions between Right and Left no longer hold up, then you can be sure that you have met a man of the Right.) Radicals like Fanon and Marcuse, like conservatives such as Burke and Hobbes in the past, have made use of concepts of human nature in their social thought. One of the merits of psychology for political thought is that it necessarily involves at one and the same time the realm of morals as well as that of science, and this will remain an enduring part of its interest.

In his *Dimensions of a New Identity* (1974) Erikson acknowledges some of the social sources of the success of his ideas in the United States. The concept of identity crisis, for example, was welcomed "because it helped to glorify the dream of youth, with all its dangers, as a semipermanent state quite desirable on its own terms."[15] However, the origins of Erikson's interest in ego identity lay within the developing body of psychoanalytic theory. Whereas early analysts had been fascinated with the repressed and the instinctual, in the 1920s the Freudian school began to turn its attention increasingly to the mind's mechanisms of adaptation, the means by which it copes with stresses. Although in its popular usage the term ego may sound synonymous with egotism and grandiosity, in Erikson's work it is defined as that "balancing function in mental life which keeps things in perspective and in readiness for action," mediating "between outer events and inner responses, between past and future, and between the higher and lower selves."[16] Ego identity secures "a sense of being at one with oneself, as one grows and develops, and it means, at the same time, a sense of affinity with a community's sense of being at one with its future as well as its history—or mythology."[17]

Moving on from Freud's concentration on the Oedipal complex of early childhood, Erikson wanted to study later stages of the life cycle, such as middle age, and also to see how identity formation could explain the traditional role of religion. Despite the obvious advantages of getting away from the undue negativism of the earlier Freudian viewpoint, the more Erikson has written about true identity being anchored in what he calls "factuality," "reality," and "actuality," the more one suspects the latent conservatism that has been built into his model of personality growth. In this book he expresses his distaste for "moralistic fervor, puritan or radical."[18] Erikson has also offset part of the uplifting flavor of his vision of human development by his concept of "negative identity," that which "each person and each group carries within it as the sum of all that it must not be." [19] It seems to Erikson that "we, the adjusted, repress in ourselves our worst potentials, and our best, in order not to endanger our adjustment," and one of his favorite notions is that of "pseudo-speciation," the way "tribes and nations, creeds and classes, each . . . . makes like being the human race with a glorious and ceremoniously hallowed vision of itself."[20]

An outsider might see Erikson as mainly a proponent of the uses of psychology in history, yet within his own profession he has tried to use history to broaden psychoanalytic understanding. Life history stands opposed to case history, representing an effort to focus on how a life hangs together rather than breaks apart. Erikson emphasized how "the whole ecology of greatness . . .transcends many of the assumptions which clinical work has suggested regarding the inner economy of a person."[21] On clinical as well as historical grounds Erikson describes how Thomas Jefferson "managed to keep together and to maintain a significant function in the lives of others," as well as how he became "prototypical for his time" in fulfilling "specific needs in the lives of those who followed him."[22]

Erikson tries to see how Jefferson's most notable neurotic symptom, migraine headaches that could be incapacitating for weeks at a time, fits in with the rest of his character in the light of the specific psychosocial con-

flicts of eighteenth-century America. But Erikson ignores the extent to
which the founding fathers necessarily relied on colonial experience, and
understates the darker side of their beliefs and actions, in order to highlight
their commitment to unlimited progress. The psychological fascination of
the American dream becomes that of "newness forever renewed," a limit-
less future; for Erikson the American world image was that of a self-made
man, "dedicated to natural labor . . . guaranteeing a reciprocation of
rights." [23]

If one reads *Dimensions of a New Identity* for the light it casts on the
historical Jefferson one is bound to be disappointed. But if one understands
Erikson's book as an ethical treatise, despite his professed dislike of moralistic fervor, what he is driving at becomes clear, for he finds in Jefferson
a valuable devotion to "the right to live in a community which chooses to
guarantee, because it knows it lives by, the fullest development of each of
its members." [24] Erikson stresses the significance of Jefferson's interest in
Jesus and especially the Sermon on the Mount. The clinical concept of
adulthood becomes Erikson's answer to the quest for "what it might mean
to be a human being," and therefore to Erikson Jefferson stands as "a man
of rare adult stature, caring intensely and competent to take care of what he
undertook—publicly and privately." [25]

Erikson insists on the necessity of America's now coming "to grips with
its own awareness of historical guilt, over having transgressed against humanity and nature." [26] Although Erikson sees that "the technologically advanced modern nations have shown themselves willing to fight world wars
and indulge in mass annihilation," he is optimistic enough to perceive in
mankind a "painfully slow progress toward unity." [27] Distinguishing himself
from "our loudest moralists," Erikson nevertheless speaks about "our slow
and zigzagging road towards the realization of specieshood for which the
creation of an American identity may well be one significant model." [28]

Clinically Erikson has stressed the key significance of the individual's
attaining inner liberation, that freedom with which one might attain the
"capacity to make informed choices." [29] Therefore to Erikson inner emancipation requires more than the promise of political and economic equality,
though it is unattainable without it. He finds confirmation of his own clinical position in Jefferson's ideals, holding that mankind possesses "a moral
core that, if given leeway to manifest itself in mutual activation with others
will tend to make ethical and rational choices. . . ." And this remains, for
Erikson, "a basic developmental truth." [30]

Erikson remains, I think, the most eminent contemporary proponent of
ego psychology. In the course of my interviews for research on Freud in the
1960s I sometimes had the feeling that a central reason for Freud being

considered significant among social scientists was that Erikson has cited him so much. Literary critics, from W. H. Auden on down, have responded favorably to Erikson's writings. Even though Erikson has grown beyond Freud's own conclusions, he has done so with enough tact and discretion so that he remains a part of what he has called "the Freudian establishment."[31]

Although Erikson has shifted the focus of his attention away from the earlier stages of life, his ethical orientation toward childhood has appealed to America's child-centered culture and its wariness of any potential prospects for the victimization of children. One of Erikson's most famous concepts is that of the identity crisis of late adolescence; while earlier psychoanalytic writers had mainly contrasted childhood with adulthood, Erikson has tried to spell out numerous intervening phases. His tendency to idealize the conflicts of youth has found a receptive audience in a society that sometimes seems willing to extend tolerance toward adolescent problems well into middle age. Erikson has revived the ancient conception of a life cycle characterized by stages. Aristotle proposed three phases, and in the Middle Ages the individual life was divided into four to ten stages. Erikson has not only ignored his predecessors, but used his notion of a life cycle to fit American optimism and meliorism, for despite his repeated reliance on the alarming word *crisis*, in the end he has sought to reassure and support, rather than challenge, preexisting social expectations.

The uncertainties of an individualistic country have helped encourage conformism, as Alexis de Tocqueville and others have long pointed out; a society relatively lacking in hierarchy and without fixed standards of status is bound to make each individual more dependent on the approval of the group. Erikson's ideas have, I believe, fed largely conservative social aspirations. In the case of contemporary psychiatry, to take only one example, practitioners are often employed by social institutions (governmental agencies, for example, the Peace Corps, and industry and colleges) as well as by individuals, and they who pay the piper get to call the tune. Middle-class mores have come to overwhelm whatever features of social deviancy might have been present in early Freudian practices.

Notable ethical positions are often taken by means of clinical concepts without sufficient awareness that the same concepts might justify very different moral outcomes. The law has been affected as well. In a famous case, *Painter* v. *Bannister*, a biological father originally lost a custody suit against his son's maternal grandparents because they had cared for the boy for two and a half years after his mother's accidental death. The home of the grandparents was said by the court to be "stable, dependable, conventional, middle-class, midwest," while that of the father was characterized as "unstable, unconventional, arty Bohemian, and probably intellectually stimulating."[32] The court relied on the warnings from "an eminent child psychologist,"[33] as it lent support to the concept of psychological parenthood. The key value of continuity, one of Erikson's central points, has become almost a dogma of psychological contributions to family law.

Among social scientists, historians have been especially receptive to new theories of motivation and have in particular responded to Erikson's special blend of psychoanalysis and history. When I participated over twenty years ago as a faculty member in Erikson's graduate seminar at Harvard, approximately half of the class listed their professional identification as historian. Psychohistory, despite its controversial status and the many methodological criticisms, has become so widely accepted in the United States that it is no longer considered necessary to hyphenate the word. Perhaps because of its still unsettled academic status, practitioners of psychohistory have defensively been too uncritical of psychoanalytic propositions. Freud and his early followers talked about the "application" of psychoanalysis to society, and even Erikson has written about the "application of psychoanalysis to politics."[34] But it seems to me that the metaphor is fundamentally faulty, as it credulously presupposes the existence of revealed psychological knowledge. In fact, psychology and history ought to make up a two-way street, and each discipline has much to learn from the other.

One of the appeals of psychohistory in the United States is the illusion that a finished technique is available to solve innumerable quandries. When most of Freud's American students came for their training he was in his last, dying phase, and it was then that he grew most grandiose about the neutrality of his so-called science. Freud also inaugurated the beginnings of ego psychology around that time, although still in an abstract rather than a clinical way. A thinker like Heinz Hartmann was true to Freud's final metaphysical intentions, while Erikson's interest in biographies is more in tune with the spirit of Freud's earlier empiricism in his case histories. In two of Erikson's studies he concentrated on the significance of techniques, that of prayer to Luther and nonviolence to Gandhi, on the model of Freud's own interest in the method of free associations.

In order to preserve his continuities with Freudian theory, Erikson has often mythologized the master, yet as an interpreter of myth Erikson can be most subtle. Unfortunately, too often people still respond to Erikson's sort of psychology in an all-or-nothing frame of mind. Erikson's example, however, like that of Freud himself, should remind us how original great psychologists strive to be; at their best both men have insisted how little we still know about the human psyche and that it is necessary for us to rely on our own experience. The motto "every man his own historian" might prepare the professional way for a similiarly independent approach—every man his own psychologist.

One of the legendary attributes of American society is its openness to diversity of opinion. Lest ego psychology be seen only as the Americanization of Freud, it is worth highlighting the extent to which Erikson has constructively helped to liberate us from the constraints of early psychoanalytic thought. Ego psychology has been a way of wriggling out of some of the dogmatism of "orthodox" psychoanalysis. In the broadest terms of intellectual history it is awkward to justify an interest in ego psychology, for earlier writers such as Jung, Adler, and Rank eloquently expressed many of the same ideas that contemporaries think of as new discoveries. But psychiatry is not a historically conscious field, and it takes considerable effort to become knowledgeable about these earlier figures in depth psychology. Yet appreciating ego psychology need not entail a lack of awareness of some of the limitations to revisionist psychoanalysis or an underestimation of Freud's own momentous contributions.

Freud was intellectually bold and unconventional, and he founded a movement at odds with the official psychiatry of his day. He was a reductionist in quest of our worst selves, and with his version of the concept of the unconscious he threw down a challenge to many assumptions about human rationality and Western values. Ego psychology, at least in the hands of Erikson, has been designed to correct some of the imbalances in Freud's thought and, in particular, Freud's negativism. Erikson does not believe that it is possible to assume, as Freud did, the presence of civilized elements in people, nor does Erikson think analysts can continue systematically to evade the problem of moral values.

Freud initially proposed that frustration of erotic life lies behind neurotic illness, and he saw this frustration as stemming from social impediments as well as from inner inflexibilities. Yet however broadly Freud conceived of sexuality, with hindsight it is easy to see that frustration cannot be defined apart from a given social and moral context, for what is considered illegitimate in one class or era will be deemed satisfying elsewhere. With all his philosophical skepticism Freud proceeded as if absolute norms could be universally agreed upon. This is a key issue, since he treated illness as a surrogate satisfaction.

In focusing on society as a source of support for the integrative functions of the ego, Erikson has tried to examine self-healing as well as self-deception. He wants to understand ego strength, what holds a person together despite conflicts, rather than concentrate on motivation manifested in stressful circumstances. (It is a part of Freud's impact on our thought that although my dictionary still does not sanction its use as a word, *conflicted* has become accepted within everyday vocabulary.) What an earlier generation of analysts might have interpreted as an illustration of pure instinctuality, whether aggressive or sexual, Erikson is likely to see as a reaction released by an impaired ego.

Many of Freud's initial, and most well-known, propositions are now clearly untenable, and ego psychology offers an alternative approach. For example, few would any longer endorse the concept of symptomatology as an expression of repressed sexuality, nor is a trauma still supposed to underlie every neurosis. In addition, the exclusively retrospective orientation, which Erikson has criticized under the heading of the fallacy of "originology," seems no longer viable. Erikson has insisted on the significance of an orientation toward the future; it is, for instance, in accord with such an outlook that blocked mastery, rather than a primal death instinct, can help account for rage.

One of the sources of the immense popularity of Erikson's ideas in the 1960s was his concern for developing an ego psychology that would bridge the gap between private and public, the individual and the social. His leadership studies and in particular his interest in explaining success rather than failure also fit some characteristically American needs, for in his fascination with greatness, originally justified in accounting for ego strength, Erikson has not been aware enough of the dangers of what sounds like an ethics of success. It would be in keeping with American pragmatism to hold, as Erikson so often does, that ethical choices can be resolved by models of personality development.

Trying to understand Erikson and his impact in the context of his times should not be misunderstood as an effort to detract from his achievement. He has succeeded in widening the scope of the influence of the clinical perspective in social science. But Erikson's own stature as an exceptionally gifted psychologist does not contradict the notion that earlier thinkers in psychoanalysis have been unduly ignored. For example, it is interesting to conjecture why Jung, who on so many subjects was more prescient than Freud, has had relatively little influence, at least on the United States. We have detailed histories of the introduction of Freud's ideas into the United States, while the bare outline of the story of Jung's American followers remains untold.

The vagaries of the history of depth psychology reveal some characteristic professional differences. As a group, psychoanalysts are more conformist than most; papers get presented and then applauded, and cited, by colleagues. The absence of normal critical challenges has meant that whereas academics regularly expect criticism, public controversies in psychoanalysis have usually meant subsequent blacklisting. Jung has received the silent treatment from "orthodox" analysts, which helps explain how someone of Erikson's temperament has feared excommunication. But it is partly because of all the idealizations of Freud that any attempts at objectivity about the early analysts appear to be shallow debunking.

Erikson's unwillingness to move too fast in inaugurating changes in psychoanalysis has been of a piece with a conformist cast to his psychosocial perspective as a whole. In shifting from a more traditional concern with the defensive ego to problems of growth and adaptation he has looked for the collective supports of ego development. He has pointed to the need for a sense of identity confirmed by social institutions and has stressed the positive role that organized religion and ritual can play. But there are those who have wondered whether the upshot of ego psychology must not be inherently conservative. Erich Fromm and Michael Maccoby, for example, have seen some of the ambiguities in Erikson's use of the concept of identity, as they warn of the consequences of evading questions of "whether or not a society stimulates or cripples the development of the individual self and whether it offers a pseudo identity in place of the original self."[35] Erikson has talked about the "genius of culture"[36] in the vein of a conservative thinker like Edmund Burke.

Erikson's system gives undue weight to conformist values. He has rightly pointed out the neglect of the role of work in earlier Freudian thinking. Yet even here it is telling of his therapeutic point of view how he looks at work individualistically and not socially; the spirit in which work gets done may matter little if its social purpose is questionable. In the end it may turn out to be an advantage not to have a secure sense of self; Erikson's own peripheral standing in a variety of fields has been a source of much of his own creativity. But alienation rarely gets praised by Erikson. Instead we find him failing to distinguish between genuine and artificial continuities, in keeping with his tolerance for myth and legend. In his own autobiographical reflections it would seem that he has thought it possible to recreate artistically his past life.

Erikson's own identity conflicts have been tied up with his attitudes toward the United States. In idealizing the United States, Erikson has assigned to this one country the creation of a new and broader identity. Erikson sees the United States as endorsing the ideal of the self-made man, and the struggle for a universally inclusive identity, in conflict with negative identities, is for him the main ethical contest in our world. (To the extent people achieve artificial wholeness by projecting their negative identities onto racial and colonial aliens Erikson's concepts can lead in a socially critical direction.)

The publication in 1967 of the Freud-Bullitt study of Woodrow Wilson was, in addition to being an attack on one of the creators of the modern

American presidency, a blow to Erikson's picture of the founder of psycho-analysis. At first Erikson did his best to dissociate Freud from his responsibility for collaborating on a polemical attack on Wilson. (Subsequently it became the official policy of the *Journal of the American Psychoanalytic Association* not to discuss this book.) Yet when Erikson reprinted his essay in 1975, he was willing to see more of Freud's hand in the Wilson book. He did not, however, alert readers to his changing ground.

Erikson's heroes have been ideological innovators like Wilson. The problem has been that Erikson has taken one-sided views of his biographical subjects. With Luther, Erikson's concentration on the young man isolates the ethical preacher from the career of an active political leader with mixed results for human betterment, and Erikson sees in Gandhi a reconciler of religious and political propensities. In each case Erikson sanctifies a hero, leaving the impression of advocating bold change while largely ignoring the reactionary political implications of the life under scrutiny.

Perhaps George Orwell's down-to-earthness can bring us up short about Erikson's kind of idealizing. Orwell began an essay on Gandhi by asserting that "saints should always be judged guilty until they are proved innocent . . ."[37] and maintains that the British handled Gandhi gently because they felt he was useful. Orwell reminds us that according to Louis Fischer, Gandhi thought the German Jews ought to have committed mass suicide in order to arouse the world to Hitler's true nature, a disturbing aspect to the history and implications of Gandhi's doctrine of nonviolence that Erikson ignores. (Arthur Koestler had a somewhat more complicated, but still distressing, version of Gandhi's attitude toward the Jews and Hitler, but Koestler added a further point that Erikson ignores: after the fall of France Gandhi praised General Pétain for having had the courage to surrender, and Gandhi thought the English should follow France's example.)

One concrete political issue, the American war in Southeast Asia, can serve to test Erikson's political convictions. No other recent event has had as momentous an impact on American life. Erikson remained publicly silent and aloof from the antiwar movement. As late as 1975 in a reprinted essay Erikson allowed himself to refer to difficulties with only "what seemed to be a senseless war."[38] In *Toys and Reasons* (1977) Erikson commented on "the fake reality of a colonial war which relied all the more on technological means of overkill as it became desperately unsure of itself."[39] But somehow Erikson perceived a similarity between Vietnam and what he called "the home-town spectacle of Watergate." Erikson referred approvingly to Seymour Hersh's 1970 account of My Lai, but one wonders how it can not have long been evident to Erikson that the American involvement in Southeast Asia was a moral disaster. Erikson's naivete can be illustrated by his repeated attempts to explain the American two-party system. His apoliticism comes out when he tells us: "Having retired from Harvard, I could on occasion even manage to peruse the Sunday papers."[40]

Erikson's concepts have always specified respect for the inner dimension of experience. But the "sense" of identity can be different from genuine identity, and illusory feelings do not equal social reality. On the other hand, Freud's own kind of hostility to illusions does not by itself guarantee that psychology will not be used complacently to justify the status quo. Freud, however, had a tragic dimension, while Erikson still believes that "human evolution has a built-in tendency—spasmodically interrupted by periods of reactionary exclusion—to create wider identities toward an all-human consciousness."[41] Along with what Erikson sees as ethical progress he detects a long-term increase in human self-awareness.

Not only is history moving in a progressive direction, according to Erikson, but each step in the life cycle has a tendency toward self-overcoming. Americans have wanted to believe that neurosis is curable and unhappiness unnecessary. Erikson's conception of growth in terms of the achievement of integration, not alienation, has fit the New World tendency to identify the healthy with the statistically average. One of the lessons of Freud is that we accept eccentricity as normal.

In getting away from Freud's pessimism, which can be damaging therapeutically, Erikson may have lost at least one valuable feature of the Freudian heritage. Erikson does not see tragedy as an ultimate conflict between mutually contradictory but equally valid norms. Rather, tragedy for him results from developmental lag. But the essence of some emotional conflicts is that they lead to no "healthy" outcome but constitute a full-scale waste of human feelings and impulses. It is difficult to see how Erikson's terminology can readily be used to suggest that people might ever have been capable of better things. He may have appealed too often to the possibilities of growth and integrity, instead of looking for signs of individual social injuries. But an earlier generation of analysts dismissed the social level as superficial and unsuitable for an analyst's inspection.

Throughout psychoanalytic thinking, and here Erikson is at one with Fromm and other revisionists, evaluative and descriptive statements are intermixed. It is a merit of this sort of psychology that its implications are not confined to abstract science. Yet confusing "ought" and "is" statements can lead to two different and undesirable consequences. On the one hand, it is possible out of utopianism to blind oneself to the practical means of implementing ethical commitments; desiring something in the future may mean little about the likelihood of its ever coming to pass. On the other hand, there is the danger of conservatism—throwing a mantle of morality over the preexisting world and endorsing everything that already "is" with an ethical sanction. Erikson's message communicates too much of what we want to hear.[42] His hopefulness is too often allied to social conservatism. He does not, for instance, confront the possibility that there may be few social groups worth being "integrated" with. It is, however, too easy to overlook how conservative a tradition Erikson has been working within. (Incidentally, Jung's politics were even more reactionary than Freud's.) I am reminded of a comment by one of the few black psychoanalysts: "In college and in medical training I had to learn how to talk white, and in becoming an analyst I had to learn how to talk Jewish." Evidently, throughout his own analysis with a Viennese follower of Freud it was always emphasized that the realities of race did not count but what mattered was how a black handles the given external situation.

One does not have to share all Erikson's values in order to appreciate the gentleness of spirit conveyed by his concepts. Furthermore, he is one of the few analysts to have ensured the vitality of the Freudian tradition. It might have reassured the scientist in Freud that his methods have led others to conclusions that he personally might never have been able to accept. Erikson has participated in the reversal of the old overconcentration on the role of fathers in personality development, yet despite the current concern with mothering we still know little about what is biologically required. Erikson's own skepticisim about clinical data is helpful, as is his willingness to bridge conventional academic barriers. There is now, for example, a regrettable gulf between my own field of political science and history. But one of the uses of psychoanalytic psychology is that it is a theory with which many professions have been acquainted and therefore it can help overcome some of the obstacles to interdisciplinary cooperation.

Notes

1. Erik H. Erikson, "Autobiographical Notes on the Identity Crisis," *Daedalus* 99, no. 4 (Fall 1970), p. 740.
2. Ibid.
3. Erik Homburger, "Review of Anna Freud's *Psychoanalysis for Teachers and Parents*," *Psychoanalytic Quarterly*, 5 (1936), pp. 292–93.
4. Erik H. Erikson, "Play and Actuality," in *Play and Development*, ed. Maria W. Piers (New York: Norton, 1972), pp. 138–39.
5. Quoted in Paul Robinson, *The Freudian Left* (New York: Harper & Row, 1969), pp. 144–45.
6. Erik H. Erikson, *Insight and Responsibility* (New York: Norton, 1964), p. 43.
7. Erik H. Erikson, *Childhood and Society*, 2d ed. (New York: Norton, 1963), p. 279.
8. Ibid., p. 318.
9. Erik H. Erikson and Huey P. Newton, *In Search of Common Ground: Conversations* (New York: Norton, 1973), p. 44, p. 142.
10. Erikson, *Insight and Responsibility*, p. 87.

11. Erik H. Erikson, *Childhood and Society*, 1st ed. (New York: Norton, 1950), p. 212.
12. Erik H. Erikson, *Life History and the Historical Moment* (New York: Norton, 1975), p. 151.
13. Erik H. Erikson, *Gandhi's Truth* (New York: Norton, 1969), p. 413.
14. Paul Roazen, *Erik H. Erikson: The Power and Limits of a Vision* (New York: Free Press, 1976), p. 157.
15. Erik H. Erikson, *Dimensions of a New Identity* (New York: Norton, 1974), p. 115.
16. Ibid., p. 92.
17. Ibid., pp. 27–28.
18. Ibid., p. 114.
19. Ibid., p. 36.
20. Ibid., p. 110, p. 97.
21. Ibid., p. 55.
22. Ibid., p. 13, p. 14.
23. Ibid., p. 79, pp. 76–77.
24. Ibid., p. 74.
25. Ibid., p. 81, p. 59.
26. Ibid., p. 111.
27. Ibid., p. 97.
28. Ibid., p. 108, p. 98.
29. Ibid., p. 108–109.
30. Ibid., p. 96.
31. Quoted in Roazen, *Erik H. Erikson*, p. 59.
32. Quoted in Joseph Goldstein, Anna Freud, and Albert Solnit, *Beyond the Best Interests of the Child* (New York: Free Press, 1973), p. 124.
33. Ibid.
34. Erik H. Erikson, *Toys and Reasons: Stages in the Ritualization of Experience* (New York: Norton, 1977), p. 172.
35. Erich Fromm and Michael Maccoby, *Social Character in a Mexican Village: A Socio-psychoanalytic Study* (Englewood Cliffs, N.J.: Prentice Hall, 1970), p. 20.
36. Roazen, *Erik H. Erikson*, pp. 45–46.
37. *George Orwell: The Collected Essays, Journals, and Letters*, vol. 4, ed. Sonia Orwell and Ian Angus (London: Penguin, 1970), p. 523.
38. Quoted in Roazen, *Erik H. Erikson, p. 49*.
39. Erikson, *Toys and Reasons*, p. 117, p. 179.
40. Ibid., p. 19.
41. Ibid., p. 148.
42. I am indebted here to lectures given many years ago at Harvard by Prof. Louis Hartz. Cf. Paul Roazen, "Louis Hartz's Teaching." *Virginia Quarterly Review,* Vol. 64, No. 1 (Winter 1988), pp. 108–25.

9

Biography

The subject of psychoanalytic biography ought to sound alarm bells in the minds of fair-minded observers. So much tendentious stuff has appeared throughout this century, under the banner of "applying" either Freud's ideas or the concepts of some of his disciples, that neutral witnesses with a concern for impartial history are entitled to be wary of what looks like zealots proselytizing in behalf of their beliefs. But if we start by asking the question of whether psychoanalytic biography still exists and, if so, whether it deserves to continue or thrive, I am hoping that the topic will hold the attention even of those most likely to scoff.

Curiously enough, Freud's most ardent so-called defenders are apt not to want to think of his own biographical studies. It is one of the few subjects on which orthodox analysts might be relieved not to have to begin with Freud. Yet I think that his studies of Leonardo and also Moses, and even his book with William C. Bullitt on Woodrow Wilson, need not cause nearly as much embarrassment as has been thought; although Freud's few comments on biography writing occasionally get quoted, his own biographical efforts rarely appear in the professional literature. If one approaches Freud not in search of infallibility but as a model of originality and daring, then his biographies begin to look as considerable as anything else he did. The Leonardo book, for example, has many things wrong with it that any beginning student ought now to be able to point out. But it remains a remarkable work of art that will nonetheless endure in intellectual history. Almost half a century later Erik H. Erikson's *Young Man Luther* had its own flaws, yet I think we would be lucky to have more such creative achievements.

The problem arises when psychoanalysis gets treated as a science, embodying a technique that supposedly can enable even the clumsiest to come up with insights. There is an illusion of omnipotence that evidently is encountered regularly in the training of psychoanalytic candidates. It is true that at the turn of the century, when, for example, members of the Vienna Psychoanalytic Society presented some of the first Freudian biographical studies, some astonishing assaults on common sense were perpetrated. The early members of the psychoanalytic movement, following Freud's lead, did aim to shake Western culture. They were nonconformists at odds with their own society, and they dredged up points that contravened traditional moral precepts, and they could do all this in the name of science without anywhere near enough appropriate evidence.

These initial efforts at psychoanalytic biography should discomfort merely true believers, who cannot tolerate past errors either in Freud or his early followers. Religious fanaticism can take the form of flattening out a sect's history, so that only what now seems defensible can be discerned in the cause's first struggles. In retrospect the first analysts did search too much for signs that might give away the existence of sexual secrets; they looked to history to find illustrative proof for Freud's concepts, such as the Oedipus complex, and they did transgress normal canons of what counts as good historical research.

Historically minded tolerance of the beginnings of psychoanalysis is in order. Such understanding does not entail that we remain unaware of the kind of mistakes that even Freud was capable of making. According to one reliable-sounding story, he once pointed to the complete collected works of Goethe and said, "All this was used by him as a means of self-concealment." [1] Presumably Freud at the moment he made that remark was in a bold frame of mind. It does not mean that Freud ignored Goethe either as a thinker or a poet. Nor does it imply that we have to overlook early psychoanalysis's own blind spots and Freud's characteristic self-deceptions.

Jones's biography of Freud, which taught us so much about the drama and struggles of the creator of psychoanalysis, did nothing to alert its readers to where Freud was apt to go wrong. Bruno Bettelheim was I believe the first to point out, in reviews of Jones that are now forgotten, that Freud's leading British disciple had failed to write an adequately psychoanalytic biography. Bettelheim had in mind that Jones had so adopted Freud's own view of things that there was not enough critical distance.

Freud's powers as a great writer make it hard for any reader to see where he might have erred. But throughout Freud's lifetime there were respectful critics of his who were willing to point out his biases. Jones temporarily succeeded in drowning out with documentary evidence any other point of view but that of Freud himself. Erich Fromm was brave enough, at the time of the first appearance of the Jones biography, to try to counteract the effects of Jones's work. Now, over thirty years later, abundant material has accumulated that successfully challenges Jones. Nonetheless, naive literary critics, as well as journalists, can still proceed as if orthodox psychoanalytic historiography were scriptural.

It is far too easy to be partisan with psychoanalytic ideas in hand, and any allegedly scientific claim to neutrality should by itself be enough to warn us about the dangers of misusing psychoanalytic concepts. To cite one example that seems notorious to me, a biographical study by a trained analyst on Alger Hiss and Whittaker Chambers appeared in 1967: Meyer Zeligs's *Friendship and Fratricide*. Hiss cooperated with this project while Chambers did not. The book is psychoanalytic from beginning to end and at the same time completely hopeless. Material about Chambers gets wildly overinterpreted, diagnostic name-calling against Chambers is frequent, and Chambers's achievements and human contacts are downplayed. Hiss is allowed to emerge as a kind of saint. It should be said that Hiss has never admitted any guilt, and there are backers of his who still swear by his innocence. Either Chambers or Hiss had to be lying in that celebrated case in the history of modern American politics, and therefore a psychological investigation does seem warranted.

The problem with Zelig's work was that he directed all his psychoanalytic fire at only one of the actors in the story. Even if Chambers were the guilty party, and the weight of the historical evidence would indicate that it is not so, more attention should have been paid to exactly how Hiss might have managed to walk into Chamber's accusatory world. But this supposedly dispassionate psychoanalytic study did not investigate Hiss with anywhere near the same kind of energy as that afforded to Chambers. Even Hiss's divorce from his wife was treated in an ethereal, unrealistic manner.

Every educated person by now has come across examples of the abuse of psychoanalytic insights in the realm of biography; biography writing itself is one of the chief means by which history gets successfully transmitted from one generation to another. Reading about other people's lives remains so fascinating that despite the fact that there are other means of communicating historical knowledge, biographies remain enduringly attractive. In understanding any life history there are bound to be gaps in material or contradictions that seem to crave psychological interpretations. It hardly requires an experienced clinician to spot areas in a life—early childhood, intimate adult relationships (or their paucity), to take some obvious examples—that benefit from a psychoanalytic perspective.

Popular biographies have in fact absorbed this point, and if one were to make a conscientious study of major biographical efforts that either were widely hailed critically or successful on a commercial level, abundant illustrations would appear of the impact of the Freudian revolution in ideas. Leon Edel wrote a multivolume biography of Henry James that, whatever its shortcomings may turn out to be, everyone agrees is a classic in its use of psychoanalytic insights. Eileen Ward's study of Keats would be another good example of a balanced literary study that has used psychoanalytic ideas with notable advantage. Joseph Frank's magnificent biography of

Dostoevsky, while it points out where Freud went wrong or psychoanalysis can be irrelevant and misleading, is clearly written with Freud's system of ideas as a background framework. If the psychoanalytic influence on biography can need to be checked, it is because exaggerated expectations lead to magical forms of thinking, which ultimately cause the bitterest disappointments.

In connection with the aliveness of psychoanalytic biography I am also thinking of work that takes place on an even more popular level. To take just some examples from American history: the affair Thomas Jefferson seems to have had with his house slave, Sally Hemmings, has become at least a part of the past, even if it is still being contested, and Franklin Roosevelt's involvement with Lucy Mercer not only became pivotal in the tale of Joseph Lash's *Eleanor and Franklin*, but went on to be a central theme of a television documentary series. (It is in keeping with this trend that the news of Mrs. Roosevelt's friendship with Lorena Hickock should have set off so much prurient sensationalism.) An examination of texts of a strictly academic nature would confirm the generalization that Freud has transformed the biographical conception of man.

The public now craves personal knowledge about historical figures and indeed in connection with all public actors, in a way that is so fully congruent with some psychoanalytic ideas that Freud is apt to take too much of the blame for the state of contemporary culture. For example, feminists are incorrect when they reprove Freud for the oppression of women, if only because he created a profession in which women advanced as far as they did anywhere in twentieth-century culture, and educators are wrong to see in Freud, who was himself an old-fashioned defender of schools as a bulwark of civilization, a primary source for the decline of civilized standards of authority. Rather than thinking that one man alone succeeded in changing history, it makes more sense to think in terms of common forces at work in Western culture that also help account for the success of at least some aspects of Freud's ideas.

Privacy now gets used in a manipulative way, and this state of intimacy is a political and social reality of contemporary life. Freud himself used his disguised autobiography, for example, in his *Interpretation of Dreams* and *Psychopathology of Everyday Life*, to establish his principles. By daring to treat dreams and symptoms as meaningful, Freud had marked the end of an era that considered such material legitimately personal and outside the bounds of historical inquiry. Although Freud worked in behalf of autonomy, the implications of his ideas may have helped undermine certain features of the ideal of individualism.

The high tide of the psychoanalytic influence on biography writing has had some unfortunate results. I am thinking here of some of the unexpected consequences of treating the biographer as a "participant" observer, to use Harry Stack Sullivan's terminology. Erikson once proposed as one cardinal rule of the psychohistorian that he state the nature of his involvement with his subject matter. But that meant, in the case of Erikson's own *Gandhi's Truth*, that a hundred pages went by in the text before Gandhi got born, and at the same time Erikson, with all his apparent openness, had evaded the issue of why that aristocratic family he stayed with in India was so receptive to psychoanalytic interpretations about Gandhi. Bettelheim has also, in his famous concentration camp accounts, failed to tell us on what grounds he was imprisoned and how he managed to be released; these omissions are all the more striking in that it is the personal nature of Bettelheim's story that has made it so persuasive that it has been hard to see around his own version of things.

The biographer's involvement in his subject matter can be so intrusive that there are times when one longs for the old-line omniscient narrator. One eminent American historian in the midst of a book felt it appropriate to announce his own homosexual nature; at least some reviewers pounced on that self-disclosure at the expense of the topic being written about. There ought to be some way of setting a limit to the extent of autobiographical information in the course of any biographical inquiry.

If psychoanalysis has helped sensitize biographers to areas that previously were apt to escape scrutiny, normal academic standards ought to be invoked as a check on the excesses involved in undertaking biographical research that is informed by psychoanalytic thought. This is a point that gets lost on clinicians who look on biography as an area in which the latest psychoanalytic thinking can be "applied." Unfortunately, some professional historians are themselves as capable of writing propagandistically in behalf of Freud as others remain highly skeptical of the entire subject of psychohistory.

The whole notion of "applied psychoanalysis," which was advanced by the early analysts, was misleading. For psychoanalysis to be capable of being applied to any of the social sciences carried the implication that it was somehow a finished or completed body of knowledge. In fact, as I trust liberal, freethinking analysts will agree, psychoanalysis is an art as well as a science and necessarily a fragile tool for carrying forward understanding. As Freud himself chose to emphasize at what turned out to be his last public lecture (in 1922), his system of thought was designed to explain how little we know, not how much. The concept of the unconscious ought not to be wielded arrogantly but should lead to genuine humility and caution.

Research does get undertaken by the bold, and Freud was himself at other moments hardly timid about the implications of what he chose to consider his "findings." Therefore it behooves social scientists to stand their ground, and talk back to their psychoanalytic colleagues; neither historians nor political scientists, for example, need to fear being open about what they consider unwarranted speculations in psychoanalytic hands.

Here I am perhaps being utopian, but I do believe it to be true that there has been nowhere near enough toleration of controversy within psychoanalysis, and if social scientists could challenge psychoanalytic ideas even as they were being influenced by them, the state of psychoanalysis itself would benefit. Although the history of psychoanalysis has been marked by a series of controversies, these struggles have not led to the kind of toleration of normal disagreement that one comes to expect in university life. The famous quarrels have been facilitated and made possible by an inadequate level of accepted everyday differences of opinion. The result is that one tends to get separate schools of psychoanalytic thought, each proceeding too independently of the other, with relatively little cross-fertilization of knowledge.

For the early analysts their profession was a calling, and this remains one of the enduringly endearing features of their lives, which has attracted so much biographical attention to them. They were not pursuing everyday careers, but mixed in with their professional commitments went a quasi-religious search for meaning, if not salvation. Melanie Klein's contention, for example, that all children ought to be analyzed may now seem quaint, but plenty of children of early analysts were sent for treatment almost as a matter of course. Even if some of the ideas of the early analysts were dotty, as people they were remarkably intriguing, and it is hard not to think that in the course of psychoanalysis becoming successfully bureaucratized it lost some of its challenge.

It is in the idealistic spirit of early analysis that I would like to return to a suggestion once put forward by Lawrence Kubie about how broadly based our psychoanalytic institutes might become. Some of us might well insist that there be an end to the difficulties in the path of lay analysis. But I am bringing up Kubie's proposal about how cultural matters should be intertwined with the communicating of psychoanalytic teachings for the sake of giving a historical underlining to how unsatisfactory a situation we find ourselves in today, for I can think of no training facilities where secure bridges have been built between psychoanalysis and social science. Psychoanalytic biography remains a subject that must be self-taught. For those of us with a professional commitment as educators it is impossible to think that things could not easily be bettered.

Psychoanalytic biography is a topic that illustrates how social science as a whole ought to be able to contribute to the development of psychoanalytic thinking. The relationship between psychoanalysis and social science should be reciprocal; psychoanalysis has something important to gain from the contact with social science. This is an aspect of the history of psychoanalysis that has not received an adequate amount of attention: the several efforts that have been made to bring psychoanalysis out of its professional isolation and into contact with academic institutions.

The problem of normality and the whole issue of the concept of maturity can be addressed in connection with psychoanalytic biography. Although Freud was ready to call feelings, acts, and even classes of people by the designations associated with the notion of neurosis, he was cautious about describing what health might consist in. Normality is one of those ideas that can be discussed endlessly, not because it is an unreal question but precisely on the grounds that psychological health remains such a challenging idea. When one thinks of what it might mean to treat patients in the context of a social environment of varying degrees of cruelty or social injustice, the significance of having some broad view of normality—as opposed to proposing a conformist adaptation to whatever the status quo might be—should be apparent.

Biographers are at their best when they are most tolerant of human diversity. This means that retrospective diagnoses, for example, should be used to promote genuine understanding rather than to stigmatize those political or social figures whom we might disapprove of. Hitler, for example, attracted the attention of a psychoanalytic study by Walter Langer during World War II; this report, commissioned at the highest levels of the American government, did actually predict that when the war came close to being lost Hitler could be expected to commit suicide. Unfortunately, the study seems to have assumed that someone as morally perverted as Hitler must have been sexually deranged as well. All the rumored oddities in Hitler's sexual tastes, which Freud is said to have thoroughly believed in himself, found their way into print. But when someone in official Washington, D.C., at the time suggested that a similar inquiry into Stalin should be undertaken, the idea was squashed on the grounds that Stalin was, after all, an ally. An approach that is suitable for enemies but not friends does not sound to me like an adequately detached one.

In the case of the Langer book on Hitler, undertaken with the help of interviews conducted with those who had known the dictator, a different kind of evidence was possible than would be the case with historical subjects whose lives took place in the inaccessible past. All biographies, however, involve a more or less implicit psychology. As our conceptions of human nature change or are influenced by modern psychological systems, the kind of behavior that will be made the subject of biographical interpretation will also alter. Nowadays a biographical study will be less likely to ignore the existence of symptoms, whether they be of a neurotic or other sort. Psychoanalytic thinking has attuned us to the meaningfulness of kinds of thinking that in an earlier time might have been discarded as simply unrealistic or eccentric.

Even biographical studies of subjects from the more distant past, whose life histories cannot be enriched through interviews, may be enhanced by means of psychological sophistication. For one of the troubles with using psychological concepts on our contemporaries is that the impact of the Freudian revolution has meant that nowadays people have fresh means of self-deception by means of diagnostic terminology. In earlier, pre-Freudian days one is apt to find evidence that is rawer and more naive, uncontaminated by our own theoretical preconceptions.

Anyone engaged in biography, whether about a subject in the relatively distant or more recent past, can be involved in the problem of dealing with a surviving family, and this necessitates an obligation of tact and discretion. The immediate survivors of any historical figure are bound to have concerns and preconceptions of their own. William James died as long ago as 1910, but although it is known that he spent a period in a private mental asylum it has still not been possible to unloosen the existing medical records. Almost fifty years after Freud's death, his family is now willing to allow editions of his letters to appear without the censorship imposed on earlier such collections, but some parts of his papers remain sealed for another century. The Jung family is at an even earlier stage of trying to protect the sacredness of its privacy. The biographer becomes a kind of sleuth, and the Henry James story *The Aspern Papers* haunts all who pursue biographical truth.

There is a politics to biography writing, and this is particularly striking since a good biography is one of the most personal matters the life of the mind can entertain. Doubtless the intimacy that the topic invites helps account for its enduring interest. A biography purports to present the experience of another human soul. It can involve so much emotional involvement that I can recall the wife of a famous biographer reporting how jealous she felt about one subject of her husband's, while she had been relatively indifferent to another of his projects. Although we ourselves can be at a loss to explain our own thoughts and feelings, a biography aims at that ideal objectivity that brings together divergent tendencies to make up a coherent picture. The deceptions that are so characteristic in autobiographies are at least in principle different from what we expect to encounter in a biography.

It is natural to wonder what makes one biography seem superior to another. Why does one account of a life strike us as more appealing and altogether memorable? This problem is one not alien to historiography as a whole; it is still a perplexing question how one particular historical narrative can seem more plausible than another. This issue cannot be resolved by two seemingly attractive solutions, an appeal to the facts on the one hand or to the degree of artistry on the other, for some biographies may be so loaded down with empirical details as to be almost unreadable and other biographies can be so compelling that they really belong in the category of fiction; some of Jean-Paul Sartre's short accounts of Renaissance figures, for instance, are masterpieces of imagination.

One way of coming at the problem of biography in a fresh way would be by considering abortive biographies. We can all think of particular biographies that strike us as failures, and the issue of models of what to avoid is important. But for the moment I would like to mention the subject of biographies that failed ever to get off the ground.

It is a fairly common experience for a biographer to deal with a living subject old enough to be venerable but adequately young to be worried about possible indiscretion. I can think of two examples, both in connection with twentieth-century American political history: Roger Baldwin, the remarkable figure in the cause of civil liberties, and Walter Lippmann, the political thinker and commentator. Both Baldwin and Lippmann were responsible for having sent aspiring biographers packing. In Baldwin's case he had at his disposal the services of an accomplished writer, Joseph Lash, and Lippmann had the chance of being immortalized by Richard Rovere.

In both cases, however, after a period of initial research the biographer came up against intransigent human vanity. Although we all know, at least as a matter of theory, that fallibilities ultimately serve to highlight strengths, neither Baldwin nor Lippmann could be detached enough to trust the biographer's judgment about how to evaluate controversial human material. The more formidable the qualities of the biographer, the more the subject may quail at the prospects of the results of the investigation. (I remember how James Strachey was initially delighted that the biographer he picked for his brother Lytton had never been to college.) In both Baldwin's case and that of Lippmann they later were subjected to books that were not as considerable as they would have been in the earlier hands.

In contrast, some people may be so eager for biographical studies as to put us on our guard. Shortly after Lyndon Johnson withdrew from the presidential race in 1968, he took into his confidence a young political scientist who was serving as a White House fellow. He told her stories about his childhood background and provided the fears and dream material that a modern psychologically oriented biographer likes to be able to have. If early psychoanalytic ideas could be used for purposes of debunking, ego psychology can too easily serve to prettify what might otherwise seem objectionable on strictly political grounds. To treat intimate material provided by President Johnson as if he were the kind of guilt-laden neurotic for whom psychoanalysis was invented would be to play into the hands of one who, now that this sort of psychology has become fashionable, wanted to use it for the sake of rehabilitating his reputation among the intelligentsia. Psychoanalytic-sounding biography could be used for the sake of rescuing Johnson's reputation from the calamity of American destructiveness in Southeast Asia by making him seem more human and sympathetic.

Psychoanalytic biography can serve the purposes of restoring the reputation of a biographical subject, idealizing in contrast to belittling a historical figure. It would seem that psychoanalytic concepts are capable of being used for a variety of moral purposes, especially when they are employed in an unspoken and undercover way. It is likely that psychoanalytic ideas will be turned in a partisan direction the more Freud's claims as a neutral scientist are taken credulously; therefore it behooves us to be on our guard lest psychoanalysis become an unacknowledged weapon in the battle of contending social forces.

Perhaps it is impossible to talk about technique in connection with psychoanalytic biography except in the spirit with which Freud approached the problem of tactics in psychoanalytic treatment: negatively. Freud's recommendations about the practice of analysis were designed to follow from a model of where a practitioner was likely to go wrong. It would seem to be as difficult to outline positively how a therapist should proceed as it is impossible to prescribe how tact should be demonstrated. At least it is in the light of that approach that I have brought up the specific examples of unfortunate psychoanalytic biography.

To enunciate a principle in an area where there are not any firm rules, no biography should be undertaken on a subject one cannot stand. (Alan Bullock's *Hitler* may be the exception that proves the rule.) Symptoms or other likely handles for psychoanalytic examination should not be used abusively, but rather contribute to an understanding of a life history as a whole. In the end biography writing does require a measure of untruthfulness; the historian chooses to introduce certain subjects into a narrative at one point rather than another. It will not do to highlight certain character features too early or in a context that would prove cruel. One tries not to hurt the feelings of living people, nor to betray confidences that have been given. Of course it is impossible to be certain about the sensitivities of other people, and it can be completely unpredictable what will cause offense. If one argues that it boils down to the amount of decency there is in the biographer, that will doubtless sound less than satisfactory as a standard. Yet decency was an ideal that was familiar to Freud, and if he had been able to be sympathetic to the problems of modern psychoanalytic biography I do not think it would be alien to him.

The subject of psychoanalytic biography may even be able to do something to improve standards of clinical case-history writing, for although pre-Freudian classical psychiatry (about which we know far too little) emphasized the significance of case histories and we appreciate how challenging Freud's efforts in this direction were, nowadays the art of case-history writing would seem to have been almost extinguished. We instead tend to get, in the course of clinical literature, fragments of material too often offered as illustrations of abstract theories.

Psychoanalytic biography, in its various forms, will survive as long as psychoanalysis remains attentive to the changing problems of interpreting behavior under different social circumstances. Within the social sciences biographical research has been a relatively neglected subject. In recent years a host of new devices have evolved for data collection and interpretation, so that students of society and politics have been tempted to try to do without the more old-fashioned means of understanding. Yet in the last analysis people make history and suffer as individuals from the unintended consequences of their actions. Human motives and feelings are entitled to as much dignity and attention as the externals of behavior. As scholars reflect over the past, they run the risk of structuring the sequence of events so that no one who lived through the period would ever recognize it as his own.

Our notions of what it is to be human are bound to influence how we reason. Biographers will turn to psychoanalytic psychology whenever they find that explanations in terms of so-called self-interest are inadequate to account for human conduct. Each of us contains within our psyches more selves than a rationalistic version of human nature can hope to deal with. To the extent that the human soul remains a mystery we will rely on psychoanalytic psychology to help us account for some of the surprises that lie in store for us as we attempt to understand the enigma with which any other human life confronts us.

Biographical reconstruction does not stop when a biography gets published, and it is a tribute to the importance of my subject, Helene Deutsch, that I was once given an opportunity by a psychiatric forum to reflect on how I had chosen to approach her life. When one reviewer called her "arguably the most important woman in the history of psychoanalysis,"[2] for a moment I felt that I had let Helene down, for although my *Helene Deutsch: A Psychoanalyst's Life* examined both her writings and her leadership, I had made no such claim for Helene. The other obvious candidate for the title accorded Helene Deutsch by that reviewer was, of course, Anna Freud. Yet, despite Anna Freud's immense public standing, especially in the United States, I do think her contribution has been exaggerated out of loyalty to her father's memory. There is no doubt that Anna Freud and her school of child analysis had a notable impact. But it is striking that virtually no critiques of her have appeared in spite of the fact that—especially in her work on jurisprudence—her ideas have enshrined middle-class values of an exceptionally conformist nature. (Some French analysts have been savagely unblinkered in their view of Anna Freud as a calamity.)

Whatever standing future historians may in the end assign to Helene Deutsch, certain features to her career are not in dispute. She was the first psychoanalyst to write a book on female psychology. When she was completing her manuscript in 1923, she wrote to her husband, Felix: "It brings something new to this *terra incognita* in analysis—I believe, the first ray of light on the unappreciated female libido."[3] For her to refer to female libido in that period was implicitly to challenge Freud's own outlook. At the same time, Helene was pioneering in her emphasis on the role of motherhood. Other analysts around that time, such as Otto Rank, Sandor Ferenczi, and Georg Groddeck, were also intrigued by the neglected role of mothering, but Helene Deutsch was the only one to insist on its significance for female psychology.

Almost simultaneously with the completion of her first book, Helene became the founding head of the Vienna Psychoanalytic Society's Training Institute. For over ten years she was the foremost leader, aside from Freud himself, in training future psychoanalysts in Vienna. When she left for Boston in 1935, Anna Freud and Edward Bibring shared the teaching roles Helene had left behind. In the United States she became a prominent analyst, helping to make the Boston Psychoanalytic Society a flourishing center for training. But Helene was not interested in founding any kind of personal school among her following. She remained tolerant of divergent outlooks and participated in no doctrinal splits. In a field as controversial as psychoanalysis, Helene Deutsch stands out for her catholicity and lack of dogma.

At the same time Helene was not a mere mouthpiece for Freud's own views. Right from the first, when she came to Freud for a personal analysis in 1918, she did so with the self-respect that accompanied her success in academic psychiatry. All her work was distinctively her own, although she expressed herself within the framework of ideas that Freud laid down. Helene's mind was subtle and well educated, and she felt no need to challenge Freud intellectually or organizationally. It is especially striking how her two-volume work, *The Psychology of Women*, which is loyal to psychoanalysis as a tradition of thought, at the same time succeeded in expressing Helene's own outlook on women, which was directly derived from her own experience. Before becoming an analyst, she had led a full and complicated emotional life, and despite her capacity for entering the lives of her patients vicariously, Helene kept on making new friends and acquaintances right up to her death in 1982 at the age of ninety-seven.

Helene's old age was as remarkable as any other feature of her life that one could talk about. In her nineties she could spontaneously burst out singing with her Armenian housekeeper. At the time I was writing my book about her, I wondered if I were not making a mistake by not interviewing even more people who had known her in the United States. But here I had to make a decision that really hinged on the kind of documentary evidence that I had available. Curiously enough, for her earlier years there was more material than for the last forty-seven years of her life. This is because after she came to the United States in 1935 she fit more or less into the culture of the New World, as a result of which there are fewer and less poignant letters from the period of her life in Boston. One of a biographer's central objectives is the re-creation of his subject, and I thought that the letters from her early Polish lover, Herman Lieberman, and the correspondence between herself and her husband, Felix, did the best possible job of presenting her personality.

The publication of my book was in itself an occasion for second-guessing, since in reading the reviews I naturally wondered whether my book had succeeded in the job as I had seen it. One old-line feminist critic of Helene's really proceeded as if my book had never been written. She ignored Helene's life and its struggles, passed over my reexamination of her writings, and proceeded to denounce her as a traitor to her sex. A woman's theoretical commitment to feminism does not seem to ensure concrete sympathy for another woman's struggles. What seems progressive in the history of women, as opposed to reactionary, depends very much on the cultural and historical sophistication in the eyes of the beholder. On the whole, I think the reviewers were generous both to my book and Helene. By coincidence, the same spring my book appeared there was an article in a feminist journal reexamining Helene's *The Psychology of Women* along the lines I myself had followed.[4]

New evidence is, from a historical point of view, especially precious, and Helene's physician—whom I had interviewed earlier with her permission and that of her son—subsequently gave me a copy of a letter Helene had sent him two weeks before she died. It seems to me remarkable that this articulate women was still capable of writing such a letter, communicating her inmost thoughts and feelings. I would have thought she had lost that capacity by then. She wrote it mostly in German; the envelope is addressed "to Dr. Zetzel with love." As I interpret her leaving him this bequest, she was trying to thank him for having been her doctor for almost fifty years. He had been a physician for many Boston analysts, his second wife had also been a psychoanalyst and his stepson had been a schoolboy rival of one of Helene's grandsons.

Dear Lou, my warmest greetings for you—
so far things in our families haven't gone so
well—
miserably in fact—.
A few days ago I saw and spoke with "the Professor"—
he also hasn't gotten any younger—
Rather a somewhat foolish old gentleman.
I have a huge correspondence to get rid of—
so greetings and love from an old, worried
woman.

                                                        Yours,

                                                        Helene

Helene was being so frank about what she considered the failure of her private life that I wondered whether I had unnecessarily failed to be more explicit in my biography. I had, however, used in a prominent spot a quotation from George Orwell: "Any life when viewed from the inside is simply a series of defeats."[5] When she commented about how she thought things had gone miserably in her family, she had in mind how she felt she had failed with her only son, Martin, as well as her two grandsons' inability to establish themselves in accord with a conventional heterosexual pattern. Like Freud, she could not reconcile herself to things in her family that she could accept clinically.

Yet no sooner had she admitted to Zetzel what she knew he would readily understand than she turned to the triumph of her life, her relationship with Freud. As a psychoanalyst she had been fulfilled. In the act of professionally living with others she had succeeded in unfolding all her talents. As a writer, she found Freud's work expansive enough to permit her to express her own thoughts and ideas. One of the books from her library that she loaned me was *How to Travel Incognito*, by Ludwig Bemelmans, and I consider it a peculiarly suitable title for the story of Helene's career as a psychoanalyst.

Helene had a remarkable sense of humor. One of the physicians who happened to see her in a hospital near the end was appalled at the shrunken size of her body but impressed enough by her name to bring her a copy of *The Psychology of Women* for autographing. She so startled him by a bit of her wit that he exclaimed, "Dr. Deutsch, you still have a sense of humor!" She quietly contradicted him by remarking, "I have a sense of humor." The doctor said that he never again treated a dying patient as if death had already taken place.

For those who knew Helene it will come as no surprise that although she remained loyal and devoted to Freud, she still could be irreverent about him. Whether she had dreamt of a conversation with Freud or had a waking vision is less important than the significance he retained in her life. She was more distant from him than many others who had surrounded him, and certainly his own daughter, Anna, could not be expected to appreciate any jokes about "the Professor."

The "huge correspondence" that Helene refers to in the letter to Zetzel means the letters from Lieberman that she had asked to be returned to her. Initially she told me, when I was interviewing her in 1964 about Freud and the history of psychoanalysis, that she intended to destroy this correspondence out of deference to her late husband. But when I was working on my biography of her I found that she had in fact been unable to do away with the letters. They were all saved, outside of their envelopes, in a separately catalogued folder that also contained photographs. Had she known she still had them she could have at least used a photograph of Lieberman for her *Confrontations with Myself*, an autobiography that appeared in 1973. Helene had obviously reread the letters over the years, and when I went over them all with her, checking them for dating as well as examining their substance and translations from the Polish, she knew some of the expressions by heart.

After her death her son and daughter-in-law could not find the Lieberman letters in her house. I had, in fact, when her daughter-in-law Suzanne told me Helene wanted the originals back, returned them to Helene's house; Helene knew that I had made Xerox copies, but nonetheless she proceeded to destroy the originals. (Incidentally, since Helene saved hundreds of Suzanne's letters to her from Los Alamos, presumably there are many letters to her from Helene that Suzanne will someday add to Helene's papers at the Schlesinger Library for the History of Women in America at Radcliffe College.)

Helene's letter to Zetzel makes me think of life imitating art, for she had not read, as far as I know, D. M. Thomas's *The White Hotel* and observed his fictional use of Freud as an old man. And she could not have known about Thomas's poem about my *Brother Animal*, which Thomas called "Fathers, Sons and Lovers," in which Helene figured, since it did not appear until after her death. Thomas in his poem was giving his rendition of the Tausk "problem" and Helene's own part in the struggle between Tausk and Freud.

Helene died having long since accepted the inevitability of death, and yet she was still searching for understanding. Perhaps she was unnecessarily harsh on herself, "masochistic" in evaluating her own human frailties. But her early psychoanalytic essay, "A Two-Year-Old Boy's First Love Comes to Grief," was an autobiographical account of how her involvement as a psychoanalytic psychiatrist interfered with her mothering her son, Martin. However much Martin gained from her, his own mature antagonism toward his mother (matched only by Helene's hostility to her own mother) serves as evidence for the extraordinary strain in their relationship. If she had neglected Martin, she overdid things with her eldest grandson, and to the end of her life she was as unforgiving of herself as of her own mother, whose dire warnings about her as a young woman seemed to have been fulfilled. In extreme old age Helene consciously regretted not having had more children, which would have suited what her husband desired as well, and she brooded over the miscarriages she had had, which were attributed by her to psychogenic causes. The absence of any great-grandchildren spoke for itself.

Yet of all the men in Helene's life perhaps Freud was the most important. In my biography I discussed how her tie to Freud was patterned on her idealized relationship to her father, and Helene consciously saw her second analysis with Karl Abraham in 1923–24 as a renewal of a father involvement. (Although she interpreted her affair at that time with Sandor Rado as a sign of her "masochism," she did not see, nor did I when I wrote my book, that for her to have a sexual relationship with another patient of Abraham's might reflect an "acting out" of her feelings for Abraham.)

Helene was so mature a woman when she came to Freud at the age of thirty-four that she could hardly blame him for any of the twisted courses her own life had taken. On the contrary, she found in his system of ideas an explanation of why things had gone the way they had. If she allowed her career to replace her life as a mother and a wife, then she need not recommend her example to others. She identified with Tolstoy's Anna Karenina's guilt feelings as a mother, and had Helene left her husband, Felix, she might have lost her son, Martin. Her writings on the conflicts in a woman between parenting and professional life remain enduring insights into human psychology, and as fathers nowadays take over more of the parenting functions, they too will experience more regularly the tensions between success in the outside world and competency at home.

Although Helene has been misinterpreted as a naive defender of old-fashioned family life, her biography shows how daring she was in defying traditional sexual roles and stereotypes. In terms of her own intimate family, it was her husband, Felix, who provided basic early mothering for their son, Martin, and Helene felt she had had to wear the pants in the family professionally. My biography and her letter to Zetzel were, in a sense, posthumous expressions of her power. Helene was convinced that her choices had been humanly costly for her. If she had been more accepting of herself, it might have led her to ideas about human development and normality that would match the unconventionality of her own experience and entitle others to feel more at ease in defying conformist pressures. Within the profession she chose for herself she became one of the best mothers in the history of psychoanalysis.

Much of my research on Helene hinged on my interviewing her. I first met her in 1964 for the sake of my research on Freud and the history of psychoanalysis. It was only in 1977–78 that that idea of a biography of her began to take shape. Perhaps she had had me in mind as a biographer long before I formally put the question to her. My interviewing demand on Helene had always been the same: that she be brilliant and original. (Sometime late in my work on Freud she jokingly volunteered to others that the evening before I used to see her weekly she would worry about what she had to offer me the next morning.) My inquiry into Helene's life proceeded on the conviction that behind all the letters she had saved, and out of the implicit autobiography of her professional writings, there had to be a story of her life as interesting as the woman I knew.

My research on Helene was part of my long-standing interest in historical underdogs. I first became interested in Freud as a neglected figure in my own profession, political science. I then wrote, with Helene's cooperation, a book on Victor Tausk's tortured relationship to Freud, on the grounds that Tausk had been neglected historiographically. My book on Freud and his circle was in large part an attempt to correct preceding distortions. And when I wrote a study of Erik H. Erikson, it was because I thought his ideas and their relationship to psychoanalysis needed clarifying.

Feminism often seems as much a political movement as an intellectual approach, and therefore we have grown accustomed to feminist writings that color reality to suit ideological purposes. When it comes to psychoanalysis feminists have already succeeded in achieving a major social impact. Starting in the late 1960s and extending throughout the 1970s, feminists established once and for all the sexist biases implicit in Freud's framework. Although women had all along held high positions as analysts throughout this century (and perhaps more so in Freud's lifetime than now), Freud's ideas were long ago challenged by a few so-called dissident analysts discontented with his approach to feminine psychology. Feminism has so fundamentally altered the way Freud's work is now perceived that Freud's stature has unnecessarily suffered a relative decline.

In recent years, however, feminist writers on psychoanalysis have tended to shift. Now that their battle against Freud's sexism has been won, feminism is allowing itself to see other aspects to analysis than those it had been assaulting. Psychoanalysis has come to be seen not just as a defense of patriarchal culture, but as a critical source of insight into traditionalist injustices.

Despite how easy it can be to pass judgment by today's standards on a woman born over a century ago, Helene Deutsch's writings were the authentic outgrowth of her most intense personal experiences. In social context she herself was a leading feminist. In 1924, when Helene had just made a presentation on the menopause, her old lover Herman Lieberman wrote her: "I was very happy and proud about your success at the conference of psychoanalysis, just like in the old times and just as if you still belonged to me. Do you remember, Halusia, your speech at that meeting in Vienna about allowing women to study law? I was very proud of you then, and now I had the same feeling when reading the report of the conference."[6]

Helene had, even as a medical student (1907–13), spoken in behalf of her sex. No doubt she would have been delighted to see Alix Strachey's comment in a letter to her husband, James, about Helene's menopause paper: ". . . a great success, only capped by her evening gown (from Paris they all said). . . . She's a remarkable woman."[7]

As a pre–World War I psychiatrist Helene had proposed founding a special institution for young girls; as she wrote to her husband:

> Young girls suffering from neuroses and psychoses are the unhappiest creatures in the world. They are sent to unsuitable places, places which make their illness worse. If they have a neurosis, they are in real trouble. They are sent to sanatoria where instead of psychiatric treatment they are given hydro-electric therapy. Flirtations with doctors and affairs with other patients spoil these girls for life. Where real medical care could bring about a miracle in dealing with the complaints, unscientific approaches cause havoc.

> And psychoses: all these schizophrenics, these split personalities who could live peacefully until they succumb entirely in their insanity! And all those in an observation period when we don't know if we are dealing with a hysteria or a dementia praecox? The many who are at the borderline and who are crying for help while they can still feel their individuality and their being. I know already: only a woman can understand and help them. That is the most wonderful aspect of my profession—I can feel my power and know what I can do.[8]

Even before World War I, Helene had grown disappointed with feminism as a movement; it was not sufficiently idealistic for her but too bread-and-butterish. She grew up in an ideology that saw the emancipation of women as part of a general human awakening. A trade-union mentality embarrassed her. It seemed to her that her freedom as a woman had followed rather than preceded her liberation as a proud individual; as she wrote Felix in 1914, "now I am a *free woman*—in order to become that, I had to be a *free human being*."[9]

In her life and career Helene became a powerful leader and an inspiration to many younger women and colleagues. In 1928 she presented a public lecture in Vienna, "George Sand: A Woman's Destiny." This paper about a great French writer filled out some of Helene's purposes as a thinker; in the course of making the subject of women her specialty, she had to come to terms with the life of a woman she credited with being "the first systematic feminist." [10] Ironically enough, George Sand herself, like Helene after her, has been attacked in our own time for not being a feminist. I think that Gustave Flaubert's memorable words about George Sand are worth repeating: "One had to know her as I knew her to realize how much of the feminine there was in this great man, the immensity of tenderness to be found in this genius." [11] Helene did herself espouse certain conventions of her time about the nature of her maleness and femaleness. But she was working from the premise of the universality of bisexual trends, and in trying to account for the sources of the formation of George Sand's conflicted personality, Helene was at the same time reflecting self-critically on the underside to her own immensely successful career.

Helene's gentleness in expressing herself meant that only in the course of a footnote did she defend herself against Karen Horney's gloss on Helene's ideas:

> I should like to defend my previous work against a misinterpretation. K. Horney contends that I regard feminine masochism as an "elemental power in feminine mental life" and that, according to my view, "what women ultimately want in intercourse is to be raped and violated; what she wants in mental life is to be humiliated." It is true that I consider masochism "an elemental power in feminine life," but in my previous studies and also in this one I have tried to show that one of woman's tasks is to govern this masochism, to steer it into the right paths, and thus to protect herself against those dangers that Horney thinks I consider woman's normal lot. [12]

For Helene it went almost without saying that "all those to whom the ideals of freedom and equality are not empty words sincerely desire that woman should be socially equal to man." [13] None of her idealism, however, meant that she did not have the courage to elaborate on what she considered some of the essential differences between men and women. The kind of masochism that afflicted her own life, for instance, would in principle be different from male masochism. (By "masochism" she was writing with a technical psychoanalytic concept in mind.) Although she has been attacked for her views on female "narcissism," Helene thought of it as a counterweight to masochism; and "passivity" was, Helene held, a special source of insight for women that led them to a kind of intuition unknown in men. But isolated terms like *masochism*, *narcissism*, and *passivity* are apt to be as misleading about Helene Deutsch's idea as Freud's concepts of id, ego, and superego are a superficial approach to the import of psychoanalysis.

Helene was in reality as surprisingly unorthodox in practice as she was in theory. She wrote about anorexia nervosa, argued against rigidities in training, and grew distrustful of long-term analyses as therapy. Only a conscientious examination of all her life and work shows how unlike a stereotyped Freudian she was. She moved beyond accepting penis envy as a biological entity or a useful theoretical construct. When she talked about a "masculinity complex" it was largely out of dissatisfaction with her own life. Feminine psychology remained her special field until the end of her life.

Helene Deutsch was an original figure in the history of psychoanalysis, and she exerted a special influence on modern psychiatry. The example of her life makes an enduringly valuable object of admiration and identification. She will be remembered as one of Freud's unusually independent followers who, without the need for rebellion, heroically coped with the idiosyncracies of her private life as she carved out of Freud's teachings a special niche for herself in the history of ideas.

It is my hope that in the course of reconsidering my biography of this pioneering psychoanalyst, additional concrete light will have been shed on the more general topic of psychoanalysis and biography.

Notes

1. Hanns Sachs, *Freud: Master and Friend* (London: Imago Publishing Company, 1945), p. 103.
2. M. Kimmel, "The Loyal Analyst," *Psychology Today*, August 1985, pp. 73–74.
3. Paul Roazen, *Helene Deutsch: A Psychoanalyst's Life* (New York: Anchor Press/Doubleday, 1985), p. 231.
4. Brenda S. Webster, "Helene Deutsch: A New Look," *Signs*, vol. 10, no. 3, Spring 1985, 553–71.
5. Roazen, *Helene Deutsch*, p. 332.
6. Ibid., p. 225.
7. Perry Meisel and Walter Kendrick, eds., *Bloomsbury/Freud: The Letters of James and Alix Strachey* (New York: Basic Books, 1985), p. 87.
8. Roazen, *Helene Deutsch*, pp. 117–18.
9. Ibid., p. 116.
10. Ibid., p. 263.
11. Ibid., p. 264.
12. Ibid., pp. 341–42.
13. Ibid., p. 342.

10

Brief Lives

Freud was a great writer, crystal clear while being most scientifically original, compelling and persuasive while being most improbable. His powerful sense of the dramatic has attracted sympathizers to his views, but the misleadingly ominous sound of some of his concepts has alienated others. Even in entitling his favorite cases he liked to shock, as with the Wolf-Man, his most famous patient. Although the name may evoke the image of a person turning into a wolf, the man in question merely had suffered as a small child from an excessive fear of wolves, about which Freud, who treated him for severe adult incapacities, wrote a case history.

The Wolf-Man, as he came to be known in the psychoanalytic literature, was in treatment with Freud from 1910 to 1914, after unsuccessful attempts at therapy by others. At this time the patient was a wealthy Russian landowner, but later the Bolshevik Revolution left him impoverished. When the Wolf-Man returned to Vienna in 1919, Freud recommended further analysis, which lasted a few months and was free of charge. Subsequently, adjusting to his financial straits, the Wolf-Man took a rather lowly job in a Viennese insurance company. After analysis with Freud, the Wolf-Man underwent two more analyses with an American physician in Vienna, Dr. Ruth Mack Brunswick, and following World War II he was in therapy with two other analysts in Vienna, where he still resided. In addition, he was frequently queried by analysts interested in the early history of Freud's work, and for over fifteen years one of them came from abroad for several weeks every summer to conduct daily sessions with him.

The Wolf-Man, by the Wolf-Man, edited by Muriel Gardiner (1971), embodies the patient's autobiographical essays on his childhood and later years, his recollections of Freud, Freud's famous case history, the supplement to his account by Dr. Brunswick, and Dr. Muriel Gardiner's record of her thirty years' contact with the Wolf-Man. Of this material, some of which has appeared previously in journals, the most interesting is still

Freud's own case paper, written on the heels of his battles with Adler and Jung to reemphasize the significance of the infantile factor in adult neurosis. Regrettably James Strachey's editorial notes have been omitted.

Freud's dream interpretations are masterful, and his reconstruction of the Wolf-Man's earliest years, if not entirely convincing, at least represents for its day a remarkably daring set of hypotheses. Typically, Freud saw the Wolf-Man as beset by ambivalent feelings toward his father and subsequent father surrogates, holding that his patient's fear of his father, and simultaneous desire for sexual gratification by him, dominated his later life. Freud announced the "final clearing up" of the Wolf-Man's symptoms in 1914 and said that he "parted from him, regarding him as cured."[1] Yet Freud conceded at the time, and this in contrast to the doctrine of some of his later disciples, that with a patient as disturbed as the Wolf-Man "psychoanalytic treatment cannot bring about any instantaneous revolution or put matters upon a level with a normal development; it can only get rid of the obstacles and clear the path, so that the influences of life may be able to further development along better lines."[2]

Ruth Mack Brunswick was one of Freud's most brilliant pupils, although the tragic circumstances surrounding her last years have contributed to her lack of recognition by the general reading public today. An intimate friend and rival of Freud's daughter, Anna, Dr. Brunswick was perhaps the single most important disciple within Freud's circle by 1930. Her case history of the Wolf-Man, who, suffering from a paranoid delusion about his nose, was referred to her by Freud in 1926, merits the closest scrutiny. (A draft of a second paper by her about him has not been included in this volume, and is not even referred to editorially.)

Unlike Freud, Dr. Brunswick was a psychiatrist with a special interest in psychosis, and she suggested that perhaps the Wolf-Man's first analysis with Freud had "robbed him of the usual neurotic modes of solution,"[3] thereby activating more primitive mechanisms. His loss of equilibrium in the mid-1920s had been triggered, she felt, by Freud's becoming dangerously ill with cancer; to her this indicated that, despite the aims of therapy, the Wolf-Man had not freed himself from the influence of Freud's personality.

Ruth Mack Brunswick's case history is rich with ingenious dream interpretations, yet for all her interest in the childhood of the Wolf-Man, in retrospect one speculates about her personal feelings toward him. It is clear that by referring to her this famous case, with the implied invitation that she write a supplement to his own lengthy essay, Freud demonstrated his esteem for the young woman. In the analysis she deliberately undermined the Wolf-Man's fantasies that he was a favorite son of Freud's by emphasizing his exclusion from Freud's social life and by pointing out that other patients had been treated by Freud for longer periods of time. The question arises whether, besides her rational objectives, Dr. Brunswick, who had herself long been a patient of Freud's, did not have intense feelings of competitiveness with the Wolf-Man, which may have influenced her treatment of him. In later years Freud grew disappointed in her, and her own inner problems were gradually to overwhelm her.

Curiously, what was probably that major romance in the Wolf-Man's life—that with Freud and psychoanalysis—is undiscussed and uninterpreted. Remembering the passionate faith of his childhood, the Wolf-Man wonders why "with no effort on my part, I discarded religion so easily. The question is, what filled up the vacuum thus created?"[4] He suggested here that perhaps literature or painting took up the void, omitting his important role in the psychoanalytic movement. He wrote articles on philosophy and art seen from a psychoanalytic point of view and also sold some of his paintings to analysts. Freud himself collected sums of money for this former patient who, as Ruth Mack Brunswick put it, "had served the theoretical ends of analysis so well."[5] Even as the Wolf-Man's life grew, according to him, less harmonious with old age, writing his experiences with Freud gave purpose to his life.

In her conclusion to his volume Dr. Gardiner stresses that "Freud's analysis saved the Wolf-Man from a crippled existence, and Dr. Brunswick's reanalysis overcame a serious acute crisis, both enabling the Wolf-Man to lead a long and tolerably healthy life."[6] Freud, however, would have been as interested in therapeutic failure as its success, and it would be in his best spirit to mention the problems the Wolf-Man failed to overcome. If a patient needed so much therapeutic propping up all these years, was psychoanalysis the preferred method of treatment for him in the first place? He did, to be sure, progress better under Freud's care than with other therapists of the day, but can one say that it was analytic insight that helped him or the continuing emotional support of Freud and the psychoanalysis movement? Freud would have wanted this question to be raised.

Karin Obholzer's *The Wolf-Man Sixty Years Later* (1982), a moving story, was immediately criticized by a handful of remaining orthodox defenders of psychoanalysis. I think it is a touching series of interviews, which were conducted by a sensitive young Viennese journalist with the Russian whom Freud treated. The Wolf-Man correctly viewed Muriel Gardiner's earlier volume as a piece of propaganda, making him into a "showpiece" of analysis. Freud had been determined to establish the importance of childhood emotional conflicts in the origin of neurosis, as well as the efficacy of rational insight as a means of cure.

The Wolf-Man Sixty Years Later will probably best be remembered for how it undermined a previous professional party line. The Wolf-Man took a highly skeptical view of Freud and his teachings. He criticized dream interpretations and transference; although he sometimes says Freud helped him, his analysis also seemed a "catastrophe"[8] as he recited how he was harmed. These interviews could only be published after his death, because he was financially dependent on orthodox analysis. Payments from the Freud archives in New York went straight to a grasping girl friend, and the Wolf-Man's paintings were bought by wealthy analysts as part of their keeping in touch with the roots of their profession. The Wolf-Man was clear-eyed enough to see how this attention exploited his dependencies.

Entirely aside from doctrinal issues, the book is a touching account of an old man's life. He sounds right in thinking he was really schizophrenic. But his struggles are also reminiscent of characters in Dostoevsky's novels who are besest by sudden ruin and enslavement to women. It is odd that after seemingly rejecting so much of analysis the Wolf-Man still accepts Freud's interpretation of a childhood trauma with an older sister. Obholzer talks about the Wolf-Man's ties to "primitive women,"[9] whom he paid for sex, without raising the issue of the peculiarities of his sexual preferences.

The interviewer won the Wolf-Man's confidence by astonishing this impoverished émigré with the admission that she too had had gonorrhoea. She treated him like an equal, and they developed what sounds like a genuine human relationship. Her account of his death in an insane asylum is sensitively done. For specialists the book will be amusing, as the Wolf-Man undermines so much that has been written about him. But in the end it is the book's tale of a suffering human being that is memorable. If the Wolf-Man could be this interesting even in extreme old age one can perhaps understand why Freud put so many years of effort into understanding him in the first place.

Patrick Mahony, a practicing analyst, is writing a trilogy about Freud's case histories; *Cries of the Wolf Man* (1984) and *Freud and the Rat Man* (1986) will be followed by a book examining Dora and Freud's other female patients. Mahony excludes Schreber and Little Hans, since Freud treated neither of them directly. By now there is a considerable literature about each of the five great case histories. Mahony mentions much of it, but ignores Henri Ellenberger's 1972 evidence that supported Jung's contention that Freud had told him Anna O. was a therapeutic failure.

The Wolf-Man subsequently figured prominently in the touching movie *1919*; in his *Cries of the Wolf Man* Mahony correctly announced that he was using "all available source material on the Wolf Man."[10] He must qualify his claim by the use of the word "available," because the sealed Freud archives contain an enormous amount of documentation about this particular patient—letters, transcripts of interviews, and even the draft of an unpublished case history by Ruth Mack Brunswick.

Freud's own case history of the Wolf-Man focused on an infantile neurosis connected with a childhood dream of wolves. Freud hypothesized that at the age of one the Wolf-Man had witnessed intercourse between his parents, *coitus à tergo*. This incident was, Freud thought at the time, absolutely essential in giving a concrete answer to both Adler and Jung, for while Jung in particular had maintained that infantile data arose defensively in a clinical context as a maneuver to distract the therapist and enable the patient to evade a current life task, Freud held to the concept that childhood incidents were in themselves capable of being pathogenic. (Mahony could have done more to make plausible the reservations by Jung and Adler.)

Freud never mentioned that as an adult the Wolf-Man practiced anal intercourse. I raised the matter parenthetically in *Freud and His Followers* (1975)—a book Mahony cites. But he does not deal with the Wolf-Man's adult sexuality. Ruth Mack Brunswick, when writing in 1929 about what the Wolf-Man, according to Freud, had seen, added: "In part this observation, in part the predominantly anal nature of the patient himself, resulted in him making this [*coitus à tergo*] his usual form of sexual intercourse. Indeed, he practiced regularly not only *coitus à tergo*, but also anal intercourse." [11] Brunswick's comment appeared in the official journal of the international psychoanalytic movement, and her name has been ineluctably linked to that of the Wolf-Man ever since Freud's referral of his ex-patient to her for further analysis. Yet the conformist pressures of the profession have ordained that the Wolf-Man's sexual preferences never receive appropriate attention.

Although Freud discusses the connections to homosexuality, he tells us nothing about the Wolf-Man's adult sexual practices. What are we to make of the contrast between what Brunswick tells us to have been true and this eerie silence elsewhere? Reticence, repression, deception, or ignorance seems as significant as any of the Wolf-Man's "cries." The Wolf-Man's sexual practices, I believe, influenced Freud's reconstruction of the supposed infantile neurosis, and nonreproductive sexuality as well seems to have played a more interesting part in Freud's thought than has been acknowledged. Freud's special interest in the Wolf-Man might have been partly fueled by, for example, the anal intercourse that Freud disguised in writing up his case. Such a curious preference in a heterosexual must have had psychological significance, and could even bear on the suicide of his wife.

Mahony considers the Wolf-Man case history Freud's "best," but does not appreciate the full imaginative quality of Freud's writing. Unlike my

own reaction to the Wolf-Man—as being a character out of Dostoevsky—
Mahony understands him as having "endured his miserable life."[12] Mahony
is correct in questioning aspects of Freud's reconstruction of the infantile
primal scene that have been too passively accepted by analysts, and he is
skeptical enough to wonder whether the toddler "saw his parents making
love one, two, three times, in a position from the rear, at five in the after-
noon. . . ."[13] Mahony is left "only blinking and wide-eyed" at "Freud's
cameo of stupendous detail. . . ."[14] Other readers, however, by the time
they get to that famous scene have been overwhelmed by Freud's literary
prowess and have more or less suspended critical judgment.

In the story of the Wolf-Man Freud trumps up his evidence in behalf of
infantile sexuality. But his sleights of hand are being overlooked in the professional literature. Muriel Gardiner—a patient of Ruth Mack Brunswick's
and apparently the model of Lillian Hellman's "Julia"—though a pillar of
integrity in contrast to Hellman's artistic lies, did shape the material about
the Wolf-Man to suit the needs of conservative psychoanalysis.

In *Freud and the Rat Man* Mahony was able to work from a copy of
Freud's original clinical notes, and his most striking conclusion is that
Freud had in his case history engaged in a "fictive manipulation of
time."[15] Freud not only changed events for the sake of constructing a better
story, but treated the Rat Man for only a few months and not the one year
that he claimed. In Mahony's view Freud's therapeutic results, again in
contrast to Freud's version, amounted to a "symptomatic remission."[16]
Freud was engaging in "therapeutic exaggeration"[17] for the sake of promoting his psychoanalytic cause, and Mahony makes no bones about Freud
having tried to indoctrinate his patient with psychoanalytic teachings.

Throughout both books Mahony objects to the translations by James Strachey, his "staid Victorian prose, its cleaning up of Viennese colloquial-
isms, its reliance on Greek and Latin to render the familiar in German . . .
and its tendency to substitute the past tense and its toning down for the
immediacy and vividness of Freud's present tense. . . ."[18] Yet like Bruno
Bettelheim, Mahony seems to forget that Freud not only picked Strachey as
a translator but was delighted with what he did.

Mahony is doubtless right in thinking that Strachey's "idealizing transference" to Freud resulted in a "doctoring up" of Freud's own words.[19]
But Mahony's point about Strachey's relationship to Freud might also be
extended to embrace Strachey's reserve about asking to see the available
Freud manuscripts. As a result, Strachey's edition for the most part was
based on the publications that appeared in Freud's lifetime. As Mahony
points out, Freud spoke about the Rat Man at six meetings of the Vienna
Psychoanalytic Society. Yet Mahony uncritically quotes from the minutes of

those proceedings without even identifying the translator, while being wary of Strachey's job, which I suspect was more literate than the one done on the minutes. Still, whatever Mahony has done with the early history of psychoanalysis, his books seem to signal a new tolerance of differing viewpoints without perpetrating the old myths about the betrayals, deviations, or heretical secessions.

Harry Stack Sullivan (1892–1949), who developed the "interpersonal" approach to psychiatry, was one of the most creative and influential psychiatrists the United States has ever had. Yet little has been known about his personal life. In *Harry Stack Sullivan: The Man and His Work* (1976), a general introduction, A. H. Chapman reveals that Sullivan's early years were lonely, tortured, and unhappy. Involved at the age of eight and a half in a sexual relationship with an older boy (who also later became a psychiatrist), Sullivan remained homosexual all his life. Chapman calls his biographical chapter "The Life and Emotional Problems of Harry Stack Sullivan" and believes that Sullivan's emotional difficulties were partly responsible for his repudiation of the illusion that the therapist automatically fulfills perfectionist standards of "normality."

Sullivan remains a hero for never writing off schizophrenics as incurable. In the 1920s orthodox psychoanalytic theory held that schizophrenics, like other psychotics, could not be helped by psychotherapy. Sullivan labored to treat some of the most seriously disturbed patients. He was, of course, working before the invention of antipsychotic drugs. Schizophrenics under his care improved significantly, and the innovative methods he used in his schizophrenic ward were to become standard hospital practice.

Shortly before the turn of the century, medicine was not among the glories of American culture. Sullivan got an M.D. from what he described as a "diploma mill,"[20] and he always suffered from a deficiency in his formal education. His lack of conventional psychiatric wisdom, however, helped him rely on his own insights and experience. Oddly enough, the self-taught Sullivan who achieved his influence by teaching disciples tried, according to Chapman, to replace the psychiatrist's apprenticeship training with neutral scientific principles. Sullivan, an artist himself, appears to have minimized the significance of the artistic component in successful psychotherapy.

Perhaps the most striking contradiction that emerges is how an interesting, eccentric, and controversial man made conformism into a psychiatric ideal. Out of his own personal difficulties, shyness, and social awkwardness he idealized the value of compromise and consensus. Although Sullivan bravely challenged the status quo of his time, Chapman remains true to the spirit of Sullivan's concepts when he claims that "to a large extent, comfortable, successful interpersonal relationships are what life is all about."[21] But conflict can be as essential to health as equilibrium.

The philosophic slack in Sullivan's thinking makes it easy to make fun of some of his formulations, and Herbert Marcuse likened them to the pious hopefulness of a Norman Vincent Peale. But Sullivan was a humanitarian who proposed social reform. He believed that if any child is afflicted by poverty, racial injustice, intellectual stagnation, or ethnic prejudice, his personality development will be blighted. Sullivan fought against racial discrimination, legal inequities, social evils, and economic deprivations. He was writing when such social factors were relegated by Freudian theory to the realm of sociology. At a time when most psychoanalysts limited their concern to infancy and early childhood, Sullivan stressed that people can change and grow throughout life. There is, he held, a natural tendency toward health, and thus "later interpersonal relationships are more likely to erase earlier damage than to erode personality strength."[22]

Sullivan was one of the first to see the weaknesses in the early Freudian dichotomy between childhood and adulthood, and he tried to spell out clearly defined developmental stages. While Freud stressed the significance of the father for the child, Sullivan insisted on the importance of the mother. Nevertheless, the reader is apt to feel uneasy when Chapman summarizes Sullivan's view of the various stages of psychological growth. As an early alternative to Freud, Sullivan was a valuable force. But one is bound to ask to what extent Sullivan's ideas were an account of what ought to happen in the developing personality, as opposed to anything that a human being has ever experienced. To be sure, Chapman criticizes some of Sullivan's ideas. But he never asks whether, to the extent Sullivan was an ethical reformer, his moral ideas could have benefited from non-American, if not non-Western, perspectives.

With the advantages of hindsight one can see that Sullivan was a leader in overselling the promises of psychotherapy. His legacy may have a dark side that we ignore at our peril, for to minimize the inevitability of tragedy, pain, and terror in human experience is to encourage a dangerous set of illusions.

Sullivan's notable contribution comes in his methods of therapy. The task of the therapist is primarily to support a patient's self-esteem; there is no more fundamental emotional need than feeling worthy, competent, and respected. Once a secure relationship with the therapist is established, the patient's emotional suffering can be reduced and he can afford to become aware of previously unknown areas of experience. Indifference on the therapist's part is disastrous, as is the therapeutic tendency to scrutinize patients as if they were specimens in a laboratory. Sullivan was opposed to exploring a patient's past through free associations. He aimed instead to remove whatever obstacles lay in the patient's path to emotional health, on the assumption that once the blocks were gone, patients could treat themselves.

At his best Sullivan insisted that a person who is observing a patient always alters the patient's behavior and emotional reactions by forming the relationship with him that makes observation possible. At his worst, however, Sullivan believed, according to Chapman, that there is no fun in psychotherapy and that "a good interview is busy and fast moving."[23] Such a work ethic would have confirmed Freud's distaste for American clinical practice.

The history of modern psychotherapy is marred by sectarianism. Worshipful biographies of leading psychologists inevitably provoke debunking books and articles—or silence. Chapman's balanced book will do much to restore Sullivan's place in history. Unfortunately, the uncertainties associated with therapy, the decline of religious beliefs, and the economic interests of the various practitioners have continued the intolerant spirit in which historical issues are too often discussed.

According to a 1976 article by David Black in *New York* magazine, Sullivan has become the center of a rigid sect of contemporary Sullivanians in New York City. The grim fate of a notable psychiatric pioneer should remind us that some of the world's greatest emancipators have ended up helping enforce new orthodoxies and tyrannies.

Coming six years after Chapman's book, Helen Swick Perry's *Psychiatrist of America: The Life of Harry Stack Sullivan* (1982) is truly authoritative; it is a splendid book that lifted the history of twentieth-century American psychiatry onto a new level of sophistication. The author's professional association with Sullivan during the last three years of his life and her editing of his posthumous works lay behind the decades of work that went into this book. *Psychiatrist of America* is a thoroughly researched, beautifully written, elegantly organized scholarly achievement; at the same time it succeeds in documenting some of Sullivan's clinical wisdom.

For all that Sullivan did to promote psychiatric research into schizophrenia, as well as his advocacy of the benefits of cooperation between psychiatrists and social scientists, he has not generally been given the credit due him. For instance, he notably helped upgrade psychiatric education in the United States. Part of this relative neglect can be traced to his being an outsider, an eclectic reformer who did not fit preconceived social roles. But his strength—not enough so-called learning to concede that his patients were incurable, as sophisticates then thought—also contributed to his insufficient recognition: Sullivan's work has suffered from his lack of a consistent command of English.

Helen Swick Perry has definitively placed Sullivan in his early years in Chenango County in upper New York State. His lonely beginnings helped him later understand what his patients felt they were up against. Although Helen Perry has been more open than most biographers usually are (about Sullivan's drinking, manipulativeness, and recklessness with money, how rough he could be on younger colleagues, and the mystery of his sexuality), she, like Sullivan, does not quite appreciate how pain and suffering can feed creativity. She does report that she at times felt "appalled by the pattern that seemed to emerge—that only with deprivation and loneliness could anyone in America break with the emphasis on being conventionally successful."[24] But she does not universalize her insight beyond America or talk about how tragedy enriched Sullivan. Whatever he himself believed, many in intellectual history have stoutly been convinced that values inevitably are "confused."

Despite the few drawbacks to *Psychiatrist of America*, its fascinating account of Sullivan's life deserves applause. He taught about "the crippling effects of poverty, restricting custom, limited schooling, accidents of geography, and the environing stereotypes."[25] We can now hope for biographies of Sullivan's friends, who, for the first time, come alive here in this book—Adolf Meyer, Edward Sapir, William A. White, W. I. Thomas, Ruth Benedict, Harold Lasswell, Erich Fromm, Clara Thompson, and Karen Horney, among others.

In the more than three decades since Jones's biography of Freud first started to appear, interest in the history of psychoanalysis has gradually accelerated. By now Jones's partisanship on behalf of the master and his consequent bias against any disciple who dared to "deviate" are easy to document. Still, an extraordinary amount of what we think we know about Freud is due to Jones's work and his gifts of exposition.

The biggest single obstacle to independent research has been the curious relationship between the Freud archives in New York and the Freud collection at the Library of Congress in Washington, D.C. Whatever the wishes of those who have given or sold material to the archives, the archives' own policy has been that the bulk of the material will only start to be available after the year 2000. The Library of Congress imposes such restrictions as are required by its official donors. In the case of the Freud collection, the principal donors are the Freud archives. A baffling system of classification means that one of Freud's letters to his deceased eldest son is restricted until 2013 and another until 2032, while a letter of Josef Breuer is sealed until 2102. Since the restrictive dates have already started to pass and a few manuscripts have become available, it is provable that this policy clearly does not stem from a wish to preserve privacy (as opposed to protecting idealizations about Freud). The Freud family's protectiveness has been complicated by the fact that the archives have allowed certain individuals to use documentation barred to scholars at large. The Library of Congress, meanwhile, houses its rich, closed collection, while the wishes of the original donors to the Freud archives are unable to gain scholars' access to them. Some of those originally involved, however, had as much savvy as the Freud archives and retained copies of letters and documents. It is in this context that, because of the primary Freud material they contain, both Vincent Brome's *Ernest Jones: Freud's Alter Ego* (1983) and Celia Bertin's *Marie Bonaparte: A Life* (1983) are important.

Vincent Brome's biography of Jones mentions twice in its preface a section of the book called "Notes and Sources"; that section's absence from the book itself is the first warning note in a volume whose production is a disgrace. It is impossible not to be irritated by the misplaced quotation marks, footnotes jumbled up or missing, passages being repeated, misprinted names, and garbled dates and quotations. The printing mistakes are so glaring that one hesitates to evaluate Brome's writing, since one cannot be sure how much of the appearance of his book is the author's responsibility.

Jones emerges from the book as more human than one might have expected from his public tenacity in Freud's behalf. Brome knows many of Jones's failings and has written a dispassionate, impartial book. It is all the harder not to be moved by the sections on Jones's tormented early love life and in particular his affair with Loe Kann, a patient of his who later became an analysand of Freud's. In the course of kidney trouble she became addicted to morphine; they lived together for years, although Jones was not always faithful to her—she was particularly wounded by his sleeping with a woman who was supposed to be taking care of her. In the end, however, Jones rose above his troubles and succeeded in making an unusually happy marriage.

Freud's initial, prescient appraisal of Jones seems to elude Brome's grasp. Freud wrote to Jung in 1908: "Jones is undoubtedly a very interesting and worthy man, but he gives me a feeling of, I was almost going to say racial strangeness. He is a fanatic and doesn't eat enough. 'Let me have men about me that are fat,' says Caesar, etc. He almost reminds me of the lean and hungry Cassius. He denies all heredity; to his mind even I am reactionary. How, with your moderation, were you able to get on with him?"[26]

Jones's professional difficulties as a neurologist in London were dismaying. Before leaving for Canada he was twice accused of behaving indecently with small children under his care. The years in Toronto (1908–13) were no more successful in fulfilling his ambitions. He was dissatisfied with his life in exile and detested the character of the Canadian people, yet he wrote forty papers there. He also paid five hundred dollars in blackmail money to a patient who had accused him of having sexually abused her, and Brome mentions evidence still to come about the final grounds for Jones's resignation from his psychiatric position at the University of Toronto.

Jones's work offended Toronto's sensibilities; in the course of one clinical paper for instance he made a connection between oral sex and Holy Communion. His commitment to the truth as he saw it was combined with a tactlessness that many of his colleagues found hard to take. On his return to London he was to rule the British Psychoanalytic Society with a firm hand, even if it meant excluding talented candidates because they might threaten his position. Starting in 1925, Jones backed Melanie Klein against Anna Freud, and Freud perceived this so-called British school of analysis as an attack on himself. Although Jones was living in the country during 1943–44, when the "controversial discussions" took place in the society over Klein's views, his own leanings were in no doubt. Yet his services in forwarding the cause, and especially his help in rescuing Freud and his personal entourage from the Nazis in Vienna, meant that despite her personal feelings about him, Anna Freud agreed that he should write the official biography of her father.

Celia Bertin's *Marie Bonaparte* is fluently written and handsomely produced, an entertaining portrait of a princess who became a psychoanalyst. It would be hard to find a greater contrast between Jones's working-class origins and Bonaparte's family tree. Marie was a direct descendant of Napoleon's brother Lucien and married into one of the most eminent of European royal families; Prince George, her husband, was a member of the Danish royal family and also a brother of the late king of Greece. Prince Philip, a nephew of her husband, spent a good deal of his childhood in Marie's house in Saint-Cloud, and his marriage to the future Queen Elizabeth II was only one of the royal occasions that this book is inevitably much taken up with. Bertin fails to mention that in Marie's own world of the international aristocracy her credentials were damaged by the fact that her maternal grandfather had been the (Jewish) founder of the Monte Carlo casino.

As in Brome's book, passages from Freud's letters are cited here that have never appeared before. In her early forties Marie Bonaparte had gone to Vienna for an analysis with Freud, and afterward she was a leading figure in the founding of psychoanalysis in France. As Bertin notes, after encountering Freud in 1925, she was "able to do research, to lecture, to present papers at congresses, to publish articles on psychoanalysis."[27] Freud complimented her on her masculinity, as he sometimes praised men for their femininity—the early analysts used the concept of bisexuality to try to free people from conventional stereotypes of the distinctions between the sexes.

Bertin's well-paced narrative concentrates on Marie's colorful private life. During her treatment with Freud, for example, she for some reason showed him one of her breasts, and at another time he had to argue against her son's idea of overcoming his incestuous fantasies by sleeping with his mother. Both before and after her analysis Marie carried on a number of love affairs; the most eminent of her lovers was Aristide Briand. But she also had more than her share of sexual difficulties, undergoing repeated surgery on her clitoris in an effort to combat frigidity. Her husband was predisposed to homosexuality, and her most faithful lover suffered from potency problems.

Although by 1953 she could write privately that Freud had been "wrong" [28] and had overestimated the therapeutic power of psychoanalysis, this did little to diminish the force of her conviction that the people she loved and cared for ought to be analyzed. She quotes Freud as having wisely told her, in the course of her training analysis: " . . . more important than what one does is what one is." [29] She sent chauffeurs in expensive cars to bring patients to her for treatment. She saw no contradiction between her own idiosyncratic experience as an analyst and leading the battle in France to establish orthodox standards of training for others—she helped to exclude Jacques Lacan from official circles both in Paris and the international psychoanalytic movement.

While neither *Ernest Jones* nor *Marie Bonaparte* can rank as true intellectual biographies, these accounts of the lives of pioneering figures in psychoanalysis make fascinating reading.

Jelliffe: American Psychoanalyst and Physician and His Correspondence with Sigmund Freud and C. G. Jung by John C. Burnham, edited by William McGuire (1984), is an interesting and important book that comes in two sections: the first, longer portion consists of a biographical essay about Smith Ely Jelliffe, a pioneering psychoanalytic psychiatrist, and the second part is made up of Jelliffe's surviving correspondence with Freud and Jung. So little has generally been known about Jelliffe (1866–1945) that students of either the history of American psychiatry or the story of Freud's movement require self-restraint not to leap immediately to the documentary evidence in the last part of the work.

Within the context of rival ideologies Jelliffe ranks as "unorthodox" and eclectic. His last letter to Freud, in 1939, has a passage in which Jelliffe tries to counter the founder of psychoanalysis's dim view of how his work had deteriorated into being "the handmaid of psychiatry in America." [30] To Jelliffe the general charge of the "superficiality"[31] of American thought meant that the values of catholicity and tolerance were being underrated. In the history of the reception of psychoanalysis in America, Jelliffe had been a major source by which European developments in neurology and psychiatry came to the United States through the printed word. Jelliffe was a prominent editor, journalist, teacher, and publicist; he appeared in court, treated distinguished patients, knew celebrities (like John Barrymore), and coauthored an influential textbook.

Burnham's biography is a good, solid piece of historical reconstruction. One wishes, though, that Burnham had explored Jelliffe's religious background, and it is curious that Burnham makes no mention of Horace W. Frink, a cosmopolitan American psychiatrist far more important to Freud than Jelliffe. Although Frink's career ended tragically, Burnham does not discuss him or even footnote a reference to his name in a passage he quotes from Karl Menninger's reminiscences.

Burnham's biographical material is invaluable as one reads through the correspondence, but readers will, of course, evaluate the letters for themselves. Jelliffe at times seems not just an "extremist"[32] but dotty. He once advised using psychoanalysis for senile patients, even when there were signs of organic degeneration. All innovators have defects. Jelliffe led the way in psychosomatic medicine, yet he went so far as to discuss the psychogenic constituents of myopia (castration) and color blindness, as well as the so-called irreversible conversion processes in dermatology, allergies, and arthritis. One wishes he had had more sense of limits—in talking about parkinsonism, for instance.

It is hard to deny the merits of intellectual radicalism in contributing to the enduring liveliness of the early Freudians. Still, one short paragraph from a letter to Freud illustrates how different their world was from our own: "This patient, in my opinion, would have been a schizophrenic if he had not displaced the whole conflict to the myopia-producing process. As it is he remained with a part of the unresolved conflict as a 'pathological blusher.' It all came on when he renounced masturbation."[33]

Freud's letters always fascinate. One of the more striking passages occurs when he says of Paul Schilder; "I must declare him unsuited to teaching psychoanalysis, quite regardless of whether others are more or less suited than he."[34] Freud was obsessed with the problem of priorities, and in this work are found further grounds for believing that he could not let the issue of Pierre Janet, a French rival, alone. On the whole, however, the Freud who wrote to Jelliffe is an aging and distant old man. The Jung correspondence is the more interesting. Jung's emphasis on the need for synthesis and cohesion fits in with recent developments within ego psychology. Jung also understood how infantile clinical material could be an evasion and defensive. One of Jung's letters is remarkable for its subtle bitterness over the accusation of being a "mystic."[35]

Jelliffe was not a great writer, either in letters or his publications. Yet he stands in the American tradition of the spirit of William James. Jelliffe's judgment about people was unusually sound. He was open-minded, if sometimes credulous; it is wonderful to read him worrying about trying to keep up with European thinkers like Edmund Husserl or Karl Jaspers. Burnham is balanced in concluding that Jelliffe's model as a thoughtful, cultured physician means that "this ideal of clinician as intellectual was one of the lasting legacies not merely of Jelliffe but of Victorian science and medicine in general."[36]

With the publication of Susan Quinn's fine biography, *A Mind of Her Own: The Life of Karen Horney* (1987), Horney's reputation reaches a new peak. She started off as a pioneering analyst in Freud's movement. Born in a town just outside Hamburg in 1885, when women could only go on to higher education in a few places in Germany, Horney became first a physician and then a psychiatrist. By 1910 she was studying psychoanalysis in Berlin, long before being an analyst was any kind of conventional profession.

Horney's main claim to fame comes from the distinctive approach to feminine psychology that she started to outline in the late twenties. Freud himself was reluctant to publish much about women and only got pushed into it when otherwise he was in danger of being preempted in the field by some of his promising young female followers. Unlike Freud, who steadfastly defined libido as masculine in nature, an idea that embodied all sorts of patriarchal biases, Horney increasingly struck out on her own in exploring the social and cultural sources of feminine problems.

Other psychoanalytic writers beside Horney found they could express their own distinctive contributions within the broad conceptualization that Freud had initiated, without repudiating his basic concepts; for example, by following up on the unexplored female libido (as Helene Deutsch did), which to Freud had been a contradiction in terms. But Horney threw aside what she regarded as the compromises of theoretical mumbo jumbo in order to highlight the legitimacy of a distinctively female perspective, and this courage has subsequently earned her a secure stature in modern feminism.

Freud himself did nothing special to combat Horney's work, although he is known to have muttered his private misgivings; Freud and Horney had no personal relationship, as she had emerged on the international scene after he had already contracted his cancer. His disciples, however, objected to what they regarded as Horney's "watering-down" of Freud's teachings and either wrote critical reviews or simply ignored Horney's work in their professional bibliographies.

As in each of the many controversies in the history of psychoanalysis, it is never easy to untangle who initiated which of the difficulties. Today Horney's views are widely acknowledged, and this book of Susan Quinn's was even published with the endorsement of an organizationally orthodox analyst, the son of a Freud favorite. Fifty years ago, though, after Horney had immigrated to the United States, she had severe problems with analysts in Chicago and New York until she was forced out of the New York Psychoanalytic Society, which objected to her training students with her "deviant" approach.[37]

In the church that psychoanalysis became Horney was a leading heretic, and she went on to establish her own training institute for analysts. That was not to be the end of the bickering, though, and there were further secessions within her own group. Entirely aside from the divisions, which were in large part personal and unbecoming in a movement with aspirations to be scientific, it is important to remember that Horney took a more humanistic view of psychotherapy than was then generally accepted. She believed that the personality of the therapist and not some neutral-sounding technique was the essential constituent of care. While others within the establishment knew as much, Horney had boldly sought to separate herself from those who pretended they had access to privileged knowledge. Worse, from the standpoints of insiders, was the way Horney succeeded in writing for a popular audience. Her books were accessible and sold widely.

Quinn's biography is both smoothly written and well organized. In the early chapters, in which she relies primarily on Horney's adolescent diaries for evidence, it is striking how Quinn manages to rework previously published material. Even when there is no new raw data available Quinn is able to make her subject live.

Like other early analysts, Horney led a colorful private life; although her marriage was a relatively early failure, she successfully raised three interesting daughters, in addition to carrying on a number of rewarding love affairs.

Unfortunately, Quinn is not successful as an intellectual historian. Too often she isolates Horney from other analytic thinkers of her time. For example, Wilhelm Reich's remarkable early hypotheses about what he called character analysis get a wholly inadequate amount of attention here, even though Horney's writings would be inconceivable without Reich's innovations; and although Quinn tells us, for the first time as far as I know, about a sexual affair between Erich Fromm and Horney, no attempt whatever is made to relate Fromm's theories to the direction that Horney's own later concepts were to take. It looks like the success of feminism has organizationally served to rehabilitate Horney, while Fromm still remains—like Jung—in outer darkness for orthodox analysis.

Quinn is working in a miserable area of scholarship. Accounts of the early history of psychoanalysis are marred by sectarian bias; partisans of different schools teach and propagate their own versions of events, omitting rival perspectives by means of the most deadly silent treatments. While Quinn herself would seem to have no special ideological ax to grind and has succeeded in producing a splendidly written account of Horney's career, *A Mind of Her Own* needs to be balanced against other texts about the same period and similar pioneers.

Notes

1. Muriel Gardner, ed., *The Wolf-Man* (New York: Basic Books, 1971) p. 226, p. 262.
2. Ibid., p. 259.
3. Ibid., p. 305.
4. Ibid., p. 20.
5. Ibid., p. 266.
6. Ibid., p. 366.
7. Karin Obholzer, *The Wolf-Man Sixty Years Later: Conversations with Freud's Patient*, trans. Michael Shaw (London: Routledge & Kegan Paul, 1982), p. 231.
8. Ibid., p. 172.
9. Ibid., p. 118.
10. Patrick J. Mahony, *Cries of the Wolf Man* (New York: International Universities Press, 1984), p. xi.
11. Ruth Mack Brunswick, "A Note on the Childish Theory of Coitus A Tergo," *International Journal of Psychoanalysis* 10 (1929), p. 93.
12. Mahony, *Cries of the Wolf Man*, p. 4.
13. Ibid., p. 5.
14. Ibid.
15. Patrick J. Mahony, *Freud and the Rat Man* (New Haven: Yale University Press, 1986), p. 70.
16. Ibid., p. 82.
17. Ibid., p. 85.
18. Mahony, *Cries of the Wolf Man*, pp. 159–60.
19. Ibid., p. 116.
20. A. H. Chapman, *Harry Stack Sullivan: His Life and His Work* (New York: G. P. Putnam's Sons, 1976), p. 27.
21. Ibid., p. 15.
22. Ibid., p. 164.
23. Ibid., p. 208.
24. Helen Swick Perry, *Psychiatrist of America: The Life of Harry Stack Sullivan* (Cambridge: Harvard University Press, 1982), p. 4.
25. Ibid., p. 68.
26. Vincent Brome, *Ernest Jones: Freud's Alter Ego* (London: Caliban Books, 1982), pp. 58–59; *The Freud/Jung Letters: The Correspondence Between Sig-*

mund Freud and C. G. Jung, ed. William McGuire, trans. Ralph Manheim and R. F. C. Hull (Princeton: Princeton University Press, 1985) p. 145.

27. Celia Bertin, *Marie Bonaparte: A Life* (New York: Harcourt, Brace Jovanovich, 1982), p. 176.
28. Ibid., p. 248.
29. Ibid., p. 176.
30. John C. Burnham, *Jelliffe: American Psychoanalyst and Physician and His Correspondence with Sigmund Freud and C. G. Jung*, ed. William McGuire (Chicago: University of Chicago Press, 1983), p. 279.
31. Ibid., p. 282.
32. Ibid., p. 132.
33. Ibid., p. 242.
34. Ibid., p. 269.
35. Ibid., p. 232.
36. Ibid., p. 168.
37. Susan Quinn, *A Mind of Her Own: The Life of Karen Horney* (New York: Summit Books, 1987), pp. 328–50.

11

Heretics

Freud was an original thinker who liked to joke that he had created psychoanalysis because it had no literature. For years now, however, the field he originated has been marked by the deficiencies of scholasticism. Technical papers typically begin by citing earlier writings, but these scholarly-looking references are misleading, since they selectively ignore the context surrounding the isolated citations.

It is in such a situation that the penalties for being a heretic and the advantages of conformism are particularly striking. Those writers in the history of psychoanalysis who ran afoul of Freud personally, or the organized movement he led, have been systematically ignored in the training of future analysts. Although, for example, it has been customary to mention cursorily the work of Alfred Adler, Carl G. Jung, and Otto Rank in lectures on "deviant" thinkers at training institutes, it is inconceivable that these authors actually be read by trainees. The same general point can be extended to more recent so-called controversial analysts; therefore, Karen Horney, Erich Fromm, Harry Stack Sullivan, and Clara Thompson have generally not received the professional recognition they deserve. (The status of Wilhelm Reich and Melanie Klein is somewhat more complicated.) Although there are of course exceptions to generalizing about the state of organized psychoanalysis, the existence of an informal Index banning certain works is impossible to contest.

The excommunication of psychoanalytic heretics is made easier by the characteristic nature of terminological innovation in the course of the clashes that have so often taken place. Freud invented a specialized vocabulary, and in the act of challenging him former disciples of his created a set of categories that were designed as substitutes for his formulations. As a result those who are training in competing schools of these thinkers would be hard-pressed, if the occasion ever presented itself, to understand one another's writings.

Paul E. Stepansky's *In Freud's Shadow: Adler in Context* (1983) is a sign
that psychoanalysis may be moving into a different period. At the outset he
declares his belief that "the history of psychoanalysis represents unex-
ploited terrain for the historian of ideas."[1] Adler led the first of the "deviations" within Freud's earliest group of disciples, and his work has
unquestionably not received the attention it deserves. If, however, Stepansky is right in believing that one of the main contributions Adler made was
in pointing toward a modern psychosomatic orientation, Stepansky is evidently not conversant with the medical literature on mind-body problems,
and this oversight on his part indicates just how right he is in thinking that
intellectual historians have important scholarship ahead of them.

Stepansky holds out the hope of a "comprehensive history of the psychoanalytic movement that remains to be written," and he is correct in seeing
his own contribution as a "useful building block" for such an ideal
project.[2] But he does not acknowledge how far distant such a proposal must
remain. His own rather awkwardly written book succeeds in inadvertently
reinforcing some of the blindspots he should have been trying to counteract.
It is simply wrong to write of Adler as in any sense a "psychiatrist."[3] A
few pages later Stepansky acknowledges that Adler "received no psychiatric training."[4] A modern audience is bound to be confused about the professional direction from which Freud, a neurologist, and his early followers
(many not physicians) had come. The central major psychiatrist in Freud's
pre–World War I movement was Jung, but Stepansky only pays the most
nominal attention to Jung's work. This is particularly regrettable since the
Adlerian split in psychoanalysis was preceded by Freud's having chosen to
favor Jung and his Swiss associates ahead of Adler and the members of the
almost wholly nonpsychiatric Vienna Psychoanalytic Society.

Assuming the isolated deficiencies in Stepansky's book are readily tolerated, we can be grateful for having a careful analysis of all the texts of
Adler's writings. Adler started off with an interest in social medicine, and
his Social Democratic outlook colored his subsequent ideas. One of the first
treatises—before meeting Freud—was on the demoralized plight of the tai-
lor trade. Adler was interested in a prophylactic approach that took as its
premise a medical science devoted to the amelioration of social misery. For
Adler physicians were really educators, and he thought that through educational guidance they could best practice preventive medicine. Stepansky is
convincing that Adler's later psychology was intended to fulfill these early
aspirations.

After Stepansky gives a summary of Adler's prepsychoanalytic work, he
offers two chapters about Adler's system of Individual Psychology. (The
title heading for the chapters, "From Medicine to Psychiatry," continues to
obscure the gulf between psychiatry and psychoanalysis in Central Europe.)
Adler was a better theorist than a writer, and he had valuable, practical

therapeutic purposes. He is perhaps best known for the idea that neurotic symptoms are the result of organ inferiority—as Stepansky summarizes it, compensations attempt "to energize the inferior organ through heightened activity."[5] Adler made other suggestions that have been built on subsequently, such as the notion that aggression is an interpersonal safeguard serving to elevate feelings of self-esteem by means of degrading others.

Even before their falling out, Adler's clinical orientation differed from that of Freud. Adler thought that sexual factors, for example, should not be taken at face value but could express a latent content as well. Adler proposed the term *masculine protest*,[6] a concept he thought could explain a variety of different forms of emotional expression. Chronic neurotic suffering stemmed, he wrote, from psychological oversensitivity, and feelings of inferiority were often compensated for through protest and fantasies of greatness. Adler had clinical points to make: patients, he held, manipulated therapists by a variety of strategies. Sexuality itself could be "arranged"[7] to express sham feelings. Adler's prose is often inaccessible, but Stepansky's discussion has the great merit of taking Adler's work seriously; it is still ritualistically dismissed in psychoanalytic circles as mere "common sense."

Although due to his chronological outlook it takes Stepansky's book a while to get to the actual quarrel between Freud and Adler, the four chapters on their intellectual difficulties are the most original part of the book. Stepansky has done an enormously conscientious job of trying to understand the language of that far-off conflict, which is apt now to sound theological in character. Stepansky is fair-minded: "Freudians, no less than Adlerians, have polemicized about Adler's departure from the Vienna Society to the point of utter caricature."[8]

Although Stepansky claims that "Freud was too adroit to excommunicate Adler outright. . . . ,"[9] Freud's dramatic reassessment of Adler's work in the spring of 1911 led to the resignation of almost half of the membership of the tiny Vienna Psychoanalytic Society. Stepansky shows that criticisms of Adler that Freud delivered at the time of their public confrontation could have been formulated almost anytime for over four years. Freud was, Stepansky says, engaging in "a political maneuver of the first order."[10] Freud wanted to put an end to Adler's collaboration in psychoanalysis, and Stepansky illustrates how in the proceedings a lot of terminology became reified. Although Stepansky apparently does not like the implications of the image of excommunication he writes that Adler's "departure from the group was the product of a premeditated assault engineered entirely by Freud."[11]

Stepansky effectively demonstrates the disparity between what Adler was actually saying and that which Freud ended up criticizing in his polemical tracts. Freud characteristically used disparaging clinical terminology to stigmatize his ex-disciples. Adler was the occasion for the first schism within the psychoanalytic movement, although not the first ally Freud felt obliged to lose. Stepansky has been working from within the broad "mainstream" of contemporary psychoanalysis and is the first within the fold to take such care with Adler's ideas.

After the struggle with Freud, Adler wrote mainly about the education of the child. Adler had long viewed psychotherapy as concentrated education, and now as a social reformer he sought the prophylaxis of neurosis. A famous experimental school in Vienna was founded on Adler's principles, and Adlerian educational guidance clinics were also set up. Although Adler's early death in 1937 cut short his possible influence, many post-Freudian writers have implicitly followed in his direction.

The impartiality of Stepansky's book should contribute to a less blinkered view of other aspects of the history of psychoanalysis.

Although Jung's stature in intellectual history is even larger than that of Adler, still the literature dealing with Jung is relatively scanty—certainly as compared with what scholars have done for Freud. To be sure, Jung lacked Freud's profoundly original vision and his clarity as a writer; the Swiss thinker tends to appear muddled in his formulations. Nevertheless, in the history of modern psychotherapy Jung pioneered in short-term treatment, and clinical concepts of his that were considered by Freud grounds for excommunication have now, seventy-five years later, quietly found their way back into orthodox analysis.

The publication of Jung's *Letters*, vol. I: *1906–1950* (1973) should have done much to help us evaluate Jung's place in modern thought. Unfortunately, prejudices die hard and biographical material is still relatively scarce, so one wishes the Jung family would authorize an official biographer to fill the gap, as the Freuds did Jones. The Jung heirs have not released for publication Jung's letters to his family. (The earliest, 1896, is to his mother, but most of them are to his wife.) Jung was assailed by Freud's students for his timidity in shying away from Freud's theory of infantile sexuality, but Jung lived a far less sexually restricted life than Freud. A married man, for many years Jung had an affair with a psychiatrist and former patient of his, Antonia Wolff. After her death in 1953 Jung's letters to her were returned to him, but he destroyed them along with her letters to him.

Jung, who claimed to have treated Freud for a neurotic complaint, acknowledged the personal element in his break with Freud; as with other especially creative analysts, Jung's admiration for Freud eventually led to an attempt to be as independent as the master. Jung wrote in a 1909 letter that "it is a hard lot to have to work alongside the father creator."[12] Although in later years Jung could at times acknowledge Freud's accomplishments and even claim to have carried on in the best Freudian tradition, he could also seek to minimize his intellectual debt to the originator of psychoanalysis. "I would like to take this opportunity," he wrote in 1933, "to rectify the error that I come from the Freudian school. I am a pupil of Bleuler."[13]

No better critique of Freud's excessive rationalism can be found than in the body of Jung's collected works; to Jung it seemed that the "intellect is a great sorcerer. . . . "[14] He also contributed positive clinical concepts of his own to psychotherapy. Long before orthodox analysts could see the point, Jung argued that current anxieties are capable of reactivating infantile material. Besides, he was interested in other stages of the life cycle than the Oedipal one. It is still not widely known that Jung was the first to insist on analysts themselves being analyzed as part of their training, and Jung came to emphasize the importance of personal rapport between patient and analyst. "Faced with the patient, you see at once, if you are not totally blinded, that all theorizing is absurd. Everything depends on how you strike the patient as a human being. In the end the personality is the most powerful therapeutic agent."[15]

Yet for all his independence in trying to treat schizophrenia and his stress on the importance of helping neurotic patients with problems of philosophic meaning, Jung could correct a disciple's overzealousness: "You *wanted* to help, which is an encroachment upon the will of others. Your attitude ought to be that of one who offers an opportunity that can be taken or rejected."[16] Far less suspicious of the unconscious than Freud, indeed sometimes Pollyannaish in his emphasis on the mind's compensatory functions, Jung concluded that "symptoms are always justified and serve a purpose."[17]

Like other Central European intellectuals of his era (including Freud), Jung felt compelled to speak out prophetically on social and cultural matters. His correspondence, however, came to be increasingly with pastors and theologians; many of the letters are dull and verbose. (Whatever Freud's faults, he is rarely boring.) Nevertheless, some of Jung's clinical vignettes are wonderfully alive.

After Hitler came to power, Jung accepted the leadership of a German psychiatric association, in what he described as an attempt to protect psychotherapy there. Continuing to live in Switzerland during this time, he helped numerous Jewish therapists escape to England and elsewhere. Jung had described some of the characteristics of Freud's psychoanalysis as Jewish, but complained that "the mere fact that I speak of a difference between Jewish and Christian psychology suffices to allow anyone to voice the prejudice that I am an anti-Semite."[18] At the same time Jung allowed his comments on the differences between Jewish and "Aryan" psychology to appear in an article published in Nazi Germany. The closeness of Jung's distinction to the Nazi one between "Jewish science" and "German science" is chilling. Jung tried to hold dissenting Dutch psychiatrists within his psychiatric association based on Germany, yet it is hard to admire the principle Jung invoked of the apolitical and neutral character of psychiatry when the political regime was Hitler's. But despite the abhorent collaboration with the Nazis, which has inevitably damaged Jung's historical standing, his genuine contributions to intellectual life deserve to be acknowledged.

Carl G. Jung still remains a relatively neglected figure, and his "analytical psychology" is little understood not only among political scientists but also among people in North America generally. Freud never had a more incisive or more profound critic than Jung; Jung appreciated Freud's special strengths as well as his key weaknesses and proceeded to work out an alternative psychological system. Jung had an elusive and often poetic style, which has not helped ensure his impact on social science. As a writer Jung is often hard to follow, and up to now his conception of human nature, with its implications for social and political thought, has been almost wholly unexamined.

The miserable state of Jungian scholarship has not made things easier. Huge volumes of Jung's work have been published almost entirely without editorial apparatus, whereas Freud's disciples have been sure to annotate elaborately even the most casual of his essays. The Jung family allowed the centennial of his birth to pass without the appearance of an authorized biography, and they have been reluctant to have discussed in print aspects of Jung's life that might conflict with bourgeois Swiss morality. (Barbara Hannah's *Jung: His Life and Work,* which was published in 1976, is the broadest biographical memoir to have appeared.) While the Freud family, as of *Freud-Jung Letters* in 1974, stopped its practice of tendentiously editing Freud's letters, the Jung family still insists on its power of editorial censorship.

A book on Jung's social and political ideas is unusually timely. Yet partly because of the rich opportunities of the subject matter, Volodymyr Walter Odajnyk's *Jung and Politics: The Political and Social Ideas of C. G. Jung* (1976) is a disappointment. It is far too narrowly conceived, as it presents Jung's ideas in skeleton form apart from either the tradition of social philosophy or the history of ideas. Jung is a more interesting thinker than this book makes him appear, and he deserves fuller treatment. Jung's conception of the unconscious was very different from that of Freud, and they disagreed, for example, in their outlooks on normality and rationality; many of the ideas of post-Freudian writers prominent in social science were in fact anticipated by Jung. *Jung and Politics* offers us few references outside of Jung's own writings, and under the circumstances the absence of a bibliography is hard to understand.

Unlike many other students of Jung's ideas, Odajnyk does not try to dodge the question of Jung's involvement with the Nazis. Freud had charged Jung with anti-Semitism before World War I, and during the 1930s Jung in Switzerland collaborated with Hitler's regime. Perhaps no other feature of Jung's life has so justifiably damaged his reputation among intellectuals. Odajnyk's chapter 6, "The German Case," presents some of the available evidence; he accurately described Jung's decision to publish a paper in Nazi Germany, where he discussed the characteristically Jewish features of Freud's psychoanalysis, as "a stupid and callous act for which there is really no excuse." [19] Jung was so naive that in later years he did not realize that his best defense would be to plead political stupidity.

Freud's own practical politics were not particularly admirable; his support of an authoritarian Austrian regime, and his attitude toward Mussolini, ought to leave his orthodox followers uneasy. Although the longest chapter in *Jung and Politics* is a comparison of Jung and Freud, Odajnyk does not seem to realize how alike they were, especially in their concrete political and social convictions. It makes little sense for Odajnyk to conclude his book with the claim that whereas the implications of Freud's psychology are "reactionary," Jung's conceptions of the psyche "could lead to a harmonious and democratic resolution of the political and moral conflicts of mankind." [20] We need no more trots on Jung, but rather presentations of his ideas that make his work come alive, and then it should be possible, as in the case of Freud, for people of various ideological persuasions to find interesting points in Jung's system of thought from which they can build.

For political scientists it will be disappointing to be told again, as in the foreword by Marie-Louise von Franz, that "to a great extent all political dissensions and conflicts are exteriorizations of inner conflicts. . . . " [21] It would seem from this remark that Jung's loyal disciples have not gone much further than devout early Freudians. Harold Lasswell was a brave and eclectic pioneer in 1930, but by now one would hope for more sophisticated conceptions of the interrelations of psychology and politics.

Although Odajnyk tells us he came to Jung after being disenchanted both with behaviorism and with Freud, he does not seem to recognize adequately that his calling as a political theorist obliges him to be more self-conscious about the uses of psychology for partisan or moral purposes. Instead of defending Jung for having supposedly created a "science" and not a "cult," [22] Odajnyk would do better to see how features of both played a part in Jung's psychology. Such a mixture would not be unique even in contemporary academic life.

Otto Rank was a brilliant psychologist, one of the founders of twentieth-century depth psychology. Rank stands along with Freud, Jung, and Adler as an explorer of the unconscious. Unlike these other three better-known figures, however, Rank has only now been rewarded with a comprehensive biography. Thanks to E. James Lieberman's *Acts of Will: The Life and Work of Otto Rank* (1985), Rank will now be securely established in intellectual history.

Before the falling out between Rank and Freud in the mid-1920s, Rank had spent far longer in Freud's circle than any other of the so-called dissidents in the history of psychoanalysis. Part of Freud's genius lay in the different kinds of people that he succeeded in attracting. With Rank, he found a thinker who would centrally concern himself with the issue of creativity.

Rank was the first Freudian to analyze art. He was full of fascinating ideas, although he expressed himself in prose that proved too dense for most readers. Yet in recent years there has been a revival of interest in Rank's work.

For almost twenty years Rank functioned in Vienna as Freud's personal favorite. Rank performed the duties of Freud's assistant and secretary to the Vienna Psychoanalytic Society, as well as undertaking his own writings. Four editions of Freud's *The Interpretation of Dreams* contained two chapters by Rank, and it is almost always forgotten that Rank's name appeared below Freud's on the title page. Rank was so close to Freud as to be almost a son, and the other psychoanalytic leaders were jealous of his special position.

Once Freud fell ill with cancer in 1923, there was bound to be a problem with his chosen successor, for, contrary to the early medical expectations, Freud did not die but lived on for another sixteen years. As Freud struggled to hold Rank within the psychoanalytic movement, other analysts—especially Jones—stigmatized every original idea of Rank's as heresy.

Eventually Rank succeeded in establishing his own following, notably at the Pennsylvania School of Social Work. As a therapist, Rank was far more optimistic than orthodox analysts of the time. His book *The Trauma of Birth* highlighted the significance of mothering and separation anxiety in human development, when Freud was concentrating on the father's role in early childhood.

Analysts since then have often been at pains to reinvent the Rankian wheel. Rank advocated shorter analyses and the use of termination dates as a way of speeding psychotherapy. He was altogether more interested in the here and now of his patients, as opposed to the Freudian ideal of reconstructing the past.

Rank sounds like a contemporary of ours in his dubiousness about the therapeutic power of rational insight. He highlighted the significance of emotional reliving rather than the place of reason in therapy. Rank was a pioneer in revising Freud's notions of female psychology, and in recommending an attitude toward "cure"[23] that was flexible instead of static. Rank thought of a patient's resistance as a force to be mobilized in behalf of self-development, and saw neurosis as a failure in being creative. Conscious self-formation was to Rank an act of will.

Lieberman's book succeeds not only in reviving the human meaning of Rank's concepts, but in documenting an important chapter in the history of psychoanalysis, for once out of the fold of Freud's faithful followers, this original writer was to be branded as insane. Freud used psychoanalytic terminology on his wayward pupil, and Jones went the furthest of all in diagnostic name calling. There is no historical evidence for Rank's alleged mental illness. Nonetheless, as late as 1957, Lionel Trilling in a *New York Times* review of Jones's authorized biography of Freud wrote that Rank had died insane. And *Time* magazine echoed this judgment in a 1958 review of an early book about Rank.

Lieberman's biography is thorough and conscientious. The early discussion of Rank's adolescent diary is particularly moving. Lieberman might have explored further the remarkable personality of Rank's first wife, Tola, who after their separation went on to become a leading child analyst in Boston, Massachusetts. Others will, in assessing Rank's stature, pay more attention to the legitimate contributions of such earlier psychoanalytic "heretics" as Jung.

It is Otto Rank's achievement that he understood not only how art and psychology interact, but that he wrote about the limits of the two, from the perspective of one who developed with Freud and then outgrew him.

Wilhelm Reich is one of the most popularly known of the many prophets to have emerged from within psychoanalysis. A steady stream of books about him in recent years has helped satisfy the public's legitimate curiosity. So far the best of them is Reich's son Peter's poetic memoirs, *A Book of Dreams* (1973). Yet Myron Sharaf's *Fury on Earth: A Biography of Wilhelm Reich* (1983) is far and away the finest book on both Reich's work and his life. It is a professional piece of scholarship that may well, until the Reich archives are finally opened, remain definitive on the subject.

The history of Freud and his circle has by now become a scholarly industry. Because of the persistence of sectarianism, though, it is not as easy as it should be to become acquainted with the growth of the tradition of depth psychology. Entirely aside from the continuing fascination with the founder of psychoanalysis, biographies of his followers—and the "heretics"—are steadily being published. Otto Rank has been reassessed by Esther Menaker's *Otto Rank* (1982); a good sympathetic book about Alfred Adler, *Masks of Loneliness* (1974), was written by Manes Sperber; we also have Jack Rubins's *Karen Horney* (1978); and Paul Stern's *C. G. Jung: The Haunted Prophet* (1976) was fascinating.

Reich is remarkable in that all his books, even the ones from the early 1920s, have been reprinted recently. His *The Mass Psychology of Fascism* anticipated the more widely used *Escape from Freedom* by Fromm and *The Authoritarian Personality* by Adorno, Frenkel-Brunswick, Levinson, and Sanford.

Readers of Sharaf's *Fury on Earth* ought not to be put off by the acknowledgments with which the book begins; a tone of sentimentality damages it, and part 1, "The Viewpoint of the Observer," consists of two chapters that appear to herald an amateurish piece of work. It would seem that the success of psychohistory has gone too far, in that biographers can feel obliged to offer material that is not, in my judgment, a part of serious historiography.

The first chapter, "Introduction," sets forth the main outlines of Reich's achievement and the vicissitudes of his reputation. It is not true, however, that "in the early 1920's many regarded him as 'Freud's pet', destined for a position of leadership within the psychoanalytic movement."[24] To be sure, Reich was a brilliant young analyst, full of ideas, and Helene Deutsch in particular did all she could to encourage and shelter her protégé. But as far as his relation to Freud himself went, by the 1920s Freud was concentrating on his patients and pupils from abroad; within the Vienna Society Reich was always controversial, and Freud held himself at some distance from Reich personally.

The problem with part 1 is partly an excessive claim in behalf of Reich's significance; we are told in the first chapter, for example, that "he had disturbed the sleep of the world more fundamentally than Freud or Marx had done."[25] Equally unsettling is the whole of chapter 2, "My Relationship with Reich." Perhaps, but maybe not, it was necessary for us to know that Reich had an affair with Sharaf's first wife; the special mental illness of Sharaf's mother did play a part in his receptivity to Reich's thinking. But there is a limit beyond which historians need not go, and Sharaf has overstepped that boundary. I do not think we had to hear about the tragic death of one of Sharaf's sons. I see no reason for our finding out that Sharaf's mother had an affair with one of his fellow students in college. When Sharaf tells us that he himself went into analysis because of a difficulty in completing his Ph.D. dissertation, he is inadvertently calling attention to one of the cultural curiosities of American society; not only is it hard to believe that Freud would have viewed such a problem as a "symptom" requiring analysis, but common sense suggests that other authorities than analysts have better training in helping students over such blockages. If it is true, as I think is the case, that a whole generation of analysands tended to seek treatment for such a sublimated incapacity, then that is telling about how oversold the claims of analysis as therapy once were.

After the biography itself is under way, Sharaf's work picks up. Yet it is not clear why he has chosen to retranslate Reich's first published analytic paper, which is particularly self-revealing, when an English version of that essay is readily available. These earlier years of Reich's career, which Sharaf does an excellent job of reconstructing, will have the most interest for intellectual historians. Reich was a genuine pioneer in modern psychotherapy. He was interested in character structure more than in isolated symptoms; he emphasized nonverbal communication and the need to release blocked feelings; finally, he insisted on the significance of negative reactions in patients toward their therapists. Late in life, Freud himself admitted that he had neglected to interpret negative transferences. In general, Reich concentrated on the degree to which earlier analysts, including Freud, had not begun to systematize their knowledge of therapeutic technique.

Long before Masters and Johnson, Reich wanted to conduct laboratory experiments in human sexuality. In addition, Reich thought that bridges needed to be built between Freud and Marx; Reich came to hold that the Oedipus complex was a product of patriarchal culture and that neurosis could be prevented if Western culture were to allow a change in its family structure. Freud wrote *Civilization and Its Discontents* (1930) to underline the differences between his own views and those of Reich.

Sharaf has done a thorough research job on Reich's personal life, although for some unexplained reason he failed ever to meet Reich's first wife, a former patient of his. (Sharaf also did not succeed in interviewing Helene Deutsch; it is not true, as he claims, that she was "of Reich's generation."[26]) Reich preached in behalf of sexual liberation; he advocated liberalized abortions and easier divorces, and also thought that most people missed out on the involuntary aspects of orgastic satisfaction. It turns out that although Reich himself was not promiscuous, he had his share of multiple affairs, as well as several stormy marriages. Sharaf is writing in behalf of Reich, and therefore the author is kind and understanding rather than moralistic.

It is regrettable that Sharaf takes so seriously Reich's work on orgone energy, which was Reich's hobbyhorse during the years Sharaf knew him. Although Sharaf states at the outset of the book that Reich "never claimed the [orgone] accumulator could cure colds, cancer, or impotency,"[27] the publisher's flier for *Fury on Earth* states that Reich was a "pioneer in the treatment of, among other diseases, mental illness and cancer. . . . " When Reich becomes mentally unbalanced, if not paranoid, Sharaf speaks of Reich's "erroneous"[28] views, and he uses technical terminology to excuse

Reich's pathology: "In his jealous rages, his violence, his bullying, his demand for confessions, Reich was under the spell of, and identified with, his introjected father."[29]

The story of the persecution of Reich by the American Food and Drug Administration, which sought to bar the sale of orgone accumulators although Reich thought they would help cure cancer, makes worthwhile reading. Reich refused to be properly defended legally and ended up being sentenced to two years in jail, where he died in 1957. According to Sharaf it was a "fantasy,"[30] not a delusion, that President Eisenhower was a secret friend. It remains at least an open question whether Sharaf is correct in distinguishing between so-called "classical"[31] science and Reich's supposedly "scientific" writings. But there is no disputing the violation of Reich's civil liberties or the social cruelty toward Reich that extended even to having copies of his writing destroyed at the order of the FDA.

Sharaf's biography is a large, sprawling book that makes for a good read. Despite its flaws, it remains a fine book, the most authoritative and informative study about Reich to have appeared. Someday perhaps Reich's works can be cited, along with those of Adler, Jung, and Rank, without any possible fear that one is thereby in danger of being contaminated by one of the prime heresies in the history of Freud's school.

Notes

1. Paul E. Stepansky, *In Freud's Shadow: Adler in Context* (Hillsdale, N.J.: Analytic Press, 1983), p. x.
2. Ibid., p. 5.
3. Ibid., p. 4.
4. Ibid., pp. 10–11.
5. Ibid., p. 53.
6. Ibid., p. 57.
7. Ibid., p. 75.
8. Ibid., p. 112.
9. Ibid., p. 130.
10. Ibid., p. 136.
11. Ibid., p. 146.
12. C. G. Jung, *Letters*, ed. Gerhard Adler, trans. R. F. C. Hull (Princeton: Princeton University Press, 1973), p. 15.
13. Ibid., p. 122.
14. Ibid., p. 134.
15. Ibid., p. 112.
16. Ibid., p. 84.
17. Ibid., p. 53.
18. Ibid., p. 161.
19. Volodymyr Walter Odajnyk, *Jung and Politics: The Political and Social Ideas of C. G. Jung* (New York: Harper & Row, 1976), p. 107.

20. Ibid., p. 187.
21. Ibid., p. x.
22. Ibid., p. xiv.
23. E. James Lieberman, *Acts of Will: The Life and Work of Otto Rank* (New York: Free Press, 1985), p. 290.
24. Myron Sharaf, *Fury on Earth: A Biography of Wilhelm Reich* (New York: St. Martin's Press/Marek, 1983), p. 5.
25. Ibid., p. 10.
26. Ibid., p. 117.
27. Ibid., p. 2.
28. Ibid., p. 435.
29. Ibid., p. 404.
30. Ibid., p. 413.
31. Ibid., p. 418.

12

Loyalism

Max Schur's *Freud: Living and Dying* (1972) was written by Freud's personal physician from 1928 until 1939; the book had been long anticipated. Schur had already composed an as yet unpublished "Medical Case History of Sigmund Freud," as well as a lengthy and informal memoir in the form of a letter to Jones in 1955 (which Jones considered the finest commentary on his biography of Freud), and before Schur's volume on Freud appeared Schur had also made use of some unpublished portions of Freud's correspondence with Fliess in order to understand Freud's account of his early patient "Irma." In *Freud: Living and Dying,* which appeared posthumously, Schur undertook the ambitious task of understanding "the development of Freud's own attitude toward all aspects of living and dying."[1]

The broad influence of psychoanalysis has encouraged the publication of many essays and memoirs about Freud. Unfortunately, however, too much research has been infused with unspoken partisanship. For example, despite Schur's explicit aim, he omits any references to Freud's curious reaction to his mother's death at the age of ninety-five in 1930. Freud had repeatedly worried, as he aged and was afflicted with cancer, that he might die before her. Freud was hoping to protect her from suffering. When she died he felt liberated: "I was not free to die as long as she was alive, and now I am."[2] Freud's mother's funeral was held in Vienna; despite his love and concern for her, and in contrast to his glowing description of the tie between mothers and sons—"the most perfect, the most free from ambivalence of all human relationships"[3]—Freud chose not to attend. He considered it suitable to send his daughter Anna; she "represented"[4] him. Surely if Schur's book were to live up to its goal it should not have so entirely ignored such an incident.

Unlike other hagiographical accounts of Freud, however, Schur tried to put Freud's own self-analysis into the center of Freud's creation of therapeutic technique. When Schur tells us that in the 1890s Freud "had com-

215

pletely abandoned hypnosis, and demanded of his patients that they withhold nothing,"[5] he communicates the authentic tone of Freud's enlightened despotism. However, Schur loyally shares the ideological blinders of many of his colleagues when he puts forward, in discussing Freud's dream interpretations, the supposedly new concept of "resistance downward": *"the emphasis on infantile factors can be used successfully as a defense against recent conflicts. . . . "*[6] (italics in original). This idea is undoubtedly clinically correct, but Schur was lacking in historical perspective: for what is presented as a clinical principle for orthodox psychoanalysis in 1972 was first proposed by the heretic Jung sixty years earlier.

Taking into account the context of the original publication date of *Freud: Living and Dying,* perhaps the most valuable part of the book consisted in the appearance of numerous letters from Freud to Fliess that had not been allowed in print until then. Freud himself had not wanted this intimate set of letters to his friend to come out. The Freud family cooperated in a partial publication of the correspondence in 1954. But if they defied their father's wishes they did so with a clouded conscience, so the letters to Fliess came out, but bowdlerized. Freud was not even allowed to joke at his own expense.

Through its inclusion of hitherto unpublished letters of Freud, Schur's book was the first to give a glimpse of what we had missed. For example, Freud's earlier friendship with Josef Breuer had turned into an intense loathing. Evidently this experienced physician was dubious about a patient of Freud's entering a fifth year of treatment. When a daughter of Breuer was about to marry someone close to Fliess, Freud was worried about "the prospect of being pushed still further from you [Fliess] and your family through the impending 'Breuerization.' "[7] Freud is known to have disliked Fliess's wife; little mention of either man's wife appears in print. But Schur quotes Freud as writing of Breuer: "I do no longer despise him. . . . If he is dead as far as you two are concerned, he is still exerting his power posthumously. What else is your wife doing but working out, under a dark compulsion, the suggestion Breuer planted in her soul when he congratulated her on the fact that I was not living in Berlin and could not disrupt her marriage?"[8]

Schur is too literal-minded in seeing Fliess as an object of Freud's transference feelings on the model of the analytic situation; Jones and other loyalists had taken a similar tack. Fortunately, at the time Schur thought that "nothing can convey better the interplay between Freud's self-analysis and his relationship to Fliess than his own words,"[9] and we thereby had access to much new raw historical data. But for all Schur's accuracy, and indeed sometimes pedantry, he used psychiatry for polemical purposes when he dismissed Fliess as having had an "unmistakably paranoid character."[10]

One might have thought Freud's discussion of his tie to his nephew John—about whom Freud wrote that "My emotional life has always insisted that I should have an intimate friend and a hated enemy"[11]—would have been relevant to an understanding of what went wrong between Freud and Fliess, as would some consideration of Freud's preoccupation with the theme of plagiarism. Schur might then have paid some attention to the Swoboda-Weininger controversy, which he omits almost entirely from his book, and have better understood the inner meaning to what he describes as: "One of Freud's stubbornly held beliefs that Shakespeare had not been the author of the plays attributed to him. . . . "[12]

Schur does try to deal at some length with Freud's obsessive preoccupation with death and, in particular, with dying at a specific date. Here Schur departed from Freud's own view of things and that of Jones in hypothesizing a coronary thrombosis behind Freud's cardiac symptoms. Since Schur was fully aware "how difficult it is to arrive at a valid differential diagnosis some seventy-five years after the events,"[13] additional medical opinion will be of help in deciding whether to reject Freud's own interpretation of an anxiety neurosis. At least Freud's fainting spells had a clear psychogenic component.

It is obvious that Schur represents an important witness of Freud's health in his last years. One rather biased theme in this book concerns the behavior of Schur's predecessor as Freud's physician, Felix Deutsch, on Freud's first contracting cancer in 1923. Deutsch was a kindly man who did not want to tell people bad news. When Freud first showed a growth in his mouth to Deutsch, Freud said, "For what I intend to do I need a doctor. If you take it for cancer, I must find a way to disappear from this life with decency."[14] This appeal was all the hint Deutsch needed; he had a rather dictatorial way about him and could easily think he knew best. Although Deutsch soon perceived the need for an even more radical operation than Freud's first, he did not tell Freud the truth about the malignancy.

Deutsch feared that Freud might prefer to die rather than be operated on again, and so he thought it better to make the necessary arrangements without Freud's knowledge. Schur clearly implies that it was because of Deutsch's being in a personal analysis at that time that he "could not 'face reality' when he saw the ugly lesion in Freud's mouth. . . . "[15] According to Deutsch's own account, locked away in the Library of Congress because Anna Freud disapproved of its appearance in print, Freud was a fighter who could not countenance weakness in himself any more than in others. To Deutsch it seemed that Freud was angry with him precisely because Deutsch had caught him out in a weak moment; the physician had seen him as a man whose normal fears and reactions had to be taken into account. Once Freud had recovered his former life and was able to practice and write again, he was able to live heroically with the knowledge and suffering of his cancer. In a letter Freud acknowledged that from the beginning he had known his growth was cancerous.

Schur was aware that Freud's "behavior in 1923, just after the detection of his cancer, was unusually fatalistic."[16] In criticism of Deutsch's treatment of Freud, Schur goes so far as to claim that "the thought of suicide never entered his mind. . . . "[17] One would have thought that if it were not for the ties of loyalism the principles of psychoanalysis would have made such an incautious assertion unlikely. Deutsch may have badly misjudged Freud's capacity to face the truth, but the elevated version that Schur presents is unnecessarily one-sided.

In Schur's account of Freud's last years the figure of Ruth Mack Brunswick is strangely relegated to the background. She and her husband were simultaneously in analysis with Freud, and then in a reversal she analyzed both Schur and his own wife. Ruth Brunswick was one of the most important pupils of Freud's last years, but because of her personal tragedy she plays little part in the history books. Schur was still in analysis with her when he became Freud's physician, and she must have had something to do with his appointment to Freud. Schur quotes Freud in 1931 referring to Ruth Brunswick and Schur as "my two *Leibärzte*"; as Schur explains, "*Leibarzt* was the term which royalty used to designate their personal physician."[18]

Although Schur intended "not to withhold any of the tragic details of his [Freud's] prolonged suffering and dying,"[19] he omits his own feeling that Freud's illness was permitted to go on for so long. Freud died after horrible suffering; he was so old and sick that it was a deliverance finally to die. Schur more than once said that he would have ended the suffering weeks earlier, but such a human reaction was excluded from his book. Perhaps we should just be grateful for his having given us as much unpublished material as he did.

Richard Sterba's memoir, *Reminiscences of a Viennese Psychoanalyst* (1982), is exceptionally interesting. A tiny group of Freud's followers helped transform the twentieth century's image of human nature. Beyond the students they trained in Europe, they later filled positions of considerable psychiatric power, especially in the United States. Even though the high point of the psychoanalytic revolution seems long past, its principles are well known and widely understood.

Sterba gives an honest and insightful account of the years 1924–38. During that period psychoanalytic theory, at Freud's initiative, changed "from the concept of the ego as a victim to the concept of the ego as the controller of the id."[20] The *esprit de corps* about which Sterba writes meant that the members of the society altered their thinking as a group. From the point of view of the history of ideas, what counts more than any individual theory is the remarkable general atmosphere: Sterba does a fine job of recreating the ambiance of the society, seen from the perspective of one of its younger members, and writes about his colleagues with objectivity and sympathy.

Sterba is particularly decent in respect to the memory of Wilhelm Reich, whose innovations in clinical technique have too often been neglected because of his later, widely criticized ideas. Sterba cites examples of how therapeutically clumsy other early analysts could be. He also describes some of the tensions between Freud's older disciples, who gathered around him before World War I, and those newer ones like himself who arrived on the scene after the great ideological battles with Adler and Jung were past.

One chapter is devoted to Freud himself. After getting cancer in 1923, he remained distant toward newcomers to his society. Although Sterba therefore had relatively little personal contact with him, the accounts of the occasional small meetings Freud held at his apartment sound altogether plausible. In private, Freud was often more ironic than in print. For example, in defending his approach in *Civilization and Its Discontents* he said, "Actually, the truth is that we do not have so much culture that we could really feel uncomfortable in it."[21]

In connection with the Viennese analytic approach to therapy, Sterba is a true representative of Freud's notion that the analyst "can do little more than patch up things."[22] Like others, Sterba is convinced that "the 'blank screen' attitude of the analyst was not what Freud considered the optimal position."[23] The analyst, while not burdening the patient with extraneous problems, should be "continuously accompanying, comforting, fortifying, explaining and encouraging."[24] Sterba states that "Freud did not hesitate to transcend the so-called classical or orthodox behavior of the analyst. . . ."[25] To my knowledge, Sterba is the first analyst to discuss "the parameter phobia": "It is certain that Freud did not suffer from the parameter phobia that became rampant among analysts in the fifties and sixties."[26] Sterba remained loyal to the spirit of Freud's therapeutic practices at their best, in contrast to those devotees of a technique who look warily on each departure from the allegedly standard approach and are suspicious of any breach beyond the sterile so-called psychoanalytic parameter.

In my opinion Sterba's *Reminiscences of a Viennese Psychoanalyst* is a reliable and pleasurable guide to that fascinating group of people who made up the Vienna circle around Freud.

A series of bold assertions mark the first paragraph of the preface to *Freud: The Fusion of Science and Humanism* (1976), edited by John E. Gedo and George H. Pollock. "Analysis," it is claimed, "is unique as an intellectual discipline in having been entirely created by one man; critics who attack present-day psychoanalysis by alleging that Freud's inheritors have erected a cult with the founder as hero have simply ignored this unparalleled aspect of the origin of this field of science.''[27] The authors of this collection of essays, who present their work as a ''sampling''[28] of what has been done on the history of psychoanalysis in Chicago over the period of a decade, say that it represents an effort to revive Freud's original aim of scientific self-examination, and they regret the degree to which ''narrow clinical pragmatism''[29] has overtaken the broadest concerns of analysis.

Assessed by the standard the authors set for themselves, the book is a failure. The bibliographical references display their hidden sectarian partisanship. To cite a few instances, there is no mention of the writings of Alfred Adler, Erich Fromm, or even Karen Horney, who once taught at the Chicago Institute of Psychoanalysis; only a casual nod is made to a few works of Otto Rank (stigmatized here as supposedly having ''defected''[30] from Freud) and Carl G. Jung, and no references are made to independent historians who had been proscribed as heretics. The authors are right in believing that ''it is not deductive reasoning which constitutes the antiscientific core of a dogma—it is the refusal to submit the conclusions to appropriate validation studies,''[31] but they do not recognize that their own methods of research advance the purpose of dogma by this precise means. The contention that analysis is ''unique'' as a discipline has been propagandized by the Orwellian device of the creation of nonpersons. Earlier historical figures are distorted to suit today's ideological purposes.

But these papers are not wholly without value. The authors concentrate on Freud, and while they exclude many other features of the history of psychoanalysis, at least this approach invites inquiry into the degree to which Freud's personality left its mark on his ideas and limited the validity of his hypotheses. But the authors stop at the water's edge. They do not ask, for example, to what extent Freud deceived himself about the scientific status of his findings. Although they do cite Freud's peculiar belief that Shakespeare's work was really written by the Earl of Oxford, they ignore existing literature that investigates Freud's need to find heroes of high social status and his preoccupation with priorities in science. Furthermore, although they mention Freud as a moral theorist, they fail to explore his complicated critique of Christianity and his ambivalences as a Jew. Nor do they perform any service in expanding our understanding of Freud's relation to Nietzsche. Montaigne is patronizingly examined as a precursor to the ''progress''[32] to be found in Freud; Montaigne is not studied to expand the imagination but rather to pigeonhole his ideas in terms of contemporary orthodox psychoanalytic categories. Although the theme of twinship in Freud's life is touched upon, it is neither broadly explored nor examined with critical faculties.

These writers note how magical thinking can serve defensive purposes, without being aware that hidden polemics cannot blind the vision of scholars. These psychoanalysts have been, like others recently, fascinated with the psychology of narcissism, and they announce; " . . . it is most difficult to value anything different from oneself. . . . "[33] The central defect to his volume is, in my judgment, a narcissistic one; otherwise they would be able to acknowledge the contributions of others to the neutral quest for the history of their science. Despite the numerous flaws that this book contains, nonetheless serious scholarship in continuing to proceed for the sake of genuinely expanding our understanding of the history of analysis.

John E. Gedo's *Conceptual Issues in Psychoanalysis: Essays in History and Method* (1986) is a particularly outspoken version of loyalist historiography; more crudely than Max Schur, but wholly in contrast to Richard Sterba's humility, Gedo, presumably with the encouragement of some allies of his at the Chicago Institute of Psychoanalysis, feels free to express prejudices that are especially illuminating about some prevalent common biases. Gedo's book is written, for example, from the side of the Big Battalions; that is, he assumes the merits of an orthodox view of the history of psychoanalysis, even though what is acceptable to those traditionalists has always varied from one decade to the next. Since I do not subscribe to the central beliefs of Gedo's wing of psychoanalytic thinking, my reaction to his book has to be critical. I did not, however, sit down to read it with any ideological preconceptions in mind, and therefore I think that the issues that arise in challenging his theses extend beyond the confines of the book itself and merit consideration in as dispassionate a manner as possible.

It is striking how Gedo repeatedly invokes with favor what he calls the "mainstream"[34] in psychoanalysis and how even more often he cites instances of what he chooses to call "dissidence."[35] A so-called dissident is to Gedo hardly someone to be admired or emulated. Yet usually it is politically authoritarian regimes that stigmatize dissent. Gedo seems to think he adequately distinguishes his own approach from that of the Catholic church by his disclaiming any need in psychoanalysis for the proscription of heresy.

I believe that in a democratic community of ideas any majority thrives on conformity. It does not seem to occur to Gedo that his very attention to instances of "dissidence" implies that a nonconformist in this field is by definition someone with ideas; otherwise logic would entail that he pay attention to scrutinizing the work of those he calls "conservatives."[36] Gedo never subjects such conservatism to any kind of critical attention or examines some of the damage it has done. Gedo rightly bemoans those instances of "civil wars," marked by the repeated threat of psychoanalysis' fragmenting into hostile factions heatedly defending ideological *partis pris*.[37] Yet Gedo does not realize that it is partly the pressure of conformism, and the lack of the open-mindedness usually found elsewhere in the human sciences that breed the disputatious factionalism that he laments.

Gedo speaks of himself as an amateur historian, but then does not follow through with an appropriate attitude toward professionals in the field. His attack on the historian of science Frank Sulloway is an outstanding example of Gedo's lack of decent reserve. He lumps Sulloway with Jeffrey Masson and then throws in Peter Swales as well, as if it were possible to tarnish them all with the same stroke of a broad brush.

The book is, unfortunately, laden with instances of false scholarship. Chapter 4, for example, is titled "The Loyal Opposition of Louise von Salomé"; the idea that she was part of any "opposition" to Freud would have struck even him as novel. Sandor Ferenczi gets treated as "the first psychoanalytic dissident," apparently on the grounds that Adler, Jung, and others were so beyond the pale that their "secessionist" ideas are not worthy of reconsideration.[38] Gedo's bibliography is woefully inadequate, as he offhandedly chooses, for example, to cite an article on Wilhelm Reich rather than any of the available books.

The sections on Heinz Kohut will make required reading for anyone concerned with the state of Chicago psychoanalysis, even if it does look like a tempest in a teacup. As interesting as anything Gedo tells us about, however, is the absence of the apparently dread name of Franz Alexander. Gedo has not placed Kohut's work in the context of the history of the Chicago Institute or scrutinized the basis of the fears Kohut seems to have had about being categorized as a deviant. The Kohut I met admired Erik H. Erikson; evidently Gedo thinks Erikson does not qualify as a "secessionist" only because Gedo bullies him as "a peripheral figure."[39]

I have singled out in Gedo's book an unmistakable tone of authoritarianism. Too often judgments are maintained as if they are in no need of being defended, much less rationally argued, and Gedo is not reliable on many specific issues, for example in connection with the details of the censorship of Freud's published correspondence.

Yet at the same time the book does have many amiable passages in it, as he makes concessions that would have been unthinkable among orthodox analysts even a decade ago. The ideas of Ferenczi and Melanie Klein get treated with reasonable sympathy. Gedo alludes to the "secretiveness" of the Freud family and even mentions what he calls "the miseries" of Freud's "sour marriage;"[40] when it comes to Freud's relationship to his wife, Gedo loses the cultural perspective he elsewhere admonishes us to keep in mind. Gedo does once acknowledge the "ossification" of the Freudian mainstream: "yesterday's mainstream," he also admits in a footnote, "may easily become a backwater by tomorrow. . . ."[41] (That line of argument, to me, still smacks too much of an appeal to power and success.)

Gedo can pay tribute to some of the contributions of "dissidence," over-looked by what he calls "the defenders of analytic orthodoxy,"[42] without naming any of the reactionaries or being conscious of the full implications of the metaphor of "dissidence." Gedo does once state: "Nor should we assume that in scientific controversies the majority is more likely to be right than in political ones. . . . "[43] And he concedes that "authoritarian attitudes to the analytic task . . . are practically ubiquitous in a profession that draws upon the traditions of clinical medicine."[44]

It sounds as if Gedo thinks of himself as a peacemaker. But when he tells us that "in the current atmosphere of sectarian rancor, we can only feel nostalgia for the tolerance of diversity implicit in Freud's attitude,"[45] Gedo is indulging in a kind of myth making about the past that reflects his own intolerance and that can serve no emancipatory purpose for the future of analysis. Unfortunately, *Conceptual Issues in Psychoanalysis* does not form part of the growing body of new literature that genuinely enriches our understanding of the Freudian tradition.

W. W. Meissner's *Psychoanalysis and Religious Experience* (1984) seeks to overcome the traditional Freudian iconoclasm toward religion. An early section devotes a great deal of attention to explicating Freud's published writings, as well as his letters, on the subject of religion. Fifteen years ago no orthodox analyst would have dared take anything like this sort of care with Freud's interest in the matter. Meissner, however, feels wholly at ease about subjecting this important side of Freud to exegesis. Although he considers Freud's biography a legitimate avenue to understanding his writings, which once would have been taboo as a textual approach, Meissner curiously fails to explore the subjective components that played a part in the construction of Freud's peculiar thesis in his *Moses and Monotheism*.

An especially admirable section of Meissner's text is devoted to quoting from the much neglected work by Oskar Pfister, a Lutheran pastor who wrote a reply to Freud's *Future of an Illusion* while at the same time remaining a thoroughly loyal disciple to the founder of psychoanalysis. While Meissner highlights portions of Pfister's argument, he does so in isolation from others in the psychoanalytic movement who had made similar points to Freud. Earlier James Jackson Putnam, for example, had, in correspondence with Freud, failed to persuade him to an almost identical point of view. Incidentally, as Meissner quotes so carefully from the Freud-Pfister letters, he might have alerted the reader to the problem of the tendentious editing of this correspondence, like most others that are publicly available to us.

The major figure with whose relevant ideas Meissner seems to be unfamiliar is Carl G. Jung. It is still unfortunately the case that orthodox Freudians cannot allow themselves to begin to treat Jung's text seriously. Otherwise, Meissner would find that much of ego psychoanalytic thinking, which he studiously links to his own interest in religion, had been anticipated long before in Jung's works. Even D. W. Winnicott, a brilliantly fresh, if not scholarly, British analyst whose concepts about transitional phenomena Meissner thinks well of, had far more inkling about the significance of Jung in revising Freud's theories.

Still another bibliographic and conceptual blind spot in Meissner's book is Erich Fromm. (The loyalist pattern of selective omissions came up in Schur, Gedo and Pollock (eds.), and Gedo as well). Fromm's own *Psychoanalysis and Religion* first came out in 1950; as much as this heretic wanted to change the direction of Freudian thinking, he, like Meissner, did not admire Jung's earlier achievements. Fromm, I think, misunderstood Jung's psychological thinking, partly because of Jung's unfortunate political commitments in the 1930s, but Meissner takes a different tack from Fromm by simply ignoring Jung's ideas and does not even mention Fromm's name. Oddly enough, the same publisher that brought out Meissner's book was responsible for Fromm's as well. Meissner expresses an interest in the moral values implicit in the psychoanalytic treatment setting, even while avoiding the brilliant papers on the same subject that Fromm published in the 1930s.

It is no wonder that it is so hard to follow the history of psychoanalysis, because cultism has allowed its thinkers to become like ships passing each other in the night. The real danger of heresy for writers in psychoanalysis is that they will be forgotten in the future technical literature of the profession. Psychoanalysis became a church with its own Index of prohibited writings. The omissions in Meissner's own bibliography become ridiculous given the scholarly-seeming approach he takes to Freud's own references to religion.

Meissner obviously has a genuine talent for exploring the implications of psychoanalytic theory, and if he had permitted himself to break free from the conceptual mold of what a thoroughly respectable analyst of the 1980s is supposed to think, read, and cite, he would have written a different book. His genuine admiration for Erik H. Erikson's concepts logically entails a toleration for a variety of other psychoanalytic writers, even if these earlier thinkers did not remain organizationally as loyal. After all, one way of paying tribute to Freud as a model is by being independent.

Someday a wholly original contribution will be made on the subject of psychoanalysis and religion, but first its authors will have to be aware of the full variety of arguments that have been advanced in the past.

Literary critics have always been attracted to Freud's genius as a writer and continue to do much to spread psychoanalytic teaching. It would be hard to contest the proposition that Freud's capacities as a stylist were un-matched both during his lifetime and since his death.

In 1961 Steven Marcus, along with Lionel Trilling, edited an abridged version of Jones's three-volume official biography of Freud. Both Marcus and Trilling had impeccable academic credentials, yet somehow, for all their literary sophistication, neither Marcus nor Trilling seemed to have re-alized how partisan a version of events Jones had set forth. For example, Freud remembered in the course of a dream that it had seemed remarkable to him how like Garibaldi his father had looked on his deathbed. To Jones this literally meant that Jakob Freud bore a resemblance to Garibaldi, an example of how any fancy in Freud's head could emerge in books as his-torical fact. Marcus and Trilling accepted unquestioningly Jones's version of this matter, among all others, in their abridgment of his biography.

Freud and the Culture of Psychoanalysis (1984) is a collection of Mar-cus's essays on Freud that does not purport to contain a conceptual unity. Marcus treats a few of Freud's texts as self-contained entities, entirely apart from any perspectives that might fundamentally challenge the founder of psychoanalysis. The central portions of Marcus's book examine Freud's correspondence with Fliess, *Three Essays on the Theory of Sexuality,* and the case histories of Dora and the Rat Man. One might have thought that these works by Freud were so well known by now that there was no special point to recapitulating their general arguments.

Marcus's work fits in too closely with other books, already discussed in this chapter, of a similar ideological persuasion, for the problem with Mar-cus's interpretations is that he seems wedded to psychoanalytic orthodoxy and too naive in terms of intellectual history. Even while Freud was still writing, thoroughly respectful critiques of him were being published. Freud knew the difference between literature and science, and it is no tribute to his memory to ignore the places where Freud's imagination went too far.

At a couple of points Marcus does grow cross with the powers-that-be in classical psychoanalysis. He has one paragraph, for example, that thunders against the systematic laundering of Freud's published correspondence. Yet an appreciation of Marcus's outrage needs to be tempered by an awareness that he himself wrote a preface to a paperback edition of Freud's selected letters without finding it necessary to alert the reading public to the edito-rial bowdlerizations in the text he was recommending. Marcus has so narrow a vision that in *Freud and the Culture of Psychoanalysis* he quotes a famous September 1897 letter of Freud's to Fliess without realizing that in 1966 James Strachey had printed a critical passage in the letter that had been censored from the published volume of Freud's correspondence with Fliess.

Marcus is right in thinking that no other writer in modern psychology can match Freud in terms of the power of his pen. But one might have thought it would not seem shocking to Marcus for others to have tried to view the conception of the Oedipus complex, for example, with cultural distance. In these essays Marcus elegantly defends fundamentalist Freudianism. He does not seem able to abide any breaks with orthodoxy, which lends a religiosity to his treatment of Freud's texts. If someone outside the faithful, like Harry Stack Sullivan, advocated doing without the couch in therapy, to Marcus this means it was merely because Sullivan saw the couch as an "inconvenience."[46] Important questions of technique, about which a considerable agreed-upon body of knowledge exists, cannot be settled by such an offhanded use of words.

Although Marcus makes no attempt to present a principle that might justify the selection of texts he has chosen to reexamine, his essays are linked together by smooth and easy-to-read prose.

Didier Anzieu's *Freud's Self-Analysis* (1986) first appeared as two volumes in France in 1975, and it will soon be apparent that the problem of orthodox psychoanalytic historiography is hardly confined to the North American continent. It is unusual, however, that Anzieu, apparently no radical toward the establishment within international psychoanalysis, takes Henri Ellenberger's *The Discovery of the Unconscious* as a serious source; that in itself represents a step in the right direction. It is also in Anzieu's favor that he does not hesitate to discuss Freud in relationship to traditional Jewish culture, although not long ago such a standpoint would have given rise to accusations of anti-Semitism. *Freud's Self-Analysis* is a labor of love and dedication; it concentrates almost entirely on the later 1890s and attempts to interpret all the autobiographical material that Freud used in *The Interpretation of Dreams*. *Freud's Self-Analysis* makes for compellingly detailed reading, and one finishes it feeling almost as if one had reread Freud's greatest book.

Yet I believe that Anzieu has nowhere near enough critical distance from Freud's own account of his dream life. When in 1954 Erik H. Erikson first published his version of Freud's "Irma" dream, Anna Freud was privately horrified; in those days it was still lèse-majesté to try to understand Freud himself psychoanalytically. But she also made the legitimate point that one cannot understand a dream without a dreamer's free associations. Surely such restraint should be an elementary principle in psychoanalysis. It is not enough, therefore, for Anzieu to take Freud's published accounts of his associations to dreams as if they were identical to clinical material.

Throughout this dense and long book Anzieu can be strangely credulous in accepting Freud's own view of things. Years ago Otto Rank, whom Anzieu deems a "dissident,"[47] pointed out that everything Freud wrote about the significance of the death of his father in 1896 ought really to be understood as a defense against the almost simultaneous loss of Freud's mentor,

Breuer. (Anzieu completely ignores the significance of Freud's putting Rank's name with his own on the cover of some later editions of *The Interpretation of Dreams* and Freud's incorporating Rank's texts with his own.) Jung had pointed out before World War I that Freud was apt to ignore how infantile material could be used as an evasion of current reality—a point that over half a century later an orthodox analyst like Schur, without mentioning Jung, singled out as an important defense mechanism. It would, I think, be characteristic of Freud to try to place in the distant past what was in fact a recent conflict. Anzieu, however, does not seem even to know about Rank's hypothesis concerning Freud's account of the significance of the death of his father being a cover for the break with Breuer. Instead Anzieu proceeds as if the "discovery" of psychoanalysis were to be understood as a part of Freud's parental mourning reaction. As a result very little about Breuer appears in *Freud's Self-Analysis,* certainly not enough to match Breuer's full standing in Freud's life. (But given Anzieu's obsessively methodical approach to trying to cover every possible line of thought, broad-mindedness would add hundreds of extra pages to his book.)

Anzieu is, like his fellow countrymen at large, ignorant of the contributions of Jung. I remember once pointing out to Paul Ricoeur that his own attempt to find Christian theology in Freud might have been better rewarded by an investigation of Jung's works; Ricoeur's interest in Freud reminded me of the Christian faith that the New Testament must be implicit in the Old. Ricoeur maintained that Jung was, as of the early 1980s, forbidden for Parisian intellectuals. The time may still come when Jung's naive and offensive politics of the 1930s will not obliterate an appreciation of him as Freud's most powerful and original critic. Anzieu, like so many others within psychoanalysis, confines himself to the image of "dissidence." "I would tend to think, " Anzieu writes, "that the cause of his quarrels with Adler, Jung, and others should be sought less in his own neurosis than in that of his ex-colleagues: it was the dissidents who quite clearly acted towards Freud as an object of 'transference.' "[48] Anzieu offers no evidence whatsoever for his contention and appears to rely merely on loyalist myth, but it needs to be pointed out that when he finds Freud himself behind the patient Freud is examining in a dream, that is for Anzieu unknowingly to follow an innovation of Jung's own that characters in dreams stand for aspects of the dreamer's own ego.

Anzieu is not emancipated enough from psychoanalytic orthodoxies to be able to deal with some of the most important human relations that Freud had. To be sure, Anzieu does not share Jones's contempt for Fliess, and Anzieu does go into a bit of the sublimated homosexual link between Freud and Fliess, but only to support what Freud himself has told us in his letters. As for Freud's sister-in-law Minna, Anzieu cannot quite make up his mind about how important she was. He does follow Jones's view that, as Anzieu puts it, "there was never any emotional or sexual relationship between Freud and his sister-in-law."[49] Anzieu says of one of Freud's dreams: "This dream confirms that there could have been nothing between them. . . ."[50]

In real life one would think that someone was pulling one's leg if he tried to argue that a dream could possibly confirm the absence of a liaison or an emotional involvement. Elsewhere I have written how I think that despite how worried Minna sounds when she consulted Jung about the problem of Freud's relationship to her, things stayed on an emotional rather than a physical level. But a dream or a whole batch of them cannot settle any such matter, at least as long as we only have Freud's written version of the dream and the associations he chose to give us.

It seems to me indefensible at this stage of our knowledge for Anzieu to propose about Freud that "the setting up of a relationship with his wife . . . was lastingly happy, fertile, and stable"; it was impossible, if we accept the tormenting implications of Freud's own theory of bisexuality, for him to ever have "fully satisfied," as Anzieu believes, the sexual instinct with Martha.[51] The issue of Freud's sexuality of course bears on his thesis of the 1890s that neurosis reflects an unhappy sex life. It was Wilhelm Reich, who Anzieu labels a "pre-psychotic,"[52] who first raised the problem of sexual discontent among the early Freudians.

Throughout Anzieu's book one does have the feeling that he has somehow mixed up the woods for the sake of the trees. *Freud's Self-Analysis* is so full of Freud's account of things, which is admittedly fascinating, that one almost does not realize how much Anzieu is failing to explore. Despite the fact that Anzieu's narrative contains inconsistencies and repetitions that may be inevitable in a book of such great length, *Freud's Self-Analysis* is full of genuinely hard work. Unfortunately, Anzieu believes that "Freud did not need to undergo psychoanalysis. . . . ,"[53] whereas one would have thought it part of the tragedy of Freud's originality that he would be uniquely incapable of being analyzed. If other of Freud's correspondences, such as those to Jung, his wife, and his daughter Anna, not to mention all the many sets of letters that will someday be in print, get as much attention as Anzieu gives to Freud's exchanges with Fliess, we can securely look forward to the Freud "industry" flourishing on both sides of the Atlantic. It is, I think, a tribute to Freud's genius and the vitality of the creative life he exemplified that despite all the reservations I had about this book, I read it straight through without extraneous interruptions.

I am not sure exactly what it says about a field when an important book is as excruciatingly painful to have to read as Adolf Grünbaum's *The Foundations of Psychoanalysis* (1984) is, but I suspect that altogether too many psychoanalytic books get bought and then put unperused on impressively filled shelves. *The Foundations of Psychoanalysis* has attracted a lot of general book reviewing attention; in behalf of its significance the editor of the *Journal of the American Psychoanalytic Association* published an editorial for which I can recall no precedent, and an issue of *Behavioral and Brain Sciences* contained a précis of the book along with commentary from thirty-eight experts, as well as a reply by Grünbaum.

Psychoanalysis has always had at best an uncertain relationship with universities. Training institutes have by and large not been connected with normal academic institutions, and liberals within the psychoanalytic movement have long thought that the isolation of analysis from university life perpetuated sectarianism and ideological intolerance. Adolf Grünbaum is a trained philosopher who has come also to hold a research professorship in a department of psychiatry, so on the face of it one would expect to be able to welcome his contribution to our understanding of psychoanalysis.

Unfortunately, however, what we have here is a demolition job, a work of intellectual fanaticism. Grünbaum uses the equipment from academic life, and in particular from his specialty in the philosophy of science, to assault a variety of writers for their logical unsoundness. He begins by tearing apart the "hermeneutic"[54] approach of Jürgen Habermas and Paul Ricoeur, but it is clear he has others (like Bruno Bettelheim) in mind as well. Their central defect, according to Grünbaum, is a wooly-minded inability to stick to the version of science that Grünbaum chooses to admire in Freud. In a passage from Freud that Grünbaum likes to quote, the founder of psychoanalysis is indeed making a bold defense of the neutrality of his "findings"; but Grünbaum does not emphasize how old and close to death Freud was at the time, nor how disillusioned with his therapeutic success Freud was by then. (Grünbaum does not mention that on the same page Freud even repudiates intuition.) Of course Freud was great enough as a writer to know how to sound, when he wanted to, like a philosopher of science might like to find him. Grünbaum especially likes to quote from Freud's papers in the 1890s, although Freud subsequently was to repudiate most of what he stood for then.

Grünbaum is determined to extract from Freudian theory the absolutely central significance of the concept of repression, as if that one solitary notion had a life of its own. Only in the course of polemicizing against Adler and Jung does Freud say anything that could be interpreted so extravagantly, and then Freud goes on from there to insist on other points that Grünbaum ignores. But as Grünbaum would have it, Freud's theory stands or falls on the issue of causation; any writer who has tried to get away from that side of Freud's theory is being untrue to what Grünbaum finds to be the essence of Freud's contributions. People like Roy Schafer, George

Klein, and Erik H. Erikson take a beating here, and by the implication of Grünbaum's argument the schools of self-psychology and object relations theory are no better off. Allegedly all these writers have unnecessarily feared Freud as a scientist.

In reality there is no such ideal figure as the "mature Freud"[55] Grünbaum has in his head. Freud was divided between being an artist and a scientist, and he dealt with that struggle prophetically in his book on Leonardo. The strength of Freud's approach came from his ability to bring a profoundly humanistic bent to bear on empirical problems. One would never guess from Grünbaum's book or the writings he cites that Freud could ever have written any of his social tracts, not to mention his critiques of religion and his assault on Christian ethics. Moral dilemmas are implicit in every therapeutic encounter, and we know that this is true in practice even if Freud was loath to admit it in principle. Psychoanalysis has attracted so much interest because it has entered into the age-old debate about how we ought to live, and although the Freud who succeeded in changing our attitude toward such diverse subjects as biography writing and morality does not exhaust all that can be found in him, it will not do to reduce Freud down to the cut-and-dry scientistic machine that Grünbaum finds comfortable to agree with.

The clinical method of psychoanalytic investigation is, to be sure, hardly without its many flaws, and Grünbaum's discussion of the role of suggestion, or what he calls the "placebo effect,"[56] is I think the most valuable part of his book. Clinical work and free associations can be "contaminated,"[57] as Grünbaum puts it, by extraneous influences, but a different evaluation would be that the impact of these forces constitutes what is apt to be most therapeutically enriching. Grünbaum does not seem to have the center of gravity of the spirit of Freud's approach as an analyst; Grünbaum neither understands the central role of the concepts of transference and resistance in Freud, nor does Grünbaum acknowledge the unique kinds of self-deceptions Freud's reasoning led him into. Grünbaum's version of psychoanalysis leaves out the mystery as well as the necessary cynicism—in short, everything that makes it interesting. Instead of Grünbaum reiterating how Freud has to have held that correct etiological insight was therapeutically indispensable, he might have cited any number of occasions when Freud expressed his lack of taste for therapy, not to mention his proclaimed dislike for philosophy.

I feel pretty confident in maintaining that had Freud started out with the aim of trying to live by Grünbaum's standards of scientific propriety, Freud would never have published a line. I am not saying this because I think psychoanalysis is in need of any special protectiveness. The state of organized psychoanalysis may be worrisome, but as an influential doctrine psychoanalytic thinking will continue to survive.

What is really disturbing, however, is that such an abominably badly written book should somehow appeal to some people's sense of what science is supposed to be about. *The Foundations of Psychoanalysis* is filled with barbarisms, nouns and verbs the likes of which I have never seen allowed in print. It seems to me regrettable that reviewers have been too craven to be outspoken enough about Grünbaum's unnecessary abuse of the English language.

Since Grünbaum feels able to be so tough on other writers by the standards he calls philosophical, I feel entitled to say a bit about his own work in the light of my knowledge of the history of psychoanalysis. When Grünbaum tells about a lawyer having asked Freud for a "psychiatric"[58] opinion or writes that Freud had "his own modality of psychiatric treatment,"[59] it is as if Grünbaum did not know that Freud lacked psychiatric training and viewed psychoanalysis as at odds with psychiatry. Grünbaum has come across the term *narcissistic neurosis* in Freud, although Grünbaum neither relates this to a modern notion of psychosis nor seems to realize that Freud early on was so ambitious as to try to include old-fashioned psychosis within the psychoanalytic theory of neurosis. The distinction between neurosis and psychosis bears in a critical way on the problem of repression and whether Freud has to be taken as recommending that it be lifted or not. Since Grünbaum seems obsessed with the idea of testing psychoanalytic doctrine by whether or not a reduction in social stigmas associated with homosexuality leads to a lessening of instances of paranoia, one would expect him to start being concerned with clinical theories of paranoia.

Grünbaum chooses to quote Freud as modestly claiming that he never meant to try to explain everything, but the historical evidence cannot sustain any such pretension. Even Heinz Hartmann was willing to admit that he knew better. Hartmann was trying to explain why Julius Wagner-Jauregg was hostile to Freud's psychoanalysis. Wagner told Hartmann that Freud was a great man, but that his aims were too broad; Hartmann quoted Wagner as having said that Freud thought that psychoanalysis could do everything, and Wagner was sure that it was not so. Hartmann went on to declare that Freud's desire to go beyond all limits of knowledge was not shared by an old colleague like Wagner. I mention this anecdote because it not only undermines Grünbaum's version of Freud as a cautious man of science, but on the grounds that Hartmann was the source. The relevance of Hartmann is not just that he was a politic and loyal disciple of Freud and interested in the philosophy of psychoanalysis; most important, he is not even once cited in Grünbaum's book. Although twenty years ago psychoanalytic literature was filled with references to Hartmann and also Ernst Kris, now it would seem that we have new fads to contend with. Loyalist orthodoxy has its fashions. Grünbaum has not been well served by allowing himself to be influenced by a tiny band of currently prominent analytic writers who are fundamentally ahistorical and as exclusively concerned with abstract logic as Grünbaum himself. It is Grünbaum's kind of neglect of the historical literature that feeds intolerance when on the contrary skepticism ought to be the hallmark of a truly scientific orientation.

One suspects that the major enemy Grünbaum has in mind with this book is the philosopher of science Karl Popper, whose long-standing dismissal of Freud (as well as Adler) has rankled some students of psychoanalysis. For myself I can accept Popper, who considered psychoanalysis unfalsifiable and therefore no science but still containing some truth to it, more easily than go along with Grünbaum's own well-meaning attempt to rescue Freud by transforming him into something so alien to anything recognizably human. At any rate, it sounds to me that Popper has a sense of humor when talking about Freud and Adler, and as a Viennese Popper knew at first hand what he was dealing with; it is surely no answer for Grünbaum to cite a casual article or two about the issue of Adler.

To return to my point at the outset of considering *The Foundations of Psychoanalysis,* it might be possible to forgive much in this book were it not so horribly written. The mountain of Grünbaum's argument brings forth a familiar mouse: the necessity of the validation of psychoanalysis beyond what can be learned from the couch. Since Grünbaum has been so rough on other writers, I hope he will see that to me that justifies the toughness of this examination of his book and that he will not misunderstand my intentions.

It is obvious that there are many grounds for being legitimately worried about the clinical foundations of psychoanalysis, and Grünbaum has performed a real service in emphasizing some of the difficulties. He might look at the writings of Freud's earliest critics. Grünbaum should look at the minimal existing literature on clinical follow-ups or the problem of multiple analyses of the same individual. Grünbaum obviously has completely honorable intellectual purposes, and his work may lead to less complacency. Grünbaum's Freud is not, however, mine, nor do I think that shrinking psychoanalysis down to the bare outlines Grünbaum has in mind could do anything to explain why this school of thought has had such an impact on twentieth-century thinking.

Notes

1. Max Schur, *Freud: Living and Dying* (New York: International Universities Press, 1972), p. 138.
2. *Letters of Sigmund Freud,* ed. Ernst L. Freud, trans. Tania and James Stern (New York: Basic Books, 1960), p. 400.
3. Sigmund Freud, "New Introductory Lectures on Psychoanalysis," *Standard Edition,* vol. 22, p. 132.

4. Ernest Jones, *The Life and Work of Sigmund Freud,* vol. 3 (New York: Basic Books, 1957), p. 152.
5. Schur, *Freud: Living and Dying,* p. 111.
6. Ibid., p. 170, p. 167.
7. Ibid., p. 204.
8. Ibid., p. 216.
9. Ibid., p. 76.
10. Ibid., p. 243.
11. Sigmund Freud, "The Interpretation of Dreams," *Standard Edition,* vol. 5, p. 483.
12. Schur, *Freud: Living and Dying,* p. 489.
13. Ibid., p. 55.
14. Paul Roazen, *Freud and His Followers* (New York: Knopf, 1975), p. 492.
15. Schur, *Freud: Living and Dying,* p. 354.
16. Ibid., p. 197.
17. Ibid., p. 353.
18. Ibid., p. 426, p. 287.
19. Ibid., p. 12.
20. Richard F. Sterba, *Reminiscences of a Viennese Psychoanalyst* (Detroit: Wayne State University Press, 1982), p. 7.
21. Ibid., p. 116.
22. Ibid., p. 111.
23. Ibid., p. 122.
24. Ibid., p. 123.
25. Ibid.
26. Ibid., p. 124.
27. John E. Gedo and George H. Pollock, eds., *Freud: The Fusion of Science and Humanism, The Intellectual History of Psychoanalysis* (New York: International Universities Press, 1976), p. 1.
28. Ibid., p. 5.
29. Ibid., p. 1.
30. Ibid., p. 86.
31. Ibid., p. 173.
32. Ibid., p. 15.
33. Ibid., p. 33.
34. John R. Gedo, *Conceptual Issues in Psychoanalysis: Essays in History and Theory* (New York: Analytic Press, 1986), p. 36, p. 41, p. 89.
35. Ibid., p. 33.
36. Ibid., p. 102.
37. Ibid., p. 160.
38. Ibid., p. 39.
39. Ibid., p. 77.
40. Ibid., p. 29.
41. Ibid., p. 164.
42. Ibid., p. 43.
43. Ibid., p. 138.
44. Ibid., p. 120–21.
45. Ibid., p. 12.
46. Steven Marcus, *Freud and the Culture of Psychoanalysis* (Boston: George Allen & Unwin, 1984), p. 240.

47. Didier Anzieu, *Freud's Self-Analysis*, trans. Peter Graham (New York: International Universities Press, 1986), p. 243.
48. Ibid., p. 526.
49. Ibid., p. 328.
50. Ibid.
51. Ibid., p. 52.
52. Ibid., p. 577.
53. Ibid., p. 208.
54. Adolf Grünbaum, *The Foundations of Psychoanalysis: A Philosophical Critique* (Berkeley: University of California Press, 1984), p. 1.
55. Ibid., p. 88.
56. Ibid., p. 180.
57. Ibid., p. 211.
58. Ibid., p. 108.
59. Ibid., p. 117.

13

Political Psychology

Political psychology makes a fertile field for those political theorists who understand their work as preeminently conceptual: thinking about how we think. One of the merits of psychological thought is that it provides a framework for addressing both empirical and ethical considerations. Fortunately, political science has always been interdisciplinary. The question today is not whether but in which ways psychological understanding of human nature can help illuminate political and social behavior.

Psychoanalytic thinking continues to influence public life. One should not have to look for uses of this system of thought that deserve unqualified approval, such as balanced biographical efforts; nor is it necessary to concentrate on spectacular trials like that of John W. Hinckley, Jr., involving variations on the insanity defense and diminished responsibility. The Freudian revolution in ideas is a feature of contemporary intellectual history, and the issue is how to ensure that these concepts get invoked with sophistication. Even the reasoning at child custody case hearings has been touched by modern psychodynamic thinking. Political studies are inevitably affected by our conceptions of human nature, and if one is trying to anticipate the behavior of a contemporary or attempting to reconstruct the character of a past political actor, it is inevitable that our notions of what it is to be normal—or even human—are bound to influence how we reason. Even though, at least since the earliest work of Harold Lasswell over half a century ago, political scientists have been intrigued by depth psychology, still there has been relatively little professional legitimization associated with writing in this area.

Despite all the controversies in the psychoanalytic literature, certain clinical modes of thinking are widely established and potentially enlightening to political observers. The concept of "as if" was first presented by Helene Deutsch before the Vienna Psychoanalytic Society in 1934; subsequently, her polished views came out in 1942: "Some Forms of Emotional Disturbance and Their Relationship to Schizophrenia ('As If')." Although Deutsch became widely known for her writings on female psychology, her notion of "as if" remained her most famous single clinical contribution. The topic of "as if" became so much a part of professional thinking that in 1965 a special panel was devoted to reconsidering her concept at a meeting of the American Psychoanalytic Association. By then her term had acquired a life and literature of its own, and her early work had been succeeded by an efflorescence of interest in the self, authenticity, and identity.

In her concern with "as if" problems Deutsch was trying to describe a false affectivity that was neither neurotic nor psychotic. (Later the term *borderline* entered the literature.) She had picked a rare pathology in order to say something general about people, for although she thought she was talking about an exceptional phenomenon hard to diagnose correctly, at the same time she held that as a transient experience "as if" is nearly universal. The patients in question make an impression of "complete normality": "They are intellectually intact and gifted and show great understanding in all intellectual matters. When they try to be productive—and efforts in that direction are always present—their work is formally good but totally devoid of originality. It is always a laborious though skillful imitation of a model without the slightest personal trace."[1]

Their relations with people are also intense, in terms of friendship, love, understanding, and sympathy, but still something is chillingly absent. True warmth and inner feeling are missing, although outwardly these people could behave "as if they possessed a fully felt emotional life."[2] A key point was that the patients themselves were not aware of any impoverishment, but believed that their empty performances were the same as the feelings and experiences of others.

Deutsch distinguished what she was talking about from old-fashioned instances of repression: those who hoard their emotions. The difficulty with "as if" cases lay not in the buildup of barriers against their instinctual life, but rather with the emptiness of their relations with themselves and others. The concept of "as if" was designed to refer to people who are capable of powerful identifications that are peculiarly imitative and lacking in character: "Their morality, ideals, beliefs are also mere shadow phenomena. They are ready for anything, good or bad, if they are given an example to follow, and they are generally specially apt to join social, ethical or religious groups in order to give substance to their shadow existence by identification."[3]

Long-standing membership in an organization can be dropped in favor of another of opposite standards "without any change of heart."[4] No disillusionment or internalized experience need take place, but rather a regrouping in the environment of the person's circle of acquaintances.

In terms of childhood development, Deutsch traced the origins of "as if" personalities to the inability to develop a normal Oedipus complex. Freud's theory did entail that truly civilized conduct meant a degree of neurosis, but many did not live up to that ideal of an inner life, with all its conflicts, and yet could not be called crazy. The phenomenon of "as if" was an expression of the human propensity to be imitatively suggestible, passively in wait of outside influences; such people validate their existence by identification. This tendency toward mimicry substituted for genuine relations with people as well as causes. One patient Deutsch wrote about, for example, could "be anything, and her emotional life remained unaffected. She never had cause to complain about lack of affect because she was never conscious of it."[5]

Deutsch's tolerance led her to expand preexisting psychoanalytic thinking. Freud had such high standards for people that his ideas could neglect the way human beings can sometimes fail to experience emotions intensely felt in great literature. In an article on absence of grief[6] Deutsch discussed remission in the work of mourning. The refusal of someone to grieve can be a defense serving to protect a severely threatened ego. The omission of reactive responses to the death or loss of a loved one was to her as much a variation on the normal as excessive grief, either in time or in intensity. Such delayed mourning will, she held, seek an outlet; she proposed that grieving that cannot be manifestly expressed may find vicarious satisfaction through identification with the sad experiences of others, which might also account for the existence of intuition and empathy.

Politics admittedly involves the existence of forces that are independent of the people involved. One of the misleading appeals of personality theory for the liberal mind is the illusory notion that the psyche is the only source of limitation and failure. This kind of utopianism can lead to discounting the relevance of social forces, to the belief, for example, that the limits to an office are simply set by the officeholder's own personality. A focus on personality factors need not entail a version of the great-man theory of history. Moreover, it is possible to describe many human qualities as psychologically mature and yet not conclude that they underlie successful political leadership.

Political leadership, especially where controversies tend to be less about rival ideas of how one ought to live and more about mundane matters, requires an ability to manipulate people. Politicans seem to need to be characteristically egotistic and nonintrospective. They have, of course, a great deal of savvy and are able to put themselves in another person's place. But their empathy is goal-directed, instrumental, and action-oriented. They have been rewarded for their abilities at externalizing—debating, arguing, verbalizing, convincing. For them to shift political positions, to move toward the right, left, or center, can entail no more inner turmoil than for a lawyer to defend a new client or to invent a fresh ploy. Politicians seem exempt from many contraints of conscience that one might want to expect from them.

Yet this tendency of public officials to behave in an "as if" fashion, to refuse to internalize problems in a way that we might think of as ideally healthy, can be peculiarly adaptive in political life. The true politician must be able to fight hard for his position, without becoming too personally involved in it. He needs a talent for self-effacement. He must be able to maintain a distance from whatever he defends or proposes if he is going to be able to compromise later in order to help reach a tolerable solution. In order to function in institutional life, one must be able to make judgments on a fairly impersonal basis. Principles of everyday personal behavior can interfere with the politican's role as a broker among competing groups.

But, from a traditional clinician's point of view, what is adaptive politically may look pathological under the scrutiny of psychoanalytic thinking. The demands of functioning in democratic systems may be at odds with (and question) some psychological concepts of normality. It is not so much a matter of politicians being motivated by an elemental power drive. A public figure has a special need to verify self-respect through external activities. In order to validate such self-esteem through achievements in the outside world, it is necessary to sustain a wide gulf between one's inner self and one's behavioral life, which is why some politicians come to seem frighteningly empty as human beings. Martin Luther King acknowledged the difficulties involved in distinguishing between public and private life: "When you are aware that you are a symbol, it causes you to search your soul constantly . . . to see if you live up to all the high and noble principles that people surround you with, and to try at all times to keep the gulf between the public self and the private self to a minimum."[7]

Whatever such a split may look like psychologically, treating oneself as an object is politically desirable, and the ability to use people as things is part of the politician's great art as a mediator.

Opportunism, we might sometimes like to think, is altogether a different matter. Long before Watergate it should have been evident what kind of false contrivances someone like Richard Nixon was so expert in; Joe McGinniss in 1969 quoted the following exchange between Nixon's staff members during the 1968 campaign:

You're not going to believe this but Nixon hates psychiatrists.

What?

Nixon hates psychiatrists. He's got this thing, apparently. They make him very nervous. You should have heard Len [Hall] on the phone when I told him I had one on the panel. Did you hear him? If I've ever heard a guy's voice turn white, that was it.

Why?

He said he didn't want to go into it. But apparently Nixon won't even let one in the same room.[8]

Nixon is hopefully more extreme in hollowness than the general rule of public figures, and yet, on a spectrum of psychological consciousness, I wonder if he is not more a representative man that we want to believe. Relatively nonintrospective people are more common politically than one thinks; certainly, by the standards of earliest psychoanalytic theory few leaders fulfill expectations about private conduct in the public realm. The concept of "as if" comes to mind because of how frighteningly detached some decision makers come to seem. Stalin reportedly told Churchill how pained he was by the necessity of forced collectivization in the Soviet Union; as the late C. P. Snow observed:

> . . . it is almost certainly wrong to imagine that Stalin felt it as a personal suffering. Men of action are not made like that. If they were they would not be men of action. Decisions involving thousands or millions of lives are taken without emotion—or, to use a more exact technical word, without affect. This was true of Asquith, an unusually amiable man, who presided over the Somme offensive in 1916; or of Churchill in the second war; or of Truman signing the order to use the atomic bomb.
>
> Men of action may, and often do, cry easy; but they don't lose sleep and they don't worry. If you worry, I once heard a leading English statesman say . . . you oughtn't to be doing the job. These homicidal decisions are taken by men capable of, to use one more technical term, horizontal fission. They act; and the rest of their mind is at rest. It might be better if men weren't constituted like that. But they are.[9]

One assumption that does not stand up to scrutiny is the ideal that public life and the norms of individual psychology are automatically identical. The good man, as Aristotle insisted long ago, is not the same as the good citizen. It is as easy to use psychology to encourage preferences and values as it is for any other ideological system of thought to promote ethics; whatever may have been the hopes of early proponents of using psychology in understanding politics, by now it is evident that the distinction between a talent for inner realities versus the understanding of external political life is directly relevant to why the prospects of using psychoanalysis in political science are not rosier than they are, for the abilities that make one sensitive to inner realities are likely to make one obtuse to external ones, and vice versa. There can even be periods in a lifetime when an individual is especially sensitive to emotional nuances and times when one is expertly attuned to external power relations.

The relationship between psychology and politics ought to be looked upon as mutually beneficial for each other. A lot of propagandistic nonsense was proposed by early analysts; Ernest Jones, for example, asked in 1948; "How many years will pass before no Foreign Secretary can be appointed without first presenting a psychoanalytic report on his mental stability and freedom from complexes?"[10] Nowadays most clinicians would consider Jones's proposal naive, but even so, in general, social scientists have a great deal to teach clinicians about power and responsibility. Yet at the same time clinical thinking has its utility for the study of politics. Each person has in him or her something of the manipulating politician, just as we all share elements of "as if" experiences; everyone plays roles that events assign.

Walter Lippmann, who deserves credit for being one of the first students of politics to appreciate the potential significance of psychoanalytic thinking, pointed out in 1922 that "the character in which men deal with their affairs is not fixed. . . . Nobody confronts every situation with the same character. His character varies in some degree through the sheer influence of time and accumulating memory, since he is not an automaton. His character varies, not only in time, but according to circumstances."[11]

Lippmann went on to dissolve some of liberalism's preconceptions about selfhood; before we concede the significance of "self-interest" in determining opinion, for example, it is critical to know "which self out of many selects and directs the interest so conceived. Religious teaching and popular wisdom have always distinguished several personalities in each human being."[12]

Lippmann did not have to cite any literature about so-called multiple personalities in order to assert that normally "there is no one self always at work."[13]

> People differ widely . . . in the consistency of their characters. . . . If the selves are too unrelated, we distrust the man; if they are too inflexibly on one track we find him arid, stubborn, or eccentric. In the repetory of characters, meager for the isolated and the self-sufficient, highly varied for the adaptable, there is a whole range of selves . . . the characters take their form from a man's conception of the situation in which he finds himself.[14]

Imitativeness can lead both to the tragedy of hypnotic-like cults and to the comic possibilities of people misconstruing new circumstances and therefore imagining "their characters for situations that are strange to them; the professor among promoters, the deacon at a poker game, the cockney in the country, the paste diamond among real diamonds."[15]

Helene Deutsch's concept of "as if" was intended to highlight the significance of chameleonlike conduct. To the extent that someone fails to develop a genuine interior being that becomes a psychological phenomenon as much as any other. The first American secretary of defense, James Forrestal, committed suicide shortly after resigning from public office, and his pastor went further in accounting for his death than cautious clinicians might; "Very few tragedies indeed do not have a personal and intimate side to them and it is not often that a man takes his own life if the inner fortress of his personal happiness is still secure. For this gives him a place of refuge; a life within a life, from the joy of which his strength is renewed and he finds fortitude. But in the case we are considering, devotion to the public service had been substituted for the forlorn hope of personal happiness."[16]

With Forrestal, the normal politician's gap between the inner and the outer became so great as to smash the inner citadel completely. Exceptional though his life was, it does suggest the way in which the separation between public and private can be a special way of relieving inner tensions; people externalize for inner motives. Yet to some extent success in politics requires the externalization of the self and the acceptance of one's identity as defined by one's political position. The ability to sustain a rich inner life while still functioning in public is that rare talent that makes for true greatness.

It is hard to think of fulfilling the ideals of autonomy and self-realization that Freud's theory would impose on us, but even as we each to some degree derive our identities from the outside environment, so we pay a price in terms of the abundance of our inner life. The concept of "as if" can help make understandable not just the extraordinary but the everyday, and directs our attention to one of the points of intersection between psychology and politics.

Political theorists adopt the historical texts they study by the standard of survival; therefore, if a book like Harold D. Lasswell's *Psychopathology and Politics* (1930) was still being reissued in 1986, then there is a substantial case to be made in behalf of its having endured long enough to belong within the realm of political theory. But in the case of Lasswell and his particular subject matter there are special difficulties in relating him to political philosophy. He thought of himself as a scientific innovator able to proceed independently of the great tradition of political thought, and although he makes numerous references in *Psychopathology and Politics* to the implications of his argument for political theory, he had helped initiate a movement of thought within social science which by and large was content to sweep aside those who defined themselves as theorists.

In part the clash between Lasswell's outlook and that of traditional political theory was a question of social class; the study of the great texts in the history of political thought has been pursued as the snob aspect of political science, and Lasswell's concentration on psychopathological concepts could hardly endear him to the most intellectually conservative members of the discipline, who were apt to dismiss out-of-hand the whole Freudian school of thought. By now political scientists have swallowed the odd term *empirical theory*, so a pigeonhole exists today in which Lasswell's work might be examined. But he had in mind moral purposes as well as more purely scientific ones, and this particular book of his has lived long enough to be entitled to the analytic care that students of political theory are accustomed to bring to bear on works of an equally venerable age.

In his 1960 "Afterthoughts" Lasswell remarked that initially he had been more impressed by the observational methods implicit in the psychoanalytic approach than by any specific theoretical formulation that then existed. *Psychopathology and Politics* appeared the same year as Freud's *Civilization and Its Disconents,* yet the latter was written in a vein more likely to attract the attention of traditional political theorists. Although Freud's text has secured an acknowledged place within the canon of books studied by political philosophers, Lasswell's own book still remains outside this realm.

It is remarkable how, even after all these years, Lasswell's book poses a challenge to conventional professional practices. For example, he declares in his first chapter on life histories that "the richest body of psychological and sociological facts is found in the files of the institutions for the care of the mentally disordered. . . . "[17] He then alludes in passing to the "usual routine"[18] by which patients are presented at psychiatric facilities and the procedures by which knowledge of clinical material gets taught by senior practitioners to students in apprenticeship.

Although the training of mental health professionals in this regard has remained constant over the past century, I would estimate that only a handful of political scientists have ever tried to learn about psychopathological concepts by actually participating in clinical conferences. Yet such sessions offer a unique opportunity for learning how clinicians actually use theoretical constructs, and the clinical material to be observed from the life histories of patients is absolutely fascinating. If political scientists have by and large ignored this source of instruction, it should also be pointed out that relatively few psychiatric training centers have made any serious effort to offer opportunities that might suit the needs of social scientists. This absence of institutional centers for learning about other fields—for clinicians also need the sophistication that comes from contact with social science—remains, I think, a major roadblock to the enhancement of political psychology.

So, although Lasswell's writings made him one of the pioneers in modern social science, and his work came subsequently to endorse and legitimize many of the most distinctive features of American political science, his example was in fact followed by relatively few others. In his "Afterthoughts" he raised the issue of "why the study of politicians (and of politics in general) by methods largely inspired by psychoanalysis has made but modest progress to date."[19] Yet I do not think that he went anywhere near far enough in exploring why his 1930 initiative had not born more fruit.

To be sure, the psychological principles that seemed so radical in 1930 have long since passed into conventional wisdom. But that does not by any means settle the issue of the extent to which those particular ideas need to be reexamined, and it is still not the case that in political science legitimacy has been fully extended to the subject matter that Lasswell had been opening up in 1930. He was not, of course, entirely alone at the time, and perhaps had he couched his work more in line with that of Walter Lippmann and Graham Wallas, not to mention the tradition of political theory that has been discussing concepts of human nature ever since the ancient Greeks, he would have been more successful. In the end he spent most of his academic life at a law school, and his contributions to political science journals grew progressively sparse.

Looking at *Psychopathology and Politics* in hindsight, Lasswell was remarkably emancipated from the sectarianism that has beset the history of psychoanalysis. He is, for example, respectful toward Adler and Jung, as well as Rank, and he was already heavily influenced by the ideas of Ferenczi, Sullivan, and Horney. (At Anna Freud's London clinic in 1965 I heard someone publicly single out Lasswell as a leader of a heretical school, although Freud's daughter, familiar with Lasswell's standing at the same law school she also had been invited to teach at, was quick to squash the suggestion.)

Lasswell does sound a little naive about Freud as a scientist, and he could have been more sensitive to the ethical dimensions connected to the whole notion of "normal" personality development. He once told me, in describing how he had undergone training analyses in Europe during the late 1920s, that he had done so under several different names; he did not seem to realize how such a procedure might have contaminated the supposedly neutral psychoanalytic setup. Yet his manner of proceeding was in keeping with what he writes here about political agitators needing to master the art of successful impostorship.

Lasswell's case histories in *Psychopathology and Politics,* which made him sound professionally disreputable in the political science of the day, read remarkably convincingly now. I remembered them being more simplistic, but I think they can still serve to introduce beginning students. The hardest part of the psychoanalytic framework to communicate to outsiders is in my opinion the spirit of the clinical give-and-take, and although Lasswell's aim lay in reconstructing life histories, he was savvy enough about the field to have penned portraits whose artistry belies his commitment to science.

For those with an interest in Lasswell's later writings, *Psychopathology and Politics* contains nuggets that foretell his full career. He writes in "Afterthoughts" about a 1938 truck accident that destroyed valuable clinical research records, but by then he had embarked on so ambitious a scientific course as to conflict with the humanistic principles that I think are an essential constituent of the orientation in psychopathology with which he started out. Too many people who have used psychiatric knowledge in political science have proceeded without adequately rethinking whether their techniques might be at odds with the theoretical structure they intend to implement.

In contrast to what Lasswell and others might once have hoped, there is no magical psychological method that can be mastered and communicated to resolve the dilemmas of understanding political life. Despite the arrogant attitude on the part of old-fashioned political theorists toward Lasswell's subject matter, no substitute exists for the sophistication about moral values that comes from the exploration of ethical alternatives in the course of the traditional study of the history of ideas.

It is beyond my competence to examine the full influence Lasswell had on subsequent social science, although his notion here of a politics of "prevention" obviously prefigured the later development of the policy sciences. In subsequent publications he became explicit about the origins of specifically political talent arising from problems of maintaining self-esteem.

My aim here has been to point out and celebrate what he did achieve in *Psychopathology and Politics.* The intellectually generous spirit that pervades the book inspired others after him, even if *Psychopathology and Politics* did not have the professionally successful impact one might like. It looks as if the book is going to have a securely long life, and for future editions it would be nice if the wonderful saying by Freud could be restored to the title page, where Lasswell originally intended it to appear: "From him who has eyes to see and ears to hear no mortal can hide his secret; he whose lips are silent chatters with his fingertips and betrays himself through all his pores."

* * *

Walter Lippmann (1899–1974), one of the most interesting political thinkers in American history, in 1922 published a great text, *Public Opinion*. By the test of the capacity of a book to survive over time, other works by Lippmann—some written as long ago as before World War I—also deserve critical scrutiny. If one tries to take a long view and think about all the books, some of them bestsellers, that Lippmann wrote, it seems to me that *Public Opinion* stands out as preeminent. Although the outline of his argument may now seem familiar, the ideas he advanced, as well as some of the conclusions he hesitated to draw, have implications both for democracy and political science that are still challenging today.

Although it should be hard to underestimate Lippmann's standing, the simplicity and lucid unpretensiousness of his prose have not invited the exegetics afforded more obscure thinkers. His official biographer, Ronald Steel, did little to ensure Lippmann's intellectual reputation. Steel did refer to *Public Opinion* as a "great work" and considered it "probably his most enduring,"[20] yet Steel's massive and detailed biography gives the book itself only the attention of a few pages. (Lippmann told an interviewer for the Columbia oral history unit that *Public Opinion* was his "first serious big book"[21]; to another interviewer Lippmann classed it as one of his four "major"[22] books, along with *A Preface to Morals, The Good Society,* and *The Public Philosophy.*)

In general Steel chose to interpret the significance of Lippmann's career in terms of his practical political involvements. It is true that Lippmann became such a figure of renown that his endorsement of a candidate for the presidency (like Gen. Dwight Eisenhower in 1952) was a newsworthy event, and when Nikita Khrushchev asked Lippmann in 1961 to delay for a few days a meeting that had been planned between them, Lippmann refused and the Soviet leader rearranged his schedule. It seems that Lippmann always was at ease with men of great power. His authorized biographer, however, along with writing a fascinating history of twentieth-century American politics, also constructed what amounts to a report card of Lippmann's position on various issues, and the most prominent reviewers kept track of the results.

Steel's biography can be contrasted with the tone of Lippmann's literary executor's novelistic account of him: Louis Auchincloss's *The House of the Prophet* is an excellent rendition of the workings of a political thinker's mind. Steel, however, did not himself see the need for the tools of an intellectual historian. Lippmann's talents, his biographer held, "lay in coordination and synthesizing ideas."[23] It is generally agreed, nonetheless, that absolute orginality is unknown even in the lives of acknowledged geniuses.

Without Steel discussing what he meant by political theory, he maintained that Lippmann's great strength was "in analysis and explanation, not theorizing."[24] Supposedly Lippmann "responded to events like a pragmatist; he did not form patterns like a philosopher."[25] Steel went even further: "despite the books that had taken him on excursions into philosophy and morals, he was primarily a journalist."[26] Yet in 1973, when Steel asked Lippmann whether he considered the writing of books or his journalism the more important, Lippmann answered: "I considered writing books the more important thing. I always viewed journalism as the place where I accumulated facts and information that I used for my books. Being a journalist was rather like the doctor, you know, who has to go and practice."[27] Despite the conclusion Steel came to in his immensely successful biography, in an appreciative obituary notice he had written: "He once described himself as a man who led two lives, one of books and one of newspapers. It was the combination that made him unique and give him his unparallelled voice of authority."[28]

Biography writing is itself a key subject in political psychology; in this case Lippmann must himself bear some of the responsibility for the damage that his biographer did to his stature. Initially Lippmann undertook to work with Richard Rovere as his biographer, but Lippmann's second wife was so sensitive in his behalf that the project aborted. Lippmann had long been narrowly self-protective; he allowed at least one book concerned with his ideas to appear without granting an interview to the prospective author. No doubt Lippmann was fully aware how an interviewer might use material in unexpected ways. Yet in the end he wound up with a biographer whose multifold distaste for him took several forms, one of which was the underestimation of the quality of Lippmann's mind.

As a young man at Harvard Lippmann made a legendary impact on those around him. He impressed people like William James, George Santayana, and Graham Wallas (as well as John Reed and Lincoln Steffens). Soon Lippmann was making regular visits to talk with Justice Oliver Wendell Holmes, Jr. But Steel prefers to quote Teddy Roosevelt's flattering appraisal of Lippmann's gifts, as Steel interprets Lippmann's involvement with philosophers negatively—in terms of the failure of his social ambitions and his keen eye for worldly advancement. Steel's biography remains consistently thin in its understanding of the history of ideas. Thorstein Veblen's framework, for example, plays no adequate part as an indispensable background to Lippmann's work. In one of Steel's howlers he has Freud, when Lippmann eventually visited him in the later 1920s, introducing the American to Jung and Adler, although it was over ten years after they had ceased to play any part in Freud's circle.

Lippmann was one of the first in the English-speaking world to recognize the significance of Freud's contribution. During the summer of 1914 Lippmann failed to interest George Bernard Shaw in Freud. In 1916 Harold Laski complained by letter to Holmes: "I wish Walter Lippmann would forget Freud for a little—just a little."[29] Lippmann had been a friend of one of the earliest translators of *The Interpretation of Dreams.* Also, he introduced Freud's disciple in the United States, A. A. Brill, to Mabel Dodge Luhan's pre–World War I Greenwich Village salon. Lippmann's participation in the life of the mind played a part in his later relationships with John Maynard Keynes and Charles de Gaulle, to name only two figures that featured prominently in his life.

Portugal's Salazar was also an acquaintance; it has often been pointed out how conservative Lippmann became. Although in the end Lippmann broke with Lyndon Johnson over the war in Southeast Asia, he had long moved far from his early brand of socialism. Starting with *Public Opinion* Lippmann grew increasingly critical of liberalism's naive hopes for public participation in decision making. Yet even by the time of his *The Public Philosophy* (1955), when he had to reassure his readers that he was not advocating the withdrawal of the electoral franchise from anyone, in a special way he still remained dedicated to the ideal of enlightenment. He was attempting to instruct educated people through his steady stream of commentary; his widely syndicated column, "Today and Tomorrow," appeared three times a week for years. Lippmann sought to serve by elucidating issues by making more rational the way political life is discussed.

Although Lippmann had begun to test the problem of publicity and propaganda in his *Liberty and the News* (1919), *Public Opinion* was centrally concerned with the role of the irrational. He had been taking notes for the book since 1914. His experience of psychological warfare, and his witnessing the conduct of World War I itself, had forced him to crystallize his thoughts. But he had long been dissatisfied with the academic approach to the study of public opinion:

> Bryce, Lowell, Dicey, Le Bon, Tarde, and others are interested in describing it as more or less static. This should be a functional description. Must begin by a search for method. It is the great variable in modern political science, usually . . . as an abstraction, because it eludes measurement and description. Rather than deal with the thing itself, writers deal with its machinery. Even then they deal only with legal and institutional forms. The reason for their failure is that they themselves are not makers and leaders of opinion, but observers. They regard it as something given.[30]

Years of such jottings lay behind the writing of *Public Opinion.*

Lippmann's first chapter introduced an unforgettable contrast between the complexities of the outside world and the distortions inherent in our need for "pictures" in our heads. This antithesis between the immense social environment in which we live and our ability to perceive it only indirectly has continued to haunt democratic thinkers. Not only do our leaders acquire fictitious personalities, but symbols govern political behavior. "Under certain circumstances" people "respond as powerfully to fictions as they do to realities, and . . . in many cases they help to create the very fictions to which they respond."[31] Lippmann specified that by fictions he did not mean lies. (The Treaty of Versailles had been a disillusioning education for Lippmann. In *Public Opinion* he remarked that Machiavelli was "a man most merilessly maligned, because he happened to be the first naturalist who used plain language in a field hitherto preempted by supernaturalists. He has a worse name and more disciples than any political thinker who ever lived."[32])

Between each of us and the environment there arises what Lippmann called a "pseudo-environment." He thought that political behavior is a response not to the real world but to those pseudo-realities that we construct about phenomena that are beyond our direct knowledge. As he described his conception years later, he was working with "the Platonic idea that you never see anything but the shadows on the wall. You can't see the reality of the world because it's all over the place and it's too much. So you have to have it reported to you . . . you live in that kind of world which is a society in which the environment is invisible, and the junction between the invisible environment and our own human action is the problem of public opinion."[33] In *Public Opinion* Lippmann was writing in a relativistic spirit that emphasized the significance of the subjective psychological dimension: "The only feeling that anyone can have about an event he does not experience is the feeling aroused by his mental image of that event. That is why until we know what others think they know, we cannot truly understand their acts."[34]

Lippmann maintained that "the way in which the world is imagined determines at any particular moment what men will do."[35] The implications Lippmann drew went beyond the importance of propaganda, although he— like Harold Lasswell—would be permanently affected by the use of public relations devices during World War I. Along with other critics of utilitarian psychology, Lippmann held that social life cannot be explained in terms of pleasure-pain calculus. Despite all the criticisms of Benthamism that many writers have advanced, self-interest still dominates the motives social science is apt to attribute to people; yet advantage, Lippmann believed, is itself not an irreducible concept: " . . . how do men come to perceive their interest in one way rather than another? The desire for security, or prestige, or domination, or what is vaguely called self-realization? How do men conceive their security, what do they consider prestige, how do they figure out the means of domination, or what is the notion of self which they wish to realize?"[36] In contrast to the central assumption of classical liberalism about the existence of a unitary self, Lippmann supposed that several personalities could coexist in each human being; therefore if advantage were to play a part in explaining politics, it would be necessary to establish which self out of the many selects and directs the interest so conceived.

Lippmann's mind was that of a fox, not a hedgehog, to use Sir Isaiah Berlin's famous distinction between types of thinkers, and *Public Opinion* teems with insights. He was, for example, trying to confront the difficulties of "adapting the psychoanalytic scheme to political thought. . . . " As Lippmann saw it, "the Freudians are concerned with the maladjustment of distinct individuals to other individuals and to concrete circumstances." They "assumed that if internal derangements could be straightened out, there would be little or no confusion about what is the obviously normal relationship." Further, "the psychoanalyst . . . almost always assumes that the environment is knowable, and if not knowable then at least bearable, to any unclouded intelligence." But in public life reality is itself the problem: "Instead of taking for granted an environment that is readily known, the social analyst is most concerned in studying how the larger political environment is conceived, and how it can be conceived more successfully. The psychoanalyst examines the adjustment to an X, called by him the environment: the social analyst examines the X, called by him the pseudo-environment."[37]

Censorship posed a special threat for a functioning democracy; news from a distant psychological world can be arranged to suit practical and ideological purposes. Lippmann was troubled by the distinct limits he perceived to the possibility for the circulation of ideas and the difficulties in the path of genuine tolerance. Limited time and attention, combined with the impact of our different social circumstances and modern means of communication, mean that each of us is necessarily far less open and responsive than we usually choose to think.

> Thus the environment with which our public opinions deal is refracted in many ways, by censorship and privacy at the source, by physical and social barriers at the other end, by scanty attention, by the poverty of language, by distraction, by unconscious constellations of feeling, by wear and tear, violence, monotony. These limitations upon our access to that environment combine with the obscurity and complexity of the facts themselves to thwart clearness and justice of perception, to substitute misleading fictions for workable ideas, and to deprive us of adequate checks upon those who consciously strive to mislead.[38]

Lippmann successfully established the role of stereotypes in the making of public opinion; we simplify perception in terms of our preferences, as well as to defend our position in society.

But Lippmann went further, for he questioned the plausibility of empiricism; he doubted that facts make up social reality. "Few facts in consciousness seem to be merely given. Most facts in consciousness seem to be partly made. A report is the joint product of the knower and known, in which the role of the observer is always selective and usually creative. The facts we see depend on where we are placed, and the habits of our eyes."[39] Lippmann's position still conflicts today with much of accepted social science: "For the most part we do not first see, and then define, we define first and then see. In the great blooming, buzzing confusion of the outer world we pick out what our culture has already defined for us, and we tend to perceive that which we have picked out in the form stereotyped for us by our culture."[40] For Lippmann interpretations make up much of what we look upon as the external world. Political life is full of arbitrary perspectives and foreshortenings, which Lippmann thought were "a great barrier between peoples."[41] He contended that "almost nothing that goes by the name of Historic Rights or Historic Wrongs can be called a truly objective view of the past."[42] What he wrote then is still alive and relevant—for example, in Arab-Israeli conflicts: "If you are using the argument from history you are fairly certain to select those dates in the past which support your view of what should be done now."[43] It is so hard to be ideally rational since "the evidence available to our reason is subject to illusions of defense, prestige, morality, space, time, and sampling."[44]

In the light of the psychological insights he was emphasizing it is no wonder that Lippmann questioned idyllic conceptions of democracy. He was not constructing a straw-man theory of self-government, as V. O. Key once alleged, but rather trying to rebuild an enduring image of public knowledge and participation that still persists widely today. In the United States he thought that Jeffersonianism was behind what he called "the doctrine of the omnicompetent citizen."[45] It is still hard for many people to accept the degree to which democracy, designed for harmony and tranquility, rests on symbols of unity, the manufacture of consent, and the manipulation of the masses. Yet Lippmann offered reasons enough for permanent skepticism about dogmas of popular sovereignty.

For all the trenchancy of its critical analysis, in the end *Public Opinion* shared the commitments of the liberal culture from which it arose. Lippmann still sought to study the world in order to govern it. He wanted to find clues to help "in detecting the false absolutism of a stereotype."[46] His optimism about the possibilities of the truth persisted although he knew some of the inadequacies of the classic doctrine of civil liberties and how stylized a version of reality gets reported in the bulletins that pass for news.

He concluded *Public Opinion* with an extensive plea for organized intelligence. He proposed that some neutral method must be devised for preparing information to be used by men of action. Like Veblen with his engineers and Lasswell's later faith in what psychiatrists and political scientists could learn from one another, Lippmann retained a belief in the efficacy of experts. His ideal remained "controlled reporting and objective analysis,"[47] as he refused to yield to the relativity of pragmatism. Despite the questioning of the existence of "facts" and his doubts about the possibility of democracy, Lippmann advocated the creation of an independent organization of truth gatherers whose work would presumably save representative government. If he had stuck to his guns about the inevitably subjective nature of what we take to the environment in which we live, he would have arrived at less amiably democratic conclusions. Enlightenment is still an essential ideal if we are to retain even a limited belief in the role of the public in governing.

Public Opinion arrived at no neat solutions, which need bother us as little as it did Justice Holmes, one of the many contemporary admirers of Lippmann's book. (Years later Lippmann would call his more skeptical *The Phantom Public,* which came out in 1925, the proper conclusion to *Public Opinion.*) It is in the nature of political theory to pose questions rather than concoct prefabricated answers. For all the wide appeal of his book, he was writing with an eye cocked at the tradition of "political thinkers who have counted, from Plato and Aristotle through Machiavelli and Hobbes to the democratic theorists. . . . "[48] No successful account of Lippmann's life and work can slight the books he had absorbed as well as those he wrote.

Political psychology is concerned not just with traditional issues of an abstract and theoretical nature, but can focus on concrete political actors, and Joseph Lash's *From the Diaries of Felix Frankfurter* (1975) can help illustrate this proposition. Lash found the diaries among the justice's papers deposited in the Library of Congress. Frankfurter, an energetic extrovert, was almost proud of his lack of introspectiveness. He began his first entry in 1911 expressing his dislike of diaries, and his own are not notable as an intimate personal memoir. He kept his diaries intermittently until 1948, making detailed accounts for short stretches of time; he destroyed portions he decided should not be preserved. Law and politics have been so intertwined in American history, and Frankfurter played such a significant role in the public life of his era, that anyone interested in intellectual history will relish Frankfurter's fragmentary reflections. Lash's lengthy introductory essay, especially because of its critical distance toward Frankfurter, is biographically fascinating.

Frankfurter repeatedly upheld the ideal of disinterestedness. Early on he had been repelled by what he saw as Woodrow Wilson's doctrinaire approach to politics, and Frankfurter remained opposed to self-rightousness and moralism in public officials. During World War II he disliked what he called the "sentimental humanitarianism"[49] of Henry Wallace. When it came to constructing standards for the Supreme Court, Frankfurter was an insistent defender of judicial self-restraint. Although he opposed activism by the court and wanted judges to be impartial and restrained in order to safeguard the law from excessively personal judgments, nevertheless Frankfurter was extraordinarily involved in behind-the-scenes politics, even while serving on the court.

Frankfurter was known for his good-naturedness and talent for getting on with different kinds of people, yet in his diaries he could be rancorous. His judicial differences with Hugo Black did not lead to a personal break. But he accused Black of having an "irascible and snarling tone of voice," at his worst being "violent, vehement, indifferent to the use he was making of cases," and capable of delivering "harangues" championing "justice and right and decency," implying any opposition amounted to supporting the side of exploitation.[50] In addition Frankfurter was exceptionally harsh about William Douglas's nonjudicial activities and especially his presidential ambitions, on the grounds that it interfered with the proper role of a justice. A born teacher, renowned as one of the greatest law professors in our century, Frankfurter could not resist lecturing his colleagues on the court and grading people in his diaries.

Many liberals who had considered Frankfurter solidly committed to social reform became disillusioned with him. Yet his defense of Sacco and Vanzetti in the 1920s prefigured his later stress on procedural niceties; Frankfurter was chiefly offended that during the trial due process had been violated in defiance of the laws of evidence. In particular, he objected to the unprofessional conduct of the district attorney, and Frankfurter held that both the judge and the prosecutor had fostered prejudice against the defendants, associating them with the guilt of social radicalism rather than just convicting them of crime. To defend Sacco and Vanzetti as Frankfurter did threw him in opposition to the Brahmin establishment with which, Lash argues, Frankfurter ultimately sought to identify himself. But even when it came to Frankfurter's later opposition to capital punishment, it was in characteristically narrow terms that he took his stand: he opposed the death penalty because it inherently sensationalizes the trial process.

During the New Deal, while Frankfurter was still a professor at Harvard Law School, he built a reputation that in the end contributed to the disappointment of many of his supporters. Although from 1933 until 1939 he held no official position in Roosevelt's government, Frankfurter served as a one-man recruiting service for the New Deal. He spotted talent for public service, admiring the "Wisconsin Idea"; as he wrote in 1911: " . . . the union between politics and the university, energizing organized knowledge in the interest of the state as LaFollette has done in Wisconsin is to me one of the most vital contributions he has made."[51] But in a series of diary entries in 1928 we find Frankfurter objecting to having a political leader on his faculty because it was important to keep the university "free from the taint of suspicion of partisan or political motives."[52] It would not be enough for someone so committed to the life of reason to reconcile the inconsistency over the involvement of universities in politics, or the contradiction between his view of the Supreme Court as a "monastery"[53] with his own extrajudicial role, by falling back for legitimacy on the particular kind of politics advocated. Frankfurter did distinguish between the merits of public service as opposed to the temptations of moneymaking in the practice of law. Nevertheless, the unresolved tensions in Frankfurter reflected a broader ambivalence toward power within American liberalism.

Even in the midst of the national emergency of the Great Depression, Walter Lippmann had warned against the dangers for intellectuals associated with public life. In 1936 he opposed Frankfurter's kind of political engagement, and according to Lash Frankfurter never forgave the implied criticism. In his diaries Frankfurter attacks Lippmann's habitual detachment; Lippmann wrote in a soundproof room, evolving drafts that might look worthy but did not need to be implemented in action. Also, Frankfurter was disgusted at what he considered Lippmann's contempt and cynicism toward congressional committees, especially since Lippmann's private opinions were at odds with the noble language in Lippmann's newspaper columns. Frankfurter remained committed to the democratic faith of the rationality of the public, and for him publicity and openness were the prerequisites for sound policy-making. As a publicist, however, Lippmann continued to try to educate the public, and Frankfurter's opposition to the court's taking part in overseeing the redistricting of gerrymandered congressional seats, because it supposedly short-circuited the public's own responsibilities for correction, amounted to a self-destructive use of the philosophy of self-government.

Lash's introductory essay does not make too much of the differences between Frankfurter and Lippmann, but it underlines a comparison with Morris Raphael Cohen that is unflattering to Frankfurter. Cohen was, like Frankfurter, a brilliant Jewish immigrant who had graduated from City College; he and Frankfurter were later roommates at Harvard Law School. Cohen named his firstborn after Frankfurter. Cohen had the more academic interest in jurisprudence, and Lash effectively cites Cohen's critique of Frankfurter's judicial conservatism. According to Cohen, it was only by accident that men like Oliver Wendell Holmes, Jr., Louis Brandeis, and Benjamin Cardozo got to sit on the Supreme Court, and then they were apt to be in the minority. For Cohen, it was dishonest for the Supreme Court to pretend it was saying what the constitution requires when it was in fact deciding what was good for the nation.

The rift between Cohen and Frankfurter was dramatized in their differences over the flag salute cases during World War II. Although Cohen visited the Supreme Court at this time, he did not see his old friend and instead asked to meet Hugo Black. According to Lash, Frankfurter had an immigrant's gratitude behind his nationalism; committed to the assimilationist function of the public schools, Frankfurter held out for the right of the state to require flag saluting even over the objections of a religious minority. (Frankfurter's stress on public education in a democracy helped lead him to play a notable role in ensuring unanimity in the Supreme Court's desgregation decision.) Lash objects to Frankfurter's having held that the Supreme Court had no more scope to protect civil liberties than property rights. Lash's imagery, however, makes one suspicious of the logic of his argument, even if one agrees with his overall judgment, for he tells us that Frankfurter's stand in the flag salute cases "uncoupled him from the locomotive of history."[54] One can question whether anyone should be certain what the future will bring, and the decision of history is not necessarily a just one. Lash's praise for the group led by Hugo Black is narrowly success-oriented. Black and his supporters were, Lash argues, "willing to take larger risks with the Court's authority than was Frankfurter, and history thus far has proved them right."[55] Yet Frankfurter's own experiences with activist courts led by conservatives between the world wars may turn out to be equally relevant today.

Lash soundly distinguished between the philosophies of Holmes and Frankfurter. Although Frankfurter hero-worshiped Holmes, Lash thinks this not so much an ideological affinity as a yearning in Frankfurter to become socially accepted. Undoubtedly Frankfurter, who came to the United States at the age of twelve, felt powerfully drawn to the ideal of the gentleman-scholar and public citizen. Frankfurter shared Holmes's admiration for the British legal system and in particular for England's procedures of criminal justice. But Holmes was a skeptical Olympian who never read newspapers, an ironist who enjoyed cosmic speculations, and a writer excelling in pithy utterances. Frankfurter, on the contrary, was a convinced democrat who devoured every bit of reading matter that came into his house, and his influence on the court was weakened by the tendency of his opinions to be too discursive. Like Holmes, however, Frankfurter was childless, and both had a great need for legal disciples.

The urge for followers in Frankfurter went hand in hand with a tendency to idolize, and Lash is highly critical of Frankfurter's capacity for being sycophantic to Franklin Roosevelt. Frankfurter had not shared the anitimperialist sentiment of the early twentieth century and lacked a suspicion of

presidential leadership. Until the New Deal, Frankfurter had been independent, an "archetypal mugwump."[56] But during the court-packing controversy Frankfurter privately advised the president how to formulate his
position, while remaining publicly neutral. According to Lash, there were
"elements"[57] of the courtier in Frankfurter's relationship to Roosevelt; the
reward for loyalty, in this account, was Roosevelt's nomination of Frankfurter to the Supreme Court seat previously held by Joseph Story, Holmes,
and Cardozo. The significance of the role of the individual in history, and
the influence presidential choices can have over future generations, can be
supported by the careers of any of these great justices.

Adlai Stevenson's life, like that of Frankfurter, is so illuminated by psychological examination that one begins to think that the closer one inspects
any political life history, the more apt it is to yield psychological treasure.
Reading John Bartlow Martin's *Adlai Stevenson of Illinois* (1976), a major
biography, evokes nostalgia. Yet one wonders whether the character of recent American history has not misled our memory about the politics of a
little over a quarter of a century ago. It is possible to romanticize the past
as a lost part of youth. In the case of a man like Stevenson, who as the
Democratic party nominee twice failed to win the presidency, there is in
addition the attraction of an antihero; so much history gets written from the
perspective of success that losers attract special sympathy. Martin is not a
great biographer, neither succinct as a writer nor brilliant as a conceptual-
izer. But his book is impossible to put down. If it is burdened with too
many details, especially about the 1952 campaign, much of the nitty-gritty
will be unforgettable for all who seriously follow American politics. Despite occasional lapses into hero worship, Martin succeeds in assembling all
the documents that should accompany an authorized life. Martin was working under the disadvantage of writing a relatively early appraisal of a politician's career, and in the end one is left with admiration, if not
idealization, for Stevenson.

Stevenson was born in 1900 and grew up in Bloomington, Illinois, which
contains some of the richest farmland in the world. His ancestors were distinguished, and a grandfather had served as vice president under Grover
Cleveland. But Stevenson's parents had early marital difficulties. His father
suffered from migraine headaches that could last for days, and he entered at
least one German sanatorium seeking relief. Stevenson's mother was also
troubled. At times she overprotected her son; as Franklin Roosevelt's
mother moved to Boston during part of his years at Harvard, while Stevenson was in Princeton his mother lived there, too. Later she entered many
sanatoriums and spent months in mental institutions; she ended up unable to
manage her own affairs and was medically treated as insane. As Martin

256   Encountering Freud

observes, "in Adlai's childhood he caught the scent of public greatness and private misery; his own life went much that way."[58]

When Stevenson was almost thirteen years old, while examining a rifle he accidentally shot and killed a cousin. Stevenson's devoted sister thought that amateur psychoanalyzing overstressed the significance of this tragedy, and perhaps, as she contended, his own divorce had a more profound later influence on him. But one loyal psychoanalyst friend of Stevenson's thought that the accident had been lastingly traumatic. Arthur Schlesinger, Jr., conjectured that this childhood accident left Stevenson with guilt feelings over the exercise of power. Some admiring friends wondered whether the accident had not scarred him with a basic insecurity, which would help account for his adult need for feminine support. Martin himself proposes that "a touch of guilt may explain his self-doubts and his protestations of unworthiness."[59] Significantly, nobody in Stevenson's family discussed the shooting incident afterward. Evidence exists that he did not mention it to his wife. Such striking silence can express pain. In 1955 Stevenson wrote to a stranger whose son had had a similar experience; "Tell him that he must live for two."[60]

Although his parents were opposed to the match, Stevenson married Ellen Borden in 1928. Bitterness developed between Stevenson's wife and sister, and Ellen's financial extravagance contrasted with his own tightfistedness about money. From an extremely pretty and appealing young woman Ellen became increasingly unpleasant; the more prominent he became, the more difficult she grew, and many parallels appeared between Stevenson's mother and his wife. She became unpredictable, sharp-tongued, and then vindictive and unbalanced. While he worked in Washington, D.C., during World War II, the couple lived apart as his parents had. She disliked the duplicity of politics, grew jealous of her husband's position, and felt neglected. She developed suspicious feelings, held herself responsible for his successes, and simultaneously suffered a loss of her own identity. Ellen had illusions of martyrdom, thought other men were in love with her, and seemed a classic paranoid case. Convinced she was hemmed in and unable to find self-expression, Ellen resented Adlai's achieving anything on his own. Toward the end he was involved with other women. The Stevensons were divorced on grounds of mental cruelty in 1949, during his term as governor of Illinois. Adlai had problems with her until his death in 1965, although he retained her mother's friendship. Her mental condition became as deteriorated as his mother's had been, and for someone identified with Abraham Lincoln the reality of mental instability in a wife made a distressing analogy.

In the 1930s Stevenson had worked for the New Deal. But the major turning point in his public career had been his joining William Allen White before World War II, setting up the Committee to Defend America by Aiding the Allies. It was a period when American public opinion was divided between "interventionists" and "isolationists," and such men of goodwill as Chester Bowles and Norman Thomas chose to join the cause of America First. As a governor, Stevenson failed to separate his private life from his official activities on the grounds that a friend was a friend, and doubtless this trait helped finally undermine his marriage. He remained deeply committed to civil liberties, and although he fought Communism he attacked McCarthyism. As governor he vetoed a bill that would have made it a felony to belong to a "subversive" group and which required loyalty oaths of public employees and political candidates. Reading another of his veto messages, concerning a bill that would have prohibited cats from running at large in order to protect birds, one cannot help believing there was a rare quality of wit to the man.

The year 1952 saw the first televised presidential campaign in American history. President Truman was offended at Stevenson's vacillation and procrastination over whether to accept the Democratic nomination. All his political life Stevenson had sought posts and then pretended reluctance and self-deprecation when they were offered. His style appealed to those Americans who distrust professional politicians. In 1952, however, it would have been fatal to be seen as the candidate of an unpopular incumbent president, not to mention being forced to defend the war in Korea. Stevenson feared almost certain defeat if Eisenhower rather than Robert Taft were to be the Republican nominee and therefore realistically hesitated as the draft for himself took shape. To his loyal friends he was always being called to more public service, but to his critics he appeared indecisive, a political Hamlet. According to Martin, Stevenson "presented the appearance of a man gay and insouciant, funny and brave. The inner man was at times unhappy, frustrated, lonely, self-doubting."[61]

Although Stevenson appealed to intellectuals he was not one himself. He learned more from listening than from reading. Despite unexceptional academic performance at college and law school, Stevenson possessed that mysterious capacity for growth and change; he was an almost compulsive letter writer and constantly rewrote his own speeches. He undoubtedly exaggerated what public eloquence can hope to accomplish, but during that first presidential campaign Stevenson delivered some enduringly fine oratory. Unfortunately, it left the electorate with an impression of him as cold and remote.

Stevenson was accused of being an "egghead" in 1952, and that insult to humane intelligence helped obscure the future dangers for intellectuals publicly associated with power. The anti-intellectualism that accompanied Eisenhower's electoral victories made it harder to appreciate some memorable words from his Farewell Address as president. From the perspective of those who during the war in Southeast Asia objected to the partisan role of professors in American government, as well as those who accused the so-called New Left of having "politicized" the universities, it is worth remembering how in 1960 Eisenhower declared that in universities government contracts can come to substitute for intellectual curiosity; he was acutely sensitive to how federal money could dominate this nation's scholars.

Stevenson's 1952 speeches were glitteringly brilliant, but Eisenhower's personal warmth and humanity came through. Yet Stevenson's honor and gallantry in defeat remain unforgettable. When he lost he remarked in private: "After all, one has to live for oneself, and the satisfactions of a proper race seem to me greater than victory."[62] In publicly conceding defeat Stevenson said he was reminded of a story Lincoln used to tell: "They asked him how he felt once after an unsuccessful election. He said he felt like a little boy who had stubbed his toe in the dark. He said that he was too old to cry but that it hurt too much to laugh."[63]

Stevenson had sides to him that are less worthy of his memory. When he died he had on his night table a copy of the Social Register. (Many of his friends listed there had voted for Eisenhower instead of himself.) There are too many anti-Semitic comments, even fairly late in Stevenson's career, to leave one uncritical. Perhaps Stevenson allowed himself to be too swept up in American anti-Communism and in imperialist expansion abroad. But he was not the only one to be misled by apparent humanitarianism. Politics remains the art of the possible, and Martin is right in concluding that Adlai Stevenson was "a man who behaved and talked unlike almost any other candidate in recent memory."[64] His humor and dedication make one question whether politics and politician have to connote disrespect and contempt.

Notes

1. Helene Deutsch, "On a Type of Pseudo-Affectivity (the 'As-if' Type)," trans. Eric Mosbacker, manuscript.
2. Ibid.
3. Ibid.
4. Ibid.
5. Ibid.
6. Helene Deutsch, "Absence of Grief," in Helene Deutsch, *Neuroses and Character Types: Clinical Psychoanalytic Studies* (New York: International Universities Press, 1965), pp. 226–36.
7. William Miller, *Martin Luther King, Jr.* (New York: Weybright & Talley, 1968), p. 112.
8. Joe McGinniss, *The Selling of the President 1968* (New York: Trident Press, 1969), p. 100.

9. C. P. Snow, *Variety of Men* (New York: Charles Scribner, 1967), p. 260.
10. Ernest Jones, "A Valedictory Address," *The Yearbook of Psychoanalysis*, vol. 3 (New York: International Universities Press, 1948), p. 54.
11. Walter Lippmann, *Public Opinion* (New York: Macmillan, 1922), p. 172.
12. Ibid., p. 173.
13. Ibid.
14. Ibid., p. 175.
15. Ibid.
16. Arnold Rogow, *James Forrestal* (New York: Macmillan, 1963), p. 43.
17. Harold D. Lasswell, *Psychopathology and Politics* (Chicago: University of Chicago Press, 1977), p. 3.
18. Ibid.
19. Ibid., p. 290.
20. Ronald Steel, *Walter Lippmann and the American Century* (Boston: Little Brown, 1980), p. 152, p. 180.
21. Columbia oral history interviews with Walter Lippmann, p. 18.
22. Interview with Gary Clarkson, May 19, 1966 (Yale University Library).
23. Steel, *Walter Lippmann and the American Century*, p. 140.
24. Ibid., p. 324.
25. Ibid., p. 490.
26. Ibid., p. 513.
27. Interview with Ronald Steel, February 25, 1973 (Yale University Library), p. 28.
28. Ronald Steel, "Walter Lippmann," *New Republic*, December 28, 1974, p. 6.
29. *Holmes-Laski Letters*, ed. Mark de Wolfe Howe (Cambridge: Harvard University Press, 1953), p. 36.
30. Walter Lippmann, "An Approach to the Study of Public Opinion" (Yale University Library).
31. Lippmann, *Public Opinion*, p. 14.
32. Ibid., p. 264.
33. Interview with Gary Clarkson, May 19, 1966 (Yale University Library), p. 15.
34. Lippmann, *Public Opinion*, p. 13
35. Ibid., p. 25.
36. Ibid., p. 26.
37. Ibid., pp. 27–28.
38. Ibid., p. 76.
39. Ibid., p. 80.
40. Ibid., p. 81.
41. Ibid., p. 144.
42. Ibid.
43. Ibid., pp. 144–45.
44. Ibid., p. 154.
45. Ibid., p. 273.
46. Ibid., p. 132.
47. Ibid., p. 289.
48. Ibid., p. 262.
49. *From the Diaries of Felix Frankfurter: With a Biographical Essay and Notes*, essays and notes by Joseph Lash (New York: Norton, 1965), p. 187.
50. Ibid., p. 283, p. 227, p. 174.
51. Ibid., p. 121.
52. Ibid., p. 131.

53. Ibid., p. 155.
54. Ibid., p. 73.
55. Ibid., p. 84.
56. Ibid., p. 20.
57. Ibid., p. 61.
58. John Bartlow Martin, *Adlai Stevenson of Illinois: The Life of Adlai E. Stevenson* (New York: Doubleday, 1976), p. 35.
59. Ibid., p. 43.
60. Ibid., p. 45.
61. Ibid., pp. 512–13.
62. Ibid., p. 763.
63. Ibid., p. 759.
64. Ibid., p. 763.

14

Psychohistory

Many people have praised the merits of interdisciplinary collaboration, and certainly one would expect to find that workers in fields like psychoanalysis and history would have much in common. For instance, both analysts and historians seek to reconstruct the past on the basis of fragmentary evidence, yet in as scientific a spirit as is compatible with the frequently subjective nature of the material they have at hand. Earlier in this century professional historians were rather standoffish about what seemed to them the grandiose social speculations by Freud and his early followers, yet in recent years, partly due to the influence of Erik H. Erikson but also traceable to the growing understanding of the significance of unconscious motivation for all the social sciences, historians have shown an exceptional receptivity to the possibilities inherent in a depth psychological perspective.

If such interdisciplinary work is to accomplish some of its objectives, however, the relationship between psychoanalysis and history has to be more than a missionary one. If each of us can hope that through the study of another professional discipline we can be partially freed from the parochialism of our own educational background, then the analytically oriented worker must expect to change and broaden his scope through contact with the historian every bit as much as the latter has had to adapt his own earlier preconceptions in the light of psychoanalytic insights.

By and large historians have been more receptive than most other social scientists to the achievements of depth psychology. Yet they have also, like others, often been credulous about the allegedly scientific findings of clinical practitioners. David E. Stannard's *Shrinking History: On Freud and the Failure of Psychohistory* (1980) is an enormously lively, well-written book; Stannard, a distinguished historical scholar, is determined to undermine the fallacies committed by so many of his colleagues in the name of psychohistory.

Stannard is a friend of interdisciplinary research and teaches in an American studies department. However, he cannot stomach the wilder abuses of psychoanalysis. Although his book starts out objecting to the prevalence of pretentious nonsense in this area, it rapidly becomes a full-scale assault, not only on the so-called applications to history of Freud's work but on the reasoning of psychoanalytic thought itself.

Stannard begins with an examination of Freud's famous essay on Leonardo da Vinci and, not surprisingly, finds that not much of the argument is left standing today. Yet even if, as seems likely, the essay was partly autobiographical, Freud's artistry commands respect, especially when understood in the context of the period in which he was writing. As a contemporary historian, however, Stannard has little tolerance for what he sees as Freud's misguided purpose.

Stannard assembles evidence that psychoanalytic therapy is highly suspect; he also attempts to show that psychoanalytic theory cannot withstand ruthless logical examination. Philosophic scrutiny damages the status of the concept of the unconscious until major parts of the psychoanalytic edifice become quasi-mystical. (Somehow Freud's dream theory escapes examination here.) Propositions that resist disconfirmation are bound to be scientifically less than satisfying.

Stannard marshals his argument with verve; this admirable book is the product of a civilized intelligence, and it is a pleasure to read. Yet the author does not seem to realize that many others have shared his doubts about psychoanalysis and its historical uses. By being apparently unaware of the elaborate history of critiques of Freud, Stannard ironically shares in the ahistoricism that he finds in the work he set out to combat.

The brute fact of the matter is that Freud has somehow survived these many years of criticism, which must mean something to a historically sensitive observer. Trade unionism and the power of therapeutic suggestion can have an impact of their own. But Freud also had a central philosophic vision, more tragic than his North American audience might always want to acknowledge, which also helps account for the vitality of his ideas.

One could cite, almost endlessly, grotesque uses of Freud, and any thinker does bear some responsibility for the way his work gets implemented. But Stannard ignores, for the sake of his polemic, the ways in which biography writing has benefited from Freud. One thinks, to take only a few examples, of Winthrop Jordan's subtle essay on Thomas Jefferson, Justin Kaplan's book on Mark Twain, and Leon Edel's multivolume biography of Henry James. More popular biographies have also been enriched by the broad impact of psychoanalytic thought.

A catalog of studies that have benefited from psychoanalysis does not itself establish the scientific claims of Freud. But such a procedure might make one pause in evaluating the overall place of psychoanalysis. Even if the Freudian revolution in ideas could be shown to have been on balance a negative contribution, it has been one that is so pervasively a part of our culture that some satisfactory historical inquiry is going to be necessary to account for the prevalence of this ideology.

My reaction to Peter Gay's *Freud for Historians* (1985) is somewhat less unfavorable on a second reading, but I fear that my point of view will be misunderstood; therefore I would like to spell out what I found unsatisfying about it. Presumably the author was writing with a sophisticated audience in mind, which is why I find his approach hard to appreciate.

Gay tells us in the preface that by psychoanalysis he means "more than the body of work done by Sigmund Freud and his immediate disciples alone."[1] I wonder how he can think he is being tolerant when he explains that he has no intention of "reading" one "psychoanalytic historian" and another "Kleinian biographer" "out of the club." He goes on to explain that "apart from the essentials about which no compromise is possible, psychoanalysis is not a fixed body of doctrines but an evolving discipline of research and theorizing."[2] He does not detail exactly what the "essentials" may be, but given the history of sectarianism in psychoanalysis, the idea that "no compromise" can be "possible" does send a shiver down my spine. When he later declares that "the object relations school remains firmly within the Freudian ambiance,"[3] it sounds to me too much like an ex cathedra declaration.

Also distressing is Gay's inability to distinguish between psychoanalysis as an intellectual entity and as a trade union. Even in 1939 Hanns Sachs, one of Freud's loyal disciples, wrote about how the scientific movement and the organization had drifted apart. Gay implies that the "highly specialized technical periodicals"[4] make great reading on which the professional historian has unfortunately missed out. I suspect, however, that one ground for some of the skepticism about psychohistory stems from the disquieting state of contemporary psychoanalysis.

Any sense of reciprocity between psychoanalysis and history is missing in the book. Gay does declare at the outset that "an exploration of just what psychoanalysis could learn from the historian, fascinating though that would be, lies beyond the scope of this work."[5] Yet without understanding what some of the defects in current psychoanalytic thinking might be and how social scientists can help to correct the situation, a book like this reads too much like a propaganda tract. Gay shows no signs of sharing any of Erikson's own subtle unhappiness with many aspects of psychoanalysis, which makes one wish that Erikson had been temperamentally able to be more outspoken about the implications of his point of view.

It is a small but telling detail that Gay lists the Freud-Bullitt book on Woodrow Wilson under Bullitt's name first, although that reverses the order of the text itself. I suppose it is a sign of progress that the book can now be discussed. It will not do, however, for Gay to cite Erikson's 1967 essay on the collaboration between Freud and Bullitt without being aware of the key changes Erikson introduced when he reprinted the essay in 1975.

Gay seems oversocialized to current psychoanalysis, and so there is a conformist ring to his explications of the Freudian model of personality development. If psychoanalysis was once "an eminently subversive science,"[6] what did it become in North America? Gay's reasoning is too dovetailed to the current organizational powers-that-be. Psychoanalysis does focus on the presence of inner conflicts, and one wishes there were more signs in Gay of ambivalence, if not dissent from orthodoxy. He tells us that Freud's "successors have not questioned"[7] the concept of the unconscious in his theory, but throughout the history of psychoanalysis there have been respectful critics of Freud who took a different approach to what they thought the unconscious consisted of. No one book, and surely not a methodologically oriented presentation like Gay's, can be expected to turn the tide of historians about the role of psychology. But if Gay set out in some sense to answer David Stannard, for example, he would have done better to assume that unbiased readers were more astute than this book seems to think.

Having expressed my serious reservations about *Freud for Historians*, I hope my praise will not ring hollow or forced. Gay is obviously an important acquisition to the ranks of psychohistory. He has kept careful track of know-nothingness about Freud among historians. The section of the book that discusses the defects of the notion of self-interest is superb. Gay tell us that he was once "a devotee of the revisionist psychoanalytic views of Erich Fromm;"[8] it is regrettable that in Gay's ideological change of heart he has swung so far in an orthodox direction. He may have found his years of psychoanalytic candidacy at the Western New England Institute of Psychoanalysis unqualifiably satisfying, but some of the most talented analysts I know have complained of how stultifying their training experience was. When Gay tells us that his reception at the New York Psychoanalytic Institute and at the American Psychoanalytic Association was "unfailingly cordial and never condescending,"[9] one might never guess at how horrible the fanaticism of an aroused orthodoxy can be. Fromm endured the fate of his heresy, and Erikson paid his own price for trying to evade being stigmatized as a so-called deviant. There is much to be said about the role of a kind of Stalinism in psychoanalysis, and therefore when Gay writes that "irrelevance, irresponsibility, and vulgarity remain the principal counts in the indictment against the psychoanalytic historian,"[10] it sounds too polemical for my taste, unlikely to persuade, and reminiscent of the intolerant religious wars of the past.

* * *

William McKinley Runyan's *Life Histories and Psychobiography* (1982) is, like the volumes of Stannard and Gay, methodologically oriented, yet it so crosses interdisciplinary boundaries that it is relevant to all the human sciences. Runyan has tackled the basic problems encountered in the study of individual lives. With a secure grasp of the relevant literature, Runyan sets out to lay the conceptual foundations for the study of lives as he seeks to evaluate and improve available methods. By the end of his work he proposes criteria and standards for making case studies as rigorous as possible.

Ideologically Runyan is clearly on the side of the angels. He acknowledges that it is legitimate for there to be a diversity of accounts about individual lives, but he does not lapse into a relativism that sees no way out of the possible quagmire of subjective interpretations. He gives examples of alternative versions of historical figures in order to demonstrate "the crying need for standards of critical biographical inquiry."[11] Value commitments and social concerns are, he emphasizes, bound to shape biographical treatments of single lives.

Evidence, he argues, has to be critically evaluated within the context of a particular perspective; alternative avenues of thought also serve as a crosscheck. He gives an especially good model of a balanced evaluation of competing explanations in a chapter titled "Why Did Van Gogh Cut Off His Ear?" He is right in contending that the method of the life history narrative, so central to practicing historians as well as clinicians, has received little conceptual attention in the social sciences.

Runyan proposes to define a case study as "the systematic presentation of information about the life of a single unit. . . . "[12] As illustrations of how case histories can be "formulated and reformulated in light of changes in scientific beliefs," he uses George III, Dr. Daniel Paul Schreber, and Little Hans. Difficult though his objectives may be, the "emergence of additional historical evidence can serve to revise prior understandings of a particular case."[13]

It is perhaps telling about the current state of psychiatry, with its attention to the elaboration of rival theoretical points of view, that Runyan can use relatively few recent examples of psychiatric case histories. Oddly enough, old-fashioned psychiatrists, at least those trained in Europe before the impact of the Freudian revolution in ideas, were expected—more so than nowadays in North America—to present their material in vivid narrative form.

Runyan sets out a series of rules for writing life histories that are lucid as well as admirably restrained and sensible. His purpose is to rehabilitate what seems like an unduly neglected scientific method. The concern for patterned individuality is a perfectly respectable endeavor. In a crucial chapter titled "The Psychobiography Debate," Runyan uses biographies of

Woodrow Wilson, Emily Dickinson, and Wilhelm Reich in order to assess how evidence ought to be weighed. Sometimes the biographer has access to material unavailable to the therapist, while on the other occasions clinical material is richer than historians know what to do with. Runyan is as open to the contributions of psychoanalysis as he is to the significance of nonpsychoanalytic approaches. In setting up eleven criteria for the case-study approach, Runyan lists, for example, providing "insight" into the person, deepening our empathy for the subject, portraying the social and historical world that the person lives in, delineating "problems" requiring action, identifying the need for additional information, and sensitizing us to the likely consequences of alternative courses of action.

One wishes, though, that Runyan had paid more attention to the vexing problems associated with training: how social scientists can be expected to learn about advances in psychotherapeutic thought and the equally important issue of how clinicians can come to feel at home in the various aspects of social science.

Runyan has succeeded in clearing the underbrush of basic concepts encountered in the study of individual life histories, and he has demonstrated that qualitative, descriptive, and interpretative approaches are legitimate avenues of knowledge for the study of life histories.

Methodology about psychohistory, no matter how sophisticated Stannard, Gay, and Runyan might be, can in the end only take us so far. In the end it is concrete illustrations that will finally convince, since the power of example teaches at least as much as, if not probably more than, the most elaborate of conceptualizations. It is in this context that I think that the issue of contemporary racism and the roots of its psychology in the past can do much, as the model of a psychohistorical argument, to illustrate the proposition that there are critical aspects of social life that require depth psychological understanding.

It has often been pointed out by critics that North American psychiatrists have, at their worst, been preoccupied with the problems of the rich and the well-to-do, while becoming secure members of the establishment themselves. They have been content—again at their worst—with the therapeutic goals of adjustment and conformism to the status quo. Too often psychiatry has been irrelevant to contemporary social problems, refining its own dry theories for the sake of a professional in-group.

Black Rage (1968), by William Grier and Price Cobbs, uses the best of modern psychiatric ideas for the sake of understanding the consequences of American racism. It was written by two Negro psychiatrists and is an urgent and moving account of what it means psychologically to be black in today's society. Committed and partisan, filled with valuable case illustrations from clinical practice, *Black Rage* is well worth reading and listening to.

Although they are advocates of racial justice, Grier and Cobbs do not indulge in any phony moralizing. Drawing on relevant elements of the Freudian tradition and displaying an acute sensitivity to the social environment, they try to cope with the black man's suffering and pain. Their main concern lies in exploring the depths of human ailments and the sources and effects of racial cruelty. American history has a savage side to it, which many of us have been too slow in realizing.

The book is short, unpretentious, and contains no pious hopefulness about the consequences of that eagerly awaited inward look at what we have done to the Negro. Nor does *Black Rage* make any empty claims about how much the Negro has gained from the aims of integration and the civil rights movement. Instead this book tolls the consequences of America's ghastly racial record; slavery does terrible things to people.

At the same time the authors do not superciliously dismiss the strengths of Negro family life or ignore the courage and integrity that stem from Negro culture. Many of the most distinctive achievements of our society, in fact, may stem from those we have most exploited. Surely our music and writing would be inconceivable apart from the black man.

As psychiatrists, though, Grier and Cobbs focus on disharmony and failure, the ways in which American life works against the humanity of its Negro citizens. The job of the psychiatrist is healing, so the authors have appropriately focused on the apathy and self-hatred, on all the insecurities and distorted self-perceptions, that our history has fostered within the Negro's soul.

This book not only eloquently teaches us about the plight of the American Negro, but its authors join that small body of workers who use psychiatry in behalf of the poor and the downtrodden. They demonstrate that psychiatry need never endorse the status quo, either explicitly or implicitly. A little more relevance in our psychiatry and a little less conformism in our thinking may help us avert social disaster.

Every profession has its strength as well as its illusions. Modern psychiatry's concern with crucial areas of our lives tends to evoke magical expectations and consequent disappointments. Grier and Cobbs, however, represent the best of balanced psychodynamic thinking. They make use of their training and clinical experience in examining an immensely complicated political and social issue, the American racial question. In their second book, *The Jesus Bag* (1971), they illustrate a kind of idealism that so often gets lost in the course of professional psychiatric practice.

The Jesus Bag is not a summary of other people's findings; it is an original and thoroughly serious book, which has something to say to even the most sophisticated student of contemporary America. Like Frantz Fanon, Grier and Cobbs use clinical vignettes for socially radical purposes, although unlike the famous prophet of the Third World they are not explicitly writing autobiography. Those who sympathize with the racially oppressed will be glad to find here a reasoned attack on the intellectual apologists of the Nixon administration and subsequent reactionary thinking. This book tells us more about its subject than any that has been written by a white psychiatrist, since along with the authors' understanding of the human suffering inflicted by racial injustice goes a full appreciation of the special strengths that accompany social alienation.

"Black children from birth," the authors begin their book, "are exposed to heavily systematized hostility from the nation and for their own survival must reject the community's code of behavior. . . . ''[14] Religion, although only one technique of survival, is in the view of Grier and Cobbs so central to the black man's experience that they have drawn on it for the title of their book. Like Nietzsche and others, they see in Christianity an instrument of psychological bondage. Child rearing also plays its part, and the authors describe the institutions—such as "the dozens"—that black culture has developed to teach its young to react with stoicism to humiliation. Since the United States has by and large excluded the Negroes from positions of political importance (on the assumption of their lack of talent), it is not surprising that in response to this devaluation blacks at critical points frequently do not take the white world seriously.

One of the anomolies of America's liberal heritage is that though the nation has been dedicated to the proposition that all men are created equal, this moral absolutism has required, paradoxically, that black men be ejected from the realm of humanity. Once blacks could be regarded as subhuman, the grounds had been laid for the white man to use the Negro as a special target for violence and for the black man to incorporate this typical American prejudice in his attitude toward himself. Accordingly, high blood pressure and hypertension—associated psychologically with repressed hostility—are medically more serious among blacks.

There may be more political polemic in this book than in the authors' best-selling *Black Rage*, yet when one reads the superb chapter on the white expert little of their argument seems superfluous. By juxtaposing the stock sayings of some social scientists with the realities of clinical life, the authors level serious strictures at the school of thought associated with the name of Daniel P. Moynihan. For Grier and Cobbs, the notion that the primary problem is class discrimination rather than race is obviously unsound, as they try to prove by specifying the unique uncertainties and dangers that in the past have surrounded the lives of black people. It has taken fancy footwork on the part of some political scientists to argue that those who perform the drudgery of American society are also guilty of an inability to postpone gratification. Despite all the attacks on Benthamism in the nineteenth century, "self-interest" as an explanation of human behavior is still riding high, and according to certain upwardly mobile and calculating social scientists, defects in Negro culture must be responsible for its failure to grasp the opportunities the United States has offered. As psychiatrists, Grier and Cobb are acutely sensitive to the subjective element, the way one's world is viewed, and they maintain that not only are the so-called opportunities largely illusory but that wounded egos lead the blacks to react to a set of realities very different from what might seem to be.

Grier and Cobbs, however, are too upright (and moralistic) to see that much of the social science they deplore is the result of a special system of rewards. It is not so much that professors are for sale as that established social science is by and large not aware of its ideological purpose, and many hardworking students, as a result of their thorough professional training, take years to discover the hidden biases in the premises of their disciplines. For some of course it is convenient never to wake up, since acquiescence on their part paves the road to success.

So psychiatry is not alone as a field in which most practitioners use the tools of their discipline too credulously; Grier and Cobbs stand out professionally because of their commitment to understanding the society around them. They illustrate how dedicated intellectuals can overcome the stultification of career training and the seductiveness of conventional advancement. True to their craft as healers, Grier and Cobbs are aware of some of the psychological dangers of the new black militancy, for instance the irrationality of black anti-Semitism; in the end these psychiatrists' books stand as disturbing reminders of all the appalling consequences of the racist side to American history.

Freud's impact on his followers was overwhelming, and perhaps as a result many of his pupils did little more than consolidate and preserve the master's findings. The relative absence of original thinking within psychoanalysis has become all the more distressing as psychoanalytic concepts have permeated the Western world. Freud himself was a great revolutionary who, for the sake of exploring new areas of man's relation to society, challenged conventional ways of thinking and defied all established professional organizations. Yet as his own ideas influenced modern psychiatry his formulations became part of a new conformism.

Bruno Bettelheim stands as one of Freud's few genuine heirs in our time. Fearlessly independent and yet working within Freud's general system, Bettelheim has sought to think through all of human psychology for himself. Once again like Freud, Bettelheim has not been content to remain a closet philosopher but has sought to test his insights in a clinical context. By the time he appeared in Woody Allen's movie *Zelig* Bettelheim was probably the most famous analyst in the West.

In addition to being a prolific writer—*The Children of the Dream* (1969) was his eighth book—Bettelheim was an ardent clinician. His Orthogenic School at the University of Chicago, which he headed until his retirement, is a brave enterprise devoted to the conviction that it is possible to help autistic children overcome the severest possible emotional conflicts, and the assistance Bettelheim's school offers is as unconventional as the very notion that these children can be rescued at all. The Orthogenic School tries to perform as an institution those parental functions that have misfired in the child's natural home.

Bettelheim's career and the evolution of his work have not been without changes in course. He has himself described in *The Informed Heart* how the experience of being an inmate in the Nazi camps at Dachau and Buchenwald shook him out of his earlier dogmatic slumbers. If the environment of a concentration camp could have a radical effect on the personalities of its inmates, he reasoned, could not some positive lessons be gleaned from this for the creative use of institutions to promote human autonomy? The origins of the Orthogenic School lie in what Bettelheim had learned about the effects institutional life can have on mental functioning.

Bettelheim has not been shy about speaking out on problems beyond the strictly therapeutic, and he is having a growing influence on social scientists throughout the world. Quite unlike many other post-Freudian thinkers, Bettelheim has never indulged in any soupy moralism. Drawing on his experiences with the children of his school, he has become a severe critic of many middle-class American child-rearing practices. In fact, he has never taken for granted the special virtues of middle-class life and has made himself into a trenchant critic of the standards of contemporary culture.

The communal method of education developed in the Israeli kibbutz (*kibbutz* is a Hebrew word meaning "group"), although involving only a small fraction of Israel's total population, was almost bound to seem to Bettelheim a fascinating experiment in nature. His *The Children of the Dream* asks: to what extent is man the father of society or society the father of man? Bettelheim's own experience with the institutional rearing of children had contradicted earlier claims that rearing children in groups must be damaging to their mental health. Moreover, the children of the kibbutz had been reared according to a variant of Freudian teaching. Like it or not, psychoanalysis has become a part of the modern world, and perhaps no one is more equipped to assess the effects of kibbutz society on personality formation than Bruno Bettelheim.

Not surprisingly, his fascinating account of communal child rearing in Israel is appreciative of the best elements of kibbutz education, which takes place in a restricted society of high consensus functioning as an extended family. "Kibbutz children live from birth on (usually from the fourth day after delivery) with their age group, not at home with their families. That is, they are reared as a group, in separate children's houses, by members of the community assigned to the task."[15]

Although kibbutz parents play a distant role in the upbringing of their children, by a conscious act of will the community is charged with assuming the overall functions of direction and control in the life of its children. The kibbutz, and not the parents, provides the basic security for the child. Peer groups play a central role in the upbringing of children, while maternal substitutes by and large take over the mothering function.

Social philosophers over the centuries have speculated on the possibilities of human development in small societies, and Bettelheim has a keen eye for the gains (as well as the losses) of this unique Israeli subculture. In the kibbutzim he found an absence of drug addiction, juvenile delinquency, and the kinds of cultural deprivations that have beset the young in our own society.

The kibbutzniks seem to have many fewer emotional disturbances than one would expect to find in a comparable group in the United States, although in a culture as different as the kibbutz it is difficult to say what would count as a sign of symptomatology. Freed from the anxieties bred by a competitive social order and the American premium on possessing things privately, the kibbutzniks have worked cooperatively in behalf of a joint community effort; their very consciences have been so formed by their society (instead of their parents) that to oppose the group would be to risk the greatest loss imaginable.

The ostensible purpose of the kibbutz movement had been to create a new way of life in a very ancient and hostile land. In fact, the dream of the first generation of kibbutzniks to found a new society has succeeded in contributing much to the uniqueness of modern Israel. Bettelheim puts this whole movement into the context of the revolt of Eastern European Jews against the constraints of ghetto life.

It took the deep devotion to a secular religion to undercut the faith of their fathers; instead of the unity of the ghetto, they evolved the solidarity of the kibbutz. Instead of the open show of familiar feeling, they substituted the calm detachment of comradeship, and in place of the values of intellectual achievement and the acquisition of property, they turned to physical labor and set themselves the task of transforming their physical environment. In the Promised Land former ghetto Jews could avoid overintellectualization by becoming farmers. Above all, the kibbutzniks rejected the powerful ghetto mother and gratified their own fears of inadequacy as parents by turning child rearing into a specialized role.

Bettelheim ruthlessly pursues the psychological consequences of the special conditions of kibbutz life. These latter-day Puritans deliberately aimed to alter the relations between children and parents as typified in Freud's conception of the Oedipus complex. If they succeeded in removing some of the worst aspects of the hostility and ambivalence between child and parent while protecting the child from fears of parental desertion and abandonment, the kibbutzim also managed to destroy the intimacy and deep attachments of traditional family life.

The author observed in the kibbutzniks an emotional flattening out and a fear of deep attachments, as they seemed to find it difficult to be fully intimate or autonomous as feeling human beings. To the degree to which they had given up to the community problems that in our society the individual must struggle over and internalize, the people of the kibbutzim lack a capacity for deep empathy with others. As critical as Bettelheim is of middle-class child rearing, he is fully appreciative of some of the best aspects of our own culture, where in exchange for all the parents' dependent care the child gives in return—ideally to be sure—through the full flowering of his personality.

No doubt other observers of kibbutz life will find much to quarrel with in Bettelheim's account. He freely admits that his report is very personal and impressionistic, based on an all too brief seven weeks' fieldwork, mainly in one kibbutz settlement. Others may well challenge the particular assets and liabilities of group rearing that Bettelheim found in Israel, but they should be grateful for his clarity, lucidity, and boldness in stating an argument. As long as we have workers like Bruno Bettelheim the Freudian tradition will remain very much alive.

Curiously enough, Bettelheim's work has evoked little critical commentary. Among professionals, however, there is more than a suspicion that most genuine autism in children has to be accounted for by organic factors and that Bettelheim's approach left many anguished parents with an unnecessary burden of guilt feelings. None of these reservations has succeeded, though, in reaching the general reading public, and, in particular, Bettelheim's concentration camp study has gone unchallenged; the "he was there" line of reasoning has choked off many would-be doubters. Terence Des Pres's *The Survivor: An Anatomy of Life in the Death Camps* (1976) did so fundamentally question Bettelheim's orientation that he felt obliged to pen an answer to Des Pres in the *New Yorker*, although Bettelheim failed to mention in his devastating account of *The Survivor* that he had been in any way discussed by Des Pres.

The Survivor is, I think, a beautifully written analysis of the literature about the death camps, which begins with a proposed change in our conception of heroism. Twentieth-century instances of genocide have, Des Pres believes, undermined the traditional grandeur of death; mass murder makes dying less a victory and survival more than victimization. Existence under the most extreme circumstances of degradation poses the dilemma of reconciling the desire for life with the quest for self-respect, and therefore to Des Pres the endurance of survivors results from acts of moral choice.

Des Pres thinks that in order to protect the everyday conception of life we repress the testimony of survivors as disturbers of our psychological peace. The need so many survivors felt to bear witness to their experiences by writing books seems itself an example of modern heroism. As survival in the camps was a collective act, so the memory of the camps becomes a social achievement. The remembered past is an essential component of the conscience of civilization. In contrast to what Des Pres considers the aims of psychotherapy—adjustment, acceptance, and forgetting—the survivor as witness has rejected conformist goals.

Throughout *The Survivor* Des Pres criticizes psychoanalytic thinkers, and in particular Bettelheim, for having emphasized the supposed regression of inmates to infantile levels of conduct. Des Pres believes the survivors are reminders not of human guilt but of objectively evil circumstances. Nazism and Stalinism subjected prisoners to filth for the sake of ultimate humiliation and debasement. Des Pres hypothesizes that genocide is more tolerable to murderers as the victims look less than human. The totalitarian objective is to crush the human spirit. Des Pres argues that prisoner behavior was not childish but a heroic response to dreadful necessity. He not only cites Treblinka, where the inmates burnt down the camp, but throughout the literature he finds instances of prisoners having maintained a sense of inward inviolateness. Just to care for one's appearance became an act of resistance; human dignity endured in the form of freedom from the entire control by external forces.

Older prisoners often died of grief, mourning for lost family and friends. Des Pres looks on the fate of inmates too much from the point of view of youth, for whom it more readily seems worthwhile to wait for the healing of time to reawaken the desire to live. It sometimes took years to accumulate the weaponry for active resistance; in the meantime death proved the success of totalitarian evil. At Auschwitz "Canada" was the slang expression for a storage depot where abundant supplies, seized from incoming prisoners, were accumulated to be shipped for the Nazi war effort. Prisoners not only stole from "Canada" but developed an underworld of risky activities essential to the maintenance of life. Instead of blaming the victims for imitating the conduct of their captors, which is how Bettelheim's reasoning proceeds, Des Pres stresses how life's resiliency coped with absolute power to cheat death. Survivors helped one another, engaged in sabotage, and at Buchenwald made contact with the Allies for a bombing raid on SS sectors of the camp.

Bettelheim's thesis has become widely influential. But Des Pres insists that Bettelheim was himself imprisoned in a special period when criminals among inmates were in positions of power. It was not true, Des Pres argues, that social bonds among prisoners were absent; nor was it the case that camp inmates did not hate their oppressors and sometimes revolt. The psychoanalytic viewpoint misleads the unwary because it assumes human nature in a civilized context. Under extremity people act not symbolically but because of external necessity. Bettelheim, Des Pres believes, felt superior to fellow sufferers, and Bettelheim's account, according to Des Pres, is marred by an egotistical obsession with autonomy, blinding us to the extent of mutual aid in the camps. Bettelheim "wishes to rouse us from our sense of victimhood; but by claiming that pressure reduces men and women to children, and by praising a heroism based on death, he tends instead to support what he fears." [16]

At the end of *The Survivor* Des Pres conjectures about the biological, as opposed to cultural, sources of survival. One can set aside such controversial scientizing and come away from his book with a moving defense of the survivor as a significant moral type. Under the worst pressures of dehumanization at least some can preserve themselves in recognizably human ways. Des Pres's book is a needed corrective to fashionable views and a tribute to the soul's life-affirming tendencies.

Psychodynamic formulations have met with some justified skepticism throughout the social sciences, yet historians trying to cope with the lives of political leaders have been long aware of the need for additional tools. Des Pres's questioning of Bettelheim makes for an intriguing debate within psychohistory, but the disagreement cannot by itself close the door that Freud's work opened for historians. Even in a book as professionally widely recognized as Robert Blake's *Disraeli* (1967) one finds that author entering into matters that, in the hands of someone less sensitive, would rouse cries of protest. For example, Blake informs us of Disraeli that "it is clear that he did not get on well with his mother." [17] Such a proposition can be validated by traditional means of scholarship. But Blake goes on: "Precisely what went wrong with their relationship no one can now tell. But something went wrong. There is no record of his ever talking about her after her death. . . . Indeed, one might almost think that he wished to obliterate her memory." [18] At this point the student of modern psychology feels on home ground. When Blake further maintains how deeply Disraeli felt maternal "deprivation,'' and how ''all his life he seems to be searching for a substitute for the mother he was somehow missing,''[19] one wonders whether a psychoanalyst who made the same kind of (undoubtedly correct) point would not be hooted at for his simplemindedness.

However, Blake has not written a biography to prove any theory, for to do so would be bound to distort a human life. More important to a biographer than any psychological principles is the amount of sediment that felt human experience has left in his bones. In Blake's case he has created a rich and complex portrait of Disraeli, flamboyant and cynical, resilient and reckless, extravagant and shady at the same time. In addition, Disraeli shone in feminine society and had a facility for conquering elderly ladies. Queen Victoria was only the most famous of a long line of such conquests.

Disraeli's wife was a rich widow; she was twelve years older than himself, and their marriage was a great success. It is often quite rightly pointed out that past historical material will elude psychological categories to the degree that one cannot check interpretations as one can hopefully do in a clinical context. Yet the impact of the Freudian revolution has also meant that nowadays people have a whole armory of new defenses, enabling them to deceive themselves by means of fancy terminology. In the middle of the nineteenth century, however, Disraeli's wife could be so touchingly open as to conclude a letter to him: ''Good angels guard my dearest. A thousand and a thousand kisses. Good night. Sleep and dream of—your Mother.''[20] Few wives would express themselves that way anymore. As Blake notes, ''the signature is revealing. Disraeli needed not only a mistress but an adoring mother, someone to look after him in illness, sympathize with him in adversity, encourage him when he was in a mood of despondency, admire him when he was successful.''[21]

I have singled out this maternal theme to show how even the most highly acclaimed political biographies touch on controversial psychological subjects, where a degree of sophistication will at least lead one to pose questions that might otherwise go undiscussed. For example, Disraeli seems to have had few friendships with equals, although he exerted charm and influence over younger men; at the end of his life one man in particular devoted himself to Disraeli ''as few sons ever do.''[22] Yet Blake does not discuss how the Disraelis might have felt about not having children. Whatever such omissions, Blake has given a superb portrait of the statesman as improviser, a man who, for all his eccentricities, contributed much to modern British parliamentarianism. Psychology can be helpful in understanding not only idealists like Erikson's Luther and Gandhi, but also a pragmatic politician such as Disraeli.

Like Blake, Fawn Brodie in *Thaddeus Stevens: The Scourge of the South*

(1959) writes absolutely fascinating political history, though she is far more explicitly psychodynamic in orientation. Originally published before ego psychology became as popular as it later became, her work demonstrates that even the earlier Freudian approach was capable of being used with biographical profit. Without any pretense of "absolute detachment,"[23] Fawn Brodie admires the aims of the Abolitionists and welcomes the Fourteenth and Fifteenth Amendments as bulwarks against the tyranny of state governments. As chairman of the Ways and Means Committee of the House of Representatives during the Civil War and then as a leader during Reconstruction, Stevens left an imprint on his era.

An inveterate gambler with a reputation as a rake, Stevens was nonetheless a teetotaler determined not to follow his father's path into drunkenness. Fawn Brodie is especially eloquent in her treatment of Stevens's clubfoot. She cites the "old superstition that cripples are really demons in mortal form"[24]: "A lame man is a minority of one wherever he walks. And there was, in fact, no persecuted minority in America for whom Stevens did not at some time speak out. Over and again in his speeches the words 'branded' and 'marked' crop up like specters that will not be exorcised."[25] Fawn Brodie observes of the crusader that "his crusade is likely to be a substitute for deeper needs, and there is no success but finds him empty and lonely still."[26] In Stevens's case he first participated in free-school agitations and then "embraced the cause of antislavery in a decade in which it was not merely inexpedient but dangerous . . . Fate had branded him with a mark of inequality, and it must have eased his torment to strike against another kind of branding, which he also pictured in terms of shackled limbs and a longing for freedom to dance."[27] As much as Fawn Brodie admires Stevens, still she writes that "indignation served him instead of love, and a sense of injustice was his substitute for hope."[28]

Stevens had been suspicious that Abraham Lincoln's gentleness would let the revolutionary gains of the Civil War go for naught. Once Andrew Johnson became president, Stevens's problem was compounded. The only Southern senator not to go over to the Confederacy at the outbreak of the war, at his inaugural ceremony Johnson was roaring drunk. As Fawn Brodie sees it, "it may well have been . . . ravaging self-contempt that was responsible for the blunder of his drunkenness at the inauguration."[29] After Johnson tried to get the Southern states to reject the Fourteenth Amendment, punishing the president became Stevens's obsession. Not surprisingly, as he aged Stevens grew "more irascible, waspish, and defiant."[30] But "at no other time in his life did he show more dramatically the destructive flexibility of a truly revolutionary leader"[31] than in his war against Johnson. Fawn Brodie thinks the impeachment proceedings were not the inevitable result of the vendetta between the two men, but rather the outcome of a collusion between Stevens's skillful vindictiveness and Johnson's ineptness and masochism.

Joseph Lash's *Eleanor and Franklin: The Story of Their Relationship, Based on Eleanor Roosevelt's Private Papers* (1971) is an excellent example of the penetration of a popular political study by psychiatric ideas. The most humanly moving part of the book consists in Lash's reconstruction of the pain and suffering of Eleanor's lonely childhood. Her mother separated from her wastrel father, and then the family had had to go to court for fear he would dissipate what remained of his estate. Orphaned by the age of nine, Eleanor "wept for her father, not for her mother,"[32] and we are told that she kept his letters with her for the remainder of her life, reading and rereading them. A neglected child, she seems to have been disliked by her schoolmates (who nicknamed her Granny). Altogether too serious and too good, she later recalled that as a small child "I seemed like a little old woman entirely lacking in the spontaneous joy and mirth of youth."[33] In turn Eleanor was terribly stern with her own children: "Playing with children was difficult for me because play had not been an important part of my own childhood."[34]

If it is no surprise that she grew up with a puritanical and jealous disposition, disliking good food and considering sex an ordeal to be borne, it is at first sight strange that she should have appealed to someone of Franklin Roosevelt's playboy inclinations. Socially, of course, it was a good match for both of them, and a politically ambitious man like Franklin is not apt to have overlooked the fact that her uncle Teddy, who was only a distant cousin to Franklin, was in the White House. (Characteristically Franklin was annoyed at the way the president stole the show at their wedding reception.) Another worldly consideration may have been that her annual income from trust funds was larger than his.

If the marriage was a good one from Franklin's point of view, it may have been also partly because he sensed in Eleanor a woman of sufficiently dominating will to help him get free from his mother's power. Initially Eleanor was subordinated to her husband and her mother-in-law, Sara, who later used her money to influence Eleanor's children. Once Franklin fell ill with polio, it seems clear that without Eleanor's help he probably would have succumbed to Sara's reported intention that he be an invalid and thereby dependent on her, for unlike his mother, Eleanor approved of Franklin's political aspirations. But Lash is uncritical of her relationship with Sara; for example, he says of Sara's having argued in favor of hiring a nurse for Eleanor's children that "later . . . [Eleanor] bitterly regretted yielding on this point,"[35] as if it were not entirely consistent with her character to have wanted to abdicate from this maternal sphere. It is also a bit implausible to accept at face value her contention once that she never wanted to be the wife of a president.

One of the most remarkable features of Lash's book is his discussion of Eleanor's discovery at the end of World War I of Franklin's affair with Lucy Page Mercer, Eleanor's social secretary. Although it might seem bold for a book officially authorized by the Roosevelt family to discuss such a delicate matter, the relationship between Franklin Roosevelt and Lucy Mercer had been made public earlier by Jonathan Daniels. If a psychiatrically oriented writer were to make as much of this affair as Lash does it would probably be attributed to an excessive preoccupation with sex: "In the shaping of Eleanor Roosevelt the Lucy Mercer affair, while neither hammer nor anvil, was the flame whose heat hastened and fixed the change from private into public person. Franklin's love of another woman brought her to almost total despair, and she emerged from the ordeal a different woman . . . Franklin did not offer the love for which she yearned, and she had to build her life around the acceptance of that fact."[36] When, however, Lash tells us that even during Franklin's presidency, when Eleanor was under the mistaken impression that the relationship had been terminated, "the wound left by the Lucy Mercer affair was still open, still painful" and that Eleanor kept seeking to "at last efface the hurt he had done her,"[37] it is hard not to think that Lash is overstating his case. It is true, however, that, unknown to Eleanor at the time, Lucy Mercer visited Franklin at the White House, and that she was with him at Warm Springs when he died.

There is a story that contrasts a Protestant minister's attitude toward the confession of a murderer with the reaction of a Catholic priest; while the former shrank from the news, the latter tolerantly inquired, "How many times, my son?" Is it possible that in forty-five years of marriage Lucy Mercer was the only other significant woman in Franklin's life? Understandably enough for someone in Lash's position vis-à-vis the Roosevelts, he does not broach the question.

Lash does quote a catty (but perhaps honest) relative as saying Franklin "deserved a good time. He was married to Eleanor."[38] Here one wonders if Lash has not let Eleanor down, for at no point does he discuss how widespread at the time her sexual attitudes were. Though Eleanor echoed conventional sentiments in discussions about sex with her daughter, is it not nonetheless possible that her actual experience had been somewhat different? And might that help account for how wounded she felt by her husband? Or else, if Lash is correct about her lack of sexual feelings, might there not have been some failure on Franklin's part in not helping her to overcome her early upbringing? Such questions as these are undiscussed by Lash. We can believe his account, though, that in reaction to Franklin's self-centered and mischievous flirtatiousness, Eleanor responded with depressions, a form of passive reproach.

As Lash sees it, "public office had a disciplining effect on . . . [Roosevelt], and when he was out of office he was restless, reckless, irrepressible."[39] The excitement and variety of politics was one of the attractions public life had for him. As with so many imaginative people, he enjoyed his inconsistencies and had an ability to tolerate the discomfort of dissonance. But if Franklin was the consummate politician, Eleanor saw herself as an agitator, "always the teacher."[40] It is a testimony to the mystery and resiliency of the human spirit that Eleanor Roosevelt could, out of the miserable childhood that psychoanalysis might see as a grim harbinger, fashion herself into the remarkable lady we all admired.

Isaac Deutscher's *Lenin's Childhood* (1970) owes its title to the author's early death, rather than from his conceptual intentions. This posthumously published fragment by a biographer of Stalin and Trotsky is all we have of his intended full-length study of Lenin. It is a beautifully written book and a tribute to the historian's art. Thanks to Deutscher's profound knowledge of Russian social conditions, as well as his understanding of the emotions of childhood, from an ounce of recorded fact he has been able to yield a pound of credible interpretation.

Deutscher is especially sensitive about Lenin's rivalry with his older brother, explicitly referring to the contributions of Alfred Adler to the understanding of sibling problems. When Lenin was seventeen, not long after the death of his father, Lenin's brother was hanged for his political activities. This event has long been acknowledged as a turning point in the young Lenin's life. But Deutscher's perception of unconscious motivation, inferred at one point from a slip of the pen, is remarkably keen:

> . . . although one may assume that Vladimir Ulyanov would have become Lenin even if his brother had not died on the gallows, there can be no doubt about the impact of Alexander's martyrdom on his early development as a revolutionary. Lenin himself was aware of this and very briefly spoke about it to his wife and sisters; all the more significant is the circumstance that throughout his political career he never evoked, in public, or even mentioned, his brother's life or death. The name of Alexander does not occur in any of Lenin's books, articles, speeches, or even in his letters to his mother and sisters. In all the fifty-five volumes of the latest and most complete Russian edition of his *Works*, Alexander is mentioned almost incidentally and only twice; in a purely factual statement in which Lenin answers a questionnaire (never completed or sent out); and in a letter in which Lenin, in 1921, recommended a certain Chebotarev: "I have known Chebotarev," wrote Lenin, "from the 1880's in connection with the case of [my] elder brother Alexander Ilyich Ulyanov hanged in 1887. Chebotarev is

undoubtedly an honest man." The omission of the "my" in the sentence is characteristic. So extraordinary a reticence could not be ascribed to frigidity of feeling: on the contrary, it covered an emotion too deep to be uttered and too painful ever to be recollected in tranquility.[41]

Philosophers and Kings: Studies in Leadership, edited by Dankwart Rustow (1969), is testimony to the wide range of scholars—some more psychologically than historically or politically inclined, others more historical or political than psychological—who find the intersection of psychology, history, and politics relevant to their work. This collection, valuable to anyone interested in the methodology of leadership studies, not only examines the lives of such figures as Newton, William James, de Gaulle, Bismarck, and Atatürk, but also treats such thematic problems as charismatic leadership, the nature of psychohistorical evidence, and Marxist leadership patterns.

As Rustow points out in his essay introducing this volume, "the politician who operates the rules of the game successfully is just as much of a psychological being as the one who runs afoul of them." This statement about leadership studies can be extended to the general contribution of psychology to history and politics, for psychological understanding is not only relevant to the bizarre and supposedly pathological circumstances of a Hitler, concentration camps, assassination, totalitarian systems, and socially or political deviant behavior, but it can also help illuminate more everyday occurrences such as the conduct of race relations and the acceptance of societal norms and ideologies, as well as the more problematic areas of rationality, freedom, democracy, and individualism. Bringing together psychology with history, as well as politics, it should be clear by now, will ensure no intellectual millennium, but it can benefit and enrich us as it helps to free us from some of the narrowness inevitable in professional training. The study of psychology can sensitize the political scientist (as well as the traditional historian) to an additional dimension of human experience, while reminding him of what we cannot know or assert.

Notes

1. Peter Gay, *Freud for Historians* (New York: Oxford University Press, 1985), p. ix.
2. Ibid., p. x.
3. Ibid., p. 93.
4. Ibid., p. 45.
5. Ibid., p. xvi.
6. Ibid., p. 58.
7. Ibid., p. 124
8. Ibid., p. xii. .

9. Ibid., p. xv.
10. Ibid., p. 4.
11. William McKinley Runyan, *Life Histories and Psychobiography: Explorations in Theory and Method* (New York: Oxford University Press, 1982), p. 30.
12. Ibid., p. 127.
13. Ibid., p. 133, p. 139.
14. William H. Grier and Price M. Cobbs, *The Jesus Bag* (New York: McGraw Hill, 1971), p. 1.
15. Bruno Bettelheim, *The Children of the Dream* (New York: Macmillan, 1969), p. 335.
16. Terrence des Pres, *The Survivor: An Anatomy of Life in the Death Camps* (New York: Oxford University Press, 1976), p. 162.
17. Robert Blake, *Disraeli* (New York: St. Martin's Press, 1967), p. 15.
18. Ibid.
19. Ibid., p. 16.
20. Ibid., p. 99.
21. Ibid.
22. Ibid., p. 755.
23. Fawn M. Brodie, *Thaddeus Stevens: Scourge of the South* (New York: Norton, 1966), p. 10.
24. Ibid., p. 19.
25. Ibid., p. 26.
26. Ibid., p. 22.
27. Ibid., p. 68.
28. Ibid., p. 374.
29. Ibid., p. 221.
30. Ibid., p. 309.
31. Ibid., p. 292.
32. Joseph Lash, *Eleanor & Franklin: The Story of Their Relationship, Based on Eleanor Roosevelt's Private Papers* (New York: Norton, 1971), p. 44.
33. Ibid., p. 28.
34. Ibid., p. 198.
35. Ibid., p. 155.
36. Ibid., p. 220, p. 297.
37. Ibid., p. 358, p. 338.
38. Ibid., p. 226.
39. Ibid., p. 265.
40. Ibid., p. 420.
41. Isaac Deutscher, *Lenin's Childhood* (New York: Oxford University Press, 1970), p. 67.

15

Sages

Walter Lippmann is the foremost American political pundit of our century. For over sixty years he surveyed public events with detached intelligence. Never temperamentally happy with muckraking, his courage came instead in his ability to think through issues with clarity, consecutiveness, and, above all, independence. In the light of the readiness with which established academicians let themselves be used by politicians, Lippmann, who needed the cooperation of politicians for his kind of work, becomes all the more noteworthy in his achievement.

A founding editor of the *New Republic,* later an editor of the *New York World,* and for more than three decades the author of a celebrated syndicated column, Lippmann became an institution in American politics. Such a career within the establishment requires (and enables) a man to keep his ear very much to the ground. At least until his final retirement from Washington he regularly dined out in political society and remained on intimate terms with the major policymakers of the Western world.

Yet Lippmann always held back a portion of his mind from the treadmill of column writing and political reportage. During his undergraduate years at Harvard, in the famous class of 1910, Lippmann had genuinely impressed men like William James, George Santayana, and Graham Wallas; they immediately recognized the quality of his intellect, and he remained loyal to their spirit in his continuing concern with serious political and social thought. His *Public Opinion,* published in 1922, is by now a modern classic in the use of psychological insights to illuminate problems in political theory, and it remains his greatest single contribution to social philosophy. There is an inevitable gap, Lippmann had argued, between the complex outside world and the stereotyped pictures we carry around in our heads, so that we can know only indirectly the confusing environment in which we nevertheless live. A pseudo-environment comes to govern our behavior. For half a century Lippmann pondered the implications of this for his own democratic convictions.

In the course of his long career Lippmann was involved with almost every major trend in American political and social thought. Certainly he was unable, or too honest, to be a consistent system builder. A socialist in college and subsequently an admirer of Teddy Roosevelt's New Nationalism, Lippmann later became an eloquent advocate of Woodrow Wilson's internationalism. (Lippmann is said to have had a major hand in drafting the Fourteen Points.) In addition, he ranks as one of the 1920s' most brilliantly skeptical commentators on the vulgarities of Babbittry.

Lippmann after the 1929 crash was an early pre-Keynesian proponent of countercyclical economic planning, but then he turned into a tough critic of the whole New Deal. Always cosmopolitan, he did not hesitate to propose American involvement in Europe in the late 1930s, and yet after World War II he was one of the earliest to caution against the extent of American overinvolvement in the affairs of the world. In each of these very different and often inconsistent phases Lippmann did not try to be a moral prophet, but expressed his likes and dislikes in terms of a reasoned understanding of the issues he saw at stake. A full-scale biography of Walter Lippmann amounts almost to an account of the history of political ideas in the United States over the better part of this century. Unfortunately, he was guarded and protective about the intrusions of scholarship and so standoffish as to refuse even to be interviewed. This author of about two dozen books started depositing his papers at Yale, and intellectual biographies of him have emerged, but they will be the poorer for not being infused with knowledge of the man.

Perhaps the peak of Lippmann's conservatism came during the Eisenhower years, when the incompetence of small-town businessmen in high public office helped to evoke his most elitist proclivities. His *Public Philosophy* (1955) was a natural law critique of democratic government, and yet his writing continued to belie his most reactionary principles; in seeking all those years to be a public educator, Lippmann never lost the rationalist faith that clearheadedness on public matters can be communicated to the people effectively. He did not relinquish the democratic ideal that the people can be rallied in the defense of the public interest.

Lippmann's *Early Writings* (1970) is a collection from his first few years of work, when he struck many as a most precocious young man with an inborn talent for writing serious prose. All these articles appeared in the *New Republic* during the years from 1914 to 1920; many of them were published anonymously at the time, so it is only now that we can be certain of their authorship. The whole course and rationale of America's initial emergence from isolationism can be found reflected here, along with an account of the hopeful attitude liberals adopted to the increased central power of the modern presidency. Some fifty-odd years later Lippmann might no longer have complained of the dangers of the paralysis of government: the end of his Washington career was preceded by a well-publicized controversy with President Johnson over Lippmann's lack of subservience on the issue of Vietnam.

Aside from acute commentary on current events in that long past era, none of which has grown stale, some memorable pieces in the collection can stand on their own: an account of the fight to appoint Louis Brandeis to the Supreme Court; descriptions of the presidential conventions of 1916 and 1920 rivaling the pungency of H. L. Mencken at his best; thumbnail sketches of forgotten political leaders like Leonard Wood, Frank Lowden, and W. G. McAdoo; essays with barely suppressed indignation at the quality of the arguments used to oppose progressive social legislation such as child labor bills and minimum wage proposals; and a perceptive and generous appraisal of Freud's stature in the modern world. The whole collection is lively and spirited and a welcome reminder of the tribute due to the entire corpus of Lippmann's writings.

It is not unusual for the reputation of a writer to go into a slump shortly after his death. When Lippmann died in 1974, he had been retired from his famous column "Today and Tomorrow" since 1967; a handful of his many books were still in print, and the reading public could be expected to remember both the unusual lucidity of his prose as well as the broad scope of thinking that his journalism reflected. Louis Auchincloss, his literary executor, wrote a novel about Lippmann, *The House of the Prophet,* which remains the most successful re-creation of Lippmann that we have, particularly moving in its depiction of the deterioration of a powerful intellect in his last months. Yet *The House of the Prophet* sold unusually poorly, did not appear in paperback, and is not even mentioned in the excellent notes to John Morton Blum's *Public Philosopher: Selected Letters of Walter Lippmann* (1986).

A temporary sag in Lippmann's public standing was transformed into a solid downward reappraisal with the appearance of the widely heralded authorized biography by Ronald Steel, *Walter Lippmann and the American Century* (1980). Steel's unspoken antipathy to his biographical subject took multiple forms: instead of seeing Lippmann as a precocious young man who immediately impressed eminent thinkers of the time, Steel alleged social climbing; he constructed a virtual scorecard that tallied occasions when Lippmann was right on public policy, offset by where he went wrong; Steel seemed to relish the details of the way Lippmann escaped regular military service in World War I; Steel emphasized the scandal of Lippmann's marriage to his best friend's wife; and Steel placed an uncharitable interpretation on Lippmann's anti-Zionism, as well as his whole relationship to his Jewishness.

Even if one puts aside biographical questions that presumably might be decided in Steel's favor, it is undeniable that the official biography seriously distorted Lippmann's contribution by underestimating the value and significance of the books Lippmann wrote. Steel, himself a journalist, interpreted Lippmann's career by his practical political involvements.

John Morton Blum lauds Steel's biography in his preface to *Public Philosopher*, saying that he could have cited it "twice as often."[1] Yet, in the course of over six hundred large pages of Lippmann's letters, Blum's conscientious notes refer to Steel's biography less than two dozen times. Robert O. Anthony, who was responsible for setting up the collection of Lippmann's papers at Yale University, has claimed that Blum edited out of Steel's early draft of the biography a number of diminishing remarks about Lippmann, preventing the book from becoming an even greater betrayal of Lippmann's trust than it in fact was.

Steel has, for the sake of this edition of Lippmann's letters, shared with Blum the notes and transcripts used in the biography of Lippmann. Yet Blum's extensive introduction to *Public Philosopher* not only makes no mention of Steel, but concentrates on the side of Lippmann that Steel had neglected—the books. Blum treats Lippmann as an intellectual historian should, by accounting for the structure, antecedents, and influence of Lippmann's ideas. Blum appreciates that Lippmann was a political theorist as well as a columnist, and his introduction emphasizes a few key texts in Lippmann's output: *A Preface to Politics* (1913), *Public Opinion* (1922), *The Phantom Public* (1925), *The Method of Freedom* (1934), *The Good Society* (1937), *U.S. Foreign Policy* (1943), *U.S. War Aims* (1944), and *Essays in the Public Philosophy* (1955). Blum utters not a word of criticism of Steel's biography, yet his whole introduction emphasizes a side to Lippmann's work that should help restore his intellectual standing. The argument of other of Lippmann's books would also be worth considering. *A Preface to Morals* (1929), for example, was a remarkable achievement, even if Steel is right in proposing that its origins can be found in the breakdown of Lippmann's first marriage.

For those interested in twentieth-century American politics, these letters make fascinating reading. Lippmann's comments about public figures and world issues are always noteworthy, even if he was fallible. Lippmann was involved with Woodrow Wilson's administration, disillusioned by the Treaty of Versailles, and scathing about the Republicans in the 1920s; he detested Mussolini, was extraordinarily prescient about Charles de Gaulle, and, at the same time, could be notoriously wide of the mark about Franklin D. Roosevelt, whom he called "a kind of amiable boy scout"[2] not to be recommended to become the Democratic candidate for the presidency.

Blum has done an almost impeccable job of identifying people and issues that come up in the course of Lippmann's correspondence, much of it to the great and the famous. One notable lapse, however, is Blum's acceptance without comment of Lippmann's false belief that Sigmund Freud had reviewed *A Preface to Politics*. Lippmann did once visit Freud in Vienna, but the author of the review of that early book of Lippmann's was in fact Freud's own future biographer, Ernest Jones.

Although some of Lippmann's letters are particularly interesting, he was not a master letter writer like Freud. (Blum, to be sure, excluded "intimate"[3] as well as routine letters from this volume.) Readers with special interests will single out different items for praise. There is a fine 1922 letter on the teaching of English in New York public schools and a strong letter to Marcus Hannah's daughter, who Lippmann thought—without rancor—had so debased her campaign for the Senate that he told her she was not worthy of election. His Harvard classmate John Reed once sent Lippmann an accusatory letter; portions of Lippmann's 1916 reply are, I think, memorable:

> I continued to believe in you even though many times I have felt that you had acted like a fool or a cad. . . . I watched you at college when a few of us were taking our chances. I saw you trying to climb into clubs and hang on to social position by your eyelids, and to tell you the truth I have never taken your radicalism the least bit seriously. You are no more dangerous to the capitalist class in this country than a romantic guerrilla fighter. . . . I got into this fight long before you ever knew it existed and you will find that I am in it long after you quit.[4]

Plenty of the greatest political theorists have been actively concerned with following practical politics; Machiavelli would have understood Lippmann's career, although not perhaps why Lippmann felt able to decline high public office. Yet it is because of Lippmann's full stature that Blum's selection of letters remains somehow disappointing. He has chosen for publication from among twenty thousand letters. But only a passing familiarity with the full body of Lippmann's letters at Yale indicates that what might have been included in this volume would have made it more actively a part of the life of the mind. For example, with all Lippmann's concern for the problems that the conduct of foreign policy poses for democracy, Lippmann's contact with the political scientist Hans Morgenthau should certainly have been included. Any remarks by Lippmann about books would have been welcome. When Arthur Schlesinger, Jr., wrote to Lippmann for comments about an introduction he had drafted for an edition of Herbert

Croly's *Promise of American Life,* Lippmann's answer to Schlesinger showed an awareness of his own limitations as a scholar, even though Lippmann had worked with Croly at the *New Republic* for years. I certainly think that space should somehow have been found for Learned Hand's altogether remarkable letter on Lippmann's *Phantom Public,* a book that Lippmann had dedicated to Hand. And not only did Lippmann write to McGeorge Bundy on the immediate political issues that are included in *Public Philosopher,* but also Lippmann had earlier requested and received Bundy's help on a proposed revision of *The Good Society.* This selection from Lippmann's letters does not contain enough that touches on the themes in his books, and therefore Blum's narrowly political principle of selection seems to have been at odds with the character of his own introduction to *Public Philosopher.*

Lippmann's career was unique in American history. Although Lippmann became doubtful about the capacity of democracy to survive under the complicated conditions of twentieth-century life, he devoted his journalistic talents to the democratic ideal of purifying the news for the public's consumption. He remained troubled by the inability of a modern electorate to secure the needed information on which to act rationally. Lippmann's was a disciplined life, a rare example of someone who did not waste his talents. These letters enrich our understanding of one of the most interesting political thinkers in American history.

Political philosophy has fallen on bad times. There has been, as Sir Isaiah Berlin once put it, a slump in sages. In pragmatic America it is always easier for scholars to gain support and recognition for narrow empirical research projects than for more speculative examinations of the fundamental premises of our political and social thought. But when political philosophy is pursued, too often it is simply academic and irrelevant to the contemporary world.

Hannah Arendt was that rarity, a public philosopher with an audience. She fully earned the right to be considered one of our ranking social thinkers. Her *Origins of Totalitarianism,* which examines the link between anti-Semitism, imperialism, and totalitarianism, is a splendid study, full of ideas. Her *Eichmann in Jerusalem* was capable of upsetting intellectuals, especially Jewish ones, all around the world; this book remains a shocker— for the terrible historical tale it tells, for the trial it records, and for the viewpoint it presents.

Men in Dark Times (1968) is a collection of assorted essays about leading Central European intellectual figures of the last century (with the exception of the opening essay on Lessing.) Despite an occasional tendency to pontificate, Arendt can be a very moving and eloquent writer. Some of these essays were originally written in German, and their English translations do not read as smoothly as the ones composed in English. Though this is not a major book of the author's, it does present some of her most characteristic outlooks.

A refugee herself, Arendt was a messenger of ill tidings. The rise of Hitler put an end to the rich cultural life of a Continental intelligentsia, forcing many of its members to flee and scatter abroad. Other men at other times have found it easy to perceive and break in their personal lives as a shattering of the Western tradition. Maybe each of us is doomed to nourish his own provincialism. For those educated in the best of Western culture, the disruptions of their own societies was almost bound to foretell the decline of the West. It is perhaps unnecessary to point out that, despite the holocausts of this century, culture—even of a distinctively Western variety—has in fact succeeded in flourishing outside the German-speaking world.

Against the background of her general theme that our era is one of public darkness, Arendt's form of cosmopolitanism has given us some brilliant essays on individual figures. The study of Rosa Luxemburg, for example, is wonderfully evocative of a human being and presents an outstanding account of a great and neglected leader in the history of socialism. A few pages on Pope John XXIII make him live as a simple man of faith and humanity, at the same time a most impressive Prince of the Church.

A very long and devoted chapter on Walter Benjamin attempts to give this man of letters his due recognition, although her essay fails to convey persuasively the sources of her enthusiasm for his talent. (Arendt was responsible for some of Benjamin's work appearing in English for the first time, and a debate has been under way over his contribution to literary and moral life.) A fine, clear essay on Bertolt Brecht illustrates her range of appreciation; she is most interested in him for his political and social convictions, and the way his ideology could conflict with his art. Yet it is the poet in Brecht, as well as his playfulness, that has captured her imagination. Arendt also sensitively treats Isak Dinesen, Hermann Broch, and her teacher Karl Jaspers, as well as her personal friends Waldemar Gurian and Randall Jarrell.

No such book of reviews, addresses, essays, and tributes can be expected to have the satisfying coherence of a sustained or developed argument. Such a collection almost necessarily acquires a continuity more of mood than of logic. These articles do form a piece, however, with her larger body of work, which has focused on defining the limits of the public realm. Although she writes so often on literary subjects and demonstrates a real talent for understanding the artist's dilemmas and inner conflicts, in the end Arendt took her stand on moral and political grounds. As a public philosopher she toiled on, contributing by her illumination to relieving public darkness.

Elisabeth Young-Bruel's *Hannah Arendt: For Love of the World* (1982) has been so widely discussed and acknowledged that it seems fair to examine at the outset its shortcomings. Many authors lack distance from their subject, and Young-Bruel cannot understand Stuart Hampshire's outspoken reservations about Arendt's work. (The author neglects to mention that Sir Isaiah Berlin also once singled out Arendt as an overrated writer in the *Times Literary Supplement*.) The book is too long; for example, the last hundred pages should have been sharply abbreviated. Despite all the detailed material that might have been appropriate toward the making of a life study, the author stuck to her project of producing a "philosophical biography."[5] It succeeds in being a thoroughly absorbing account of the development of Arendt's mind, even if the people who play a part do not rise above a wooden level. Her involvement with Martin Heidegger, with whom she had an affair as a young woman, remains hard to fathom, as do other friendships. (The breakup of her first marriage is described in particularly "highfalutin" terms.) The anti-Communist climate of opinion in which *The Origins of Totalitarianism* first appeared does more to account for its reception than the author seems willing to concede.

Unlike the approach of so many who have written on Arendt, who at her death in 1975 was showered with tributes, Young-Bruehl takes seriously *Eichmann in Jerusalem*. Political theorists too often ignore this book, as if it were an embarrassment in its topicality. Although the controversy may appear hard to understand today, at the time the Jewish powers-that-be were outraged by her book. Young-Bruehl not only gives a balanced account of the debate, but puts the book in the setting of Arendt's earlier concern with "the Jewish question." The discussions prior to the founding of the state of Israel are particularly pertinent today, for although much of the theorizing then might appear to have been sectarian, it has become increasingly relevant. The notion that Zionism could breed a species of fascism was raised long before the 1982 Israeli invasion of Lebanon. (In 1948 Arendt, Einstein, and others signed a letter of protest to the *New York Times* when Menachem Begin, then a terrorist, came to the United States looking for support.) Arendt considered herself an internationalist, not anti-Zionist.

Young-Bruehl also explores the earlier controversy that arose over Arendt's article "Reflections on Little Rock." Here she is not so successful in being evenhanded. Neither Little Rock nor the name of Governor Faubus appears in the index to this book, although Ralph Ellison—one of Arendt's critics— gets listed. In the late 1950s American mistreatment of its blacks had finally come to the political forefront. For Arendt to have used all her mental equipment to oppose the desegregation of public schools was more than a lapse into perversity. As she justified her position by distinguishing between "the private, the social, and the political,"[6] such abstractions sound hollow in the fact of concrete moral reality. (Heidegger's membership in the Nazi party did not destroy Arendt's bond to him.) For Arendt to invoke states rights in the midst of the struggle over the Supreme Court's rulings on segregated schools was appalling. Arendt had preserved a special sort of innocence that goes with creativity in social theory. But in stressing politics as the realm of heroism and freedom she was overreacting to her own experience of statelessness. The tradition of German philosophy from which Arendt came has an unpleasant underside that Young-Bruehl might have done more to highlight.

This book is a tribute to Arendt. Her preferences, sympathies, and eccentricities are lovingly rolled together, accepted, and made to seem coherently justified. Arendt was one of those refugees who did so much to enliven North American life. Yet she deserves to be weighed by European standards; it might be well to pay attention to the judgment of Hampshire and Berlin, as a corrective to the appreciation and gratitude of Arendt's former students. It is a shame to puff up a superb essayist into a theorist whose marginal notes in books seem worth quoting.

Hannah Arendt was a fiercely anti-Freudian lady; when she denounced the "comedy" of "soul-experts" in the Eichmann trial, she was implying that the psychiatrists who certified his sanity were themselves a part of the moral debacle of Western culture. Yet the psychology underlying her version of Jews in Europe who were allegedly complicit in their own destruction bears curious resemblances to the tendency within Freudian theory toward blaming the victim. At least the critics of Arendt's version of the Holocaust found her too hard on the Jews of Central Europe and too evasive about the realities of social cruelty with which they had to contend. Every historical narrative has to imply certain psychological preconceptions; Arendt, and as we shall see George Orwell as well, even though a declared opponent of psychoanalysis, necessarily shared in our contemporary climate of opinion, which has been so influenced by Freudian thinking. Reinhold Niebuhr, another philosopher, felt he had to come to grips more explicitly with the challenge of Freudian teachings.

Niebuhr is now one of the saints of modern American liberalism. He was a man of God with a social conscience, and his preaching and writing made him an influential force on the left. In the 1930s he wrote in a nondoctrinaire Marxist vein, but later he became disillusioned with socialist principles. Niebuhr taught that although Christianity could not prevent misfortune, it could provide the faith that gives distance to suffering. He believed that politics would fail to provide ultimate fulfillment, but that salvation was not possible apart from a life of political involvement. As the years passed *Time* and *Life* came to feature him regularly, and Richard Rovere once called him "the official establishment theologian."[7] Niebuhr was also one of the founders of Americans for Democratic Action and a thinker whose words can now be ritualistically invoked to sanction the most well-intentioned proposals. Although neoconservatives have tried to lay claim to him as well, it would be hard to find anyone who stayed more devoted to the cause of the American liberal tradition.

A study of Niebuhr therefore invites high expectations. Although Richard W. Fox denies that *Reinhold Niebuhr: A Biography* (1986) is an "official" study, he had sufficient cooperation from Niebuhr's family and friends to make it hard to envision any other book supplanting this one for its thoroughness and critical care. Despite the book's imaginative limitations (its subject does not spring vividly to life), Fox has written a fine biography of Niebuhr the intellectual. A new generation will better understand Niebuhr's texts and why he attained a revered status in the American liberal community.

Perhaps the lack of vividness is not entirely Fox's fault. Part of the problem may stem from the destruction by Niebuhr's brother of family correspondence. At any rate, Niebuhr seems to have been too controlled and rational a man for his life to have had much color. He was deeply devoted to his widowed mother and evidently remained celibate until his marriage in 1931. Niebuhr himself wrote about his marriage in cryptic terms. A woman who was in love with him in 1925, but disappointed by his reaction, described him in a way that sounds chillingly like his image in Fox's biography:

> . . . he's empty and cold and unemotional—unstirred in the depths of his being—at least only a little stirred. *Surely* with the tremendous capacity of mind—there must be this other thing dormant somewhere. But what will stir it, what will arouse it! I don't know. Or has so much gone into intellect that the other side has paid the penalty and become warped and dwarfed—and we must expect only mind! I don't know. He can *never* satisfy me, as he is today—*never*. Perhaps I could mean in part what he needs—but he too must mean what I need.[8]

Whatever this book fails to communicate about felt experience, though, it does demonstrate the origins of Niebuhr's thinking. He was born in 1892, the son of a midwestern minister of the German Evangelical Synod of North America who had come to the United States in 1881. Niebuhr was a favored child who did not need to rebel against his stern, Germanic father; they shared a liberal pietistic faith. Niebuhr was an excellent student who did not get much of a formal education until he started attending Yale Divinity School in 1913.

Fox traces some of Niebuhr's earliest inner struggles to his standing as a cultural outsider. At Yale he continued to be ill at ease in the English language, and he also had to contend with the painful subject of his German-American identity. Throughout World War I, he was a superpatriot, believing that by endorsing the American side he was simultaneously fulfilling the cause of the true German. It is an expression of this biography's genuine impartiality that Fox does not flinch at showing how Niebuhr's brand of patriotism contributed to a wave of cultural repressiveness. Endorsing Prohibition was an essential part of Niebuhr's early conception of Americanism and progressivism. It took the shock of the Treaty of Versailles to move him to question his prior liberal thinking.

During the 1920s Niebuhr's Evangelical Church in Detroit flourished. It was a solidly middle-class congregation, although an enduring myth about Niebuhr would have it that he was a preacher for factory workers. He regularly challenged the moral complacency of a prosperous culture, as he assailed the sin of pride with more than a little self-satisfaction. He had become a leader of liberal Protestantism in the United States. At a time when secular liberals were inclined to give up on politics, Niebuhr and his friends were moving leftward. He criticized modern industry, became increasingly pro-labor, and for a time even called himself a pacifist. The United States was for Niebuhr altogether too consumption-oriented and success-minded, overly interested in health rather than salvation. He fought the Ku Klux Klan and assaulted Henry Ford's pretensions to humanitarianism. By 1929 Niebuhr joined the Socialist party.

In 1928 Niebuhr had started his notable career as a teacher at Union Theological Seminary. With the publication of his *Moral Man and Immoral Society,* he explored the ethics of social change as he distanced himself from liberals who preached ideals while complacently ignoring the necessities of power. Niebuhr thought that Christians should face their moral responsibility for injustice in the world. He argued as a realist who knew that history did not have in store a community of love. As Fox so ably puts it, for Niebuhr "religion was not doing good, feeling holy, or experiencing the transcendent; it was grasping the evil in one's efforts to do good, recognizing one's finitude, realizing that the transcendent was unattainable."[9] Although Niebuhr found sentimentality repugnant, it was increasingly evident that he was part of the tradition of humane tolerance associated with the heritage of John Stuart Mill.

Like Freud in his *Civilization and Its Discontents,* Niebuhr saw the self as the ultimate basis for social tensions. For Niebuhr as for Freud, the soul was at odds with itself, unaware of its own aspirations and therefore doomed to disappointment in the search for happiness. While Freud thought in terms like narcissism and aggression, Niebuhr invoked the inevitable role of sin and evil in even mankinds' highest endeavors. Niebuhr was deeply suspicious of any calls for individual self-fulfillment. Fox believes that Niebuhr's central contribution to the intellectual life of the 1940s was the sober assertion of inevitable limits to human existence.

After the Hitler-Stalin pact, Niebuhr became convinced of the statesmanship of Franklin D. Roosevelt. Niebuhr struggled on behalf of American intervention in Europe. As in the First World War, he was a superpatriot and came to fight both Communism and Communist sympathizers. (At first he approved the execution of the Rosenbergs.) Fox suggests that Niebuhr's theology resembles that of Whittaker Chambers and that Niebuhr's friend Lionel Trilling's *The Middle of the Journey* echoed Niebuhr's point of view. Yet somehow J. Edgar Hoover continued to view Niebuhr with suspicion, and the FBI compiled a huge file on his activities.

Niebuhr grew increasingly interested in international relations. Fox concedes that too much of Niebuhr's work in this field was amateurish, and it indulged too uncritically in Cold War rhetoric. More surprising than the borrowed tone of these writings was Niebuhr's eagerness to popularize to the point of intellectual coarsening. Writing for the *Saturday Evening Post* does not seem in keeping with his status as theologian and thinker. (Alas, even the best of American thinkers seem to yearn for the "success" of mediocre journalism.) One suspects that had Niebuhr lived a more cloistered existence and been less ambitious in worldly terms, his writing would have had a better chance of sustaining his earlier promise. Fox is right to judge Niebuhr by the highest standards of intellectual achievement. Niebuhr's last books were embarrassingly thin.

Ill health dogged Niebuhr for his last nineteen years. A stroke in 1952 permanently changed his life. Subsequently he sought help in psychotherapy for depressions that were characteristic for his immediate family but also may have been organically linked to his physical afflictions. Although Niebuhr said he lacked the imagination for autobiography, he continued to publish on contemporary political issues. He detested Richard Nixon and opposed the Vietnam War. The honors that he continued to receive made his weakened powers all the harder to bear. He died in 1971.

George Orwell and Sigmund Freud seem mutually uncongenial figures in intellectual history. In print Orwell rarely referred to the founder of psychoanalysis. According to his friend Geoffrey Gorer, Orwell regarded psychoanalysis with mild hostility, putting it somewhat on a par with Christian Science. Another friend, Sir Richard Rees, had no recollection of Orwell's ever once mentioning Freud's name and considered this an aspect of Orwell's "psychological incuriosity."[10] Orwell's first wife, Eileen, had a little training in the academic psychology of the late 1920s and early 1930s. Even though some eminent English intellectuals were psychoanalysts in that period, Orwell evidently had no contact with them nor any interest in their subject. On the other side of the kinship that I would like to explore, Freud in all likelihood never heard of Orwell. Freud's taste did not include many of the most illustrious twentieth-century writers and artists. In his last years Freud liked to relax with a good mystery story and relished in particular Agatha Christie's *Murder on the Orient Express*. Orwell also enjoyed detective stories, and he wrote about some of their implications and sources of appeal. His novels that appeared in Freud's lifetime were narrowly read and artistically not unconventional; it is Orwell's masterpiece *1984*, published in 1949, ten years after Freud's death, that retains its uncanny, horrifying, and, one might say, Freudian air.

The Freud of history was a bourgeois gentleman. Freud also was a bit of a snob, excessively admiring the wealth and position of someone like his disciple the Princess George, Marie Bonaparte, who was a direct descendant of Napoleon's brother Lucien. Orwell on his part made the most strenuous effort to break away from the class system of his society. He even sought to find out what it was like at the utmost bottom of the social pyramid. Going down and out in Paris and London hardly corresponded to either Freud's ambitions or his conception of himself.

Freud conceived his role as that of a scientist and rarely lost sight of the need to systematize his ideas into a comprehensive framework. Although he might seek newspaper reviews of his books, he disdained writing for the popular press. Once in 1920, as his royalties in the United States began to mount, Freud volunteered through an American nephew, a public relations specialist, to write four articles for a New York magazine. *Cosmopolitan* then offered one thousand dollars for the first piece, but rejected Freud's suggested title, substituting its own topic. Freud was horrified at what he saw as the dictatorship of a crass and uncultivated society and drew back with shock at the venture. As Ernest Jones commented about Freud's "stinging" letter of refusal to his relative, some of Freud's "indignation emanated from feeling a little ashamed of himself at having descended from his usual standards by proposing to earn money through writing popular articles."[11]

Unlike Freud, Orwell had no medical practice to rely on; he was an immensely hardworking journalist who sometimes had to do hackwork. Orwell came to think that it was relatively easy to live by means of journalism, although his book royalties, until the end of his life, remained meager. Orwell once defined a regular book reviewer as anyone who reviews at least one hundred books a year. Orwell's vision was a sustained one, yet he was not a systematic thinker. Freud and Orwell had their respective visions in life, but Orwell's had a specifically political aim. As a socialist, he was committed to class struggle. Even in his most time-bound tracts, Orwell stands out as one of the best representatives of the humane English social tradition.

Freud was reluctant to develop the political and social implications of psychoanalysis and thought that his techniques were scientific and therefore ideologically neutral. Wherever Freud "applied" psychoanalysis to society, he made the point that his application represented merely his personal views and that others might use psychoanalytic ideas to reach different ethical conclusions. Orwell, however, became convinced that everyone is necessarily a part of social conflict. He thought that political bias is inevitable. Even in aesthetics, Orwell insisted that there can be no such thing as neutrality.

In their practical political judgments Freud and Orwell also differed. From Orwell's point of view as an opponent of all nationalisms, Freud would at best seem politically naive; at the outset of World War I, he joined in with the frenzy of enthusiasm toward the Central Powers. Like other Europeans of his day, Freud thought it well that the outbreak of warfare had swept away the artificialities of the old regime. His allegiances as a cosmopolitan soon reasserted themselves, but in his old age Freud supported a reactionary Austrian government that suppressed the socialists in a civil war. Nevertheless, Freud, who rarely even voted, thought of himself as apolitical. As an enemy of Franco's, Orwell would at least have been pleased that in the 1930s when Freud was asked for copies of signed manuscripts to be auctioned off in behalf of the cause of the Spanish Republic, he willingly complied.

Although Freud started out as a heretic in terms of established psychology and medical practice, he gained an almost hypnotic effect on his followers and succeeded in establishing an orthodoxy that exerts its power even today, fifty years after his death. Freud knew the power of legend and got his own version of the history of psychoanalysis into books long before anyone else realized that his "movement" was one that would have lasting interest. When potential renegades threatened the purity of Freud's purposes, he did not hesitate to expel deviators as "heretics." Orwell was sensitive to the ways in which would-be emancipators ended up by enslaving mankind's thought. To Orwell, unorthodoxy was a necessary part of intelligent thinking. He admired heretics as those who refused to allow their consciences to be stifled by quietly accepting received wisdom. One of Orwell's most fundamental convictions was that there were too many twentieth-century religions claiming to possess "the truth."

Though at first glance Orwell and Freud are quite different, in many ways they are surprisingly similar. As writers, for instance, they both fascinate by being masters of an unpretentious way of expressing themselves. Freud's visual talents fulfill Orwell's dictum that "good prose is like a window pane."[12] At the outset of their writing careers, both Orwell and Freud lacked sales, but by the end of their lives collected editions of their works had appeared. Orwell's triumph was a personal one, while Freud depended on the support of disciples. In Freud's case, his lively style can be discerned as early as adolescence; on the other hand, Orwell became a conscious artist. To round out the bare bones of a comparison, both of them are known to the world by changed names: Freud gave up Sigismund for Sigmund, and, more radically, Orwell had been born Eric Blair.

In their convictions Orwell and Freud had far more in common than one might suppose. Both were superlative rationalists who felt their intelligence oppressed by the weight of human stupidity. Religious belief seemed to them a particularly noxious species of nonsense. Politically, Orwell and Freud shared a suspicion of American power. Although Orwell made much more of his concern at the dangers inherent in machines, in his daily life Freud rarely relied on the use of the telephone; for both of them letter writing was an art as well as a necessity. Although Freud was far older, born in 1856 instead of 1903, each came to feel that World War I marked a watershed after which the universe was barer and more dilapidated. Freud spent the last sixteen years of his life afflicted with sickness and the approach of painful death; 1923, the year he first got cancer, is the single most important demarcation point in his mature writings. The pessimism of *1984*, Orwell's last book, has also often been traced to his intense personal suffering. Both saw themselves as outsiders in their respective societies. Both had a sense of privacy and requested that no official biography be commissioned, though in the end each family decided that the appearance of unauthorized, and supposedly misleading, biographical studies necessitated violating that request. In his lifetime Freud became the leader of a sect, and in death both men have been the centers of cults. Their archives have been jealously guarded, if not sealed, from the public's inspection.

Orwell and Freud were committed to enlightenment and the destruction of myths. They remained puritanical believers in the power and morality of honesty. Yet both—Orwell politically and Freud scientifically—were capable of deceiving themselves. While defending the cause of enlightenment, they were unable to believe fully in the reality of progress. Both cherished European civilization as a whole, retaining a special affection for England's heritage of liberties. The world before World War I was the great age of liberal bourgeois culture, but the twentieth century undermined the empires in which Orwell and Freud had been born. The Austro-Hungarian Empire broke apart earlier than the British one, yet a mood of helplessness pervades the work of both writers. In *1984* Britain has been absorbed into the

United States to help make up Oceania. Therapeutically, Freud respected and worked with "breakdown," and Orwell became convinced that while it was impossible for anyone to win, some kinds of failure were superior to others. Both men accepted the inevitability of suffering.

Orwell's socialist commitments were not collectivist but of a liberal kind; Freud had a similar moral disposition. Both Orwell and Freud were acutely sensitive to the threat to privacy posed by the conformist pressures of society. Eccentricity and individualism can be hard to sustain. Orwell's alternative title for *1984* had been *The Last Man in Europe*. In the novel "ownlife"[13] is a specially designated crime. Winston Smith's first seditious act is diary keeping; he buys a blank book in a junk shop and then a penholder and a bottle of ink. Reading is also solitary and therefore becomes as subversive as writing. Orwell refused to abbreviate the difficult portion of the novel where Winston Smith reads from Emmanuel Goldstein's book; Orwell had been under pressure to make cuts there from the Book-of-the-Month Club, but he stood ground and they adopted *1984* anyway.

As prophets, Orwell and Freud shared similar aims. Both demanded the preservation of integrity within one's soul. Their basic value was the love of liberty. Freud sought to free his patients through unearthing their childhood pasts. By reinterpreting what already exists in our mental lives and through recalling past experiences, the psychoanalyst aims to release the most vivid and genuine responsiveness. But Orwell fears in *1984* that the future holds an opposite promise. As O'Brien, Winston Smith's inquisitor, predicts: "Never again will you be capable of ordinary human feeling. Everything will be dead inside you. . . . You will be hollow. We will squeeze you empty, and then we shall fill you with ourselves."[14]

Above all, the psychologies of Orwell's *1984* and that of Freud's system are remarkably similar. Both thinkers have been accused of misanthropy; neither defends hedonism. Both are one-sidedly morbid and characteristically negative. But their pessimistic extremism rests on the skepticism of disappointed idealism; both Orwell and Freud retain a fragmentary hope that psychology can improve mankind's lot. In a painful autobiographical essay, "Such, Such, Were the Joys," written in the year he began *1984*, Orwell observed that thanks to the spread of psychological knowledge it was now "harder for parents and schoolteachers to indulge their aberrations in the name of discipline."[15] The problem for Orwell, as for Freud, was how one could ever know what someone else, in this instance a child, might be thinking. Orwell, like Freud, thought that the key issue was not behavior but inner feelings.

Freud held that an understanding of unconscious motivation was the central contribution of his psychology: "He that has eyes to see and ears to hear may convince himself that no mortal can keep a secret. If his lips are silent, he chatters with his fingertips; betrayal oozes out of him at every pore. And thus the task of making conscious the most hidden recesses of the mind is one which it is quite possible to accomplish."[16] In *1984* Freud's knowledge of unconscious means of expression is precisely what is to be feared; one might betray oneself through a mere expression in the eyes: "The smallest thing could give you away. A nervous tic, an unconscious look of anxiety, a habit of muttering to yourself—anything that carried with it the suggestion of abnormality, of having something to hide."[17] Orwell called it the danger of facecrime. Winston reflected: "Your worst enemy . . . was your own nervous system. At any moment the tension inside you was liable to translate itself into some visible symptom . . . what was frightening was that the action was quite possibly unconscious."[18] Wishfully irrational thinking, for Orwell as for Freud, became a menace.

In *1984* the ubiquitous telescreen threatens to invade the mind's inner self. But despite its constant spying, Winston believes that with planning it is still possible to outwit the authorities, for "with all their cleverness they had never mastered the secret of finding out what another human being was thinking."[19] Once imprisoned, Winston concedes, the issue would grow more acute. Even then, however, he optimistically hopes that only "facts" would be extracted: "But if the object was not to stay alive but to stay human, what difference did it ultimately make? They could not alter your feelings; for that matter you could not alter them yourself, even if you wanted to. They could lay bare in the utmost detail everything you had done or said or thought; but the inner heart, whose workings were mysterious even to yourself, remained impregnable."[20]

Liberalism historically has defended the distinction between a person's mind and his actions; a division between inner and outer states was also a part of the rise of the theory of religious toleration. Winston is even confident that confession under coercion need be no ultimate threat to human autonomy: "Confession is not betrayal. What you say or do doesn't matter; only feelings matter."[21] But one purpose in Orwell's writing *1984* was to expose the weakness in traditional liberal psychology. Does the existence of subjective feelings over which we have no control and the play of mystery reassure or undermine the liberal ideal of self-control? Freud thought that through free associations he could succeed in finding out what another human being is thinking. He too aimed to promote self-mastery, and he saw, as did Orwell, the outdatedness of any image of old-fashioned confession: "In confession the sinner tells what he knows; in analysis the neurotic has to tell more."[22]

Once Winston gets arrested his previous assumptions undergo almost clinical testing. Freud had thought of psychoanalysis, at least around the time of Adler, as an educative process; his treatment procedure was designed to combat resistances based on self-deception. "Psychoanalytic treatment," he once wrote, "may in general be conceived as . . . a *re-education in overcoming internal resistances.*"[23] Under arrest, however, Winston faces a formidable ordeal, which turns out to be brutal: "the task of re-educating himself."[24]

The demands on Winston are heavier than he, or pre-Freudian psychology, could have expected: "From now onwards he must not only think right; he must feel right, dream right."[25] It would seem that under extreme stress the ideal distinction between deeds and desires becomes meaningless. O'Brien tells Winston that "the Party is not interested in the overt act; the thought is all we care about."[26] Freud had believed that in our unconscious minds there is no difference between wishful ideas and acts, but in *1984* this hypothesis has become a working accusatory political principle. One of the terrors of captivity turns out to be that "in the eyes of the Party there was no distinction between the thought and the deed."[27]

Thought-crime could come about in sleep-talking or by any other involuntary expression. The Thought Police of *1984* are agents whose task is inner snooping. The telescreen is sensitive enough to pick up heartbeats. Once Winston is imprisoned, his dreams, which Freud considered the royal road to the unconscious, are also open to inspection. Unlike an analytic patient, Winston is not cooperating voluntarily. But Orwell described Winston's earlier diary keeping as a "therapy"[28] that has not worked. According to the logic of *1984*, Winston must now undergo a more drastic treatment.

The psychology that explains O'Brien's power over Winston is Freudian. According to psychoanalysis, neurosis binds one to the terrors one tries to master. Freud sought to understand self-destructiveness. According to him, what a man most dreads he also longs for and what someone fears can lead to what he fears coming true. Freud called this "the fatal truth that has laid it down that flight is precisely an instrument that delivers one over to what one is fleeing from."[29] Winston had written his diary for O'Brien. Later Winston's panic in recurrent nightmares of rats gives O'Brien the key to understanding his breaking point, the worst thing in the world according to Winston's psyche. This ultimate horror varies from individual to individual, which accounts for O'Brien's reference to the unknown terrors of the dreaded Room 101: "Everyone knows what is in Room 101."[30]

Freud was so preoccupied with the issue of understanding another's thoughts that in the end he came to believe in telepathy, at least in the form of thought transference; one of his more committed essays on telepathy was withheld from publication until after his death. Orwell wrote in a letter in 1949: "I can't get very interested in telepathy unless it could be developed into a reliable method."[31] Empathy, however, was one of Orwell's goals: he once objected to orthodox Marxists on the grounds that they thought they possessed a system that explains everything; therefore they never bothered to find out what is going on inside other people's heads.

If it is possible to make too much of parallels between Orwell and Freud, Winston's torture by O'Brien is clearly modeled on psychoanalytic treatment. Winston lies flat on his back as O'Brien reads his mind. To O'Brien, Winston is a difficult case. Their time together is described as a series of "sessions."[32] O'Brien's stated aim is to "cure" Winston, to make him "sane."[33] As O'Brien explains to Winston: "You are mentally deranged. You suffer from a defective memory. . . . Fortunately it is curable."[34] Winston seems to have a "disease" that gives him "delusions."[35] O'Brien is described as having "the air of a doctor, a teacher, even a priest, anxious to explain and persuade rather than to punish."[36] Orwell is reported by Richard Rees to have made one direct, dismissing reference to psychoanalysis: "A psychoanalyst would have to be cleverer than his patients."[37] A terrible feature of *1984* is precisely O'Brien's intelligence: he "knew everything."[38] Considering Winston's torture as therapy makes it even more frightening from a libertarian point of view. Even when Winston is shown in a mirror the physical wreck O'Brien has transformed him into, O'Brien insists that it is Winston who has reduced himself to such a state.

The psychoanalyst's technique of using a couch involves the patient in both social and sensory deprivation. Probably any psychotherapeutic situation, with or without a couch, evokes magical feelings. But in Freud's system of treatment, the process of overcoming self-deceptions distinctively means the arousal within the patient of resistances against the analyst; analysis then becomes a struggle. The patient makes a contract for what can, given enough sadism in an analyst and passivity in a patient, turn into an inquisition. In *1984* one of the Party's central aims had been "how to discover, against his will, what another human being is thinking."[39] In *1984* science has almost ceased to exist, but the scientist of that time is "a mixture of psychologist and inquisitor," who does research "studying with extraordinary minuteness the meaning of facial expressions, gestures and tones of voice, and testing the truth-producing effects of drugs, shock therapy, hypnosis and physical torture. . . . "[40] O'Brien aims not merely to destroy the Party's enemies but to change them.

Freud was naive politically, not just in terms of day-to-day world events but about the power elements implicit in his method of treatment. He hoped that his goal of neutrality in the analyst would be enough to protect the patient from undue influence. Orwell, however, was exquisitely sensitive to power seeking. In *1984* he observes: "Power is in tearing human minds to pieces and putting them together in new shapes of your own choosing."[41]

In a rare reference to Freud, Orwell in an essay links him with Machiavelli, perhaps not only as a false emancipator. In the therapeutic state there are neither taboos for the individual nor legal restrictions on public authority. As a friend of individualism Orwell worries in *1984:* "If both the past and the external world exist only in the mind, and if the mind itself is controllable—what then?"[42] The last words of *1984* express Orwell's warning for the future; the struggle is over and Winston has conquered himself: now he loves the mythical dictator, Big Brother.

Freud was a great psychologist of memory. The strength of his approach rests on the way our minds play tricks with us about our past. The distortions and selectivity of memory are, Freud held, the stuff of neurosis. The analyst should aim to correct false recollections and, through reawakening past experiences, repair psychological damages. At the outset of *1984,* Orwell's protagonist suffers from an unintelligible childhood. Winston makes an effort to recover childhood memories; he wonders whether London has always been the same. As he forces himself to reminisce in diary writing, new memories arise that clarify the past. At one point Winston tries to get his girl friend Julia to collaborate in retrospection; he encourages her memory to go backward. Winston feels that his own memory is "not satisfactorily under control" and therefore he has "furtive" knowledge that others lack.[43] He feels in his bones "some kind of ancestral memory that things had once been different."[44] The tormenting capacity of memory lends *1984* its nightmarish air.

Winston's sense of smell in particular evokes the past. In the Spartan world of *1984* fresh coffee succeeds in reminding him of "the half-forgotten world of his childhood."[45] Chocolate makes him think of something he once did that he would prefer to undo, but which remains inexorably a part of his past. It takes only a whiff of a scent of chocolate to stir up a personal memory that is both "powerful and troubling."[46] Dreams reawaken when Winston would like to forget. He takes his dreaming seriously as "a continuation of one's intellectual life . . . in which one becomes aware of facts and ideas which still seem new and valuable after one is awake."[47] After one such dream, Winston becomes conscious why memories of his mother had been tearing at his heart; a childhood bit of greediness for chocolate on his part had preceded the disappearance of both his mother and his sister.

Winston's concern with memory is public as well as private. In the course of *1984* he goes down and out, trying to test an old man's recollections; regretfully he finds only "a rubbish heap of details"[48] instead of a useful historical account. The Proles, who comprise the non-Party 85 percent of the population of Oceania, are no help in resisting tyranny. Winston bitterly comments that "where the Lottery was concerned, even people who could barely read and write seemed capable of intricate calculations and staggering feats of memory."[49] Winston's job as an Outer Party member is in the Records Department, where he specializes in the falsification of written material. History can be manipulated and destroyed, as evidence from the past gets incinerated in "memory holes."[50] Not only events but people as well can be made to disappear, as they are "vaporized"[51] into oblivion. Winston fears the danger not merely of death but of annihilation. Winston knows that anyone's existence can be denied and then forgotten.

During his captivity the continuity of Winston's daily memories is broken. After he and O'Brien have looked at a document incriminating to the official version of the past, Winston reminds O'Brien of what they have just seen, but O'Brien flatly repudiates the memory. After lengthy interrogation and repugnant cruelty, Winston gets physical treatment for his mind. O'Brien administers what is described as "a devastating explosion . . . as though a piece had been taken out of his brain."[52] Afterward Winston is still occasionally troubled by false memories, but if he recalls anything contrary to the Party's demands, Winston can now dismiss it as a product of self-deception.

While Freud proposed therapeutically to reconstruct personal history, Orwell feared the artificial destruction of the past. Their shared concern for memory led both to be dubious about the reliability of autobiographies, and their reticence about authorizing biographies of themselves stemmed from a similar historical skepticism. In *1984* bringing history up to date becomes one means of abolishing the past. A frightening Party slogan goes: "Who controls the past controls the future: who controls the present controls the past."[53] The past becomes mutable, and therefore Orwell considers the future unimaginable. If the past can be rewritten, does it retain any of its traditional reality?

Orwell tended to romanticize the advantages of the past, although his nostalgia is touched with bitterness. In *1984* the further back one goes the more there is of love, freedom, friendship, and loyalty. As Freud had thought that each of his patients carried within him the unconscious truths about himself, Winston proposes that the best books are "those that tell you what you know already."[54] When Winston and Julia rent a room above the antique store, they try to recapture a lost London: "the room was a world, a pocket of the past where extinct animals could walk."[55] According to Party teachings, "anything old, or for that matter anything beautiful, was always vaguely suspect."[56] The glass paperweight Winston acquires stands for his yearning for the world of the past; the Thought Police are quick to smash it when they arrest him.

Freud was fascinated by the distant past; he collected ancient statuary and likened memories to archaeological artifacts. The task of therapy was to loosen ties to the past and by reviving early emotional experiences free the individual from neurotic bondages. Unlike Orwell's fearful regret that history has lost its meaning, Freud believed in the permanency of its power: " . . . in mental life nothing which has once been formed can perish— . . . everything is somehow preserved and . . . in suitable circumstances . . . it can once more be brought to life."[59] Freud thought that each of us carried within him a kind of resonance board, so that when we see or experience anything all our past memories give their overtones to our experience. The past lives in the present through the influence of unconscious forces: "In the unconscious nothing can be brought to an end, nothing is past or forgotten."[58]

Whatever differences in their approaches to the past, for Orwell as for Freud childhood is the central, though inaccessible, period in human history. Both believe that a child's responses and misperceptions are a permanent source of adult anxiety and conflict, and both see childhood as the model of later enslavement and oppression. Although human beings may be peculiarly exploitable because of the inevitability of early dependencies, Freud and Orwell each value retaining the child's spontaneity and freshness. It is particularly significant for understanding Orwell's views that in *1984* normal family life has been destroyed. Children are dreadful savages eager to witness the spectacle of public hangings and horrible enough to become spies on the lookout for unorthodox thoughts in the minds of their own parents. When one reads Orwell's account of the sadism built into his own boarding school experience, a world to him of "force and fraud and secrecy,"[59] it is hard not to see the personal basis on which he later constructed the vision of *1984*.

Orwell's attitudes toward women in *1984* are close to Freud's. They both, for instance, conceive of mothers in terms of ideally self-sacrificing creatures. More important, the character of Julia combines a familiar set of idealized conceptions of femininity, which while they exalt women also denigrate them. Julia is noble and pure; she brings delicacies of food as well as sex. Yet she is incapable of Winston's intellectual effort; Julia falls asleep while he reads her portions of Goldstein's book. Orwell comments that "she only questioned the teachings of the Party when they in some way touched upon her own life" and that "the difference between truth and falsehood did not seem important to her."[60] Winston is wary of intimacy and links sensuality with stupidity; he tells her, "You're only a rebel from the waist downwards. . . . "[61] Julia does not care much about reading, and her docile work on the novel-writing machines in the Fiction Department is a mark of Orwell's contempt.

Women are the most bigoted adherents of the Party, the staunchest hunters of heresy, and the most credulous believers in slogans. But Julia had hopefully thought that "they can make you say anything—*anything*—but they can't make you believe it. They can't get inside you."[62] Whatever her inadequacies, Winston confides his guilt about his mother to Julia. Instead of emphasizing, as Freud often did, sex's capacity to enslave, the way passions can be bondage, Orwell saw love as capable of releasing one's best self. But Freud too could be idealistic about the emotional side of physical love, and just as Freud complained that modern civilization entailed new forms of nervousness, Orwell thought emotions flowed easier and better in the past. When he first sees the spot in the countryside that Julia had chosen for their rendezvous, it reminds Winston of a beautiful landscape he has long dreamt of.

Eroticism is the Party's enemy. Children are conceived solely for collective purposes. Pleasurable sexuality is a specious act of rebelliousness: "Desire was thought-crime."[63] The sexual act is to be eradicated, the orgasm abolished. As an animal drive, sexuality constituted a political act. *1984* has an "Anti-Sex League" and its vows of celibacy. For Freud, neurotic symptoms could be understood on the model of an already aroused energy, first suppressed and then finding devious expression. In *1984* the energy blocked by privations gets transformed into the hysteria of war fever and leadership worship. Freud and Orwell repudiate any conception of asceticism as an ideal; both think that Christian sainthood is a form of escapism from the difficult demands of love and the pain of preferring some people more than others, and both grew suspicious of humanitarianism as a form of hypocrisy.

Orwell describes the prevalent atmosphere of *1984* as controlled insanity. The power of the Party rests on its ability to dissipate discontents by turning them outward towards Oceania's rivals, Eastasia and Eurasia. The world Orwell feared in the future was filled with irrational terrors and lunatic misunderstandings. Orwell not only considered Hitler criminally insane but was inclined to the view that it was possible to describe a whole culture as insane. In 1946 Orwell wrote that "political behavior is largely non-rational . . . the world is suffering from some kind of mental disease which must be diagnosed before it can be cured."[64] Curiously, as skeptical as Orwell was about psychoanalysis, when confronted with Nazis he chose to join the school of thought that considers anti-Semitism a sickness. After observing some captured Germans in 1945, Orwell fell back on the theory of neurosis; the appropriate remedy, he argued, was not punishment or revenge but some form of psychological treatment for the prisoners of war.

The language and imagery of the psychoanalytic consulting room pervade *1984*. Winston fears that he will unwillingly betray his inner conflicts through unconscious symptoms of unorthodoxy. He is a self-deceiver subject to occasional hallucinatory experiences. Orwell describes Winston's renting a room as a "lunatic"[65] project. Irresistible impulses seize control of Winston; returning to the junk shop for antiques is seen as a form of death wish.

Although Orwell's vision of *1984* may sound extreme, he had increasingly become preoccupied with the problem of establishing truth and sanity in a universe of lies. Orthodoxy is one technique for maintaining emotional equilibrium, but Orwell rejects the option of securing sanity through lack of understanding. At the same time, Orwell disliked the idea that normality can be established by counting the number of people who share any belief. But if madness is not identical with nonconformity, what is it? Even Freud never went very far in exploring this critical line of thought. Orwell and Freud clung to the notion that there has to be some objective, external standard by which one assesses reality, perhaps because both of them were aware of the extent to which it is possible to delude oneself. Freud had stressed the way in which fantasies can cloud rationality. In *1984*, Goldstein, Big Brother, and a host of other features to life may be fictitious, the products of psychological invention; reality may become so elusive as to be defined solely by the intent of the Party.

The 2 percent of the population of Oceania who make up the Inner Party are held together by their common allegiance to a doctrine; the Brotherhood, the supposed forces of opposition, is also built on an indestructible form of ideology. But idealism leads to insanity, for once there are no longer any records that exist outside of human memory, and assuming that memories are mutable, then it becomes impossible to be sure of even the most paltry matter of fact. Orwell's objections to the way in which orthodox believers hold to the existence of "the truth" stemmed partly from his own uncertainty about how, under modern conditions, reality can ever be securely established. Becoming unbalanced was only one aspect of the problem confronting Orwell; being wrong was another. In the long run, Orwell and Freud were agreed, only the truth can make us free. In *1984* Orwell sardonically proposes warfare as a reliable guide against insanity; illusions are militarily dangerous, and therefore war kept Oceania attached to some semblance of truth.

For Orwell, sanity was part of one's humanity: "It was not by making yourself heard but by staying sane that you carried on the human heritage."[66] One gathers from Orwell's essays that he considered Freud's distinctive method as suitable mainly for understanding the exceptionally perverse or for treating those chosen spirits in search of salvation, but throughout Orwell's work he preferred to be concerned with the maintenance of the average person's ordinary human decency. In *1984* two and two can be made sometimes to add up to five, and that kind of dislocation is only a portion of what the Party can accomplish. In the face of strange events and bizarre theories, Orwell still believed that it was possible to remain a normal and decent person and yet be fully alive. Freud tended to take for granted a standard of adulthood that worthy people more or less lived up to; both Freud and Orwell disdained the weakness of the "riff-raff" and used "grownupness" as a high form of praise.

One of the triumphs of *1984* is Orwell's conception of Newspeak, a language invented not to expand but to decrease the scope of human thought. Orwell was convinced that politics and language were intimately connected and the debasement of human dignity could take place in either of these interrelated spheres. The aims of Newspeak was to render thought-crime logically impossible; by destroying old words and creating new ones, thoughts can be so narrowed that heresy becomes unthinkable. The jargon of modern ideologies, such as nationalism, leads people to repress facts for the sake of consistency of conviction.

Double-think is a Newspeak word for mastering reality by means of controlling memories. In *1984* old-fashioned contradictions become increasingly unsettling as apparent paradoxes dissolve under Newspeak logic. Since there are no laws, nothing can be illegal. The central principles of *1984*—war is peace; freedom is slavery; ignorance is strength—gain an eerie meaning by the end of the novel. Orwell once labelled schizophrenic "the power of holding simultaneously two beliefs which cancel out."[67] Double-think is described as the means by which one can hold "two contradictory beliefs in one's mind simultaneously"[68] and accept both of them as true. In this respect double-think is almost a parody of the psychoanalytic ideal of normality—the capacity to endure in the face of ambiguity, frustration, and delay. By contrast, *1984* suggests that through neutralizing knowledge and altering the past, it becomes possible to forget that one has forgotten anything.

Moreover, double-think is a concept that might well be applied to features of Freud's system of thought, which helps explain why Orwell, despite the resemblances between his own psychological beliefs and those of psychoanalysis, held himself aloof from Freudianism. If a former patient symptomatically recovers without the supervision of a psychoanalyst, then recovery can be dismissed as a defensive "flight into health." But if a patient deteriorates in the course of treatment, the problem is supposed to lie in the patient's masochism and the failure is put under the rubric of "negative therapeutic reaction." Some psychoanalytic patients have later ended up in psychiatric hospitals or as suicides, but Freud could regard such outcomes as a tribute to the efficacy of psychoanalysis: the patients' neuroses had been "cured"; only the success of the treatment had led the way to

more primitive means of coping, psychosis. The whole concept of "resistance" in psychoanalysis can be abused readily; Freud's system had too
many formulas that excused both analysts and patients from assuming full
responsibility for their actions. In addition, while Freud was alive he took
pains to doctor the history of psychoanalysis to suit his own ideological
purposes, and since his death, orthodox followers have continued the falsification of history.

The psychology of *1984*, Orwell's greatest sustained piece of work, reflects concerns that are present in earlier writings. He once even wrote a
novel, *A Clergyman's Daughter,* about a case of amnesia in a sexually repressed young woman. Freud himself readily acknowledged that "creative
writers are valuable allies and their evidence is to be prized highly, for they
are apt to know a whole host of things between heaven and earth of which
our philosophy has not let us dream."[69] Although Orwell could not endorse
Freud's psychology, implicitly he came close to several key psychoanalytic
tenets.

It need hardly be emphasized that in *1984* Orwell had composed a critique not only of Stalinism but of industrial trends in the rest of the world
as well. But Orwell's famous novel was also published at one of the high
points of Freud's influence, which may help account still further for its
immediate success. In that early Cold War period, it was fashionable in the
West for intellectuals to turn to individual psychology, and in particular to
its depth dimensions, as an explanation and rationalization for their withdrawal from earlier radical commitments. If human nature were as Orwell
and Freud saw it, then little wonder that earlier hopes for change had remained unfulfilled. Whatever their respective politics, intellectually Orwell
and Freud were iconoclasts; their differing commitments help explain their
particular visions. The extent to which, despite all their differences, Orwell's psychology reveals similarities to Freud's testifies to the pervasive
influence of psychoanalysis on twentieth-century images of human nature.
Comparing these two writers also helps show how Freud's insights fall
within the history of ideas. A passage in Orwell about Jonathan Swift illuminates the power that a certain kind of genius can have: "Swift did not
posses ordinary wisdom, but he did posses a terrible intensity of vision,
capable of picking out a single hidden truth and then magnifying it and
distorting it. The durability of *Gulliver's Travels* goes to show that if the
force of belief is behind it, a world-view which only just passes the test of
sanity is sufficient to produce a great work of art."[70] Orwell's *1984* as well
as Freud's psychoanalysis illustrate the principle that it is sometimes necessary to disproportion reality in order to heighten our perception of certain
aspects of it.

Notes

1. *Public Philosopher: Selected Letters of Walter Lippmann,* ed. John Morton Blum (New York: Ticknor & Fields, 1985), p. ix.
2. Ibid., p. 281.
3. Ibid., p. vii.
4. Ibid., p. 39.
5. Elisabeth Young-Bruehl, *Hannah Arendt: For Love of the World* (New Haven: Yale University Press, 1982), p. xxi.
6. Ibid., p. 309.
7. Richard W. Fox, *Reinhold Niebuhr: A Biography* (New York: Pantheon Books, 1985), p. 234.
8. Ibid., p. 86.
9. Ibid., p. 174.
10. Richard Rees, *George Orwell: Fugitive from the Camp of Victory* (London: Secker & Warburg, 1961), p. 12.
11. Ernest Jones, *The Life and Work of Sigmund Freud,* vol. 3 (New York: Basic Books, 1957), p. 29.
12. George Orwell, "Why I Write," *A Collection of Essays* (New York: Doubleday Anchor Books, 1957), p. 320.
13. George Orwell, *1984* (New York: Signet, 1953), p. 64.
14. Ibid., p. 195.
15. George Orwell, *The Collected Essays, Journals, and Letters,* vol. 4, ed. Sonia Orwell and Ian Angus (London: Penguin, 1970), p. 418.
16. Sigmund Freud, "Fragment of an Analysis of a Case of Hysteria," *Standard Edition,* vol. 7, pp. 77–78.
17. Orwell, *1984,* p. 49.
18. Ibid., p. 51.
19. Ibid., p. 127.
20. Ibid.
21. Ibid., p. 126.
22. Sigmund Freud, "The Question of Lay Analysis," *Standard Edition,* vol. 20, p. 189.
23. Sigmund Freud, "On Psychotherapy," *Standard Edition,* vol. 7, p. 267.
24. Orwell, *1984,* p. 210.
25. Ibid., p. 213.
26. Ibid., p. 192.
27. Ibid., p. 185.
28. Ibid., p. 55.
29. Sigmund Freud, "Delusions and Dreams in Jensen's *Gradiva,*" *Standard Edition,* vol. 9, p. 42.
30. Orwell, *1984,* p. 198.
31. Orwell, *The Collected Essays,* vol. 4, p. 537.
32. Orwell, *1984,* p. 198.
33. Ibid., p. 192.
34. Ibid., p. 187.
35. Ibid.
36. Ibid., p. 184.

37. Rees, *George Orwell*, p. 145.
38. Orwell, *1984*, p. 199.
39. Ibid., p. 147.
40. Ibid.
41. Ibid., p. 203.
42. Ibid., p. 63.
43. Ibid., p. 29.
44. Ibid., p. 48.
45. Ibid., p. 64.
46. Ibid., p. 93.
47. Ibid., p. 48.
48. Ibid., p. 71.
49. Ibid., p. 67.
50. Ibid., p. 31.
51. Ibid., p. 112.
52. Ibid., pp. 195–196.
53. Ibid., p. 189.
54. Ibid., p. 152.
55. Ibid., p. 115.
56. Ibid., p. 74.
57. Sigmund Freud, "Civilization and Its Discontents," *Standard Edition*, vol. 21, p. 69.
58. Sigmund Freud, "The Interpretation of Dreams," *Standard Edition*, vol. 5, p. 577.
59. Orwell, *Collected Essays*, vol. 4, p. 400.
60. Orwell, *1984*, p. 117.
61. Ibid., p. 119.
62. Ibid., p. 127.
63. Ibid., p. 54.
64. Orwell, *Collected Essays*, vol. 4, p. 289.
65. Orwell, *1984*, p. 78.
66. Ibid., p. 24.
67. Orwell, *Collected Essays*, vol. 4, p. 151.
68. Orwell, *1984*, p. 163.
69. Freud, "Delusions and Dreams in Jensen's *Gradiva*," p. 8.
70. Orwell, *Collected Essays*, vol. 4, p. 261.

Conclusion

My own interest in studying Freud arose out of a concern with intellectual history as a whole, and in particular the tradition of political and social thought. And just as these wider matters lend, I hope, a breadth to my understanding of psychoanalysis itself, so it is my belief that the examination of Freud should lead to a return to reflecting anew on the great figures, as well as the largest issues, of social theorizing in the past.

Dostoevsky is only one of the giants who so obviously prefigured Freud as to be a writer of immediate importance to me; the occasion for my writing about him was the appearance of Joseph Frank's superb biography. One of the most remarkable features of the first volume, *The Seeds of Revolt 1821–49* (1976) was its appendix, ''Freud's Case-History of Dostoevsky,'' an essay first published in the *Times Literary Supplement*. With a dazzling display of erudition, Frank demolished Freud's famous 1928 paper '' Dostoevsky and Parricide.'' Freud had argued that Dostoevsky's epilepsy was ''affective'' rather than organic and that the full-scale outbreak of the illness could be linked to the murder of his father. Although other of Freud's so-called applications of psychoanalysis to history have long been challenged, until now his essay on Dostoevsky had escaped critical examination.

Frank establishes that Freud was essentially using the figure of Dostoevsky for the sake of propagandizing preconceived psychological convictions. Frank begins by pointing out a fact that Freud never mentioned—Dostoevsky had a son who died at the age of three from an epileptic attack. Presumably the child inherited the illness from his father, which would bear on the hypothesis of the emotional character of Dostoevsky's own epilepsy. In contrast to Freud's approach, Frank finds that Dostoevsky's symptoms of epilepsy cannot be traced to either childhood or the death of his father, but in all probability began during his later captivity in Siberia. Furthermore,

Frank documents how Freud twisted scanty biographical evidence to prove that Dostoevsky suffered from the threat of castration by a punishing father. Frank also objects to Freud's characterization of Dostoevsky as a latent homosexual; as Frank irreverently puts it, "there are no male friendships in Dostoevsky's life comparable in length and emotional importance to Freud's own friendships with, for example, Wilhelm Fliess and Josef Breuer."[1]

In his critique of Freud's essay, Frank sticks to the material available at the time Freud wrote on Dostoevsky. A key footnote in the text of Frank's book indicates, however, that it now seems unlikely that Dostoevsky's father was in fact murdered. Yet Frank had constructed so firm a case within the terms of Freud's own knowledge that so significant a piece of new information becomes only a postscript to the way Frank has pulled the rug out from under Freud's thesis. It is unfortunate that Frank did not go further in perceiving how Freud had used Dostoevsky for the sake of disguised autobiographical understanding. *The Brothers Karamazov* was Freud's favorite novel, and he considered Dostoevsky's literary standing to be close to that of Shakespeare; the Russian could therefore serve as one of Freud's many doubles in the history of ideas and in particular as a precursor to modern psychology. Frank does not mention that Freud himself suffered from fainting attacks and urinary incontinence, as well as the personality traits of irritability and intolerance that he ascribed to Dostoevsky. Freud's interpretations of Dostoevsky's deathlike attacks go far in explaining some of Freud's own fainting spells. Finally, Freud himself fit his picture of Dostoevsky as a guilt-ridden writer who worked best after some appeasement of fate through suffering.

Although Frank's *Times Literary Supplement* article heralded the appearance of his book, it is only one illustration of the scrupulous scholarship with which he has approached his subject. To the extent that he seeks biographical understanding of Dostoevsky, Frank is, of course, compelled to come to terms with the significance of the Russian's early years. According to Frank, Dostoevsky's family did not resemble Freud's reconstruction. The Dostoevsky's were a tightly knit unit where the children's welfare was uppermost in their parents' concern. Dostoevsky's father was not the model for the dissolute patriarch of the Karamazovs, and although at the time corporal punishment was a conventional aspect of child rearing, evidently Dr. Dostoevsky never hit any of his children.

It is regrettable that while he feels obliged to dismiss the central points in Freud's essay on Dostoevsky, Frank fails to mention the way Freud projected portions of his own problems onto his account of Dostoevsky, yet paradoxically this particular weakness in Frank is an aspect of the strength of his general approach, for he is determined to avoid biographical reductionism, whether in talking about Freud, Dostoevsky, or any other thinker. Frank aims to interpret Dostoevsky's art and therefore not to "go from the life to the work, but rather the other way round."[2]

Frank sees Dostoevsky's achievement as a synthesis of the social and cultural life of his period. He approvingly quotes Jose Ortega y Gasset: "I see in criticism a fervent effort to bring out the full power of the chosen work. It is just the opposite, then, to what Sainte-Beuve does when he takes us from the work to the author and then sprays him with a shower of anecdote . . . the critic is expected to provide in his work all the sentimental and ideological aids which will enable the ordinary reader to receive the most intense and clearest possible impression of the book."[3]

Dostoevsky's stories are examined as personal expressions, but Frank sees him as oriented more than most by issues outside himself. Frank is fascinated by Dostoevsky in the context of nineteenth-century Russian culture, and his notable accomplishment is to present Dostoevsky in the milieu of his society. Where psychologists are too prone to find in the past illustrations for currently fashionable theories, Frank has sought to re-create an alien period of a great writer and in that way to expand our horizons of the humanly possible. The result is intellectual history at its best.

Frank sees the presence of serfdom in Russia and Dostoevsky's moral revulsion against the enslavement of the peasantry as one of the key aspects to his early writings. In addition, Frank emphasizes the significance of Dostoevsky's religious background; in contrast to Dostoevsky's own experience, Tolstoy and Herzen were not given religious instruction as children. Dostoevsky's respect for nonheroic suffering was a notable feature of traditional Russia, and his conception of salvation as pride surrendering to the self-sacrifice of love made on its behalf by Christ was not simply a manifestation of personal idiosyncracy. Dostoevsky's psychology of violent emotion and tortured conflict fit the reality of a society whose goals were increasingly unsettled and whose values starkly conflicted. Dostoevsky saw the torment of irreconcilable ideas, and the quest for dignity in a world of class obstacles and political repression; yet he was also aware of the human problems for which there can be no social solution.

Although earlier literature emphasized the relative harmlessness of the youthful political activities for which Dostoevsky was arrested in 1849, Frank demonstrates that Dostoevsky belonged to a secret group devoted to arousing revolutionary change in the status quo of the serfs. Dostoevsky's involvement in Russian romanticism did not mean he was insensitive to political and social injustices, and Frank reminds us that the European governments of that era were hardly unconcerned about all those who reacted against the corruption behind formal social facades. Politics and literature are still today uniquely intertwined in Soviet life.

In the mid-1950s Frank conceived the project of reexamining Dostoevsky. In the end he executed a multivolume study, of which *The Seeds of Revolt* is the first installment. He has not sought to invent a Dostoevsky at odds with the responses of intelligent readers over the past century. Rather we find Dostoevsky more present and critically alive than ever before.

As impressive as *The Seeds of Revolt* remains, Volume 2 of Frank's *Dostoevsky, The Years of Ordeal, 1850–59* (1983) is even more remarkable; probably this is because *House of the Dead,* Dostoevsky's most direct recreation of his years of imprisonment, is superior to anything he had written before. It is perhaps enough to say that Frank has continued his scholarly endeavor on the same high level.

Frank begins with "the Petrashevksy affair."[4] Earlier Frank established that Dostoevsky had not, as received wisdom understood, been engaging in harmless political dabbling. The czar's police accurately spotted a conspiracy of radicals in which Dostoevsky was one of the most devout. Although everyone knew of Dostoevsky's 1848 arrest and the czar's last-minute commutation of a death sentence into imprisonment at hard labor in Siberia, nothing prepared one for the vividly detailed description that Frank has provided.

One early footnote can illustrate the joy in reading this book. A certain Gen. I. A. Nabokov, the great-great-uncle of the novelist Vladimir Nabokov, was commandant of the Peter-and-Paul Fortress in which Dostoevsky underwent solitary confinement after his arrest. The author of *Lolita,* in his *Speak Memory!,* claimed that his illustrious relative had lent books to "the writer Dostoevsky, author of *The Double,* etc."[5] Frank puts a subtle question mark after the "etc." According to Frank, no evidence exists for Nabokov's fancy that his ancestor had loaned Dostoevsky books: "Perhaps all it means is that Dostoevsky borrowed books from the prison library."[6]

According to Dostoevsky's second wife, he told her that his arrest "broke his life in two" and that without the imprisonment he would have gone "mad."[7] When he was deprived of his freedom, he not only learned something about his own resiliency, but also discovered the power of the human spirit when forced to rely on its own resources. Dostoevsky continually struggled to get what scraps of writings he could obtain from the outside world. Increasingly he came to see Europe as the source of doctrines of egoism and selfishness, and here Dostoevsky was being self-critically censorious.

According to Frank, after the mock-execution Dostoevsky gained a new grasp of existence from his confrontation with death. The individual, Dostoevsky held, is obliged to uphold his integrity no matter what the outward circumstances might be like. Frank insists that Dostoevsky's social sense, and in particular his outrage over serfdom in Russia, was allied with religious questionings and probings about the ultimate meaning of life. Dostoevsky's understanding of the tragic dimension to human experience, the way ultimate values conflict with one another, makes him one of the immortals of Western thought.

Although Frank follows Dostoevsky's life in sequence, the biographer has more to work with now than earlier. *House of the Dead* becomes far more interesting a text than one had ever realized. He was living among some of the basest of criminals, yet he retained the conviction that "men, however, are everywhere men."[8] As far as Frank can detect, relatively early in Siberia (1850) Dostoevsky had his first genuine epileptic attack. When he was finally released from prison in February 1854, he had to serve in a lowly position in the Russian army. Not until 1859 was he allowed to return to Russia, and only then did he succeed in getting permission once again to publish his writings.

Frank contends that these "years of ordeal" brought about a transformation in Dostoevsky's beliefs and convictions. Direct contact with the people taught him the lesson of the significance of the brotherhood of man. In the absence of normal standards of morality, Dostoevsky found that the Russian peasantry was capable of expressing an outlook all its own. The idea of reformers that peasants would ever accept upper-class leadership in a struggle for freedom was clearly a delusion of a Westernized intelligentsia. After his conversion experience, Dostoevsky had faith in the ordinary Russian as a human embodiment of Christ. True social progress would only be the result of a change in the moral approach of the upper class toward the people.

Although Frank is at pains to separate his approach from that of Freud and orthodox psychoanalysis, and Frank rightly insists that an artist like Dostoevsky cannot be held to have a theory of human nature, nevertheless he points out all the features of unconscious mental life and the irrational that Dostoevsky understood. In the midst of the worst humiliations of prison life, Dostoevsky found illustrations of the need people have to affirm their dignity. He identified his prison experience with the life in an ideal socialist utopia, and he emphasized the general need of human beings to express a will of their own in defending themselves against psychological encroachment. "The prison camp," Frank writes, "convinced Dostoevsky that private work, which guarantees the individual a sense of self-possession and moral autonomy, was fundamental for maintaining the human psyche on an even keel. . . . "[9] Frank has amply prepared us for the creation of the underground man.

The Years of Ordeal also covers Dostoevsky's army life, as well as his first marriage. After his wedding, the diagnosis of epilepsy became settled, and evidently his first wife never forgave him for what she thought of as a concealment. During this formative period, Dostoevsky's belief system became established. Czar Alexander II, who abolished the serfdom that *The Seeds of Revolt* established was an essential constituent of Dostoevsky's revolutionary activities, seemed a worthy object of Dostoevsky's devotion. The Crimean War solidified the notion that Russia had a mission to redeem Western culture.

Dostoevsky's politics were such, Freud had archly commented, that "lesser minds have reached with smaller effort."[10] Although Frank is unremittingly hard on Freud, it is important that Freud's choice of *The Brothers Karamazov* as his favorite novel represented an overcoming of Freud's own values. As an Austrian Jew Freud could not share Dostoevsky's kind of patriotism, nor could he appreciate Dostoevsky as a believing Christian. Freud might have seen in Dostoevsky an admirable kind of radical skepticism, but he could never have shared the Russian's Christian convictions. Dostoevsky's remark that he would "prefer to remain with Christ rather than with the truth"[11] was antithetical to Freud's whole orientation.

Dostoevsky's beliefs were not as eccentric as they might seem. Frank performs a notable service in showing how Dostoevsky was part of the dominant trend in Russian intellectual life at the time. Literature and criticism were then, as they still are now in the Soviet Union, a political enterprise.

In Dostoevsky's life, as in the characters in his works, egoism is a dreaded fear. He especially assailed selfishness when it was garbed in noble ideals. Human beings were all too capable of self-intoxication, and ideology could allow the nastiest of actions. These volumes of Frank's are so captivating partly because of Dostoevsky's moral and psychological genius: "A base soul escaping from oppression becomes an oppressor."[12] Those who are humiliated have an instinctive impulse to hit back, illustrating, in Frank's words, how egoism can be "so self-absorbed as to be incapable of forgiveness or even of mercy."[13] Dostoevsky's work illustrates repeatedly how resentments can explode from the deepest parts of the human psyche. *The Seeds of Revolt* and *The Years of Ordeal* lay the groundwork for Dostoevsky's later and greatest works. Volume 2 ends with Dostoevsky's return to Russia, ten years after he had left as a prisoner in shackles.

My own intense fascination with *The Seeds of Revolt* and *The Years of Ordeal* stemmed partly from a long-standing absorption with Dostoevsky. Frank's two books, at least for someone like myself who had read everything by Dostoevsky I had ever been able to lay my hands on, came as a revelation. Partly it was a question of Frank having so thoroughly absorbed the historical and social background to Dostoevsky's writings; Russian culture and its history remain relatively alien, and Frank succeeded in making it accessible. But he had proceeded with such originality and artistry that there was little left about Dostoevsky's life that one once thought one knew that withstood his sensitive biographical inquiries.

Frank's volumes in some sense gave us a new Dostoevsky, in that previous biographical knowledge was no longer trustworthy. Frank's obvious mastery of the Russian primary and secondary source material made it the most authoritative study available and at the same time an intensely readable experience. Frank is so thoroughly sophisticated a literary critic that he succeeded not in trying to foist off on us an allegedly novel Dostoevsky, but has used fresh evidence to deepen our understanding of the great writer with whom we were already familiar. Frank's books revived memories of Dostoevsky's most characteristic works and reminded us of key aspects of the writings of a man whose novels are so unforgettably a part of our heritage.

Yet after a lively beginning to the opening of Volume 3, *The Stir of Liberation,* 1860–65 (1986) there is such a difference between a chunk of two hundred pages and my memory of Frank's earlier two books that I began to wonder whether my high expectations had led to some inevitable disappointment or even to a suspicion that I had assessed the other work incorrectly. That large early portion of this book lacked the narrative pace of both *The Seeds of Revolt* and *The Years of Ordeal.* Frank had accomplished once again admirable explorations in Russian intellectual history, but his concentrated analysis of Dostoevsky's journalism, within the context of its social and political background, lacked movement, and then suddenly, in the last 125 pages of *The Stir of Liberation,* Frank's biography returns to the absolutely superb level of the earlier volumes.

What had happened is that Frank's original intention to produce a four-volume work dealing with Dostoevsky's life and writings had changed to expand into five; Frank tells us in the preface to *The Stir of Liberation* that he was forced to extend the size of his project "when the present book emerged rather unexpectedly." [14] To be more precise, Frank felt he had to deal with the neglected archival material and scholarly studies connected with Dostoevsky's years as a polemicizing journalist. Frank obviously knows best how much attention has to be paid to each phrase of Dostoevsky's life and what needs to be done to prepare us for understanding the background to the immortal novels, but this alteration in Frank's original plan does, I think, show up in the flawed execution of *The Stir of Liberation.*

Overall, however, we have once again a thoroughly fresh version of Dostoevsky. One commonplace has always emphasized Dostoevsky's reactionary politics after his imprisonment. It is true that he became a fervent supporter of the czar as a liberator of the serfs; Dostoevsky did also later utter anti-Semitic ideas, and he was repeatedly to write about the moral ambiguities in radicalism. But Frank argues that in the context of his times Dostoevsky was steering a middle course within the ideological squabbles of the Russian intelligentsia. He was living in a time of revolutionary ferment, and although he distanced himself from radical thinkers, he himself had to take into account the threat of the czarist censorship. Ironically, one censor thought that Dostoevsky's depiction of Siberian imprisonment in *House of the Dead* was so rosy as to pose the threat of incitement to crime, and on a later occasion a journal that Dostoevsky and his brother Mikhail edited was closed down at the order of the political authorities. Frank says that Dostoevsky was unique among the greatest Russian artists in depicting the people of Russia revolting against their enslavement. He abhorred serfdom and all that went with it humanly. "Whatever else Dostoevsky may have been," Frank writes, "he was certainly not an uncritical defender of existing institutions. . . . "[15] Dostoevsky was never on the side of suppressing ideas, even though he might be opposed to them, and according to Frank, Dostoevsky always thought it was a mistake to interfere with the free expression of thought.

The years 1860–65 brought Dostoevsky into direct contact with some of the greatest writers in Western thought. Frank carefully depicts Dostoevsky's personal and intellectual relationships to Alexander Herzen as well as Ivan Turgenev. It seems touchingly chatty to find Herzen writing to a mutual acquaintance: "Dostoevsky was here yesterday—he is a naive, not entirely lucid, but very nice person. . . . He believes with enthusiasm in the Russian people."[16] After Dostoevsky's death Turgenev surprisingly referred to him as the Russian Marquis de Sade. Frank presents interesting material about lesser figures like Nikolay Strakhov, Apollon Grigoryev, and N. A. Dobrolyubov. N. G. Chernyshevsky is particularly significant in *The Stir of Liberation*, since it is his *What Is To Be Done?* (1863) against which Dostoevsky will be reacting with his conception of the underground man. Although by 1865 Dostoevsky's greatest writings still lie in the future, the chronology of his work was such that *The Stir of Liberation* can culminate with an impressively persuasive examination of the text of *Notes from the Underground*.

Dostoevsky's religious convictions are sufficiently different and difficult that they deserve the extended discussion that Frank affords them. Naive students of Dostoevsky, who may know little more about him than the unforgettable legend of the Grand Inquisitor, are apt to ignore Dostoevsky's hostility to Roman Catholicism; Dostoevsky succeeds so convincingly because he understood both possible sides of the argument, and he is illustrious in Western history if only because he regularly dramatized the inevitability of the tragic clash between competing moral values. When he rejected European ideas, he had in mind those that emphasized the selfishly self-regarding aspects of the human mind. For Dostoevsky, Russia was a country that could stand for the principle of community as it existed in the traditional Russian peasant commune. Dostoevsky's nationalism was part of his taking the side of the Christian ethic of love and self-sacrifice in contrast to the Benthamite utilitarian doctrine of individualism and self-interest. Yet suffering was no end in itself for Dostoevsky, but could serve as a goad to keep alive what Frank calls the "sense of moral autonomy in a world deprived of human significance by determinism."[17]

This third volume of Frank's biography covers the death of Dostoevsky's first wife, who was tubercular, as well as the fatal collapse of his brother Mikhail, it recounts a brief adulterous and unhappy romance of Dostoevsky's; and the book also includes Dostoevsky's first episode of addictive gambling at roulette, which always took place while he was abroad, where in part he went for the sake of medical treatment. In *The Stir of Liberation* Frank has let up on his criticism of Freud and of psychoanalytic thinking; when it comes to Dostoevsky's gambling, Frank wisely steps quietly past Freud's own view of it, but then relies heavily and probably correctly on the theorizing of an orthodox analyst, Otto Fenichel.

Frank's work now faces its greatest challenge, since it above all aims to use an understanding of Dostoevsky's life to illuminate his writings, and the story has come to the period of Dostoevsky's greatest creativity. Frank points out that Dostoevsky's failure, financially, as an editor and a journalist would in the end prove his salvation as an artist. It is with great anticipation that we await the completion of this biography, and that eagerness is not just due to Dostoevsky's novels and his stature in Western thought as "the Russian Shakespeare," but constitutes a tribute to the high quality of this biography.

Concentrating on Freud has led me inevitably back to the greatest figures in the history of political and social thought. It is fascinating how different psychological conceptions held by various major writers have had an affect on their views on the role of man in society. There is a seemingly endless series of ways in which psychological understandings of human nature can help illuminate the behavior of man in political and social life. The most powerful social philosophers have all been thoroughly interdisciplinary; in more recent years the unifying visions of the classical thinkers have tended to be splintered within academic specialties.

Political philosophy deals with concepts and issues as well as with the ideas of individual thinkers, and the ethics of normality, in the context of the old distinction between good and evil, plays such an inevitable role in any thinking about the moral implications of psychoanalysis that I trust it will serve as a suitable note on which to end this book.

Normality is a concern by and large invoked in everyday life by the insecure. Reality inevitably confronts us with the unexpected; Machiavelli once went so far as to ascribe half of political life to the mysterious workings of what he called Fortune. To the extent to which we are necessarily in the grip of forces over which we can have little control, there are a variety of ways of trying to manage our relative helplessness. Machiavelli in his *History of Florence* sounds blatantly superstitious. In the twentieth century, however, old-fashioned forms of magical thinking seem unattractively primitive, and different means of asserting ourselves are now in fashion. As traditional religion has become a relatively unpopular alternative, psychology has acquired a special status of its own. Psychological concepts may in fact be used for ethical purposes, as they serve to praise as well as blame, yet they can appear neutral and dispassionate, capable of being independently confirmed.

It is in this climate of opinion that the concept of normality now functions so pervasively. To take only one kind of example, young parents, unable to rely on secure traditions about child rearing, turn to manuals for reassurance and guidance. Dr. Spock may be the best known, yet he is hardly alone in the extent to which psychoanalytic thinking pervades his texts. Anxieties about a normal fetus precede those in connection with infancy and extend to all phases of human development; there is apparently no end to the uncertainties of an individualistic era. The absence of collectively agreed-upon standards feeds this lack of directedness. Such conformist pressures have direct political implications; John F. Kennedy, for example, remarked—within earshot of his wife—that he had had to get married lest the public think he was "queer."

The issue of normality often arises by means of the conceptual other side of the coin: the frequency of psychopathological terms in daily conversation as well as in sophisticated books often masks the same underlying fears about what constitutes normality. Earlier eras could be more tolerant of diversity. The Freudian revolution in the history of ideas has sanctioned a whole host of words and phrases, in addition to *neurotic* and *psychotic,* which can be used artificially to reaffirm our stability.

Even the most explicitly antipsychological thinkers, as we have seen with both Orwell and Arendt, take recourse to psychodynamic notions. It would be mistaken to suppose that psychopathological terms are only brought up in connection with spectacularly offensive political events. It is true that the more we know about Stalin, the easier it can be to see him in terms of a theory about paranoia rather than in connection with the tradition of thought associated with Karl Marx or specifically Russian national practices. Yet it requires an enormous amount of cultural savvy before we are entitled to invoke clinical concepts in connection with any political leader, no matter how offensive we may judge him.

The conditions under which psychological terms get properly used are, however, at odds with how they are regularly raised, and that remains the heart of a key conceptual problem associated with political psychology. However much we may legitimately fear the dangers of a nuclear holocaust, I doubt the scientific propriety of much psychiatric moralizing on the subject. The alleged fears of small children can of course be studied, although adequate attention has to be paid to the suggestive impact of the political values of the parents of those who are realistically disturbed about the prospects of nuclear dangers getting out of hand. On the whole, ethical utopianism can too readily be associated with the use of psychology in politics. I am thinking, for example, of the hopes of Harry Stack Sullivan about what psychiatry could do for poverty and race relations and Erich Fromm's frequent political pronouncements, as well as Erik H. Erikson's dedication of his *Childhood and Society* to "our children's children."[18] (To be sure, conservatives are also capable of abusing psychiatric terminology, as for example when Bruno Bettelheim once roundly denounced students during the Vietnam War for a disruption that he found particularly objectionable.)

As a theorist, however, I would like to call attention to the fact that ethical high-mindedness does not always serve purposes of social change or genuine reform. Grounds exist for believing that a certain kind of philosophical piousness may end up reinforcing the social status quo rather than legitimately challenging it. The alternative is not, I should hasten to add, a return to Freud's own most corrosive pessimism. As the years passed he gave up his earlier commitment to sexual emancipation, much to the distress of someone like Wilhelm Reich, and Freud ended up with a cynical conservatism that meant in the 1930s his support for an Austrian authoritarian regime.

Radicals like Herbert Marcuse could later rely on an orthodox version of Freud's viewpoint without realizing what the social implications of death instinct theory might be. The humanistically oriented revisionists of Freud's views, like Fromm and Erikson, were trying to inject genuine humanitarianism into a psychoanalytic world view that appeared to end in therapeutic despair and ethical nihilism, and in Fromm's neglected retort to Marcuse's famous dissection of neo-Freudianism Fromm accused Marcuse of ultimately advocating a nihilistic position.

However extravagant Fromm might sound in defending himself against Marcuse's strictures, which were I think largely unfair, there is less danger in psychoanalysis ever being a devastating threat to Western culture than in its lending undercover support to objectionably conformist practices. The papacy, and whatever equivalents of it as our moral guardians exist, can be counted upon to warn the public against any deterioration in existing moral standards. Psychological notions have been used on occasion to dress up radical positions. However interesting Frantz Fanon's use of psychiatry might have been, it was not a set of books or professional teachings that drove him to advocate therapeutic violence as a solution to colonialism. Societies are tough enough to withstand safely more challenges than intellectuals can readily come up with. It has been conservatives like Edmund Burke, oddly enough, who on the one hand fear the power of ideas and at the same time express the greatest confidence in the existence of social cohesion.

There is more truth to the conservative contention about the inevitable impact of society on individuals than writers on the left have usually been ready to acknowledge. As an aspect of the success of Freudian ideas psychodynamic notions of normality have become part of the prevailing social structure around us. One need only think about how Anna Freud and her collaborators at Yale Law School came up with defending the idea of psychological parenthood and used it to support the notion that continuity in child custody cases should prevail over what these experts considered mere biological parenthood. The value of continuity can be as unthinkingly enshrined as a part of middle-class morality as the alleged dangers of traumas were once used to frighten people into conformity.

It seems to me a pity that traditional political theorists have been so resistant to exploring the challenge of modern psychological thinking. One of the great strengths of the examination of the whole tradition of Western political thought is that it should promote a sophisticated view of the variety of moral positions that have been defended by thinkers in the past. A central weakness in all recently fashionable psychological theorists is a relative lack of philosophic distance from the values that are being supported. Too many psychologists do not even want to acknowledge the ethical dimension to their work, and so we have scientific arguments being used in behalf of hidden moral preaching.

Freud himself was philosophically subtle enough to be suspicious of some of his own key concepts. At least in correspondence and conversation he acknowledged that health was only one value among others and that it could not exhaust morality as a whole. At times he thought he could get away with the idea that health was only a practical notion, not a theoretical commitment at all; he treated people whom he regarded as very ill, at the same time as he was capable of dismissing patients on the grounds that they were too well adjusted to be worth his time. Freud frequently made a great display of his abhorrence of philosophy, in contrast to what we now know to have been his youthful fascination with the subject. He claimed that morality was so self-evident that he thought that he himself had never done anything ethically questionable. Unlike Jean-Paul Sartre, who was so troubled by the problem of meaninglessness, Freud found psychological significance everywhere. To question the meaning of life, Freud once wrote in old age, was to confess to the existence of a personal surplus of libido.

Nonetheless, it would be a gross mistake ever to take Freud as any kind of philistine. If he was wary about this whole subject of normality it was because he realized full well what kind of quagmire he was in danger of entering. He touched on the subject of normalcy only on the rarest occasions. Once, in an essay implicitly designed to refute Carl Jung's views on psychological types, Freud said that an ideally normal person would have hysterical, obsessional, and narcissistic layers in harmony; doubtless he was speaking autobiographically, but at the same time his idea communicated one of his characteristic demands about how high a standard he expected of mankind, for to be able to bear that much psychological baggage and still be able to function effectively presupposes a considerable degree of self-control and capacity to endure stress, as well as the presence of constitutional giftedness. Freud typically took for granted that the people he liked best to work with were creative and self-disciplined, and he replied once, when asked what a normal person could be expected to be like, with the maxim: "to love and to work."[19] This comment of his became one of Freud's most famous sayings, and I think Erikson is right is saying that it goes deeper the more one ponders it.

Psychoanalysts since Freud and the first generations of his followers have not been anywhere near as creative or as talented as their predecessors. I do not think this assessment is a consequence of the human tendency to romanticize the past, therefore overglamorizing the beginnings of psychoanalysis as a profession. The early analysts were objectively an unusually interesting lot who pursued their profession as a mission. The underside to their spiritual commitment was a degree of sectarianism that could be frightening. But whatever unnecessary ideological wars they engaged in and however they might have stifled their doubts through the adoption of questionably dogmatic beliefs, they were highly educated people completely at home in the world of ideas and general culture.

Still it was hard for these pioneers in modern psychology to accept the legitimacy of their own human experience. What makes them enduringly attractive as models is their individualistic defiance of conventional standards of how we ought to live. Therefore it is paradoxical to find, for instance, Harry Stack Sullivan idealizing "interpersonal" success, Helene Deutsch glorifying the reproductive joys of motherhood, and Erik H. Erikson making an ethical norm out of the achievement of adulthood. The private lives of the Freudian school do not support the premium that psychoanalytic theory put on the value of "genitality." It is as if these analysts forgot that tragedy can be enriching, yet doubtless Freud's emphasis on the inevitability of the tragic dimension had helped attract them to psychoanalysis in the first place.

The result has been an intellectual legacy from Freud that is less richly adequate than it might have been. The current situation of psychological theory is distressing because of the power that this conceptualization has gained. Analysts are no longer in a position of being unrecognized outsiders at odds with the social status quo. On the contrary, at least in North America, psychoanalysis has become a part of the establishment, and therefore the lack of attention to ethical alternatives, and an insensitive approach to the problem of normality, can become an invitation to an implicit celebration of conformism.

Freud feared that the most original and disturbing aspects of his ideas would be destroyed by the widespread acceptance of his work in the New World. I wonder whether he did enough to prevent precisely this outcome. By not providing more hints about normality and not owning up publicly to the wide variety of psychological solutions he found both therapeutically tolerable and humanly desirable, Freud contributed to what he most sought to prevent. He had set out, in the spirit of Nietzsche, to transform Western values; he was eager to go beyond accepted good and evil. When he assaulted the maxim "love thy neighbor as thyself" as both unrealistic and undesirable, he was explicitly trying to overturn not only Christian ethics but Western culture as well. Otto Rank thought that Freud's notion of latent homosexuality was antihumanitarian and authoritarian, and other post-Freudian writers have sought to come to a different set of moral conclusions than the founder of psychoanalysis.

It does seem somehow fitting that Freud should have been invited to testify in behalf of Leopold and Loeb for their crime in Chicago. Historically Freud was then an old man with an embittered hatred of all things American; although he appreciated the money to be earned off a nation he viewed as a land of barbarians and was concerned that Jews were involved in such a scandal, there was no possibility of his making such a trip at that stage in his life. But it is hard not to think that there had been something in Freud's psychoanalysis that too readily broke with the necessary restraints in Western culture. If one hurls thunderbolts at traditional ethics and morality, does one not in the end bear some of the responsibility for what happens?

It should be said of Carl Jung, whatever the unfortunate nature of his own political stupidity in the 1930s in connection with the Nazis, that even before World War I he had realized that people needed more than a tearing apart of their problems on the assumption that they would automatically be able to synthesize things on their own. Jung's longtime respect for religious beliefs was part of an early and prophetic effort to inject something constructive into a psychoanalytic outlook that sounded unduly critical. Much of psychoanalytic writing since Freud's death, which has sought to overcome his own personal biases and correct the unduly negativistic imbalance in his thinking, was anticipated by Jung years ago; and other respectful critics of Freud's foresaw at least some of the dead end to which his ideas might lead.

It is logically impossible to talk about neurosis without at the same time implying a standard of maturity as well, and yet despite how powerful psychology can be in outlining human defects and weaknesses, it has not been nearly as successful in coming to terms with the positive side of human strength and coherence. Ego psychology, which for a time was the most fashionable school of psychoanalytic thinking after Freud's death, aimed precisely to rectify the inadequate way he left the issue of normality. It is hard to see even how anyone could know what was pathological apart from an assumed or explicit conception of normalcy. Clinicians have been increasingly attentive to this problem, although it is historically worth remembering that one of Freud's charges against Adler had been that that disciple's interest in normal human development constituted a heretical "deviation" from psychoanalysis.

An attention to cultural differences has to be part of any outlook on normality that is going to be capable of being defensible. Here early Freudian theory was deficient, for despite all the familiarity Freud and his followers had with patients from a wide variety of social backgrounds, they were loath to take such issues into account in their theoretical thinking. They were trying to universalize their insights, and it is only with the passage of time that social changes have highlighted how much Freud took for granted that it is necessary to be more explicit about.

As much as Freud, at least toward the end of his life, thought he had succeeded in being a scientist, at the same time he always harbored the idea that his work had immense implications for social philosophy. The psychoanalytic treatment setting was, he believed, a potential basis for new values and ethics. He himself, when he attacked religion, for example in his *The Future of an Illusion,* tried to argue that he was only spelling out one possible implication of his work. When he wrote *Civilization and Its Discontents* against what he thought was the dangerous possibility of mixing up Wilhelm Reich's Marxism with the purity of Freud's own psychological "findings," Freud was once again committing himself to only one more position that he thought could be sustained by his clinical so-called discoveries. Surprisingly, Jung's own social preferences were pretty close to those of his former master; whatever the conflicts between Freud and Jung, old-fashioned gentlemen of that era shared many of the same cultural viewpoints.

In the end I think that the issue of the significance of normality and its relationship to nihilism will have to be left an open question. In some sense Freud does fit into the liberal tradition's quest for a theory of individualism; his whole therapeutic approach did encourage a kind of self-expression that was congenial to the aims of thinkers like John Stuart Mill. Whatever the excesses to which psychoanalytic ideas were sometimes put, the historical Freud did not advocate self-indulgence; he might romantically posture in defiance of Western traditions, yet he stood for order and civility. Just how conservative Freud really was can be seen in his distaste for so much of modern art and literature. But of course many of the twentieth century's most daring cultural innovators took inspiration from the psychoanalytic perspective. No philosopher ever succeeds in imposing himself on history in an undistorted form, and every writer must bear the responsibility for the uses to which his ideas eventually get put.

Freud's psychology, however it may ultimately be evaluated, did contribute to our understanding of what it can mean to be human, and in that sense his ideas will be permanently interesting to political theorists. But it is impossible to attempt to spell out in a definitive way the ideological implications of psychoanalysis. The writers who have been influenced by Freud constitute a wide range of people, and in this connection I am reminded that Herbert Marcuse told me how impressive he found Thomas Szasz, although the latter's politics were very different from those of the Frankfurt school of critical sociology.

It was an old analyst and loyal disciple of Freud's, Helene Deutsch, who had, I think, the most appropriately philosophic attitude toward the perplexing issue of normality. She once reported to me that in her earlier years, when she had been one of the most prominent teachers in the history of psychoanalysis, she used to make it a practice to ask prospective analysts in the course of interviewing them for acceptance into training what they thought a normal person would be like. It is of course an ultimately unanswerable conundrum, and yet one that as civilized people we too are obliged to raise repeatedly. Like all genuine questions in political philosophy, the problem of normality can never be solved; it remains a real issue, nonetheless, to the extent that we choose to find it intolerable to contemplate a universe lacking in moral values.

Notes

1. Joseph Frank, *Dostoevsky: The Seeds of Revolt, 1821–1849* (Princeton: Princeton University Press, 1976), p. 385
2. Ibid., p. xii.
3. Ibid., p. 2.
4. Joseph Frank, *Dostoevsky: The Years of Ordeal, 1850–1859* (Princeton: Princeton University Press, 1983), p. 6.
5. Ibid., p. 13.
6. Ibid.
7. Ibid., p. 18.
8. Ibid., p. 77.
9. Ibid., p. 156.
10. Freud, "Dostoevsky and Parricide," *Standard Edition*, vol. 21, p. 177.
11. Frank, *Dostoevsky: The Years of Ordeal*, p. 160.
12. Ibid., p. 279.
13. Ibid., p. 280.
14. Joseph Frank, *Dostoevsky: The Stir of Liberation* (Princeton: Princeton University Press, 1986), p. xi.
15. Ibid., p. 303.
16. Ibid., p. 191.
17. Ibid., p. 328.
18. Erik H. Erikson, *Childhood and Society,* 2d ed. (New York: Norton, 1963).
19. Ibid., p. 256.

A Bibliography of Paul Roazen

1960

"The Politics of Stalemate," *Oxford Opinion,* October 1960.

1968

Freud: Political and Social Thought (New York: Knopf, 1968; London: Hogarth, 1969, translated into Spanish, German, Portuguese, Italian, French, and Japanese; Da Capo Books reprint, with new preface, 1986).

Review of *Reich Speaks of Freud,* ed. Higgins and Raphael, *Nation,* April 15, 1968.

Review of Grier and Cobbs, *Black Rage, Book Week (Chicago Sun Times),* August 4, 1968.

Review of Miller, *Martin Luther King, Book Week (Chicago Sun Times),* December 15, 1968.

1969

Brother Animal: The Story of Freud and Tausk (New York: Knopf, 1969; London: Allen Lane, 1970; translated into French, German, Spanish, Italian, Portuguese, and Japanese, reprinted by New York University Press, 1986.)

"Sigmund Freud, Lou Andreas-Salomé, and Victor Tausk: A Curious Triangle," *Encounter,* October 1969.

"Victor Tausk's Contribution to Psychoanalysis," *Psychoanalytic Quarterly,* July 1969. Editor of three papers by Victor Tausk: "On the Psychology of the War Deserter," "Diagnostic Considerations Concerning the Symptomatology of the So-called War Psychoses," and "On the Psychology of the Alcoholic Occupation Delirium," *Psychoanalytic Quarterly,* July 1969.

Review of Davis, *Lawrence and Oppenheimer, Psychology Today,* January 1969.

Review of Arendt, *Men in Dark Times, Nation,* January 27, 1969.

Review of Bowen, *Biography, Book Week (Chicago Sun Times)*, February 2, 1969.
Review of Bettelheim, *Children of the Dream, Sunday New York Times,* April 6, 1969.

1970

Review of Mitzman, *The Iron Cage: Max Weber, Chicago Sun Times,* January 7, 1970.
Review of Lifton, *History and Human Survival, Book Week (Chicago Sun Times),* January 18, 1970.
Review of *Letters of Sigmund Freud and Arnold Zweig, Nation,* May 25, 1970.
Review of Rosenberg, *The Trial of the Assassin Guiteau, Columbia Law Review,* June 1970.
Review of Lippmann, *The Early Writings, Nation,* September 7, 1970.
Review of Geismar, *Mark Twain: An American Prophet, Showcase (Chicago Sun Times),* November 1, 1970.

1971

"The Legend of Freud," *Virginia Quarterly Review,* Winter 1971.
"Psychoanalysis and Moral Values," *Dissent,* February 1971 (also in *Moral Values and the Superego Concept in Psychoanalysis,* ed. Post [New York: International Universities Press, 1972]; translated into French, *le Coq-Heron,* 1988).
Review of Reich, *The Mass Psychology of Fascism, Saturday Review,* February 13, 1971.
Review of Stone, *The Passions of the Mind, Showcase (Chicago Sun Times),* March 14, 1971.
Review of *The Wolf Man,* ed. Gardiner, *Saturday Review,* August 14, 1971.
Review of Grier and Cobbs, *The Jesus Bag, Nation,* September 27, 1971.

1972

"Reflections on Ethos and Authenticity in Psychoanalysis," *Human Context,* Autumn 1972.
"Freud and America," *Social Research,* Winter 1972.
Review of Storr, *The Dynamics of Creation, Showcase (Chicago Sun Times),* August 20, 1972.
Review of Hale, *Freud and the Americans,* vol. 1, *Contemporary Sociology,* November 1972.

1973

Editor, *Sigmund Freud* (Englewood Cliffs, N.J.: Prentice Hall; New York, Da Capo Books reprint, 1987).
Review of Wolman, ed., *The Psychoanalytic Interpretation of History, Journal of Nervous and Mental Diseases,* January 1973.

Review of Wollheim, *Freud, Nation,* February 26, 1973.
Review of Jung, *Collected Letters,* vol. 1, *Nation,* June 25, 1973.
Review of Schur, *Freud, Living and Dying, Human Context,* Autumn 1973.

1974

Review of *Freud/Jung Letters, New Statesman,* April 12, 1974.
Review of *Freud/Jung Letters, Showcase (Chicago Sun Times),* April 14, 1974.

1975

Freud and His Followers (New York: Knopf, 1975; London: Allen Lane, 1976; translated into German, Spanish, Portuguese, Japanese and French; reprinted by New York University Press, 1985).
"Freud and His Money," *Practical Psychology for Physicians,* July 1975.
"Psychology and Politics: The Case of Erik H. Erikson," *Human Context,* Autumn 1975.
Review of Erikson, *Dimensions of a New Identity, Nation,* June 7, 1975.
Review of Crews, *Out of My System: Psychoanalysis, Ideology, and Critical Method, Canadian Forum,* December 1975–January 1976.

1976

Erik H. Erikson: The Power and Limits of a Vision (New York: Free Press, 1976; translated into Italian and Japanese; reprinted by Free Press, 1986).
"Psychology and Politics: Biographies of Leaders," *Contemporary Psychoanalysis,* January 1976.
"Erik H. Erikson: Psycho-Historian as Mythologist," *Reviews in European History,* September 1976.
"Erik H. Erikson's Post-Freudianism," *Psychohistory Review,* December 1976.
Review of Friedrich, *Going Crazy: An Inquiry into Madness in Our Time, Saturday Review,* January 24, 1976.
Review of Jacoby, *Social Amnesia: A Critique of Conformist Psychology from Adler to Laing, American Scholar,* Spring 1976.
Review of Des Pres, *The Survivor: An Anatomy of Life in the Death Camps, Canadian Forum,* June–July 1976.
Review of Lash, ed., *From the Diaries of Felix Frankfurter, Virginia Quarterly Review,* Summer 1976.
Review of Chapman, *Harry Stack Sullivan: The Man and His Work, Psychology Today,* October 1976.

1977

"Orthodoxy on Freud: The Case of Tausk," *Contemporary Psychoanalysis,* January 1977.
"Freud's Clark University Lectures Reconsidered," *Journal of the American Academy of Psychoanalysis,* October 1977.

Review of Maccoby, *The Gamesman, Saturday Review,* January 22, 1977.
Review of Fromm, *To Have or To Be?, Nation,* February 5, 1977.
Review of Walkenstein, *Don't Shrink to Fit!, Psychology Today,* March 1977.
Review of Szasz, *The Sacred Symbol of Psychiatry: Schizophrenia, Canadian Forum,* April 1977.
Review of Izenberg, *The Existentialist Critique of Freud, New Society,* April 14, 1977.
Review of Jahoda, *Freud and the Dilemma of Psychology, New Society,* May 5, 1977.
Review of Gedo and Pollock, eds., *Freud, Fusion of Science and Humanism, Isis,* September 1977.
Review of Frank, *Dostoevsky,* vol. 1: *The Seeds of Revolt, Virginia Quarterly Review,* Fall 1977.
Review of Martin, *Adlai Stevenson of Illinois, Queen's Quarterly,* Autumn 1977.

1978

"Reading, Writing, and Memory: Dr. Kurt R. Eissler's Thinking," *Contemporary Psychoanalysis,* April 1978.
"Orwell, Freud, and *1984," Virginia Quarterly Review,* Autumn 1978.
Review of Szasz, *Karl Kraus and the Soul Doctors, Queen's Quarterly,* Spring 1978.
Review of Robert, *From Oedipus to Moses: Freud's Jewish Identity, Contemporary Psychology,* June 1978.
Review of Martin, *Adlai Stevenson and the World, American Scholar,* Summer 1978.
Review of Odajnyk, *Jung and Politics, American Political Science Review,* December 1978.

1980

"Eriksonian Therapy," in *Psychotherapy Handbook,* ed. Herink (New York: New American Library, 1980).
"Freud and Tausk," *Historical Perspectives on Depression* (Nutley, N.J.: Roche Laboratories, 1980).
"Erik H. Erikson's America: The Political Implications of Ego Psychology," *Journal of the History of the Behavioral Sciences,* Fall 1980.

1981

Editor, "Helene Deutsch's 'Two Cases of Induced Insanity,'" *International Journal of Psychoanalysis,* Spring 1981.
Editor, "Helene Deutsch's 'Anorexia Nervosa,'" *Bulletin of the Menninger Clinic,* November 1981 (also translated into French, *Le Coq-Heron,* 1984).

1982

"On Errors Regarding Freud," *International Journal of Psychoanalysis,* 1982.

Editor, "Helene Deutsch's 'On the Pathological Lie,'" *Journal of the American Academy of Psychoanalysis,* July 1982.

Editor, "Helene Deutsch's 'George Sand: A Woman's Destiny,'" *International Review of Psychoanalysis,* Fall 1982.

"Obituary of Helene Deutsch," *International Journal of Psychoanalysis,* Fall 1982.

Review of Stannard, *Shrinking History: On Freud and the Failure of Psychohistory, Contemporary Psychology,* April 1982.

Review of Malcolm, *Psychoanalysis: The Impossible Profession, Virginia Quarterly Review,* Autumn 1982.

Review of Turkle, *Psychoanalytic Politics: Freud's French Revolution, Canadian Political Science Review,* September 1982.

Review of Perry, *Psychiatrist of America: The Life of Harry Stack Sullivan, American Journal of Psychiatry,* December 1982.

Review of Kovel, *The Age of Desire: Case Histories of a Radical Psychoanalyst, Queen's Quarterly,* Winter 1982.

1983

Editor, "Helene Deutsch's 'On Supervised Psychoanalysis,'" *Contemporary Psychoanalysis,* January 1983 (translated into French, *Le Coq-Heron,* 1987).

"In Memoriam: Helene Deutsch," *American Journal of Psychiatry,* April 1983.

"'As If' and Politics," *Political Psychology,* October 1983.

Review of Obholzer, *The Wolf-Man Sixty Years Later, New Society,* January 6, 1983.

Review of Bertin, *Marie Bonaparte: A Biography,* and Brome, *Ernest Jones: Freud's Alter Ego, Times Literary Supplement,* May 6, 1983.

Review of Roustang, *Psychoanalysis Never Lets Go, Canadian Forum,* May 1983.

Review of Young-Bruehl, *Hannah Arendt: For Love of the World, Canadian Political Science Review,* June 1983.

Review of Ostow, ed., *Judaism and Psychoanalysis, American Journal of Psychiatry,* July 1983.

Review of Hersh, *The Price of Power: Kissinger in the Nixon White House, Canadian Forum,* December 1983.

1984

"Freud e La Teorie politica," in *Freud: Gerusalemme Nella Psicianalisi,* ed. Verdiglione (Milan: vel Edizioni, 1984).

Editor, "Helene Deutsch's 'The Menopause,'" *International Journal of Psychoanalysis,* 1984.

"Les oublies de l'histoire," *L'Ane* (March–April 1984).

"A Note on the Vienna Psychoanalytic Society: Felix Deutsch's Letters, 1923 & 1935," *Journal of the History of the Behavioral Sciences,* October 1984.

Review of Sterba, *Reminiscences of a Viennese Psychoanalyst, Journal of Nervous and Mental Disease,* January 1984.

Review of Sharaf, *Fury on Earth: A Biography of Wilhelm Reich, Canadian Forum,* June–July 1984.

Review of Malcolm, *In the Freud Archives, Toronto Star,* July 14, 1984.

Review of Burnham, *Jelliffe and His Correspondence with Jung and Freud, Globe and Mail,* August 18, 1984.

Review of Eichenbaum and Orbach, *Understanding Women, Queen's Quarterly,* October 1984.

Review of Roustang, *Dire Mastery: Discipleship from Freud to Lacan, Queen's Quarterly,* October 1984.

Review of Runyan, *Life Histories and Psychobiography, Psychiatry,* November 1984.

Review of Burnham, *Jelliffe and His Correspondence with Jung and Freud, American Journal of Psychiatry,* December 1984.

1985

Helene Deutsch: A Psychoanalyst's Life (New York: Doubleday/Anchor Press, 1985; New York: New American Library, 1986; translated into German and French).

"Helene Deutsch's Feminism," *Psychohistory Review,* Winter 1985.

Editor, "Helene Deutsch's 'A Case that Throws Light on the Mechanism of Regression in Schizophrenia,'" *Psychoanalytic Review,* Winter 1985.

"Walter Lippmann's Stature," *Psychohistory Review,* Fall 1985.

"Conformity in Psychoanalysis: A Response to Jacoby," *New Ideas in Psychology,* 1985.

Review of Stepansky, *In Freud's Shadow: Adler in Context, Psychohistory Review,* Winter 1985 (also in *Philosophy of the Social Sciences,* December 1986).

Review of *The Complete Letters of Sigmund Freud to Wilhelm Fliess,* ed. Masson, *Globe and Mail,* April 13, 1985.

Review of Frank, *Dostoevsky, vol. 2: The Years of Ordeal, Virginia Quarterly Review,* Summer 1985.

Review of Sharaf, *Fury on Earth: A Biography of Wilhelm Reich, Psychoanalytic Psychology,* Summer 1985 (also in *Psychoanalytic Review,* Winter 1985).

Review of Lieberman, *Acts of Will: The Life and Work of Otto Rank, Los Angeles Times,* July 14, 1985 (also in *International Herald Tribune,* July 24, 1985).

Review of Marcus, *Freud and the Culture of Psychoanalysis, American Journal of Psychiatry,* August 1985.

Review of Gellner, *The Psychoanalytic Movement: Or the Coming of Unreason, New Statesman,* August 16, 1985.
Review of Rycroft, *Psychoanalysis and Beyond, New Statesman,* September 13, 1985.

1986

"Helene Deutsch: Biographical Hindsight," in *Women Physicians in Leadership Roles,* ed. Dickstein and Nadelson (American Psychiatric Association Press, 1986).
"Opinion: On Psychoanalytic Education," *Academy Forum,* Fall 1986 (also in *Newsletter,* Massachusetts Association for Psychoanalytic Psychology, May 1986)
Review of Horden, ed., *Freud and the Humanities,* Gay, *Freud for Historians,* and Sartre, *The Freud Scenario, New Statesman,* January 31, 1986.
Review of Kendrick and Meisel, ed., *Bloomsbury/Freud: Letters of James and Alix Strachey, Globe and Mail,* February 8, 1986.
Review of Kohon, ed., *The British School of Psychoanalysis, New Statesman,* February 28, 1986.
Review of Fox, *Reinhold Niebuhr: A Biography, New Republic,* March 31, 1986.
Review of Thornton, *The Freudian Fallacy: An Alternative View of Freudian Theory, American Journal of Psychiatry,* May 1986.
Review of Cocks, *Psychotherapy in the Third Reich: The Göring Institute, Dissent,* Spring 1986.
Review of Jacoby, *The Repression of Psychoanalysis: Otto Fenichel and the Political Freudians, Journal of Nervous and Mental Disease,* August 1986.
Review of Blum, *Walter Lippmann: Cosmopolitanism in the Century of Total War, Queen's Quarterly,* Summer 1986.
Review of Gay, *Freud for Historians, Psychohistory Review,* Fall 1986.
Review of Diggins, *The Lost Soul of American Politics, Journal of American Politics,* December 1986.

1987

"Psychoanalytic Biography: Dead or Alive?," *Contemporary Psychoanalysis,* October 1987.
Review of *Public Philosopher: Selected Letters of Walter Lippmann,* ed. Blum, *American Scholar,* Winter 1987.
Review of Torrey, *The Roots of Treason: Ezra Pound and the Secret of St. Elizabeth's, Journal of the History of the Behavioral Sciences,* Winter 1987.
Review of Wright, *Lillian Hellman: The Image, the Woman, Globe and Mail,* January 17, 1987.
Review of Erdelyi, *Psychoanalysis: Freud's Cognitive Psychology, American Journal of Psychiatry,* May 1987.

Review of Byck, ed., *The Cocaine Papers, Journal of the History of the Behavioral Sciences,* July 1987.
Review of Frank, *Dostoevsky,* vol. 3: *The Stir of Liberation, Virginia Quarterly Review,* Summer 1987.
Review of Meissner, *Psychoanalysis and Religious Experience, Journal of Nervous and Mental Disease,* August 1987.
Review of Anzieu, *Freud's Self-Analysis, Psychohistory Review,* Fall 1987.
Review of McGrath, *Freud's Discovery of Psychoanalysis: The Politics of Hysteria, Psychoanalytic Psychology,* Fall 1987.
Review of Mahony, *Freud and the Rat Man,* and Mahony, *Cries of the Wolf Man, Partisan Review,* Fall 1987.
Review of Lasswell, *Psychopathology and Politics, Political Psychology,* September 1987.
Review of Grunbaum, *The Foundations of Psychoanalysis: A Philosophical Critique, Modern Psychoanalysis,* 1987.

1988

"Louis Hartz's Teaching," *Virginia Quarterly Review,* Winter 1988.
"Memories of the Boston 'Psycho,'" *Psychologist-Psychoanalyst,* Summer 1988.
"Normality and Nihilism," *Virginia Quarterly Review,* Summer 1988.
"The American Liberal Tradition," *Los Angeles Times,* October 19, 1988.
Review of Quinn, *A Mind of Her Own: The Life of Karen Horney, Globe and Mail,* February 6, 1988.
Review of Eissler, *Freud as an Expert Witness, Contemporary Psychology,* March 1988.
Review of Sagan, *Freud, Women, and Morality, Los Angeles Times,* March 6, 1988.
Review of Gedo, *Conceptual Issues in Psychoanalysis: Essays in History and Method, Journal of the American Academy of Psychoanalysis,* April 1988.
Review of Hiss, *Recollections of a Life, Chicago Sun Times,* May 8, 1988.
Review of Gay, *Freud: A Life for Our Time, Globe and Mail,* May 14, 1988.
Review of Chesler, *Sacred Bond: The Legacy of Baby M, Boston Globe,* June 5, 1988.
Review of Kenney and Turner, *Dukakis: An American Odyssey,* and Gaines and Segal, *Dukakis: The Man Who Would Be President,* and Dukakis and Kanter, *Creating the Future: The Massachusetts Comeback and Its Promise for America, Globe and Mail,* August 20, 1988.
Review of Robertson, *Lily: A Rhapsody,* vol. 2, *Canadian Historical Review,* September 1988.
Review of Krull, *Freud and His Father, Psychohistory Review,* Fall 1988.
Review of Grosskurth, *Melanie Klein: Her World and Her Work, American Journal of Psychiatry,* October 1988.

Review of Young-Bruehl, *Anna Freud: A Biography, Globe and Mail,* December 3, 1988.

Review of Storr, *Solitude: A Return to the Self, Globe and Mail,* December 17, 1988.

Index

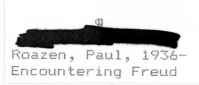